A Legal Guide to Doing Business in South America

Ricardo Barretto Ferreira da Silva
Paulo Marcos Rodrigues Brancher
Carla Amaral de Andrade Junqueira Canero
Editors

Defending Liberty
Pursuing Justice

ABA Section of
International Law
Your Gateway to International Practice

Cover design by ABA Publishing.

Printed in the United States of America.

15 14 13 12 11 5 4 3 2 1

Library of Congress Cataloging-in-Publication Data

A legal guide to doing business in South America / edited by Ricardo Barretto, Paulo Marcos Rodrigues Brancher, and Carla Amaral de Andrade Junqueira. — 1st ed.
   p. cm.
 Includes index.
 ISBN 978-1-61632-957-0
1. Business law—South America. 2. Investments, Foreign—Law and legislation—South America. 3. Trade regulation—South America. I. Barretto, Ricardo, 1949- II. Rodrigues Brancher, Paulo Marcos, 1973–III. Andrade Junqueira, Carla Amaral de, 1977–
 KH101.B87L44 2011
 346.807—dc22

2011012510

Table of Contents

Chapter 1

Chapter 2

Chapter 4

Country Coordinating Author: Marcos Ríos
Country Coordinating Author: Consuelo Raby
Country Coordinating Author: Paola Belan
Country Coordinating Author: Diego Peró

Chapter 5

Country Coordinating Author: Carlos Urrutia Valenzuela
Country Coordinating Author: Tomás Holguín

Chapter 6

Chapter 7

Chapter 8

Country Coordinating Author: Jean Paul Chabaneix
Country Coordinating Author: Mariano Fuentes

Chapter 9

Chapter 10

Country Coordinating Author: Fernando Pélaez-Pier
Country Coordinating Author: Paula Serra Freire

Acknowledgments

This project was conceived during the ABA 2009 Spring Meeting in Washington, D.C., when the editors put forward the suggestion to the ABA Publications Committee. This project was made possible thanks to the support and full commitment of the invited country coordinating authors, and we are delighted with the result.

Putting together this publication has called for a great deal of determination and enthusiasm. The work done by each of the country coordinating authors, co-authors, and contributors is acknowledged in each of the chapters. We wish to express our gratitude to each lawyer who contributed to the preparation of this book through the following country coordinating authors: Marcelo Bombau (Argentina); Pablo Rojas (Bolivia); Marcos Rios, Consuelo Raby, Paola Belan and Diego Peró (Chile); Carlos Urrutia and Tomás Holguín (Colombia); Bruce Horowitz (Ecuador); Alejandro Guanes (Paraguay); Jean-Paul Chabaneix and Mariano Fuentes (Peru); Sandra Gonzáles (Uruguay); and Fernando Pelaez Píer and Paula Freire (Venezuela).

The section's Publications Officer, the Honorable Marilyn J. Kaman, and Richard Paszkiet, Mike Burke, and Natalie Cirar provided invaluable support and contributed enormously from the inception of this book to its publication. In our role as editors, we also enjoyed the full support of other lawyers from our firm, Barretto Ferreira, Kujawski e Brancher—Sociedade de Advogados (BKBG), for the preparation of the chapter on Brazil. A warm thanks to all of them.

The chapters of this book are the result of the hard work, persistence, and cooperation of a highly experienced and skilled team of lawyers. We hope that readers will rely on the content of this guide when considering doing business in South America.

Ricardo Barretto Ferreira da Silva
Paulo Marcos Rodrigues Brancher
Carla Amaral de Andrade Junqueira Canero
Editors

About the Editors

Ricardo Barretto Ferreira Da Silva, admitted, 1973, São Paulo, Brazil. Education: São Paulo University (USP) Law School; Institute of World Affairs, Connecticut, U.S., 1973; L.LM Taxation and Corporate Law at University of North Dakota, U.S., 1974–1975. Senior and managing partner at Barretto Ferreira, Kujawski e Brancher—Sociedade de Advogados (BKBG) (www.bkbg.com.br). Editor and co-author, *Computer Law in Latin America,* published by the Computer Law Association, Inc. (www.itechlaw.org), Washington, D.C., U.S., January 1998. Co-editor of the book *Doing Business in Brazil* published by American Bar Association (www.abanet.org), 2002. Listed in *Telecommunications Industry Report, European Counsel Magazine, International Who's Who of Internet and E-Commerce Lawyers; International Who's Who of Telecom Lawyers; Telecoms; Guide to the World's Leading Telecommunications Lawyers,* edited by Euromoney Legal Media Group; *The Chambers Global—The World's Leading Lawyers; Chambers Latin America.* Member: Vice-Chair of the Inter-American Law Committee of the Comparative Law Division of the ABA, 2001-2004, Washington D.C., U.S.; Member of Board of Directors of CLA (www.itechlaw.org), 1995-2001 and 2003-2005; Vice-President of CLA (www.itechlaw.org) 2002-2003; Vice Chairman of the Technology and Information Protection Sub-committee of the Committee R of International Bar Association (IBA) (www.ibanet.org), 2002/2004; Executive Vice President of the Brazilian Computer and Telecommunication Law Association (ABDI) (www.abdi.org.br) for 1989/1994 and President of ABDI for the years 1995/1998; Representative of ABDI in the Board of Directors of the International Federation of the Computer Law Associations (IFCLA) for 8 years; Federal Communications Bar Association (FCBA), Washington, D.C., U.S. (www.fcba.org). Email: barretto@bkbg.com.br

Paulo Marcos Rodrigues Brancher is a founding and managing partner at Barretto Ferreira, Kujawski e Brancher–Sociedade de Advogados (BKBG). He holds a Ph.D. in International Law and is a professor of International Law at São Paulo Catholic University Law School. He is listed in the following international directories: *Who's Who Legal, Chambers & Partners Latin America, Practical Law*

Company—Which Lawyer? and *Best Lawyers.* Mr. Brancher assists foreign companies doing business in Brazil, is the author of many books on Business Law, and is a frequent speaker at national and international seminars.

Carla Amaral de Andrade Junqueira Canero is a partner with Barretto Ferreira, Kujawski e Brancher—Sociedade de Advogados (BKBG). She holds Ph.Ds from the Law School of São Paulo University and the University of Paris I—Panthéon-Sorbonne, as well as a Bachelor of Law from Pontifícia Universidade Católica de São Paulo and Master in Law from Paris I. She has been a Ph.D fellow at the World Trade Organization and participated in the Program for Young Brazilian Lawyers in Geneva and Brasilia. Ms. Junqueria is listed in the directory International PLC—Trade Experts Guide, Chambers Latin America, Best Lawyers Brazil and Who's Who as a reference in the area of international trade. She has been published in several collective works and speaks Portuguese, English, French, and Spanish.

In addition to serving as editors of *The Legal Guide for Doing Business in South America,* the named editors are also the country coordinating authors for the chapter on Brazil.

About the Country Coordinating Authors

ARGENTINA

Marcelo Bombau leads the mergers and acquisitions and media and entertainment departments of M. & M. Bomchil. Since joining the firm in 1981 he has worked on a number of important transactions, participating actively in some of the most important reorganizations and company purchase deals carried out in Argentina during the past decade, especially related to media and entertainment. The mergers and acquisitions field has been at the core of Mr. Bombau's activities; he has given advice on difficult negotiations and actively participated in due diligence processes, negotiations, and the structuring of complex businesses. Mr. Bombau is member of the board of directors of several local companies. Various publications have distinguished him within his area of practice. He has written many articles and has lectured both in Argentina and abroad. Mr. Bombau graduated from Universidad Nacional de La Plata in 1981. He is a member of Colegio de Abogados de la Ciudad de Buenos Aires, the American Bar Association, and the International Bar Association.

BOLIVIA

Pablo Rojas is the managing partner of C.R. & F. ROJAS-Abogados, where he has been a member of the firm since 1995. He graduated from Marlborough College, Wiltshire, England in 1989, obtained his law degree from Universidad Católica Boliviana Law School in La Paz–Bolivia, and was admitted to practice in 2002. Mr. Rojas has a master's in international legal studies from Golden Gate University School of Law in San Francisco, and he currently teaches corporate law at the Universidad Católica Boliviana in La Paz. Mr. Rojas is a Knight of the Sovereign Order of Malta. He also currently serves as Minister Counselor to the Embassy of the Order of Malta in Bolivia.

BRAZIL

Ricardo Barretto Ferreira da Silva is a founding, senior and managing partner with Barretto Ferreira, Kujawski e Brancher – Sociedade de Advogados (BKBG). He is the editor and co-author of *Computer Law in Latin America,* published by the

Computer Law Association, Inc., and editor of *Doing Business in Brazil*, published by the American Bar Association. Mr. Barretto Ferreira is a graduate of São Paulo University School of Law and the University of North Dakota. He is listed in various international directories and has served on many boards and committees.

Paulo Marcos Rodrigues Brancher is a partner with Barretto Ferreira, Kujawski e Brancher – Sociedade de Advogados (BKBG). He holds a Ph.D in International Law and is also a professor of International Law at São Paulo Catholic University Law School. He is listed in the following international directories: *Who's Who Legal*; *Chambers & Partners Latin America*; *Practical Law Company—Which Lawyer?*; and *Best Lawyers*. Mr. Brancher assists foreign companies doing business in Brazil and is a frequent speaker at national and international seminars.

Carla Amaral de Andrade Junqueira Canero is a partner with Barretto Ferreira, Kujawski e Brancher – Sociedade de Advogados (BKBG), specializing in international trade. She assists clients in trade remedy proceedings, customs procedures, and WTO and regulatory cases. Ms. Junqueira is listed in international directories as an authority on international trade in Brazil, and she is a frequent speaker at national and international seminars on international trade issues. She holds two Ph.D. degrees in WTO Law, from the University of São Paulo and from Panthéon-Sorbonne University in Paris.

CHILE

Marcos Ríos is a partner at Carey y Cía. Ltda., where he is a member of Carey's corporate, mergers and acquisitions, real estate, and government contracts groups. His practice focuses on mergers and acquisitions, project development and international finance, real estate, government procurement, corporate compliance, and gaming law matters. Prior to rejoining Carey in 2004, Mr. Ríos was a senior associate with Hogan & Hartson LLP (HoganLovells) in Washington D.C.; an international associate with Simpson Thacher & Bartlett in New York; a senior associate at Carey; and in-house counsel with Western Mining Corporation in Havana, Cuba. He is a professor of U.S. business law at Universidad de Chile and American University's joint LL.M. Program. He is co-author of *International Arbitration: Practical Considerations with a Latin American Focus*, published by the Journal of Structured and Project Finance (2003), and of *Joint Ventures in the International Arena, 2d ed.*, published by the ABA's Section of International Law (2010). Mr. Ríos is a member of the District of Columbia Bar, the Chilean Bar Association, and the American Bar Association's Section of International Law. He is fluent in Spanish and English.

Consuelo Raby is the director of the corporate, project development, and government contracts practice groups at Carey y Cía. Ltda. Her practice focuses on

commercial and corporate advisory services, capital markets' regulations and issuances, mergers and acquisitions, joint ventures, restructurings, project development
(particularly real estate and tourism), national and international finance, tourism
legislation, and gaming law matters. Among other projects, Ms. Raby has been in
charge of advising American and European companies acquiring and/or operating
real estate and hotel assets in Chile. She also represents international companies in
government contracts and bids in Chile and in other countries of Latin America.
In addition, Ms. Raby has participated as senior associate and as leading attorney
in some of the most important mergers, acquisitions, and issuances in the country
during recent years. She is a member of the arbitral corps of the National Arbitration Center (CNA), and of the Chilean Bar Association. Ms. Raby studied law at
Universidad Católica de Chile and was admitted to the bar in 1996. In 2002, she
obtained a masters of law degree from Duke University in North Carolina. She is
fluent in Spanish and English.

Paola Belan is a member of Carey y Cía.'s corporate, project development, and government contracts practice groups. Her practice focuses on project financing and
development, mergers and acquisitions, international transactions, commercial and
corporate advisory services, and recently on tourism legislation. Currently she is an
assistant professor of civil law at the Universidad de Chile Law School. Mrs. Belan
graduated from the Universidad de Chile Law School and was admitted to the bar
in 2005. She is fluent in Spanish, English, and Hebrew.

Diego Peró is a member of Carey y Cía.'s corporate, project development, and government contracts practice groups. His practice focuses on project financing and
development, mergers and acquisitions, international transactions, and commercial
and corporate advisory services. He is a member of the Chilean Bar Association.
Mr. Peró graduated with distinction from the Pontificia Universidad Católica de
Chile Law School in 2002 and was admitted to the Chilean Bar. He obtained a
masters of law degree from The University of Sydney Law School in 2008. Mr. Peró
is fluent in Spanish and English.

COLOMBIA

Carlos Urrutia Valenzuela is managing partner of Brigard & Urrutia, Colombia's
oldest law firm and one of its largest and most prestigious. Mr. Urrutia attended
Johns Hopkins University for two years of undergraduate studies, and then transferred to the Universidad de los Andes in Bogotá to purse his legal education. He
graduated in 1974 and obtained a doctorate of law degree. In 1975 Mr. Urrutia was
appointed Secretary General of the Governorship of the State of Cundinamarca, and
subsequently Secretary of Finance. In 1977, Mr. Urrutia returned to private practice at Brigard & Urrutia. In addition to being managing partner, Mr. Urrutia heads
the firm's services group. During his 33-year career at the firm, Mr. Urrutia has

advised clients on a wide variety of matters, concentrating in aviation law, commercial law, banking law, and international financial transactions. Mr. Urrutia has acted for developers as well as for banks and financial advisers. His clients are some of the world's leading financial institutions with interests in Colombia. Mr. Urrutia is fluent in Spanish, English, and French.

Tomás Holguín is an associate of Brigard & Urrutia, Colombia's oldest and one of its largest and most prestigious law firms. Mr. Holguín attended Universidad del Rosario in Bogotá to purse his legal education. He graduated in 2006 after being appointed as Colegial Mayor of the University, one of the highest recognitions that a student of that university may be awarded. In 2008, Mr. Holguín obtained a specialized degree in Finance law. After working for the Chamber of Commerce of Bogotá and the Universidad del Rosario, Mr. Holguín joined the Corporate and Antitrust teams of Brigard & Urrutia in 2006. Mr. Holguín has written the book *Carlos Holguín Holguín, Escritos*, published by Universidad del Rosario (2006) and "Disregard of the Corporate Veil in the Stock Exchange Market" in *Disregard of the Corporate Veil*, published by Universidad del Rosario (2010). Mr. Holguín is fluent in Spanish and English.

ECUADOR

Bruce Horowitz is a founding partner of Paz Horowitz, Abogados, and has extensive experience in the practice areas of anticorruption compliance, international intellectual property, and litigation risk and settlement value analysis. He has a postgraduate diploma in the prevention of public corruption from Catholic University of Ecuador Law School (2006); a J.D. from New York University Law School (1976); and a B.A. from Brandeis University (1970). He is licensed to practice law in Ohio, the U.S. Court of International Trade, the U.S. District Court (Alaska), and the Ninth Circuit Court of Appeals. In the area of anticorruption, Mr. Horowitz has been advising clients, providing workshops, and giving presentations on compliance with the Foreign Corrupt Practices Act since 1989. He is a vice-chairperson of the ABA International Anti-Corruption Committee. Mr. Horowitz has been recognized as an international leader on trademark matters by *Business Law Research* and *Euromoney* publications. Prior to founding Paz Horowitz, Abogados, Mr. Horowitz practiced law in the United States on the staff and as managing attorney of the Alaska Legal Services Corporation (1974–1983) and as the executive director of the Ohio State Legal Services Association (1983–1985). As a U.S. Peace Corps volunteer from 1970 to 1973, Mr. Horowitz worked as a land surveyor for the Shuar Indians in the Ecuadorian Amazon region. He taught philosophy, logic, and economics at the American School (Quito) from 1985 to 1989.

PARAGUAY

Alejandro Guanes Mersan is a founder and partner of Guanes, Heisecke & Piera Attorneys at Law, where he specializes in corporate law, international trade law, intellectual property law, computer law, and aviation law. He is also an arbitrator at the Paraguayan Center of Arbitration and Mediation. He earned his LL.M. in international trade law from the University of Arizona James E. Rogers College of Law. In 2005, Mr. Mersan received an award from the Paraguayan Bar Association for his prolific contribution to juridical publications. He has written many articles on intellectual property matters; computer law; Internet and domain names regulations; and law and information technology. Mr. Mersan is a founder and past president of the Paraguayan Association of Computer Law; a founder and past vice president of the Paraguayan Chamber of Information Technology; and a past member of the board of the Paraguayan Association of Industrial Property Agents. He is also a member of the Inter-American Association of Intellectual Property.

PERU

Jean Paul Chabaneix chairs the finance and mergers and acquisitions practice group at Rodrigo, Elias & Medrano Abogados, where he specializes in project finance, corporate finance, mergers and acquisitions, and oil and gas. He has extensive experience in concession processes and in mining, oil and gas, and power deals.

Mariano Fuentes graduated in Law from Pontifical Catholic University of Peru in 2010. As a law student, he worked for the Interamerican Bank of Finance (BIF) advising regular clients in banking transactions and operations. Mr. Fuentes currently works with both domestic and international clients as a legal assistant for the Rodrigo, Elias & Medrano Law Firm, specializing in Project Finance, Securities Regulation, Banking, Finance, and Taxation. He speaks fluent Spanish, English and French.

URUGUAY

Sandra González Vila is a partner with Ferrere Abogados in Montevideo, where since 2007 she has been head of the dispute resolution department, responsible for complex commercial litigation and arbitration, both domestic and international. Ms. Vila earned a law degree from Harvard University in 2000, a postgraduate certificate in administrative contracts from the University of Montevideo in 1997, and a doctorate of law and social sciences from Universidad de la República, Facultad de Derecho in Montevideo in 1996. She currently teaches at Universidad ORT Uruguay in Montevideo. Ms. Vila is a member of the Bar Association of Uruguay and the American Bar Association.

VENEZUELA

Fernando Peláez-Pier joined Hoet Pelaez Castillo & Duque in 1977, where he is one of its leading corporate partners and contributes to the strategic direction of the firm. Mr. Peláez-Pier is a prominent member of the global legal fraternity and, as an expert on inward investment, he has helped several of the largest multinational corporations develop their businesses in Venezuela. He practices in the areas of contract negotiations, mergers and acquisitions, foreign investments, project finance, and alternative dispute resolution. He is president of the International Bar Association. He has also served the IBA as vice president, secretary general, chair, vice chair, and secretary treasurer. Mr. Peláez-Pier is also a member of the American Bar Association, the Interamerican Bar Association, and the Advisory Board of the Institute of International and Comparative Law. He has received numerous professional awards. Mr. Peláez-Pier is a graduate of the Iberoamericana University in Mexico City; Paris University (diplôme d'études supérieures); and the University of the Andes in Merida, Venezuela. He speaks Spanish, English, and French.

Paula Serra Freire practices corporate law at Hoet Pelaez Castillo & Duque in Caracas. She holds a law degree from Pontifícia Universidade Católica do Paraná, and a master's degree in international private law from Université de Paris 2 (Pantheón-Assas). She is fluent in Portuguese, Spanish, English, and French.

Introduction

As the world moves closer to a global business framework, business lawyers can no longer afford to ignore the international components of their daily practices. As companies around the world move from the local to the global, lawyers and businesspeople face a myriad of new questions depending on different legal texts and, most importantly, the cultural and legal contexts that they encounter.

Amid current financial and economic hardships and against the backdrop of slow-paced recovery in the more developed regions of the world, South America has increasingly attracted the eyes of the world. In 2009, while many regions faced stagnation or recession, South America's estimated GDP growth was 5.9 percent. Though still a region of many contrasts, the subcontinent plays an increasing role in the business strategies of multinational enterprises. However, South America's legal and business environment is still highly complex for many.

This book discusses the legal environment for business in the 10 major countries of South America: Argentina, Bolivia, Brazil, Chile, Colombia, Ecuador, Paraguay, Peru, Uruguay, and Venezuela. The chapters focus on national regulations that affect the lives of companies aiming to set up operations in these countries, including the regulatory framework; purchase of property; hiring of employees; aspects of environmental, consumer, and antitrust legislation; and other matters. The objective of this book is to provide the reader with a common language for business and a road map for investments in South America.

Each chapter has been written by a country coordinating author, invited by the editors, or jointly with co-authors and/or contributors, who offer domestic law expertise and firsthand experience, drawing on the knowledge and skills obtained in their day-to-day activities advising foreign companies doing business in South America.

However, due to certain production and space limitations, the authors were asked to discuss only the issues that they consider most important in each jurisdiction. Thus, readers should not expect to find complete coverage of every legal aspect of any issue in the following pages.

Your comments on this book are most welcome, and we will endeavor to incorporate your suggestions into future editions. We hope you enjoy reading this book and find it instructive.

Ricardo Barretto Ferreira da Silva
Paulo Marcos Rodrigues Brancher
Carla Amaral de Andrade Junqueira Canero
Editors

South America Overview

Ricardo Barretto Ferreira Da Silva
Paulo Marcos Rodrigues Brancher
Carla Amaral De Andrade Junqueira Canero
Editors

South America has an area of 17,840,000 square kilometers. The region's population is approximately 390 million, with an annual growth rate of 38 percent. South America's economy is based mostly on agriculture and mineral extraction, but Brazil and Argentina stand out for their exports of manufactured and semi-manufactured goods.[1] Among the major cities of the region are Sao Paulo, Brazil with a population of 17 million; Buenos Aires, Argentina with 11.2 million; and Lima , Peru with 8.3 million inhabitants.

South America's GDP reached USD 2.8 trillion in 2009 and experienced fast recovery after the financial crisis, with an estimated GDP growth rate of 5.9 percent. Brazil, Uruguay, Paraguay, Argentina and Peru presented the highest rates. Inflation in the region fell from 8.2 percent in 2008, to 4.7 percent in 2009. The recovery from the international crisis relied on public policies intended to lower food and energy prices, as well as investment in infrastructure, mainly in roadway networks and ports.[2] Brazil has the largest ports in South America, with the capac-

---

1. Economic Development Division of the Economic Commission for Latin America and the Caribbean (ECLAC), Preliminary Overview of the Economies of Latin America and the Caribbean (2010), http://www.eclac.org/publicaciones/xml/4/41974/2010-976-BPI-WEB_upadted_12-14.pdf

2. http://websie.eclac.cl/anuario_estadistico/anuario_2009/esp/default.asp

ity to circulate over 700 million tons a year. South America is connected by regular flights and has over 100,000 kilometers of railway network.

In the energy sector, countries in the region have installed capacity for 278 thousand megawatts of energy. Brazil and Argentina obtain over 80 percent of their energy from hydroelectric power or natural gas, and Brazil's large sugar cane production also leads to significant ethanol production. Colombia has the largest coal reserves in South America, and Venezuela is one of the world's biggest oil producers. Recent discoveries of oil in Brazil may generateeven higher production levels in the region.

The region also has the largest mining companies in the world and is rich in silver, copper, and iron ore. South America produced 340 million tons of iron ore in 2008, with Brazil responsible for 20 percent of world production. Steel production is increasing due to the promotion of national public policies.

The mobile division leads the telecom sector, with about 375 million people owning mobile phones. Telecom companies in Argentina, Brazil, Chile, and Uruguay offer 3G networks[3].

South America is the world's leading producer of coffee, orange juice, sugar, and soybeans. Argentina is one of the countries which depends the most on the exports of agricultural products (about 55%).

In South America, 2009 was an important year for foreign direct investment (FDI), withUSD 55 billion invested in the region. {{Au: Correct as changed?}}Brazil, Chile and Colombia were the largest hosts with 26, 13 and 7.2 billion respectively. The main targets for FDI were natural resources, manufacturing sectors with low and medium technology intensity and services.[4]

South America remains one of the world's fastest growing consumer markets. Consumption was driven upward by increased consumer credit and the creation of public policies sustaining consumption by the poorest segments of the population.5 Cars, computers, and electronics in Brazil and Chile reached record levels of consumption.6 In 2008, Argentina, Brazil and Venezuela produced almost 900 thousand commercial vehicles. Nowadays, in Brazil alone almost 300 thousand vehicles are sold per month.

---

3. The World Bank, http://data.worldbank.org/topic/infrastructure

4. Unit on Investment and Corporate Strategies of the ECLAC Division of Production, Productivity and Management, Foreign Investment in Latin America and the Caribbean, 2009, http://www.eclac.org/publicaciones/xml/2/39422/inversion2009i.pdf

5. Economic Development Division of the Economic Commission for Latin America and the Caribbean (ECLAC), Preliminary Overview of the Economies of Latin America and the Caribbean (2010), http://www.eclac.org/publicaciones/xml/4/41974/2010-976-BPI-WEB_upadted_12-14.pdf

6. *São Bernardo do Campo*, Adiós to poverty, hola to consumption, The Economist, http://www.economist.com/node/9645142?story_id=9645142

As for regional agreements, Argentina, Brazil, Paraguay, Uruguay and Venezuela form the Southern Common Market (MERCOSUR). Eleven South American countries plus Mexico form the Latin American Integration Association (ALADI). Chile has fifty seven bilateral or regional trade agreements[7] and all countries in South America are members of the World Trade Organization.

Countries in South America are mostly Spanish-speaking, except for Brazil, Suriname, Guyana and French Guiana whose official languages are respectively Portuguese, Dutch, English and French. Languages reflect South America's colonization and ethnicity.

The majority of the legal systems in South America are based on civil law, and countries are advancing significantly on arbitration and international trade law. Important reforms to several judicial systems are being developed in order to better receive FDI.

This edition of the *Legal Guide for Doing Business in South America* covers ten countries: Argentina, Bolivia, Brazil, Chile, Colombia, Ecuador, Paraguay, Peru, Uruguay and Venezuela.

---

7. The World Bank Group, Doing Business 2011: Making a Difference for Entrepreneurs, http://www.doingbusiness.org/~/media/fpdkm/doing%20business/documents/profiles/country/db11/chl.pdf

CHAPTER 1

Argentina

Marcelo Bombau
M. & M. Bomchil*
*Contributors to this chapter: Guillermo Malm Green (Brons & Salas); Alejandro Ciero, Ramón
Moyano, Alejandro Martinez de Hoz, and Bernardo Cassagne (Estudio Beccar Varela);
Ignacio Randle (Estudio Randle); Pablo Ferraro Mila (González & Ferraro Mila); Marcelo Den
Toom, Alejandro Messineo, Florencia Pagani, and Marisa Stachuk (M. & M. Bomchil); Her-
nán Slemenson (Marval, O'Farrell & Mairal); Roberto Bauzá (Rattagan, Macchiavello, Aro-
cena & Peña Robirosa Abogados); Hernán Camarero, Alejandro Llosa, and Damián Navarro
(Richards, Cardinal, Tützer, Zabala & Zaefferer); Saúl Feibogen (Vitale, Manoff & Feilbogen);
Laurence P. Wiener (Wiener·Soto·Caparrós); and Pablo Crescimbeni (Zang, Bergel & Viñes).

COUNTRY OVERVIEW

Argentina is the eighth-largest country in the world and the second-largest in Latin
America in terms of surface area, covering some 1.5 million square miles, with
a population of approximately 41 million. It is organized as a federal republic
with a democratic political system and a government consisting of an executive
branch headed by the president, a legislative branch, and a judiciary. The president
is elected by direct vote and may serve a maximum of two consecutive four-year
terms.

Argentine Congress comprises two houses, the Senate and the Chamber of
Deputies, and has exclusive power to enact laws concerning federal legislation,
including international and interprovincial trade, immigration and citizenship,
and patents and trademarks; and to enact the civil, commercial, criminal, mining,
labor, and social security codes, which are applicable nationwide.

The judicial system is divided into federal and provincial courts, with each
system having lower courts, courts of appeal, and supreme courts. The supreme
judicial power of Argentina is vested in the Supreme Court of Justice.

Each of the 23 provinces enacts its own Constitution, elects its own governor
and legislators, and appoints its own judges to the provincial courts.

ESTABLISHING A BUSINESS PRESENCE

Permanent Structures

To conduct business on a permanent basis a foreign company can either (i) incorporate or participate in a local entity, or (ii) qualify a representative or a branch. Foreign companies wishing to participate in local companies must file and register with the Public Registry of Commerce (PRC) (i) a copy of their articles of incorporation and bylaws; (ii) proof that they are validly existing according to the laws of the country where they were formed; and (iii) the corporate resolution appointing legal representatives and fixing a local domicile. They shall also: (i) inform if they are subject to business prohibitions or restrictions in their place of origin; and (ii) demonstrate that, outside of Argentina, they either (a) have one or more agencies, branches, or permanent representations, (b) hold a participation in companies that qualifies as noncurrent assets; or (c) own fixed assets in their country of origin. In case a foreign company was incorporated for the sole purpose of being a vehicle for investing in other companies, compliance of the above requisites by its controlling entity suffices.

Suitable Corporate Forms

Commercial activities in Argentina are usually carried out through one of the following: the corporation (sociedad anónima or SA), the limited liability company (sociedad de responsabilidad limitada or SRL), or the branch of a foreign company. The first two are the most common, since they limit the liability of the parent company to the extent of its interest in the local company. Applicable rules are comprised in the Argentine Commercial Companies Act 19,550 (ACCA), which is applied nationwide. Provincial laws set forth rules for registration and other requirements.

The structure and rules for SAs and SRLs are quite similar although the latter has slightly less operational costs. Certain activities such as banking and insurance require that the company be incorporated as an SA. The minimum stock capital required for SAs is equivalent to some USD 3,000. There is no minimum requirement for SRLs. However, the stock capital needs to be consistent with the corporate purpose. SAs and SRLs can be managed and represented by one or more individuals, in which case decisions shall be adopted by majority vote. The board shall hold meetings at least quarterly, and the majority of directors need to be Argentine residents (there being no nationality requirements). The directors must also register with the tax and social security authorities.

Resolutions on matters that go beyond day-to-day decisions are to be decided by the stockholders and, unless a unanimous meeting and vote are expected, all others need to be summoned. SA stockholders shall be notified by means of notice in the Official Gazette within a specific time frame. Companies under permanent governmental supervision as well as specific situations also require notices in a nationwide newspaper. The summoning rules for SRLs are more flexible. There are certain specific statutory quorum and majority requirements depending on the kind of meeting (ordinary or extraordinary).

Wholly Owned Entities

ACCA rules require at least two stockholders. According to the regulations and policies in force in the city of Buenos Aires, the minority holder shall own no less than 2 percent of the stock capital. The two stockholders may belong to the same group; thus, ultimately, the local company may be a wholly owned entity.

Joint Ventures

The ACCA provides for contractual joint ventures, which are not granted legal personality and thus do not have a legal existence separate from their members. These agreements need to be registered with the local PRC in order to have effects vis-à-vis third parties and must contain term of duration, name, domicile, liability of each of the members, and the details on the decision-making process, among other specifications.

Investments in Mergers with Existing Entities

There are basically two ways of participating in or acquiring a local business: a) Purchase of shares: the continuity of the legal entity entails risks associated with hidden liabilities, particularly tax and social security ones; b) Asset purchase: this option provides reasonable protection against hidden liabilities if executed through the Transfer of Going Concerns Act and federal and provincial tax regulations. This alternative is more expensive than a "share" deal.

Merger processes are quite common in Argentina. Subject to compliance with certain fiscal requirements, corporate reorganizations (mergers included) can be carried out in a tax-free fashion. Corporate reorganizations encompass a number of agreements, valuations, and stages, and must be registered with the PRC.

Agency/Reseller/Franchising/Distribution Networks

Agency, distribution, and franchising agreements lack specific regulation by law in Argentina. Thus, their main characteristics and those of other distribution networks (commercial agents, licenses, etc.) have been shaped by doctrine and case law. As such, the parties can, in principle, freely regulate their relationship.

- In an agency agreement, the principal entrusts the agent with the promotion and marketing of the former's business. The agent sponsors a principal business and receives a commission from the sales of the products or services. The agent can either simply intermediate in the sale of goods by marketing the products and/or services, and/or, on the other hand, can act as attorney in fact of the principal, carrying out negotiations and executing purchase agreements on its behalf. The main characteristic of this structure is the financial and operative independence of the agent. Courts have ruled that the agent is an independent contractor, not a subordinated businessman or an employee. However, when agents are natural persons there is a potential risk that they may be considered by labor law as formal employees.

- Distribution agreements also make use of independent contractors but—in this structure—the middleman does not sponsor or handle the products or services as an attorney in fact. The distributor acquires the products or services with the purpose of reselling them. Courts have ruled that one of its material traits is the need to have an established independent organization in order to provide services related to the said products or services. As opposed to the agent, the distributor carries out the invoicing, delivery, and post-sale servicing at its own risk and receives commercial objectives, quotas, and other instructions from the principal. The distribution of certain products (e.g., newspapers, magazines, and films) requires specific regulations.

- Franchising agreements have been recognized by case law, and their use has spread out quite widely. Though the franchisee is an independent contractor, the contractual bond is stronger than in the distribution agreement, in terms of organization, trademark, objectives, and overall economic dependence. By this agreement the franchisee uses the franchisor's business model, commercialization system, and know-how.

- Absent a fixed term, said contracts are valid and enforceable until the parties decide to terminate them. However, problems have arisen when one of the parties terminates the agreement without reasonable forewarning notice and a cause for "damages" arises. Case law has provided that the lack of a specific contractual term does not imply that the bond is perpetual, but that the terminating party needs to serve the other with a reasonable forewarning notice. How "reasonable" the forewarning has been will be adjudged considering: (a) whether there is a proportional relation between the term of the agreement and the term of the prior notice; (b) the investment made by the distributor, agent, or franchisee; (c) the exclusivity, or not, of the agreement; and (d) the time that would be required for the "weaker" party to reestablish its financial situation.

Representative Offices and Other "Non-Permanent" Establishments

Foreign companies may also perform activities through a branch with a duly registered representative. Branches, as opposed to the local corporate entities, do not limit the liability of the parent company. Branches prepare their annual financial statements separately from their parent and file them with the PRC. There is no requirement for minimum branch capital, with the exception of activities such as banking or insurance.

Approvals and Registration

Argentine companies are regulated by the ACCA; resolutions are issued by the PRC of each province and, when applicable, by the National Securities Commission. The performance of regulated activities such as media, banking, or insurance also requires filings with the relevant regulatory agency. Local companies must also be registered with the Tax Authorities. Foreign shareholders are not obliged to obtain a tax identification number in order to own shares in a local entity.

Sensitive Economic Sectors/Restrictions on Foreign Ownership

Freedom to set up a business by foreign investors is the prevailing principle. However, the "equal treatment" principle recognizes certain exceptions: inter alia, in public procurement, a preference is given to goods of domestic origin and to local services ("Buy Argentina Regime"), such as media and broadcasting.

Some of the more attractive sectors for foreign investors, such as mining, forestry, leather, renewable energy, petrochemicals, agricultural machinery, biotechnology, vegetable oils, wine, cultural-related industries, software, outsourcing, and tourism, also set out some minor restrictions on foreign ownership.

Political Risk and Related Issues

Uncertainty regarding Argentina's future has increased during the past decade as a consequence of a decrease in institutional quality and the rule of law.

For instance, in 2001, Argentina's government collapsed and the country defaulted on its sovereign debt payments (over USD 100 billion was owed to domestic and foreign bondholders, of which approximately 93 percent has been restructured). Recent regulations have affected contractual relationships, casting uncertainty on the enforceability of acquired rights and protection of private property. Such regulations include decrees or laws on asymmetrical conversion of US-dollar-denominated debts into pesos; mandatory transfer of private welfare system funds to the public system; termination of concession agreements for public services, such as water and sewer and national airline; or intervention of the same. Expropriations and confiscations have not been unheard of.

This notwithstanding, Argentina has achieved a stable democratic system. The current Federal Supreme Court has shown reasonable independence from the political influence of the federal government and has decided major cases in which it did not coincide with the federal government's interest or desire.

Potential foreign investors should take into account the depicted political issues knowing, however, that Argentinean law provides an adequate legal and judicial system to mitigate them, such as, for example, the freedom of choice of venue, jurisdiction, and law applicable to international contracts, and the undisputed protection of private property (only narrowed in cases of clear national emergencies).

INVESTMENT ISSUES AND TAX INCENTIVES

Legal Treatment for Foreign Investment

As a general principle, foreign investors wishing to invest in Argentina do not require prior governmental approval, except for certain specific regulated areas (for example, media) or for general applicable regimes such as antitrust regulations (for example, the mandatory merger notification system). They enjoy the same status and have the same rights that local laws grant to Argentine investors.

Treaties on Foreign Investment Protection

Argentina has diplomatic relationships with almost all countries and is a member of several international organizations such as the World Bank, the International Monetary Fund, MERCOSUR (South American Common Market Treaty), and the International Centre for Settlement of Investment Disputes (ICSID).

Argentina has entered into several Bilateral Investment Treaties,[1] so as to improve the guarantees provided by the Foreign Investment Law to investors, by enhancing (i) protection against expropriation; (ii) free transfer of income from local subsidiaries; (iii) fair and equitable treatment; (iv) nondiscrimination; and (v) alternative dispute resolution mechanisms, whereby an investor whose rights have been violated can choose between resorting to local jurisdiction, or to have recourse to international arbitration. Since 2001, many foreign investors have asserted claims against Argentina before ICSID.

Publicly Held Companies—Capital Market Regulations

The Argentine securities market is regulated nationwide by its Securities Law whose governing body is the *Comisión Nacional de Valores* (the CNV), a governmental agency empowered to issue further regulations in the form of mandatory resolutions. Main regulations address aspects relating to transparency in the public offering regime, such as participation in public offerings, disclosure of relevant information, tender offers, insider trading, and market manipulation.

The securities market is divided from a regulatory viewpoint into a private market and a public market. This division is based on the concept of "public offer," which is the invitation made by an issuer or by parties engaged in the purchase and sale of securities, to the general public, or certain sectors thereof, through personal offers, newspaper advertisements, media, or by any other means, to enter into any transaction involving securities. The term "transaction" includes the initial issuing and placement, as well as the subsequent purchase and/or sale. Only public offers of securities are subject to the Securities Law.

Those involved in any "public" offer must be registered with the CNV. The Securities Law provides that only securities that have identical rights in each class may be publicly offered.

Securities in Buenos Aires are traded in self-regulated organizations such as the Buenos Aires Stock Exchange (BASE) and the electronic over-the-counter market in which only dealers registered with the CNV may trade securities. The clearing of transactions on the BASE is carried out through the *Caja de Valores S.A.* Settlement is carried out through the Merval, which is the company that oversees brokerage activities and transactions of the BASE. Over-the-counter transactions are cleared and settled by their respective parties, and the participants may deposit traded securities with the *Caja de Valores S.A.*

The regulations of the CNV set out specific procedures regarding the registration of debt securities, asset-backed securities, pooled funds, investment funds, direct investment funds, money market funds, and authorization of rating agencies.

Alternate Investment Structures—Investment Funds

Trust structures have become one of the most popular and effective methods to organize investments. The main feature of the trust (or Fideicomiso) is the complete isolation of the underlying assets, obtained through the transfer of said assets to a vehicle that agrees to hold or manage them for the benefit of a third party. Thus, the underlying assets are removed from the balance sheet of the settlor, creating a new independent estate. The Fideicomiso has been successfully supported by local courts through many decisions.

The Fideicomiso is not a legal entity but an "independent estate" that has the capacity to enter into agreements and act as an employer. Under local tax regulations the Fideicomiso is considered a taxpayer and, as such, must obtain its own tax identification number, prepare returns, and pay taxes.

The beneficiaries of the trust have the right to control and replace the trustee. Similarly, this flexible structure allows that newcomers can be added to an existing trust. Beneficiaries also enjoy the possibility of freely assigning the benefits over the trust, which can be organized either as a private investment mechanism or as a capital market structure offering equity parts to the public.

Securitization has had notable development in the local capital markets with a number of transactions tapping the international markets. A wide variety of underlying assets have been used as the source of repayment such as mortgages, personal and consumer loans, export receivables, future flow transactions, leasing, hydro-carbon royalties, and tax sharing revenues.

OPERATIONAL LEGAL ENVIRONMENT

Tips on Negotiation in the Country

Understanding local customs and etiquette is vital to building trust and securing an investment. Some common business practices are as follows.

1. Personal relationships are highly valued. Most people in Argentina take a sincere interest in others and spend time getting to know each other.
2. Schedules are relaxed. Argentineans have a flexible attitude toward time. Arriving 10 or 15 minutes after the scheduled time is common.
3. A handshake is the normal greeting and farewell. Once a relationship has developed, a hug or a kiss on the cheek complements the handshake.
4. Negotiations can be lengthy since Argentineans are quite detail-oriented.
5. Except for international deals, business in Argentina is usually conducted in Spanish.
6. Business organization in Argentina tends to be hierarchical. Status is important and attention is paid to appearance.
7. Arguments and debates are generally considered constructive ways of bringing about new ideas.
8. Physical proximity is used as a way of communicating. Do not be offended or surprised if an Argentine colleague is in your personal space.
9. The U.S. Embassy usually has a good read on the local political, social, and business environment.

Foreign Exchange

Foreign exchange is a highly regulated area, especially since 2005.

In terms of inflow of funds, there is a mandatory deposit of 30 percent of the inflow amount, which must be made in U.S. dollars with an Argentine bank, for a 365-day term, bearing no interest. There are, however, certain exceptions to this mandatory deposit, such as (a) Direct Investments: foreign residents making a direct capital contribution and/or purchasing at least 10 percent of shares in local companies, are exempt. Purchase of real estate by non-Argentine residents is also exempt; (b) Credit Operations: when foreign loan proceeds are used by the local borrower for investment in nonfinancial assets registered as "fixed assets," the mandatory transfer of such funds into Argentina will also be exempted from the deposit. Other exceptions are: (i) loans granted by certain foreign multilateral and bilateral lending agencies, and (ii) loans to be allocated to the settlement of external debts. Proceeds from export operations are generally exempted also.

Regarding the outflow of funds, some ad hoc requirements must be met in order to be authorized to send funds abroad. For instance: (i) dividends payable to foreign investors must arise from audited and approved financial statements of the local company; (ii) the repatriation of funds by nonresidents resulting from the sale of direct investments in local companies shall be authorized in case the nonresident investor has maintained the investment for at least 365 days; and (iii) repayment of the principal amount of a loan granted by a foreign lender, including its accrued interests, is subject to specific requirements.

There is a monthly limit of USD 2 million that can be acquired by local companies and individuals for investments of any kind of out Argentina.

Payment of fees related to services of any kind rendered by foreign residents is not subject to any specific restriction.

Immigration and Visa Requirements

A temporary residence visa allows a person to work in Argentina. For its obtainment a "residence request" must be filed by the local employer petitioning authorization for the expatriate to enter Argentina. The permit is issued within 20 to 30 days. Afterward, the expatriate must appear before the nearest Argentine consulate with the entry permit, the executed labor contract, and personal documentation. Upon submission of these documents, the expatriate will be granted a one-year temporary residence visa, which will enable him or her to work, freely enter and leave Argentina, complete procedures to obtain an Argentine ID and driver's license, and bring personal assets into Argentina.

Import and Export Issues

Argentine Customs Code and its Regulatory Decree contain the main legal framework regarding import and export of goods. The governmental body in charge of applying said legislation is the National Customs Administration.

Those wishing to perform import and/or export activities have a special registry for which purpose they must: (i) be registered before the Argentine federal tax authorities; (ii) provide evidence of economic solvency or a guarantee as mandated; and (iii) not be comprised within any of the limitations contained in the Customs Code.

There are, however, exceptions to such registration when import and export activities are (a) not performed on a regular basis, or (b) are performed under specific regimes (for example, luggage, onboard supplies, diplomatic exemptions, among others). If the import or export activities are not performed on a regular basis, a special authorization from the National Customs Administration must be obtained.

Once registered, the applicant must file annual financial statements and report managerial changes. Failure to comply with these requirements may lead to sanctions, including cancellation of the registration.

Notwithstanding special regimes contained in special laws, all means of transport arriving to Argentina must enter through authorized channels and provide the corresponding customs' authority with all the required documentation regarding the vehicle and its cargo. Another alternative is to request and obtain direct customs clearance, which is eligible only for certain goods.

Generally speaking, the export process is similar to the import process described above.

Taxation of Business and Cross-Border Transactions

Several tax aspects should be taken into consideration in connection with doing business in Argentina either with a presence in the country or directly from abroad. Argentina has three different levels of taxation: (i) the federal level with income tax, minimum deemed income tax, value added tax (VAT), excise taxes, personal assets tax, and tax on debits and credits on bank accounts as the main taxes, besides custom duties as a federal levy; (ii) the Provincial and Buenos Aires city district level with turnover tax and stamp tax as the leading taxes; and (iii) the municipal level that normally imposes taxes on services such as health and security. The taxes that may normally affect cross-border business are income tax, VAT, and stamp tax.

Argentina has adopted the worldwide principle of taxation and thus, resident taxpayers are subject to income tax on their worldwide income with an ordinary foreign tax credit as a unilateral method for avoiding double taxation. The tax is assessed on taxable income at the rate of 35 percent. Nonresident taxpayers are (a) subject to tax only on Argentine source income, which is determined under certain tests, and (b) generally subject to tax on notional taxable income at a certain percentage determined for the relevant type of income involved. The effective tax is determined applying the 35 percent withholding tax rate on such notional income.

Nonresidents are exempt from income tax on the capital gains derived from the assignment of shares in an Argentine corporation, although this exemption does not apply in the case of other securities such as quotas of a limited liability company. Dividends are, as a rule, not subject to withholding tax except for the equalization tax that may apply in certain situations.

The taxation of transfer of technology, know-how, and technical assistance is not only ruled by the Income Tax Law but also by the Transfer of Technology Law, which contains regulations with tax consequences such as deductibles for income tax purposes and for applying reduced withholding tax rates.

The taxation of permanent establishment (PE) is scarce on rules determining whether it is an Argentine or foreign PE and as to how to attribute its income since PEs are subject to tax on worldwide income, as is any corporation.

Transfer pricing rules have been adopted in Argentina and need to be checked in cross-border transactions. Different methods are foreseen for determining the arm's-length range, and the local taxpayer has to choose which is the most appropriate for the given transaction.

Though thin capitalization (2:1 debt equity ratio) rules have been adopted, not many situations are caught. When business financing interacts with treaty partner countries, some arguable rules may affect the international transaction.

Doing business either from or to a low-tax jurisdiction is always more burdensome as the income tax rules either require more evidence on the transaction or increase the taxation. Likewise, the Argentine income tax treaty network[2] needs to be analyzed in cross-border transactions since it limits the Argentine source taxing rights in many circumstances.

Minimum deemed income tax is levied on the assets held at the end of the fiscal period at a rate of 1 percent. The income tax paid during a given year is taken as credit for the minimum deemed income tax payable in such year; any excess income tax does not give rise to a credit. The minimum deemed income tax paid in a given year may be used as a tax credit toward the same tax liability of the following 10 years.

As a general rule, the Personal Assets Tax is a tax on net wealth of individuals and estates that should not affect cross-border transactions. However, in the case of participations in Argentine companies held by nonresident companies, it is presumed that the indirect owner is an individual or an estate and the obligation of the local company is to pay a tax assessed at 0.5 percent on the value of the participation held by the nonresident under certain rules. This tax liability does not apply in certain cases of taxpayers resident in given treaty partner countries (for example, Spain and Switzerland).

Though VAT (levied at the general rate of 21 percent with reduced 10.5 percent rates) is a tax that generally affects local transactions, it may sometimes affect a cross-border deal as well. Exports of goods are clearly zero-rated, but exports of services receive such treatment only when the service supplied in Argentina is effectively used or exploited abroad.

Stamp tax is a local tax levied on acts or contracts with economic content that are either executed or have effects in a given local jurisdiction. As it is a local tax, each jurisdiction has its own rules. The tax is assessed on the economic value of the contract and the average tax rate is 1 percent. The city of Buenos Aires has reintroduced this tax after several years at a general rate of 0.8 percent. Contracts implemented through an offer letter, which is accepted by an act of the addressee, have worked as a way to avoid the stamp tax and have been supported by case law.

Labor and Employment

Argentine labor legislation is mainly contained in the Employment Contract Act, the regulations issued thereunder, and the collective bargaining agreements applicable according to the employer's main line of business. Hiring alternatives under local law are the following:

    a. Permanent contract: Argentine labor law sustains the "indefinite" term contract as the rule. It is not required to be written, and it has a mandatory trial period of 90 days, within which the employer may terminate the same without severance payment. Admitted departures from this general rule are described in the following paragraphs.

b. Part-time contract: applicable to those who work for less than two-thirds of the normal working day.

c. Fixed-term contract: this type of hiring must be in writing, set its limited duration, and document its objective justification, which must be extraordinary (for example, replacement of an employee on leave). The maximum term for these contracts is five years.

d. Temporary contract: written contract used to meet extraordinary workforce needs for an indefinite period, under which: (i) the employer is not required to give prior notice of its termination; (ii) no severance payment is due when the contract concludes upon completion of the extraordinary needs; (iii) the extraordinary workforce needs must be reasonable and expressly stated in the agreement; (iv) the trial period is not applicable.

e. Seasonal employment contract: intended for activities that take place during repetitive cycles by reason of the nature of the business (for example, for ski instructors).

f. Temporary contracts provided by agencies authorized by the Ministry of Labor: the worker is considered as an employee of the agency rather than of the user company.

g. Traineeships: subject to a reduced working day; and the contract may not exceed 12 months. Traineeships are not considered employment contracts.

Termination of employment relationships can occur in different ways:

a. Resignation: valid insofar as it is reflected in formal trustworthy correspondence (telegram) from the employee, or through the Ministry of Labor. It does not generate severance compensation;

b. Termination by mutual agreement of the parties: passed before a public notary or executed before the labor courts or the Ministry of Labor;

c. Termination for cause: it can be alleged in case of failure by the other party to comply with its obligations. If the cause for termination is challenged, its merits will be eventually assessed by a labor judge;

d. Job abandonment;

e. Termination without cause: in this case the employer must pay the statutory severance compensation, as described below;

f. Termination for force majeure or lack of work non-attributable to the employer: in these cases, the employee is entitled to a compensation equivalent to 50 percent of the regular severance compensation provided for dismissal without cause;

g. Employee's death; and

h. Retirement.

Upon dismissal without cause the following severance payment items apply:

a. Seniority compensation: equivalent to one monthly salary per year of service or period in excess of three months, on the basis of the best, normal, and highest monthly remuneration earned by the employee during the last year of services;
b. Payment in lieu of prior notice: if upon termination a party fails to give the mandatory prior notice, the other party will be entitled to a compensation "in lieu of notice" equivalent to the salary that would have been payable during the applicable period had the notice been given;
c. Dismissal month's salary;
d. Compensation for pending vacations; and
e. Proportional thirteenth salary.

Mandatory employee insurance is to be hired with special-purpose insurance companies covering medical care, salary payment, and compensation in case of labor accidents or illnesses. Different regulations establish technical standards and health measures aimed at protecting the employees' physical and mental health; preventing, reducing, or eliminating workplace hazards; and at encouraging accident prevention practices.

The Argentine Social Security System is financed with monthly employee contributions (11 percent of the salary), which are withheld by the employer, as well as with monthly employer contributions (ranging from 21 to 27 percent).

Work hours cannot exceed eight hours a day, with a weekly 48-hour limit. The daily limit may be extended to nine hours, as long as the maximum weekly limit is not exceeded.

Antitrust and Competition Issues

Argentina's Defense of Competition Law reaffirms the prohibition of acts limiting, restricting, or distorting competition and abuses of a dominant position, while also addressing merger regulation. The law applies to those engaged in economic activities, to the extent these activities have local effects. All violations are assessed under a rule of reason approach, as the Competition Law does not stipulate any categories of per se illegal conduct. Prohibited acts are so qualified insofar as they may harm the general economic interest, a term interpreted as closely related to that of consumer welfare.

The National Antitrust Commission or CNDC is in charge of the investigations of anticompetitive practices and merger review. It reports to the Secretariat of Domestic Trade. Judicial review of its decisions is unrestricted in scope.

Anticompetitive agreements are included in the general prohibition of the Competition Law, which also provides a non-exhaustive list of anticompetitive practices, such as concerted practices through price fixing, market allocation, information exchange, and bid-rigging. Local Criminal Code provides for sanctions for price fixing of goods among competitors but, as a practical matter, this provision has not been applied in the past 20 years.

The Competition Law also identifies unilateral conduct patterns as abuses of dominance. Both exclusionary and exploitative types of abuse—including abusive pricing—are prohibited. Refusals to deal and price discrimination are among the most common violations brought to the consideration of the CNDC. When analyzing the existence of a dominant position, the following factors must be taken into account: (i) the extent to which other goods or services can act as substitutes; (ii) statutory restrictions limiting access to the market; (iii) whether the relevant person may unilaterally influence pricing or restrict supply or demand; and (iv) the potential market power of competitors.

Merger control is exercised over all economic concentrations of enterprises. It is understood as (i) the de jure or de facto acquisition of control over companies, going concerns or assets from which an independent turnover can be identified, by means of a merger, the transfer of a going concern, the acquisition of property or any interest rights, when such acquisition gives the acquirer control or substantial influence over the enterprise, as well as (ii) any act or agreement that transfers a decisive influence on the passing of resolutions related to the ordinary or extraordinary management of an enterprise.

Mergers and acquisitions will be subject to control if the enterprises involved in the transaction (acquirer and target companies or merging parties, but not seller) have a turnover in excess of approximately USD 50 million in Argentina, unless a special exemption applies. Exemptions from merger control are (i) acquisitions of enterprises in which the acquirer already owns more than 50 percent of the interest (or voting rights thereof), (ii) intra-group transactions, (iii) acquisition of a single enterprise by a foreign investor that has not owned shares or assets in Argentina, and (iv) situations in which the amount of the transaction and the value of the assets located in Argentina being acquired, transferred, or controlled do not exceed approximately USD 5 million, unless recent transactions in the same market exceed certain thresholds. In addition to the application of fines for late filing, the SCI may: (a) approve, (b) impose undertakings, or (c) prohibit the transaction.

Conduct prohibited under the Competition Law may be subject to cease-and-desist orders; fines for up to USD 40 million (sums that may be doubled in the case of repeating offenders and in special cases of abuse of dominance); and judicial divestiture, dissolution, or liquidation. Corporate officers, directors, managers, or proxies may also be fined jointly and severally with the company involved. Such persons may also be barred from acting in commerce for a term of one to 10 years.

Environmental Issues

Argentine Constitution recognizes the right to a healthy and balanced environment and sustainable development and it establishes a "polluter pays" principle whereby environmental damage generates the obligation to "restore" it (subject to law). Though power to legislate on environmental matters is vested upon the provinces, the federal government has the power to legislate minimum standards to be met throughout the country. This has been done through the Environmental Framework Law, which sets the following principles:

a. any work or activity that may likely significantly degrade the environment or any component thereof or affect people's quality of life, is subject to an environmental impact assessment review;

b. anyone performing activities that may be hazardous to the environment must obtain insurance guaranteeing the remedy of any environmental damage;

c. any person causing environmental damage shall face strict liability and shall be responsible for restoring the damaged environment to its prior condition. Should such restoration be technically impossible, the payment of substitutive compensation is appropriate;

d. if two or more persons are involved and the party responsible for the damage cannot be determined, or if the extent of the damage caused by each of them cannot be accurately established, all of them are jointly and severally liable without detriment, if applicable, to the right of contribution among them.

Consumer Protection and Product Liability

The Argentine Consumer Protection Act (CPA) has established some preventive norms for product liability through a system that sets forth the strict, joint, and several liability of all the participants in the different stages of the production, marketing, and commercialization for damages arising from the risk or defects of products or services.

The CPA also demands that specific information and notices be made for products or services that may be dangerous to the health or safety of consumers. Thus, the supplier must market them under conditions that guarantee consumer safety. When defective, used, or reconstituted products are publicly offered to undetermined potential consumers, their condition needs to be clearly and accurately indicated.

The manufacturer, seller, and any intermediary are subject to strict liability standards that can be individually avoided only if it is proved that the cause of the injury is unrelated to it. Lack of negligence is insufficient to be freed from liability.

There is no sharing of liability in the Argentine legal system, and the burden of proving that the product is not defective is imposed upon the manufacturer. Anticipated waivers and clauses changing the burden of proof are illegal.

Punitive damages were introduced in the Argentine legal system through an amendment of the CPA in April 2008.

Land Use and Real Estate

Ownership of land in Argentina is generally freehold and is subject to registration with the official Land Registry where the land is situated. Since Argentina has a well-developed land register system, there is no title insurance system.

Foreign ownership is unrestricted except in border areas, in which case prior consent of the National Security Zones Commission must be obtained.

The process of acquiring immovable property can be divided into three stages: (i) the precontractual stage, which normally involves initial negotiations, preliminary letters of intent, and a summary title investigation; (ii) the contractual stage, when detailed negotiations are normally completed and the contract is entered into; and (iii) the postcontractual or completion phase, which involves the execution of the notarial deed of conveyance and the registration of the deed at the Land Registry.

Mortgages are the most commonly used security in relation to immovable property. The mortgaged property, however, remains in the possession of its owner, who may transfer the same to a third party subject to the mortgage. The mortgage must cover a specific property and amount, and the underlying obligation guaranteed by the mortgage must also be certain and determined. Mortgages securing conditional, future, or undetermined obligations are permitted, provided that an estimated value of the obligation is provided upon creation of the mortgage. Mortgages must be created by means of a public deed executed by mortgagee and mortgagor before a notary public, and afterward they must be registered with the Land Registry in order to perfect the mortgage and produce effects against third parties. Foreclosure of the mortgage can be sought through special summary court proceedings, which provide for the sale of the property by public auction.

Urban lease provisions are generally of "public order" and cannot be altered by agreement of the parties. Urban leases need only be in writing, there being no notarial or registration requirements. Urban leases of commercial property have a minimum term of three years whereas residential leases have a minimum term of two years. These minimum term requirements do not apply to certain types of leases such as tourism, parking spaces, and stalls at markets. Notwithstanding the minimum terms indicated above, after the first six months' lease, the tenant has a legal right to terminate the lease by giving the landlord 60 days' prior notice. Lease agreements are subject to a maximum term of 10 years.

In general, the tenant shall be responsible for carrying out minor repairs and regular maintenance of the leased property and for those repairs caused by his fault. Any defects in the structure of the property or more serious repair works are, however, the responsibility of the landlord.

Urban development in Argentina is basically governed by municipal zoning regulations and local building codes, which vary according to each jurisdiction.

Intellectual Property

Protection of intellectual property in Argentina derives from the Argentine Constitution and from different laws, decrees, and international treaties.

Copyright is regulated by the Copyright Law and the Berne Convention, among other treaties, and is equally applicable to nationals and foreigners, except for the case in which a foreigner seeking copyright recognition comes from a country that does not have similar copyright protection. Broad protection is given to "any scientific, literary, artistic or didactic production" and it extends to the material expression of ideas, procedures, methods of operation, and mathematical concepts but not to the ideas, procedures, methods, and concepts themselves. Argentina recognizes both moral and patrimonial rights of the authors. While moral rights are nontransferable and of unlimited duration, patrimonial rights are of limited duration, freely transferable, and admit certain limitations.

Registration with the Copyright Office creates a presumption of authorship in favor of the registrant. The assignment or licensing of copyrighted works must be registered with the Copyright Office in order to be enforceable and valid vis-à-vis third parties. The standard term of copyright protection is the author's life plus 70 years counted from January 1 of the year immediately following the author's death. Nevertheless, other protection terms apply to specific cases. Software is specifically included within the works protected under the Copyright Law.

The Argentine Ministry of Foreign Affairs administers the Country Code Top Level Domain. The registration of domain names is, for the time being, free of charge.

The Trademarks and Trade Names Law and a variety of international treaties, such as the Paris Convention and the Agreement on Trade-Related Aspects of Intellectual Property Rights (Gatt-Trips), set the legal framework in the trademark field. Though not a member of any common system of trademark registration, Argentina has adopted the international classification of goods and services under the Nice Agreement.

A trademark must be registered with the Trademark Office in order to obtain property rights over it. Nevertheless, exceptions have been granted by admitting rights to nonregistered trademarks in special cases (for example, prior widespread recognition). Trademark registrations last for 10 years and they can be indefinitely renewed for identical periods. Trademark holders (as well as copyright and patent owners) can also register them with the "Customs Alert System," a mechanism under which the Customs Office will send notice and allow inspection of goods bearing the relevant trademark before they can clear customs.

The legal framework for patents and utility models is constituted mainly by the Patent Law and a variety of international treaties such as the Paris Convention and the Gatt-Trips. However, Argentina has not adhered to the Patent Convention Treaty.

Inventions are patentable when the products and proceedings reflect novelty, inventive activity, and actual industrial application. Since Argentina's entrance into the Gatt-Trips, pharmaceutical patents can be obtained in Argentina. Foreign legal entities and individuals may obtain registration of a patent, as long as they establish a domicile in the city of Buenos Aires. Patent rights can be assigned, transferred, and licensed through any means but must be registered with the Patent Office. Once a patent application is granted, it will be valid until the twentieth year counted from the application date. Renewals are not admitted. The Patent Law also regulates protection of Utility Models, which is granted for a nonrenewable 10-year term from the date of the application.

Industrial Models and Designs protect the shape or appearance given to an industrial product providing an ornamental feature. There is no examination of the application, and the granting proceedings are very fast. Protection is granted for five years from the filing date and can be renewed twice for identical periods of time.

Customs

The General Customs Administration, organized within the local IRS, is in charge of enforcing legislation related to import and export of goods, and the means and conditions under which said goods are transported. It assists the federal government in certain key areas related to national security and national health by limiting or banning goods considered dangerous or illegal.

The General Director has authority to (i) exercise powers granted by legal provisions with respect to taxes regarding import and export of goods and other custom-related activities; (ii) interpret legal provisions related to customs affairs; (iii) control international traffic of goods; (iv) apply temporary or permanent bans on import or export of goods; (v) review the customs administrators' final decisions; (vi) exercise the jurisdictional attributions granted by the Federal Customs Code; and (vii) require assistance from the security forces for the fulfillment of its duties, among others.

Internet Regulations/E-Commerce

Although no regulations currently pertain specifically to e-commerce, three main legal aspects should be kept in mind:

a. Jurisdiction: the principle is that the parties can freely agree to which jurisdiction they will submit disputes.
b. Consumer Protection: all online offers must clearly indicate their commencement and termination dates, as well as any conditions or limitations that they may have; product characteristics and availability; contracting

conditions; restrictions and limitations; procedures for early termination of the contract; returns policy; and so on; and they must provide the consumer with the technical means to identify and correct data input before the transaction is completed and to expressly state his or her decision to enter into the contract.

c. Data Protection: under Argentinean legislation, all personal data, not only "sensitive" data, is granted protection; the general criterion is that the user's consent is necessary for any data-processing procedure, with few exceptions.

Databases resulting from website information fall under the obligation of database registration. Information pertaining to the database needs to be registered rather than the database itself. Users have the right to access, rectify, update, suppress, and block their data.

Financing Issues/Payments

The Argentine government has imposed a restrictive exchange system, whose rules must be taken into consideration with regard to all kinds of transactions involving inflows and/or outflows of funds to and from Argentina, or foreign trade operations. See the section on Foreign Exchange above.

Secured Transactions

A security interest exists when a borrower enters into a contract that allows the lender, or secured party, to affect the collateral that the borrower owns in the event that the borrower cannot pay back the debt. In contrast with the open number of secured interests that can be acquired over personal property in other countries, there are a limited number of rights in rem recognized under local law.

An important feature of Argentine law is that it does not allow the secured creditor to extrajudicially repossess the collateral and resell it to pay the amount of the indebtedness. No self-help procedure is available.

The most important security interests used in Argentina are (1) mortgages (see the section on Land Use and Real Estate, above); (2) pledges, with or without delivery of the pledged asset to the creditor; and with Pledge Registry filing requirements; (3) international letters of credit; (4) warrants; and (5) trusts, understood as an agreement that does not need to be registered before any supervisory body and that carries the advantage that no judicial procedure will be necessary in case of default insofar as the trustee receives specific instructions to sell the underlying assets, pay the defaulted debt, and deliver any net proceeds to the debtor.

In case of insolvency proceedings, and unlike unsecured credits, interests on secured credits continue to accrue up to an amount not exceeding the value of the security. Secured creditors have priority on the assets securing such credits. Assets transferred to a trust will exclusively be applied to repay the secured creditor and will not be affected by the bankruptcy procedure.

Securities Laws Issues

Local regulations are aimed at preventing the misappropriation of nonpublic information and guaranteeing fair dealing in the securities market. Any fact that may have a significant effect on the trade of securities must be timely reported, there being a legal duty on certain persons to keep secret all information that has not been publicly disclosed and that may have an impact on the price of securities. The use of privileged information for the benefit of the persons who have access to such information or that of third parties is forbidden.

All persons who by reason of their position, activity, or relationship gain access to confidential information must take all necessary measures to prevent others from gaining access to the same. Such persons must inform of any fact or circumstance that may be deemed a violation of the duty of confidentiality or a violation of the prohibition against the use of privileged information.

The issuer and shareholders are entitled to recovery proceedings in case of insider use of privileged information ("short swing profits").

Government Procurement

Government Procurement is considered a typical administrative matter and thus governed by administrative law. Thus, contracts executed by public sector entities are generally ruled by provincial law rather than by federal law.

Public procurement rules are applicable to most of the contracts entered into by public instrumentalities, such as: (i) public works contracts; (ii) public service concessions; (iii) equipment supply agreements; and (iv) consulting services agreements, among others. Said rules do not apply to public finance or employment or to contracts with Sovereigns or Multilateral Organizations.

Generally, contracts executed by public instrumentalities are ruled not only by the general principles but also by (a) Specific Bidding Terms and Conditions issued ad-hoc when the bidding and tender process is called; (b) the resulting awarded contract; and (c) general administrative law criteria set forth in applicable case law.

The basic guidelines of Government Procurement are: (i) efficiency; (ii) fostering of competition for bidders and contractors; (iii) transparency and publicity of proceedings; and (iv) equal treatment for bidders and contractors. Although the general principle is that all contracts must be awarded by means of a public bidding procedure, some exceptions may be applicable. The public instrumentality is generally awarded certain unilateral specials powers vis-à-vis the private contractors. Assignments of awarded contracts require the contracting authority's express and previous consent.

Although Government Procurement and competitive bids are generally open to foreign-based companies and even in some cases specifically targeted to an international market, specific rules may award certain preferences and/or privileges to local firms.

Liabilities of Companies' Directors and Officers

The ACCA regulates the functions of the board of directors and the rights and duties of the directors. Under the same, directors and officers are jointly and severally liable without limitation to the company, the shareholders, and third parties in the event of qualified malperformance of their duties or infringement of the law or the articles of association or bylaws of the company, and for any other damage caused by fraud, abuse of authority, or serious fault.

Directors are expected to act with loyalty and under the good businessperson diligence standard. Such duty to act diligently is not a guarantee of good results in their tenure but a standard of performance with best efforts to fulfill the corporate purpose as per the circumstances of time, mode, and place. Directors and officers must give preference without exception to the company's corporate interest and the common interest of the shareholders over any other interest.

The board of directors may delegate certain functions to committees of the board or to directors, officers, and/or employees. However, the members of the board are subject to the board's ultimate responsibility for oversight. The only exception applies when the certificate of incorporation or bylaws delegate a function to a director and the same is registered with the Public Register of Commerce.

Directors' liability shall be determined by taking into account their individual performance when duties have been assigned on a personal basis, or in accordance with the articles of association, the bylaws, or a decision of the shareholders meeting. Director's liability is subject to a four-pronged test based on the existence of (i) illegal behavior (through action or omission), (ii) objective or subjective liability attribution factor, (iii) damage, and (iv) relationship link between the illegal behavior and the damage.

There are also special directors' liability regimes for criminal, tax, labor, bankruptcy, environmental, and foreign exchange–related issues.

The approval by the shareholders meeting of the performance of the directors during a fiscal year or during their tenure, or the express waiver of the director's liability approved by the shareholders meeting, shall extinguish any corporate action for directors' liability, if such liability is not due to violation of the law or bylaws and absent an opposition or challenge by shareholders representing at least 5 percent of the corporate capital. However, shareholders shall still be individually entitled to sue the directors, but the scope of the action shall be limited to their personal interests. Directors may also be exempted from liability arising from a decision of the board of directors if they have declared in writing their opposition thereto and notified the statutory supervisor of such circumstances.

Directors and officers' insurance policies are valid under Argentine Insurance Law. Willful misconduct is not covered.

Litigation/Dispute Resolution Systems

Due to its federal organization, Argentina has a dual court system. The judiciary is divided into federal and provincial courts, with each system having lower courts, appellate courts, and supreme courts.

The National Supreme Court of Justice is the highest court for constitutional and federal matters. It extensively exercises general appellate jurisdiction by deciding, as a court of last resort, cases involving matters governed by the Constitution or laws that provide for specific federal jurisdiction. The same is granted exclusive and original jurisdiction in matters concerning foreign diplomats and those in which a province is a party. Federal jurisdiction also extends to issues relating to international treaties, admiralty and maritime jurisdiction, those involving the federal government as a party, controversies between provinces, and cases involving disputes between residents of different provinces.

Each provincial constitution provides a framework for its own judiciary, and determines the jurisdiction of its courts and the rights to be guaranteed by the judicial procedure.

Proceedings before federal and provincial courts are conducted in written form and usually involve the following stages: claim, reply, defenses to the claim, counterclaim, evidence production, closing arguments, and final ruling. A mandatory 3 percent court tax over amounts claimed is payable at the time of starting a lawsuit. The prevailing party in a lawsuit is usually awarded attorney fees. The losing party must also pay litigation costs (such as expert witness fees and court tax).

For most disputes of pecuniary content, mandatory pretrial mediation needs to be exhausted prior to the initiation of lawsuits in the city of Buenos Aires.

Federal and provincial procedural codes govern arbitration in their respective jurisdictions. All Argentine procedural codes recognize the right of private parties to submit their disputes to arbitration, and they usually include a section with arbitration rules that apply in case the parties do not designate their own set of arbitral rules. Three types of arbitration are most commonly regulated by the procedural codes: (a) the *iure* arbitration; (b) amiable composition; and (c) an arbitral expert opinion procedure. There is no legal restriction for the parties to choose an institutional arbitration, to submit to institutional arbitration rules, or to appoint foreigners as arbitrators.

A foreign judgment or arbitral award cannot move against the interests or assets of a person or entity based in Argentina, unless the same is validated by a competent local court. When the foreign judgment or arbitral award originated in a country that has ratified a treaty or convention applicable in Argentina, the provisions thereof will prevail over any Argentine procedural code. Argentina is a signatory to several international treaties and conventions on the topic, including the 1958 New York Convention on Recognition and Enforcement of Foreign Arbitral Awards.

Enforcement of foreign judgments and arbitral awards requires a special proceeding in order to obtain an *exequatur*, by means of which the Argentine court authorizes the enforcement of said foreign judgment. Under the Federal Procedural Code, the requirements for recognition and enforcement are the following: (a) the judgment must be final in the jurisdiction where rendered, and it must have been issued by a court with jurisdiction in accordance with Argentine conflict of laws principles and have resulted from a personal action, or an "in rem" action with respect to personal property that was transferred to Argentine territory during or after the prosecution of the foreign action; (b) the defendant must have been personally served with the summons and given an opportunity for a proper defense; (c) the judgment must be valid in the jurisdiction where rendered, and its authenticity proven; (d) the judgment must not affect public policy principles of Argentine law; and (e) the judgment cannot be contrary to a prior or simultaneous judgment of an Argentine court. In case recognition or enforcement of a foreign arbitration award is sought, in addition to the above, the subject matter of the dispute needs to be proven as arbitrable under Argentine law.

CONTRACTS AND DOCUMENTS—FORMS AND ENFORCEABILITY

In Argentina, contracts are ruled and governed by the principle of freedom of forms, which is an expression of the principle of "free will." However, this rule has some exceptions: (i) certain agreements require a specific form in order to be valid and enforceable; (ii) other agreements require a specific form, not in order to be valid but to be able to be proven; (iii) the existence of a contract may be derived from attitudes and consent evidenced by the parties; and (iv) contracts can also be implemented through offers that are expressly or implicitly accepted by the recipient party.

ENDING/ RESTRUCTURING A BUSINESS PRESENCE

Terminating a business association involves a series of related stages beginning with an act of dissolution, followed by liquidation of assets and property, and distribution of the surplus to the equity holders.

Dissolution/Liquidation

Under the ACCA, dissolution may be either involuntary (by operation of law) or voluntary (upon majority vote of the company's equity holders). Although certain organic changes to a company (e.g., mergers, consolidations, and spin-offs) may terminate the existence of a company, they do not trigger its liquidation.

Upon the occurrence of a cause of dissolution, the company shall cease all activity not necessary to the wind-up of its business, the discharge of liabilities, and the liquidation of assets and property. Directors of a company in dissolution are limited to taking only those actions immediately related to the liquidation of the company. Action beyond this limited scope would expose them to personal liability to third parties and equity holders. The dissolution shall be effective vis-à-vis third parties only upon registration with the PRC.

Upon reaching the liquidation stage, the directors become liquidators (or, within 30 days, may appoint persons to act in their stead). The appointment of the liquidator shall be registered with the PRC, and the liquidators assume representation of the business entity, with the initial task of determining total assets and property to be liquidated. Upon doing so, a special balance sheet must be prepared. The liquidators must report to the equity holders on the status of the liquidation on a quarterly basis, and add the words "in liquidation" to the corporate name. If the proceeds from the liquidated property are insufficient to satisfy the debts, the liquidators shall demand pro rata contributions from the equity holders. If contributions are not made, the liquidator must file for insolvency protection.

Upon payment of all liabilities and the distribution of surplus, the liquidators shall certify that the liquidation process has been completed and, upon request to the Public Registry of Commerce, the liquidated entity's charter shall be canceled.

Insolvency/Bankruptcy/Restructuring

Argentine Bankruptcy Law endeavors to adapt to an economic and social reality and to recurring economic crises. It reflects two major policy principles: it allows an economically viable business the opportunity to restructure its debts; and it is predicated on equal treatment of similarly situated creditors. The Bankruptcy Law contemplates three principal types of proceedings: (i) privately negotiated prepacked proceedings; (ii) the "Chapter-11" type reorganization; and (iii) liquidation in bankruptcy.

A legal entity unable to pay debts as they become due or otherwise undergoing economic or financial problems may enter into a privately negotiated restructuring plan agreed upon with at least the majority of its unsecured creditors. When successful, this proceeding concludes with judicial confirmation of the plan and its imposition on all creditors. Unless otherwise provided, the content of the plan will be binding upon the signatories even if not confirmed by the judge. In order to obtain judicial confirmation, the absolute majority of unsecured creditors, representing two-thirds of the aggregate unsecured liabilities of the debtor, must consent to the plan. Once the plan is confirmed, it shall be binding on all unsecured creditors with prior claims, even if they were not a party to the plan.

The reorganization proceeding may be brought only through a voluntary petition filed by the debtor, admitting its inability to pay debts as they become due. Once the petition for relief has been granted, certain transactions are subject to court approval, while others are expressly prohibited. The debtor maintains control over its business but is supervised by a trustee. Upon commencement of the reorganization proceeding, all monetary claims against the debtor (except for foreclosure on security interests, which may be filed or continued upon notice to the bankruptcy court) are stayed and the claims transferred to the bankruptcy court's jurisdiction. Interest on all unsecured debts ceases to accrue.

Creditors must file with the trustee evidence of their claims, security interests, and priorities, if applicable. Said claims are subject to challenge by the debtor and the other creditors.

The debtor is granted an "exclusive period" to propose a reorganization plan. The court will establish "classes" of creditors and shall appoint a creditors' committee. The reorganization plan must be approved by a special majority of creditors within each class. If the proposed plan is rejected, a third party may offer an alternative plan to creditors under a "cramdown" process in which creditors or other interested parties may acquire the debtor pursuant to a separate reorganization plan. This process requires that an independent appraiser assess the market value of the debtor and, after considering any objections, the court will fix the market value of the debtor. This decision is final and cannot be challenged.

At this time, the debtor may also resubmit or propose a new plan to its creditors. Approval must be obtained from creditors holding at least two-thirds of the total allowed, unsecured claims and from an absolute majority of all unsecured creditors within each class. A cramdown plan must be accepted within 20 days of the court's valuation of the debtor or the proceeding will be converted into liquidation.

Before bankruptcy becomes a viable option for a company in financial distress, debtors must be insolvent. Bankruptcy proceedings are available after the failure of a reorganization proceeding, after a debtor voluntarily seeks bankruptcy, or after a creditor files a request with evidence that the debtor did not pay debts as they matured. The debtor has five days to challenge the creditor's petition.

Declaring bankruptcy immediately imposes restrictions on the debtor and its representatives and administrators. Within 24 hours of the bankruptcy declaration, the court orders its publication for public notice. A debtor who satisfies certain provisions of the Bankruptcy Law may, within 10 days of the last publication, convert the liquidation proceeding into a reorganization proceeding.

Depending on the date of insolvency, the bankruptcy court may grant a retroactive reach-back period not exceeding two years prior to the declaration of bankruptcy or the filing of a reorganization plan. All creditors must request the verification of their respective claims, and some may enjoy a privilege with respect to distribution preferences. The trustee has the option of (a) continuing a company's operations informing the court of the practicability of maintaining the company as a going concern, or (b) requesting the liquidation of the company. Proceeds from these sales will first cancel bankruptcy costs, with any surplus being distributed to creditors.

CONCLUSION

Argentina's political situation does not differ largely from that of other Latin American countries. Its proven ability to overcome very unfavorable situations has been successfully tested several times during its history. This has been possible due to its well-educated population, its abundant natural resources, its solidified democratic system, and—above all—to its legal environment headed by a very reasonable judiciary.

NOTES

1. To date, the following countries have entered into BITs with Argentina, all of which are currently in full force and effect: Algeria, Armenia, Australia, Austria, BENELUX, Bolivia, Bulgaria, Canada, Chile, China, Costa Rica, Croatia, Cuba, the Czech Republic, Denmark, the Dominican Republic, Ecuador, Egypt, El Salvador, Finland, France, Germany, Greece, Guatemala, Hungary, India, Indonesia, Israel, Italy, Jamaica, Malaysia, Mexico, Morocco, the Netherlands, Nicaragua, New Zealand, Panama, Peru, the Philippines, Poland, Portugal, Romania, Senegal, South Africa, South Korea, Sweden, Switzerland, Thailand, Tunisia, Turkey, Ukraine, the United Kingdom, the United States, Venezuela, and Vietnam.
2. Currently, Argentina has comprehensive tax treaties in force with Australia, Belgium, Bolivia, Brazil, Canada, Chile, Denmark, Finland, France, Germany, Italy, the Netherlands, Norway, Spain, Sweden, Switzerland, and the United Kingdom.

CHAPTER 2

Bolivia

Pablo Rojas
CR&F.Rojas—Abogados

COUNTRY OVERVIEW

The Plurinational State of Bolivia is a landlocked country located in the middle of South America. Bolivia has an area of 1,098,581 square kilometers[1] and shares its borders with Brazil, Paraguay, Argentina, Chile, and Peru.

Bolivia can be divided into the following regions: "altiplano" or the highlands, valleys, and lowland tropic. The states of La Paz, Oruro, and Potosi are located in the "altiplano," western part of the country, and have an average altitude of 3,500 meters above sea level. The states of Cochabamba, Chuquisaca, and Tarija are located in the valleys and have an altitude between 1,000 meters and 3,000 meters above sea level. The states of Pando, Beni, and Santa Cruz are located near 400 meters above sea level and have a tropical climate.

The population of Bolivia as of 2010 was 9,672,866.[2] The major cities in Bolivia are La Paz, Santa Cruz, and Cochabamba. La Paz is where the government is located, but Sucre is the official capital where the Supreme and Constitutional Court sits.

Bolivia is a democracy divided into nine decentralized and autonomous states. The Bolivian state is organized and structures its jurisdiction through the legislative, executive, judicial, and electoral branches.

Bolivia is a civil law country. The Bolivian Constitution also recognizes indigenous community justice as part of its judicial system.

ESTABLISHING A BUSINESS PRESENCE IN BOLIVIA

Permanent Structures[3]

The most common business enterprises incorporated under Bolivian law are corporations and limited liability partnerships (LLPs). These business entities share common aspects but differ in complexity of structure and methods of ownership.

The organizational structure of a corporation consists of the following tiers: directors/officers, a comptroller, and three or more shareholders.

Shares represent ownership interests in a corporation. They are freely transferable by endorsement, and such transfers are tax exempt.

The ownership and management structure for an LLP requires a minimum of two partners. A board of directors is optional, and no comptroller or bylaws are required.

Capital quotas represent ownership interests in an LLP. Transfers of capital quotas must be approved by all partners and are tax exempt. Each time partners transfer capital quotas, the articles of incorporation must be amended.

For the incorporation of a corporation or LLP, the following information is required:

1. Name, age, marital status, nationality, profession, domicile and I.D. number of those people who will become partners or shareholders; and/or name, nature, nationality, and domicile of those entities that will become partners or shareholders
2. There are no limitations or special restrictions for foreign partners or shareholders. In the case of a foreign entity, a certificate of good standing is required.
3. Name and domicile
4. Purpose
5. Paid-in capital

A minimum of three directors is required for corporations. Board members may be of any nationality and may reside outside Bolivia. Corporations also require a comptroller and alternate who must be domiciled in Bolivia. The mentioned corporate bodies are not required for an LLP.

The nearest Bolivian consulate must legalize the incorporation documents. Furthermore, said documents must be submitted in Spanish. Documents translated into Spanish may be filed provided a court-appointed translator in Bolivia has translated them.

A special power of attorney may be granted for purposes of incorporating a Bolivian entity. As with all other documents, said power of attorney must be in Spanish and legalized by a Bolivian consulate.

Subsidiaries and Branches

According to the Bolivian Commerce Code, a subsidiary is any company formed in Bolivia and whose main shareholder or main partner is a foreign entity. Subsidiaries enjoy the same tax treatment as any other Bolivian entity.

Any foreign company may also incorporate branch offices in Bolivia without limitation. In order to establish a branch office, the following documents are required:

1. Articles of incorporation
2. Bylaws
3. Certificate of good standing
4. Board resolution approving the establishment of a branch

The above documents must also be legalized before a Bolivian consulate. If said documents are in English, a translation must be obtained from a court-appointed translator in Bolivia.

The board resolution approving the establishment of the branch must include the following:

1. Domicile of the branch. The domicile of the branch may be in any Bolivian city.
2. Amount of capital assigned to the branch. There is no minimum capital requirement, but it must be deposited in a Bolivian bank.
3. A power of attorney for the establishment of the branch.
4. A power of attorney for the manager of the branch.

The incorporation branches may take up to two weeks from the date on which all documents are in order and ready to be submitted to the Bolivian Commerce Registry.

Companies Incorporated Abroad

Foreign companies or individuals may carry out isolated or occasional acts in Bolivia without having to register or incorporate. If, however, said acts are habitual, registration or incorporation is mandatory.

There is no precise definition or single measure that can establish whether an act is considered habitual. Certain basic parameters, however, may be identified in order to establish whether an act is habitual. Habitual acts do not necessarily correspond to quantitative criteria but to criteria such as the following: the opening of a branch office, or the registration of a company before a governmental or regulatory authority.

Joint Ventures

Law 1182 explicitly permits joint ventures between domestic and foreign investors. According to said law foreign investors entering into joint venture contracts must establish a legal domicile in Bolivia.

Foreign companies investing in certain regulated industries are required to enter into joint venture agreements. Said agreements are typically entered between local or foreign investors and the state-owned companies such as YPFB (hydrocarbons) and Comibol (mining).

Investment in Mergers

In accordance with the Bolivian Commerce Code, companies are allowed to merge. Currently, there is no comprehensive merger control system in Bolivia.

In regulated industries such as electricity, hydrocarbons, telecommunications, securities, and insurance, specific regulations are administered and enforced by newly created, sector-specific supervisory and control authorities. Mergers of Bolivian corporations are additionally subject to the Bolivian Commercial Code, requiring notice of a proposed transaction to creditors and shareholders who may lodge objections through judicial process before a civil judge.

There are market share filing thresholds for mergers in the electricity sector. A merger or acquisition in this sector market is reportable if it grants an electric generation company a market share of more than 36 percent.

Other regulated sectors do not have filing thresholds. However, parties must contact the relevant regulatory authorities prior to a merger in these sectors.

Agency and Distribution Agreements[4]

The Bolivian Commerce Code regulates agency and distribution agreements. Bolivian law does not distinguish between agents and distributors. Agents and distributors are independent persons or entities that promote or exploit businesses in a specific area within the country, as intermediaries of another entity, local or foreign.

Unless the agency agreement provides otherwise, the principal cannot use other agents in the same geographical territory, nor can it sell directly. The principal must pay the agent the remuneration indicated in the agreement and reimburse expenses as provided in such agreement. If no term has been fixed for payment of such remuneration, it should be paid within 30 days of conclusion of the business.

Bolivian law is silent as to maintenance of inventory. Said matter should be contemplated in the contract.

An agent does not acquire additional rights as an employee. If, however, the agent is on the payroll of the principal and receiving a fixed commission, the agent shall be considered an employee.

Appointment of a local agent by a foreign principal does not subject the principal to payment of Bolivian income tax. There are no limitations on the amount that may be paid to agents.

The principal can terminate agency agreements without cause provided such provision is inserted in the agreement. It is permissible under Bolivian law for the contracting parties to agree to allow the principal to terminate the agreement without cause. Notice of termination under agency agreements depends on what the parties have agreed to in the agreement.

There are no specific franchise laws. Franchise agreements, however, must be registered before the Commerce Registry. The only limitation with regard to franchise agreements is tax-related, in that royalties remitted abroad are subject to a 12.5 percent withholding tax.

Approval and Registrations

The last step in forming a local entity is the filing of articles of incorporation or bylaws, tax ID, and all other documents required by law. Said filing is done before the Bolivian Commerce Registry (FUNDEMPRESA). Provided all documents are in good standing, the Bolivian Commerce Registry shall issue a license allowing for the commencement of operations of the new entity. The license is usually issued within three weeks from the moment that all pertinent documentation has been filed.

Agency and distribution agreements must be registered before the Commerce Registry, and must be governed by Bolivian law. Notarization of the agency or distribution agreement is also required.

Sensitive Economic Sectors

Local and foreign investors have the same rights and obligations, but they may be subject to special regulations if they are involved in any of the following industries: mining, oil, gas, electricity, transport, and telecommunications.

Political Risk and Related Issues

Investments in Bolivia may be affected by policy changes that may respond to political rather than economic factors. Certain industries such as telecomunication, energy, and hydrocarbons that were privatized in 1995 are now being nationalized.

In May 2006, the nationalization of Bolivia's oil and gas reserves obligated foreign firms to renegotiate new terms for exploration and development under which Bolivia's share of revenues would increase significantly. Many issues, however, made it impossible for such generation of revenues. Among said issues it is important to mention weak judicial security, arbitrary regulatory decisions, and corruption.

During 2007 the Bolivian government nationalized the largest long-distance telephone company, Entel. The government claimed that co-owner Euro Telecom Italia had violated its contractual obligation to invest sufficiently and owed back taxes. Arbitration proceedings are still under way.

From 2008 to the present two electricity companies have been nationalized. Negotiations are under way in order to avoid arbitration proceedings.

INVESTMENT ISSUES AND TAX INCENTIVES

Incentives[5]

In September 1990, the Bolivian Congress passed an Investment Law. Under such law, local as well as foreign investment is stimulated and guaranteed. The mentioned Investment Law also guarantees the following:

Local and foreign investors have the same rights, duties, and guarantees, and no authorization or prior registration is required for any investment. Right to ownership, as well as free foreign currency exchange, is guaranteed to local and foreign investors.

Investors can freely contract investment's insurance in Bolivia or abroad. Local and foreign investors can enter into joint ventures.

Local and foreign investors can agree to submit their discrepancies to arbitration according to the Constitution and international laws. Investors, local or foreign, have equal access to the following: purchase and selling of foreign currency; taxes; right to export capital and profits; and to invest in any commercial or industrial activity, except those activities that belong to the public sector such as public services.

Foreign Investment Protection Treaties

Bolivia has entered into 24 Bilateral Investment Treaties (BITs) with countries such as Argentina, Chile, Ecuador, Uruguay, Venezuela, Costa Rica, Cuba, France, Switzerland, the United Kingdom, and the United States, among others.

Most of the BITs follow a similar format indicating that controversies dealing with investments shall first be resolved through amicable consultations. If an agreement is not reached, the door is open for arbitration before the World Bank's arbitration facility, International Centre for the Settlement of Investment Disputes (ICSID).

Bolivia, however, became the first country to withdraw from ICSID. As a result Bolivia plans to renegotiate its 24 BITs.

Double Tax Treaties

The Bolivian tax system is income-source–based; therefore only income that is of a Bolivian source is taxed regardless of whether the employee resides in Bolivia.

Bolivia has double tax treaties with the Andean countries (comprising Bolivia, Colombia, Ecuador, Peru, and Venezuela) and the following other countries: Argentina, France, Spain, Sweden, and the United Kingdom.

Publicly Held Companies

According to the Bolivian Commerce Code, a corporation can be formed by way of a sole act of its founders or through the public subscription of shares. If the incorporation is through a public subscription of shares, the promoters must prepare a foundation program that must be signed by them and approved by the Commerce Registry.

Upon obtainment of approval by the Commerce Registry to incorporate a publicly held company, the foundation program must be published in a local newspaper. A bank must thereafter prepare a subscription agreement, and the monies paid for such subscription of shares must be deposited in such bank. As soon as the capital has been subscribed, the promoters must call a shareholders meeting with the participation of representatives from the bank and Commerce Registry and the participation of the majority of the subscribed shareholders. The process of registration before the Commerce Registry concludes the incorporation of a company by public subscription of shares.

OPERATIONAL ISSUES

Tips on Negotiations in Bolivia

When doing business in Bolivia it is important to note that Bolivia is a civil law country, and as such, contracts and transactions executed under Bolivian law tend to be shorter in length and detail than those of common law countries. All agreements must adhere to the stipulations of codes and statutes whether or not those stipulations are included in an agreement.

Bolivia has the largest indigenous population in Latin America. Business etiquette, however, is very similar to that in its neighboring countries. Accordingly, the approach to business is formal. Professionalism is expected, academic titles with the surname are used, and the shaking of hands when meeting and leaving is customary.

Foreign Exchange

The Central Bank of Bolivia is the supreme authority in matters of currency. The Central Bank of Bolivia controls the entry and discharge of foreign currency through the private banks, which can freely operate in foreign exchange.

There is no foreign exchange control in Bolivia. Foreign currency can be purchased freely at any private bank or the Central Bank of Bolivia, and it can also be remitted abroad with no restrictions. Income of a Bolivian source is, however, taxed with a 12.5 percent withholding tax.

Immigration and Visa Requirements[6]

The regulation with regard to the movement of people entering and leaving Bolivia falls within the jurisdiction of the Dirección Nacional de Migración. Bolivian law contemplates the following forms of immigration: spontaneous, planned, and selective immigration.

Spontaneous immigration refers to the entrance of foreigners by their own initiative and at their own expense. Planned immigration is that which is oriented by the State. Said orientation may be conducted directly by the State, or through governmental agents or international institutions interested in migratory programs. Selective immigration is that which promotes the immigration of investors, professionals, industrial or farming technicians, and qualified labor.

Tourist Visas

Tourist visas are granted for a period of stay of 30 days. Tourist visas may be renewed in Bolivia for an additional 60 days. One may not work in Bolivia with a tourist visa.

Bolivian consulates, which are located in major capitals, are authorized to grant tourist visas. A valid passport and transportation tickets are required to obtain a tourist visa.

For the renewal of a tourist visa, proof of financial solvency is required. Said renewal must take place in Bolivia.

A fee that ranges from USD 10 to USD 50 is charged for the obtainment of a tourist visa. The mentioned fee depends on the applicant's country of residence.

Special Purpose (Business)

A special purpose visa is granted for a period of stay in Bolivia of 30 days. Said visa can be renewed once for a maximum of 30 days.

Special purpose visas may be obtained at any Bolivian consulate or in Bolivia. A valid passport and documents indicating the purpose of the visit are required. Said documents may include a labor contract or an invitation to activities related to culture, art, or sports. Transportation tickets must also be presented for the obtainment of a special purpose visa.

The fee to obtain a special purpose visa is approximately USD 50.

Permanent Visa

The following permanent visas are granted by Bolivian authorities: Fixed period of time visa and indefinite visa.

The fixed period of time visa is granted for one or two years, and is renewable. The mentioned visa can be obtained in Bolivia and is extended to the family of the visa holder.

The following documents must be presented in order to obtain a fixed period of time visa: a valid passport that must have a special purpose visa; a medical certificate; and a certificate of domicile and of good behavior. With a fixed period of time visa, a foreign ID card is issued to the beneficiary.

The indefinite visa requires ownership of real estate or a stable investment in Bolivia. Professionals or technicians involved in community services and integrated into Bolivian society may also apply for an indefinite visa. Said visa is also issued to foreigners who have obtained a university degree in Bolivia, or to retired individuals who receive income from abroad or have Bolivian children. With an indefinite visa, a foreign ID card is issued to the beneficiary.

Taxation of Business and Cross-Border Transactions

Bolivian Taxes[7]

Value Added Tax (VAT)

VAT applies to the sale of all movable goods located in Bolivia, work contracts, and imports. The standard VAT rate is 13 percent.

Company Profit Tax

Company profit tax is chargeable at 25 percent on the company's net profits. Said tax is applied on profit as shown in the audited balance sheets at yearly financial closings of legal entities.

Withholding Tax

When income that derives from a Bolivian source is paid to foreign beneficiaries, a 12.5 percent withholding tax is payable, subject to the provisions of any applicable double tax treaty.

Transactions Tax

A transaction tax applies to the transfer of ownership of movable assets or property and rights as a result of the exercise of, among others, a trade, industry, profession, or business. The standard rate for the transaction tax is 3 percent. The purchase of shares, debentures, securities, or any credit documents is exempt from said tax.

Financial Transactions Tax

Financial transactions are taxed at 0.3 percent. The transfer of funds abroad and the transfer of funds to and from Bolivian saving accounts with less than USD 1,000 are exempt from said tax.

Complementary VAT Tax

The complementary tax to the VAT is applied on the income of individuals and estates, originating from capital investment or work or the combination of both. This tax is determined by applying a 13 percent tax on said income.

The complementary tax to the VAT is applied on the totality of income derived from a Bolivian source, not mattering where the taxpayer is domiciled or residing. Payment of dividends to individuals is not subject to this tax.

Other Taxes

All entities or individuals who own real estate, registered vehicles, yachts, or aircraft are also subject to tax. Said tax is determined by the respective municipality in which the mentioned items are located.

Additional taxes also exist in relation to mining and hydrocarbon-related activities. A tax to individuals leaving the country also exists, at a rate of USD 20 to USD 40.

Labor and Employment[8]

General Principles

Specialized Labor and Social Courts adjudicate all employment disputes in Bolivia. There are seven Labor Courts, three Social Courts of Appeal, and two Social Courts in the Supreme Court for cases of annulment.

The main sources of employment law in Bolivia are codified laws, supreme decrees, resolutions, and collective agreements and individual contracts (the Labor Law). Bolivian law applies to people who work for foreign companies within Bolivian territory.

There are no Bolivian long-arm statutes. Accordingly, Bolivian law does not apply to employees of Bolivian companies working in another jurisdiction.

The Labor Agreement

For an employment contract to be enforceable under the Labor Law it does not have to be in writing. The following, however, are essential elements that an employment contract must have: capacity of the parties to contract, acceptance, object, and consideration.

A written employment contract should contain the following: employer's contact details (name, domicile, legal representative, identification number, legal representative's identification number); name of employee; identification number, age, nationality, and domicile of employee; nature of service or task and place where service or task will be performed; amount of salary; duration; place and date of employment contract; and names and ages of spouse and children.

The Labor Law also recognizes collective agreements. Associated employers must enter into collective agreements with the employees, which are considered part of an individual employment contract.

Mandatory Labor Requirements
Trial Period

A three-month trial period applies only to new employees with indefinite employment contracts. Employees dismissed during the three-month trial period are not entitled to severance or other employment benefits. According to Supreme Decree 17280 dated March 18, 1980, there is no trial period for the following individuals:

- Applicants with a university degree
- Applicants with certificates from teaching or capacitating entities
- Applicants who can demonstrate that they are suitable professionals
- Those admitted to work by means of a merit exam or competition
- Rehired employees
- Those employed on a temporary basis.

Hours of Work and Earnings

The following hours of work are set by statute: eight hours per day and seven hours per night shift (night work is between 20.00 and 06.00); 48 hours per week for men and 40 hours per week for women. Working hours do not apply to those employees who cannot submit themselves to working hours set by statute because of the nature of their work; in this case an employee may not work for more than 12 hours. Overtime and Sunday work are paid at a 100 percent surcharge.

Employees may not earn less than the minimum income set by the Executive branch of Government. Minimum income is currently set at USD 90 per month.

Holidays/Rest Periods

Employees are entitled to an annual vacation that varies according to the following length of service: one to five years' service: 15 days; five to 10 years' service: 20 days; 10+ years' service: 30 days annual vacation. In addition, employees are entitled to various public holidays and Sundays off.

Minimum/Maximum Age

Minors under 14 years old are prohibited from working. Age limit to work is 65 years unless the employer agrees to hire the employee for three more years. The normal retirement age under the social security system is 50 to 55 for men and 45 to 50 for women. Retirement age in case of pension plan depends on the amount of capital accumulated by the employee.

Illness/Disability

The Caja Nacional de Salud must provide the covered employee with all the necessary medical assistance for any illness, work-related or not.

Disability benefits are provided as part of a long-term insurance by the pension funds that cover disability, old age, and death. The benefits are monthly annuities that depend on the years of contribution to such funds by the employee. Employees must contribute to the mentioned fund, up to 12.21 percent of their monthly remuneration.

Disability benefits are paid based on the level of employee's disability as a result of the sickness.

Location of Work/Mobility

When the task or service of the employee takes place over 2 km away from the employee's residence, employers may be obliged to provide transport. When the task or service of the employee takes place over 100 km away from the employee's residence, the employer must pay food and transport expenses.

Compulsory Terms

The following compulsory provisions must be included in employment contracts: employer's contact details (name, domicile, legal representative, identification number, legal representative's identification number); name of employee; identification number, age, nationality, and domicile of employee; nature of service or task and place where service or task will be performed; amount of salary; duration; place and date of employment contract; and names and ages of spouse and children. Noncompulsory terms in addition to compulsory provisions may be included in an employment contract.

Hiring Non-Nationals

A maximum of 15 percent of the total workforce of a company registered and domiciled in Bolivia can be comprised of expatriates. Also, a company registered and domiciled in Bolivia may hire only qualified expatriates. Expatriates working in Bolivia require a visa.

Social Security Contributions and Pension Plans

The following social security contributions are mandatory by statute: employer contribution 13.71 percent; housing 2 percent; professional risk 1.71 percent; short-term insurance 10 percent; employee contribution: 12.21 percent; seniority contribution 10 percent; common risk 1.71 percent; and pension fund commission 0.5 percent.

Monthly social security contributions allow employees to retire, in which case a monthly rent is paid. Employees may opt to be paid in one lump sum.

Payments for Maternity and Disability Leave

Disability benefits are provided as part of a long-term insurance by the pension funds that cover disability, old age, and death. Disability benefits are paid based on the level of the employee's disability as a result of the sickness. Accordingly disability benefits are paid as follows: absolute disability, two years of salary; permanent disability, one year of salary; partial disability, 18 months of salary; temporary disability, salary is paid for duration of disability for a maximum of six months.

In the case of maternity leave the employee is entitled to receive the necessary medical attention. Maternity leave begins 45 days prior to the child's birth and ends 45 days after the child's birth. During said period the employee's salary must be paid.

An employee on maternity leave has a right to receive milk products prior to the birth of a child. The value of the milk products must be at least equal to one month's salary of minimum wage, and the products must be given to the employee starting the fifth month of pregnancy and up to the day of birth.

A postnatal subsidy and a milk subsidy are also provided to the employee on maternity leave after the birth of a child. The postnatal subsidy is given once, and must be at least equal to one month's salary of minimum wage. The milk subsidy consists of milk products that must be equal in value to one month's salary of minimum wage, and they must be provided on a monthly basis until the child is one year old.

It is important to note that both father and mother may not be dismissed from their place of work until their child has reached the age of one year.

Termination

Procedures for Terminating the Agreement

Termination of an employment contract is the result of a dismissal or a voluntary withdrawal. In either of the mentioned cases, the employee is generally entitled to severance and other benefits.

According to the Labor Law dismissal of an employee proceeds only if the following occurs: intentional material damage caused to work instruments; disclosure of industrial secrets; negligent acts that may affect industrial security and hygiene; unjustified absence for more than six days; failure to comply with work agreement; and theft or robbery by the employee.

If dismissal is for a reason not contemplated by the Labor Law, the employee may ask to be reinstated in the workplace by the labor authorities or for payment of corresponding social benefits. Upon dismissal or resignation, the employer and employee must file a form (finiquito) before the Bolivian labor authorities.

Termination on Notice

Fixed-term employment contracts require a 30-day notice of termination by the employer and 90 days notice of termination by the employee. Temporary employment contracts and employment contracts for a specific task or service require a one-week termination notice after one month of work, 15 days' termination notice after three months of work, and 30 days' termination notice after one year of work.

Severance Payments

If the duration of a labor agreement has been left open, upon an unjustified dismissal accepted by the employee, said employee may be entitled to an indemnity for lack of prior notice (three months' severance payment) and an indemnity for length of service. An indemnity for lack of prior notice applies only to those workers who have been working for more than three months. The equivalent of a three-month salary is given as an indemnity for lack of prior notice. An indemnity for length of service applies to those who have been working for more than three months. The equivalent of one month's salary for every year worked is given, but such payments are granted only if requested by the employee and if the employee has been employed for more than five years.

Antitrust and Competition

There is no specific Bolivian set of statutes with regard to competition law. Provisions included in the Constitution, Commerce Code, Criminal Code, Law 1600, and Resolutions that refer to unfair trade apply when resolving competition issues.

Article 314 of the Bolivian Constitution prohibits private monopolies and oligopolies and all forms of associations that aim for total control and exclusivity in the productions and commercialization of goods and services.

Under Bolivian law certain industries such as telecommunications, banking, insurance, transportation, electricity, and hydrocarbons are regulated by a specific set of regulatory statutes known as Law 1600, aimed to regulate competition issues. Title V of Law 1600 applies when resolving competition issues of regulated industries.

Article 68 of the Commerce Code provides as a general rule that the use of trademarks, signs, labels, and drawings that may induce the public to confusion with regard to the quality, origin, or quantity of the goods offered or sold may constitute a crime sanctioned by the Criminal Code. According to Article 236 of the Criminal Code, sanctions may include imprisonment of six months to three years.

Environmental Matters

Environmental Law No. 1333 of April 27, 1992 (the Environmental Law) was enacted in order to achieve the protection and preservation of the environment and natural resources, promoting sustainable development with the purpose of improving quality of life. There are certain activities, such as the pollution of air and water, that are susceptible to generating environmental liability.

According to the Environmental Law, companies involved in activities that may generate an environmental liability must obtain an Environmental Impact Evaluation (EIE). The EIE consists of a group of administrative procedures, studies, and technical systems that appraise the possible adverse environmental effects resulting from the execution of a determined work, activity, or project.

The works, projects, or activities that due to their characteristics may require an EIE previous to their execution must be evaluated with the Environmental Impact Declaration (EID). The EID issued by competent environmental authorities includes studies, technical recommendations, regulations, and limits, within which the works can be developed.

A breach of the Environmental Law and its dispositions will be considered an administrative infraction. In some cases the mentioned breach may constitute a crime punishable by law.

Consumer Protection and Products Liability

Product Liability is regulated by the Bolivian Civil Code (the Civil Code). The Civil Code's chapter entitled "Illicit Acts" specifically deals with product liability. Illicit acts are referred to as extracontractual responsibilities. Article 984 of the Civil Code provides that a person shall be held liable for any willful or negligent act that causes damage. Accordingly product liability is based on intent and negligence.

According to Article 999 of the Civil Code, joint liability shall apply if more than one person is responsible. If one person has indemnified the total amount of damages, said person may thereafter recover from the other wrongdoers. If it is not possible to determine the amount of damages owed by each wrongdoer, the total amount of damages will be divided equally.

Any product that threatens health or life of individuals must be recalled from the market. If damage has been caused as a result of failure to recall a certain product, the affected party may file suit for damages incurred.

The burden of proof lies with the victim who has suffered damages as a result of a willful or negligent act. The existence of causation between a person's acts and the damage caused is necessary for responsibility to arise.

With regard to illicit acts as they would apply to product liability, the following defenses are available: force majeure or acts of God. Compliance with regulatory or statutory requirements may also help prove that no negligence was involved.

Under Bolivian law, damages include both the actual (damnun emergens) and future (lucrum cesans) loss, detriment, or injury the plaintiff's person, property, or rights suffer. Moreover, damages under Bolivian law must be direct and foreseeable.

Accordingly, Bolivian law does not contemplate damages that are punitive, indirect, incidental, or consequential.

Supreme Decree No. 0065, dated April 3, 2009, regulates and determines user and consumer rights, the competent authority to resolve consumer conflicts, and the proceedings pursuant to consumer or user complaints. Supreme Decree 0065 is enforceable in the entire Bolivian territory and is applicable to every natural, corporate, private, and public person or entity that performs commercial, importation, and industrial activities destined to consumers and users in Bolivian territory. Any natural or corporate person who acquires or uses services, products, or goods, movable or nonmovable, in the condition of final recipient, is considered a user or consumer.

The following are some of the most important rights granted by Supreme Decree 0065 to users and consumers:

- To have access to truthful, reliable, and timely information regarding price, conditions, and characteristics about the offered products and services.
- To obtain instruction regarding optimal and responsible use of the product and/or service.
- To receive and/or acquire the products and/or services in the conditions, deadlines, form, and any other circumstances in which the product and/or service has been offered, agreed upon, or advertised.
- To return a product and obtain its reparation, or the restitution of the infringed right, in a timely fashion.

Land Use and Real Estate

For many reasons, such as relatively low property prices, extensive uncultivated land, cheap labor, and a very lax tax system, Bolivia can be considered an attractive jurisdiction for foreign investors wishing to operate in the real estate sector. The Bolivian government and the banking sector have implemented strong financial programs to support medium- and small-scale agricultural projects. However, due to the existing legal uncertainty and lack of regulation, many new investments could be considered as possibly high yield but also high risk.

The new Constitution passed in January provides for a special agricultural regime and guarantees individual and collective private property, subject to the fulfillment of an economic and social purpose. The law limits private properties to 5,000 hectares but larger pre-existing properties will apparently not be affected. Foreign citizens may not acquire land owned by the state; thus, they may enter into exploitation joint venture agreements with the state, or acquire land from private owners.

Intellectual Property[9]

Patents

Under Bolivian law, for an invention to be patentable, it must be new; it must involve an inventive step; and it must be capable of industrial application. The patent must not be specifically excluded from protection.

The owner has the right to use a patented invention and prevent unauthorized third-party use (Article 52, Decision 486, Andean Pact). In order for a patent to be protected it must be registered with the Bolivian Patent Office.

A patent owner can enforce his rights through an action for revindication. An action for revindication means that a patent owner can claim affected rights from the competent national authority and request the following: the transfer of the applications being processed or the rights being granted; and recognition as co-applicant or co-owner of those rights when patents or registration of industrial designs have been applied for or obtained by persons with no right to those patents or registrations.

Compensation for damages can be requested in the same claim, if the domestic legislation of the member country permits this (Article 237, Decision 486). A patent owner can also enforce his rights through Bolivian criminal courts (Article 363, Bolivian Criminal Code).

Patents under Bolivian law are protected for 20 years, subject to the payment of renewal fees. An annual maintenance fee must also be paid.

Trademarks

Under Bolivian law a trademark must be capable of graphic representation, and of distinguishing the goods or services of one undertaking from those of another undertaking. The owner of a registered trademark has the exclusive right to use the trademark and prevent all unauthorized third parties from doing any of the following with the trademark: using, removing, and manufacturing (Articles 153 to 155, Decision 486).

Trademarks are protected under Bolivian law provided they are registered with the Bolivian Trade Mark Registry. Unregistered trademarks can be protected by means of an action for passing off, but the limitations of this action make registration advisable.

Trademarks are enforced under Bolivian law through an action before the competent authority (Chapter I Title XV, Decision 486). A trademark owner can also enforce his or her rights by Article 362 of the Bolivian Penal Code.

Trademarks under Bolivian law are protected for an initial period of 10 years. Said period is renewable indefinitely for further 10-year periods.

Registered Designs

Under Bolivian law a Registered Design must relate to the appearance of all or part of a product resulting from certain features of the product or its ornamentation. The design must be new and have individual character.

The owner of a registered design has the right to use and prevent unauthorized third parties from using, manufacturing, importing, offering for sale, marketing, or making commercial use of products that incorporate or reproduce the industrial design (Article 129, Decision 486).

Bolivian law protects designs through their registration with the Patent Office. If the design is already registered, a priority certificate must be enclosed in the application for registration. Protection lasts for an initial period of 10 years and is renewable at 10-year intervals.

Unregistered Designs

Unregistered designs must be original and relate to the shape or configuration of an article. The owner has the right to use and prevent unauthorized third parties from using, manufacturing, importing, offering for sale, marketing, or making commercial use of the design (Article 129, Decision 486).

Unregistered designs must be registered with the Patent Office. Unregistered designs are protected for a for a maximum of 10 years, subject to renewal at 10-year intervals.

Copyright

Under Bolivian law a copyright subsists in original works of literature (including computer software), drama, music, and art, as well as sound recordings, films, broadcasts, cable programs, and the typographical arrangement of published works. The owner of a copyright can oppose any modification of his or her registered work.

A copyright is protected by a resolution issued by the Bolivian Copyright Registry. Protection of a copyright lasts for the life of the author plus 50 years.

Confidential Information

Information that is confidential in nature, and that was initially communicated in circumstances importing an obligation of confidence, can be protected. The rightholder is entitled to the protection and enforcement of this right for as long as the information remains confidential and there is a legitimate interest that requires protection.

There are no formalities required for protection of industrial secrets. Employees or managers are prohibited from revealing trade secrets to third parties, and Decision 486 grants express protection to trade secrets. Also, Articles 257 and 267 to 269 prohibit disloyal competition.

Customs

Imports of capital goods are subject to an import duty of 5 percent on CIF value plus 10 percent of the Value Added Tax (VAT), 2 percent transactions tax, 0.5 percent warehouse fee, and 1.5 percent customhouse agent's fee. Imports of noncapital goods are subject to a 10 percent import duty, plus the mentioned VAT, transactions tax, and the other charges.

The import of vehicles is subject to an 18 percent special consumption tax. However, passenger-carrying vehicles and heavy-load vehicles are subject only to a 10 percent special consumption tax. All tobacco-related products are subject to a 50 percent special consumption tax.

Internet Regulation and E-Commerce

Bolivian law does not have legislation directed at Internet regulation or e-commerce.

Secured Transactions

Bolivian civil code regulates secured transactions in which the lender acquires a security interest in collateral owned by the borrower and is entitled to foreclose on or repossess the collateral in the event of the borrower's default. Specifically articles 1360 to 1396 and 1401 to 1408 of the Bolivian Civil Code regulate pledges and mortgages, respectively.

Securities Laws

The Bolivian Commerce Code in general regulates securities. The securities exchange, however, is not fully developed in Bolivia. Currently only stocks and bonds are traded in the Bolivian stock exchange.

The Superintendency of Pensions, Securities and Insurance is the securities regulator in Bolivia. Its role as regulator is set out in Law No. 1834 (the Securities Market Law).

The Bolivian Stock Exchange (the BSE) is the only stock exchange operating in Bolivia. According to the Securities Market Law, the BSE may establish its own internal regulations that govern its activities as well as the activities of its members that include brokerage houses and its shareholders. The BSE's main functions include registering securities, providing trading facilities to its members, providing information about securities, and supervising brokerage houses.

Government Procurement

Government expenditure in Bolivia is high due to extensive purchases of machinery and other goods and services. Products produced in Bolivia are given preference in government purchases. Priority in government purchases and simpler prerequisites are also granted to small and micro-producers.

Importers of foreign goods can participate in government procurements only where locally manufactured products and service providers are unavailable. In such cases, the government may call for an international tender. Foreign companies that want to submit a tender must do so by way of a joint venture or "asociación accidental" with a local company.

Liability of Company Directors and Officers

According to Article 321 of the Bolivian Commerce Code, the directors of a company have joint and unlimited liability before the company, its shareholders, and third persons in the following cases: failure to carry out functions; noncompliance with laws, bylaws, statutes, regulations, or resolutions; damages that are the result of negligence, intentional negligence, or fraud; and the unlawful distributions of profits.

A claim against a director may proceed only with the authorization of the shareholders who shall name and appoint the plaintiff. Likewise a claim against an officer requires the authorization of the board of directors. The statute of limitation to bring a claim against a board member or officer is three years.

Litigation/Dispute Resolution

The basic source of Bolivian law dealing with arbitration, in both domestic and international contexts, is Law No. 1770 of Arbitration and Conciliation (the Arbitration Law). The Arbitration Law was enacted in 1997.

The Arbitration Law, in accordance with international arbitration conventions, recognizes the validity of arbitration agreements that provide for foreign law and arbitration proceedings. Such arbitration agreements are referred to as "international commercial arbitration clauses," and are valid so long as no grounds exist at law for the revocation of the general agreement.

According to article 12 of the Arbitration Law, an arbitration agreement between the parties prohibits them from initiating judicial procedures over the subject matter or controversies submitted to arbitration. In the event that court proceedings are initiated despite the existence of an arbitration agreement, the affected party must submit a motion to dismiss based on an existing arbitration agreement.

Bolivian Arbitration Proceedings

Article 3 of the Arbitration Law establishes that controversies emerging out of contractual or extracontractual obligations may be submitted to arbitration. The only issues that may not be submitted to arbitration are those relating to labor relations and capacity of individuals.

Chapter 4 of the Arbitration Law deals with rules regarding arbitral process. Said rules, for example, include instructions for filing the complaint and instructions regarding the giving of adequate notice. Rules of discovery are also included in Chapter 4 of the Arbitration Law.

Arbitral Tribunal

Chapter 3 of the Arbitration Law deals with arbitral tribunals. Arbitral tribunals must impel arbitration proceedings and preside over them.

Arbitral tribunals are composed of natural persons who are designated by the parties or by third persons. The members of an arbitral tribunal are known and referred to as "arbitrators."

Arbitral tribunals have the authority to adjudicate a dispute between the parties, and to resolve the controversies submitted to them. The jurisdiction granted to arbitral tribunals includes the power to summon the parties, to order all necessary precautionary measures, and to render the corresponding arbitration award.

The parties are obligated to abide by the resolutions rendered by the arbitral tribunal. The arbitral tribunal may ask for judicial assistance in executing its orders.

Conciliation

Pursuant to Article 51 of the Arbitration Law, the parties are free to come to an independent settlement or conciliation during the arbitration proceedings. A conciliation or an independent settlement concludes an arbitration proceeding.

Expenses and Fees

According to Article 58 of the Arbitration Law, the involved parties must equally pay costs and fees involved in the arbitration proceedings. The parties, however, can also agree on the payment of expenses and fees.

Arbitration Award

The arbitration award concludes the arbitration proceedings. The arbitration award must be given by the arbitral tribunal based on the merits of the case and in accordance with what was stipulated in the general agreement. In the event the parties to the agreement submit their controversies to an arbitral tribunal, such tribunal must base its decision on the merits of the case and in accordance the agreement's clauses.

Arbitration awards are mandatory. Judicial assistance and public force may be used in executing an arbitration award.

Foreign arbitral awards are enforceable in Bolivia and must follow the same procedure as the one established for foreign judgments.

Enforcement and Foreign Judgments and Awards

With regard to the enforcement of foreign judgments, Article 553 of the Bolivian Civil Procedure Code provides that where there is a treaty between Bolivia and the country where the final judgment was issued, the judgment will be enforced based on such treaty. In the absence of a treaty, Article 553 the Bolivian Civil Procedure Code provides that the final judgment of the foreign court may be enforced in Bolivia according to the principle of "reciprocity." This term is used to denote the relationship existing between two states where each state gives the citizens of the other state the same privileges. Where such reciprocity exists, the judgment of the foreign court will be enforceable in the same way as a Bolivian judgment would be in the foreign state.

In the absence of reciprocity, any foreign judgment must comply with the requirements of Article 555 of the Bolivian Civil Procedure Code in order to be enforceable in Bolivia. The requirements are as follows: (a) the action that resulted in such judgment was an "in-personam" action, or an "in-rem" action relating to a movable good transferred to Bolivia during or after action was initiated in the relevant foreign jurisdiction; (b) any defendant in the action that resulted in such judgment having a residence in Bolivia has been duly served to appear in court in Bolivia; (c) the obligation to which such judgment relates is valid under Bolivian law; (d) such judgment complies with all relevant requirements of the laws of the jurisdiction in which it was rendered so as to be considered authentic under Bolivian law; (e) such judgment has the effect of res judicata, in consistency with the laws of the country where it was rendered; (f) such judgment would not violate Bolivian law or public policy; and (g) such judgment would not be incompatible with a prior decision rendered in Bolivia.

The Supreme Court may take eight or more months until it resolves to accept the foreign judgment. Once such recognition is rendered, the judgment must to be delivered to a lower court for its enforcement. This may take at least three additional months.

CONTRACTS AND DOCUMENTS—FORMS AND ENFORCEABILITY

According to Articles 454 and 519 of the Bolivian Civil Code, contracts among parties are mandatory, and the parties are free to determine the content of their agreements. Contractual liberty, however, is subordinated to the limits imposed by law, and the realization of interests worthy of judicial protection.

ENDING A RESTRUCTURING BUSINESS PRESENCE

According to the Bolivian Commerce Code, companies may be dissolved and liquidated prior to their expiration date. The partners or shareholders of a company may dissolve and liquidate a company provided an agreement exists. Mandatory dissolution and liquidation exists and is regulated by the Commerce Code if a company's capital is reduced by more than 50 percent or if the company is declared bankrupt.

NOTES

1. http://en.wikipedia.org/wiki/List_of_sovereign_states_and_dependent_territories_by_population_density.
2. http://www.trueknowledge.com/q/population_of_bolivia_2010.

3. Book 1, Title III, Chapters 1, 4, and 5, Bolivian Commerce Code (Decree No. 14379).
4. Book 3, Title VI, Chapter 4, Bolivian Commerce Code (Decree No. 14379).
5. Law No. 1182, September 17, 1990 (Investment Law).
6. Law 2445; Supreme Decree 26973, 24423, 25150 (Immigration Law).
7. Law No. 843, May 28, 1986; Law 1606, December 22, 1994.
8. General Labor Law, December 8, 1942 (Labor Law).
9. Decision 486, Andean Pact; Book 2, Title I, Chapters 3–7, Bolivian Commerce Code.

CHAPTER 3

Brazil

Ricardo Barretto Ferreira da Silva
Paulo Marcos Rodrigues Brancher
Carla Amaral de Andrade Junqueira Canero
Barretto Ferreira, Kujawski e Brancher– Sociedade de Advogados (BKBG)*
The following additional members of Barretto Ferreira, Kujawski e Brancher—Sociedade de Advogados (BKBG) have contributed to this chapter: Fabio Kujawski (regulatory and government procurement); Lionel Zaclis (insolvency, real estate, and litigation); André Fernandes (corporate); Luiz Antonio dos Santos (labor and employment); Flávia Rebello (intellectual property, IT, and Internet regulation); Valéria Galindez (dispute resolution); Celso Grisi (tax); Ricardo Inglez de Souza (antitrust and products liability); Cristiane Costa (corporate); Manuela Tavares (labor and employment); Alexandre David (banking/financing/agribusiness); Marina Carvalho (trade and customs); and Elizabeth Fernandes (environmental and products liability).

COUNTRY OVERVIEW

Brazil is the largest economy in South America and one of the largest in the world. This former agricultural colony has evolved into a power in agribusiness and, more recently, in the oil and gas sector, with the discovery of new oil reserves. The country's modern industries and service sector are also booming.

Brazil has a population of approximately 192 million inhabitants, which is concentrated largely in the Southeast region, mainly São Paulo, which is the largest city in Brazil and in South America.

Over the past 30 years, Brazil successfully completed its political transition from a military regime to a full democracy. The government is committed to strengthening financial stability and to assuring the protection of national and foreign investments.

Brazil's major trading partners are Argentina, China, and the United States. Brazil is also a member country of MERCOSUR, an international trade zone with an extensive agenda that includes not only trade, but environmental, educational, and cultural policies. Other MERCOSUR members include Argentina, Paraguay, and Uruguay.

Brazil is a federative republic, comprised of states, municipalities, and the Federal District. The country is governed by a presidential system and has three branches: the executive, legislative, and judiciary, at the federal, state, and municipal levels.

The president is elected for a four-year term (reelection being permitted), and is the head of the executive branch, which is the government branch charged with direct and indirect administration. The legislative branch is formed by a bicameral National Congress, which is responsible for passing proposed legislation before it receives presidential sanction. The judiciary system is composed of federal and state courts. In addition, Brazil has a federal law that permits arbitration to solve conflicts involving disposable patrimonial rights.

The Brazilian legal system is based on civil law and is founded on the Brazilian Constitution of 1988.

ESTABLISHING A BUSINESS PRESENCE

Permanent Structures

Suitable Corporate Forms

Brazilian law provides for different forms of association for the conduct of economic activities geared to the production or circulation of goods and services. Among the corporate-entity types of companies, the most common are the corporation (sociedade anônima or SA) and the limited liability company (sociedade limitada or LTDA).

LTDAs are disciplined by the Brazilian Civil Code. The minimum number of partners is two in this type of company. The capital of an LTDA is divided into proportional parts (quotas), distributed among the partners (quotaholders), and not represented physically by certificates. The number of quotas held by each partner is established in the company's articles of association, and any transfer or assignment of ownership over the quotas is subject to an amendment to the articles of association. The corporate name may include the name of the partners or a fictitious name, but it is always accompanied by the expression "limitada" or its abbreviation, "Ltda." The corporate name shall also indicate the purpose of the company in summarized form.

LTDAs are managed by one or more administrators, who shall be Brazilian or foreign individuals residing in Brazil (with a permanent work visa) and who need not necessarily be partners. Brazilian law permits the creation of an Advisory Board and Audit Committee for the LTDA, whose respective duties and operation shall be regulated in the articles of association.

SAs are governed by Law 6,404/76 (Brazilian Corporation Act). An SA operates under the corporate name indicating its corporate purpose, with the addition of the expressions "sociedade anônima" or "companhia," in full or in abbreviated form. There is no minimum capital requirement for the formation of an SA, except in special cases (for example, financial institutions and trading companies). SAs may be organized with "authorized capital," that is, with less subscribed capital than the amount authorized by the bylaws. In this scenario, an increase of the subscribed capital up to the authorized limit will not be subject to an amendment to the bylaws. The capital stock is divided into shares, which may or may not have a face value. The minimum number of shareholders is two. Shares may be common, preferred, or fruition shares according to the nature of the rights or benefits that they confer on their owners, and registered or book-entry, with respect to their form. Brazilian law prohibits the issuance of bearer shares.

SAs may be of two kinds: publicly held or closely held, depending on whether or not the securities issued by them are listed for trading on the securities market (stock exchange or over-the-counter market). Publicly held corporations are authorized to raise funds with the investor community and are currently submitted to the legislation that disciplines the capital market, and also to the supervision of and registration with the Brazilian Securities Commission (Comissão de Valores Mobiliários or CVM), which is an independent administrative authority in charge of regulating, controlling, and supervising the Brazilian capital market.

The administrative bodies of SAs are the board of directors (conselho de administração), which is mandatory for publicly held companies and for those with authorized capital, and the board of executive officers (diretoria). The board of directors is responsible for determining the company's general business orientation; the board of executive officers is the company's executive body, with the exclusive responsibility of representing the SA before third parties. The members of the board of executive officers (diretores) will be individuals residing in Brazil, whereas the members of the board of directors may be individuals residing and domiciled abroad, provided that they are represented by an attorney-in-fact residing and domiciled in Brazil, duly empowered to receive summons. The board of directors shall be composed of at least three members, who must be shareholders, and the board of executive officers shall be composed of at least two officers, who may be shareholders or not. The SA may optionally have an advisory committee, whose members may reside abroad and be remunerated by the Brazilian company.

SAs shall have an audit committee, whose formation, when its operation is not permanent, may be called for at any shareholders meeting, as provided by law.

Shareholders in an SA generally enter into shareholders' agreements, which typically deal with such matters as the purchase and sale of shares, the preemptive rights related thereto, and exercise of voting rights. The company must comply with the provisions of the shareholders' agreement whenever it is registered with the company's head offices. The protection of minority shareholders is provided for by law, and may be extended through provisions in the corporate bylaws and shareholders' agreements.

Brazilian law considers companies regularly registered with the competent public registry office as legal entities. Companies that develop business activities are subject to registration with the Board of Trade (Junta Comercial).

Wholly Owned Entities

The organization and operation of LTDAs are more flexible and less burdensome than for SAs. An SA involves more formalities than an LTDA as regards its organization and operation, bearing in mind that the publication of certain corporate acts and documents is mandatory in the case of SAs. Consequently, the publication and general operating costs of an SA tend to be higher than those of an LTDA.

For the purposes of possible entry into the Brazilian market and if the foreign investor intends to incorporate a wholly owned subsidiary in Brazil, it is recommended that the LTDA-type of business organization be adopted.

Joint Ventures

In Brazil, the use of the corporation (sociedade anônima) is recommended for cases of joint ventures.

Contractual joint ventures normally take the form of a secret partnership (sociedade em conta de participação) or consortium. Secret partnerships do not have a legal personality and have the nature of a simple partnership agreement. The partnership has two types of partners: the ostensible partner, which conducts the corporate business on its own behalf, appears to third parties, and is responsible for the obligations assumed with third parties; and the secret partner, which contributes cash or assets and participates in the results of the company business. The consortium, on the other hand, is a group of companies formed with the purpose of accomplishing a specific undertaking. The participating companies continue independently, but the consortium has a common administrative direction. The consortium does not have a legal personality; it is formed by a contract that disciplines the obligations and responsibilities of the participants; and it has a limited duration.

Normally, joint ventures imply the existence of a complex contractual structure formed by (i) a base agreement, which will define the purpose of the association (project); the existence or not of a company; the type of company to be created; the procedures for setting up the joint venture; the management rules, rights, and obligations of the parties; the duration; rules regarding the dissolution of the joint venture; the profit/income sharing method; and rules concerning dispute resolution; and (ii) such agreements as the corporate bylaws or articles of association of the legal entity; partners' or shareholders' agreements; technology transfer or trademark and patent licensing agreements; agreement for the supply of machines and equipment; financing instruments and guarantees; and others, depending on the project.

Investments in Mergers with Existing Entities

Foreign investors may decide to enter the Brazilian market through a mergers and acquisitions (M&A) transaction. M&A transactions may have as their subject matters the assets of a Brazilian company (certain specific assets or a group of necessary assets for the development of a particular activity or business), establishment of a Brazilian company; or purchase of equity interests (shares or quotas) representing the capital of a Brazilian company. The purchase of assets, establishment of a Brazilian company, or purchase of equity interests must be formalized via the execution of a purchase agreement. The subscription of the equity interests of an SA (shares) or LTDA (quotas) should be formalized through the execution of a subscription agreement.

It is advisable that a legal, financial, and accounting due diligence investigation of the target company be carried out in order to identify contingencies and potential risks related to the business of the target company, and also to help prospective buyers decide whether or not to go ahead with the deal. If the acquisition involves an industrial plant or establishment or even a piece of land, it is advisable to conduct a specific environmental investigation, with a view to identifying any existing hidden liabilities. This investigation should include the execution of a soil and groundwater contamination analysis (phase I and phase II) on the sites of the business units or manufacturing plants, as well as an analysis of the waste disposal procedure of the target company or establishment and its compliance with the legislation concerning postconsumption liability, if applicable to the products of the target company or establishment.

The negotiation process of an M&A transaction is normally lengthy and complex. During the negotiation progress, it is common for different contractual instruments (confidentiality agreement, letter of intent, and memorandum of investment) to be drafted and signed. The definitive contracts of M&A transactions, especially the purchase agreement, generally follow international practice, but without prejudice to the application of the legal provisions of the Brazilian Civil Code relating to contracts, conditions precedent, indemnification, and losses and damages, for example.

When involving the purchase of the entire equity interests, the buyer assumes control of the legal entity along with all its assets and liabilities. In the case of the partial purchase of the equity interests or capital subscription, the foreign investor assumes an equity interest in the capital of the target company together with other partners or shareholders, in a situation similar to a joint venture, which should be regulated by a partners' or shareholders' agreement.

Agency, Distribution, Franchising, and Reseller Agreements

The main characteristic of agency, distribution, franchising, and reseller agreements is that they enable the supplier of a product or provider of a service to expand its presence in the marketplace by contracting with a third party to develop certain activities. Following is an overview of each contract and its particularities.

Agency Agreement

In Brazil, under an agency agreement, an independent agent works as an intermediary in the sale of products or services. Agents may be individuals or legal entities that, without the existence of an employment relationship, are responsible for negotiating commercial transactions and soliciting purchase orders on behalf of one or more principals. The agent's role is to be the liaison between the principal/manufacturer and the customer, so that the principal can sell directly to the customer. The agent's representation must occur according to the principal's guidelines, and the agent is not allowed to grant rebates or discounts without authorization from the principal.

The agent is entitled to a commission, usually calculated on the purchase price, which shall be paid by the fifteenth day of the month following payment of the invoice by the customer. The relevant agency agreement must specify the general terms and conditions of the representation; identify the products, term (definite or indefinite), and, territory; specify whether it is exclusive or nonexclusive; and define the duties and responsibilities of each party.

Brazilian law also provides for the indemnification of the sales agent upon termination of the agreement by the principal without cause, or by the agent for cause, and establishes the minimum indemnification amount at one-twelfth of the agent's total payment during the representation term, in the case of indefinite-term agreements. In the case of termination of a fixed-term contract, the indemnification shall correspond to the monthly average of the commissions paid on or before the termination date, multiplied by one-half of the remaining contractual months, duly adjusted for inflation.

Moreover, pursuant to the Brazilian Civil Code, in the case of termination of an indefinite-term agency agreement without cause, the terminating party is required to give 90 days' prior notice of termination to the other party.

Distribution Agreement

Under a distribution agreement, the distributor purchases products and resells them under its own name and at its own risk and expense. Brazilian laws do not afford to independent distributors the same protection afforded to agents. Distribution agreements are governed by the Brazilian Civil Code, except when involving the distribution of automotive vehicles, which is subject to specific regulation.

The distribution agreement must outline the terms and conditions of the relationship between the parties. Brazilian law does not establish statutory indemnification in the case of early termination of a distribution agreement. Nonetheless, in the case of breach of contract or termination without cause, the breaching or terminating party may be required to indemnify the innocent party for damages arising from the breach.

In the case of termination without cause of distribution agreements for indefinite terms, (i) the termination can be effective only after a reasonable period of time has elapsed that is consistent with the nature of the business and the investments made by the distributor; and (ii) the terminating party is required to give reasonable prior notice of termination to the other party.

Franchising Agreement

The Brazilian Franchise Act defines the franchise as a system whereby a franchisor grants to a franchisee the right of use of a trademark or patent, associated with the right of exclusive or semi-exclusive distribution of products or services and, in some cases, also with the right to use certain technology for the implementation and management of a business or an operational system developed or owned by the franchisor.

Under Brazilian law, the franchisor is required to disclose to the franchisee, through a franchise offering circular letter (COF), in great detail, all the information concerning the business, the franchise, and the franchisor. The COF must be delivered to a prospective franchisee 10 days before the execution of any agreement between the parties or payment of any amount by the franchisee to the franchisor.

Franchise agreements are subject to registration with the Brazilian Patent and Trademark Office (BPTO) to be effective vis-à-vis third parties. In the case of an agreement with a foreign franchisor, registration of the agreement with the BPTO and the Central Bank of Brazil is also a condition precedent to enable the remittance of payments abroad and the deductibility of payments by the Brazilian franchisee for Brazilian corporate income tax purposes.

Reseller Agreement

The reseller agreement is very similar to the distribution agreement from the point of view of independence from the manufacturer and risk of the business. As there is no specific legislation for reseller agreements in Brazil, general contract law applies as well as the regulations applicable to distribution agreements, by analogy.

Representative Offices and Other "Nonpermanent" Establishments

A foreign company may directly operate in Brazil through a representative office or a branch office, that is, through an extension of the foreign corporate entity itself.

However, this procedure presents some disadvantages when compared with the establishment of a permanent structure in Brazil through the formation of a company, for the following reasons: (i) need for prior authorization through an act of the Federal Executive Branch, which is a red-tape and time-consuming process; (ii) prohibition of the remittance of royalties to the head office abroad for the use of trademarks and exploitation of patents, and (iii) tax disadvantages.

Approvals and Registrations

Certain procedures must be observed for companies to establish operations and start their activities in Brazil, regardless of the type of business organization. The first refers to the registration of the incorporation/formation documents (public deed or private document), with the body responsible for such.

Registration of Companies, for the filing of acts of business companies (including corporations sociedades anônimas), is carried out by the Boards of Trade (Juntas Comerciais) of the states in which the registered offices of the business companies are located.

Civil Registration, for the registration of the acts of general partnerships (sociedades simples), is carried out by the Civil Registry of Legal Entities (Cartórios de Registro Civil das Pessoas Jurídicas), which are jurisdiction bodies in the judicial districts to which they belong.

Amendments to the articles of association/corporate bylaws of business companies must be presented to the Board of Trade of the state in which the registered office of the company is located, through a specific application.

In the case of corporations, in addition to the aforementioned filing, the company is also required to arrange for the publication of its corporate bylaws in the official body of the location of its registered office.

Subsequently, the companies whose acts have been filed with the competent bodies (Commercial Registry or Civil Registry, as the case may be) must arrange for their enrollment with the competent federal, state, and municipal authorities and obtain the registration of their tax and accounting books. These procedures begin, as a rule, with the enrollment in the Federal Register of Corporate Taxpayers of the Finance Ministry (Cadastro Nacional de Pessoas Jurídicas do Ministério da Fazenda or CNPJ/MF), which will also enable the company to open a bank account.

Companies are also required to register with other public agencies, including the Brazilian Social Security Institute (Instituto Nacional de Seguridade Social or INSS), Federal Savings and Loans Bank (Caixa Econômica Federal) for purposes of the Length of Service and Guarantee Fund (FGTS), and local government authorities (prefeituras municipais) of the cities in which the registered and branch offices of the companies are located. In addition, considering the companies' corporate purposes, the companies must also arrange for their registration with the Secretariat of Public Finances (Secretaria da Fazenda) of the state and with other bodies and/or public agencies, such as the environmental agency if an industrial activity, National Sanitary Surveillance Agency (Agência Nacional de Vigilância Sanitária or ANVISA) if an activity involving drugs, and others, as the case may be.

Companies that have foreign partners (natural persons or legal entities) shall register the foreign capital with Central Bank of Brazil, which will serve as a basis for the repatriation of the investments, remittance of dividends, and so on.

The foreign capital must be registered through the Electronic Declaratory Registration–Foreign Direct Investment (RDE–IDE) Module, which is part of the Central Bank Information System (Sistema de Informações do Banco Central or SISBACEN).

Sensitive Economic Sectors/Restrictions on Foreign Ownership

Some sectors of the Brazilian economy, such as telecommunications; mining and the exploitation of the hydroelectric power grid; journalism and radio broadcasting companies; activities related to the oil and gas by-product production chain; and public air services, are especially regulated by the Brazilian state, with partial or total restriction on foreign capital.

Brazilian law does not define a single regulation model for foreign capital in Brazilian companies, but rather, restrictions established in some specific sectors of the national economy, which may be more or less rigid in accordance with the sector-specific legislation.

Political Risks and Related Issues

Since the enactment of the Constitution of the Federative Republic of Brazil in 1988, the country has been experiencing one of the longest periods of its history under the positive effects of a Legal Democratic State and stability in the conduct of the country's economic policy.

Various factors contributed to this present reality. Brazil today has the ninth-largest GDP in the world, is the third-priority destination for foreign investments that will be made during the period 2010–2012, and the conservative growth tendency of its economy, at least for the next two years, is over 5 percent annually. International investment banks, for the first time, classified Brazilian sovereign papers as investment grade, giving them access to international pension fund investments.

The foreign exchange and macroeconomic policies prevailing in Brazil are no longer as sensitive to partisan interests as they were in the past. This means that, regardless of the political party in power, the socioeconomic foundations and democratic regime rest on solid institutional bases. Thus, the country presents a very low risk, particularly if Brazil is compared to other South or Central American countries.

Nevertheless, Brazil has been a signatory of the Multilateral Investment Guarantee Agency Convention (MIGA) since 1992. The purpose of this agency, among others, is to grant guarantees against political risks that are generally not covered by traditional insurance companies, in international investments. The Convention determines that MIGA may insure investments considered eligible against losses resulting from one or more of the following types of risks: (i) currency transfers and convertibility; (ii) expropriation and similar measures; (iii) breach of contract; and (iv) wars or civil disturbances.

INVESTMENT ISSUES AND TAX INCENTIVES

Legal Treatment of Foreign Investment

In Brazil, the agency responsible for the registration, control, and monitoring of investments made by means of foreign capital is the Central Bank of Brazil, and, with regards to the monitoring of the fiscal aspects related to foreign investments, the Finance Ministry, through the Brazilian Internal Revenue Service (Secretaria da Receita Federal).

Foreign capital is regulated in Brazil by Law 4,131/62 (Foreign Capital Law) and Law 4,390/64, which, among other provisions, define foreign capital as any assets, machines, equipment, financial, or monetary resources that are brought into the country, to be used for the production of goods or services, or for investment in economic activities, provided that, in any of the cases, they belong to individuals or companies resident, domiciled, or based abroad. Under the aforesaid law, foreign capital is ensured identical treatment to that afforded to national capital, and any discrimination not provided in law is forbidden.

All foreign capital must be registered. No movements of the resources received and remitted abroad may be made without the registration, with special emphasis on the remittance of profits, dividends, interest on net equity, reinvestment of this profit in the recipient company in which they were generated, repatriation of capital, and others. The registration of foreign capital is currently done electronically, through the Central Bank Information System (SISBACEN), specifically in the RDE–IED Module, as seen earlier.

Accordingly, foreign investment may be made automatically, without the need for any prior analysis or authorization of the Central Bank. The foreign investment to be made and registered is not subject to prior analysis and verification by the Central Bank, being merely declaratory; that is, the recipient company of the foreign investment and/or representative of the foreign investor shall conduct the respective registration directly with SISBACEN.

The declaratory nature of this registration, however, implies the responsibility of the applicants for the veracity and legality of the information provided.

In addition, the registration by the RDE–IED Module assumes the prior registration of the responsible person with the Central Bank, for access to the SISBACEN to be authorized, in accordance with the rules currently in force. It is characterized by the assignment of a number for the "national recipient–nonresident investor," under which all the changes and subsequent inclusions relating to the registered investment must be recorded.

For the registration of a foreign direct investment in the RDE–IED, prior registration of the parties involved in the Cademp–Cadastro de Empresas da Área do DESIG is necessary.

Treaties on Foreign Investment Protection

Although Brazil has signed agreements for the promotion and reciprocal protection of investments (Bilateral Investment Treaties or BITs) with 14 countries, these agreements have never been ratified by the Brazilian National Congress and, therefore, are not in force. Brazil, together with other member countries of MERCOSUR, signed the MERCOSUR Protocol of Colonia on Reciprocal Promotion and Protection of Investments within MERCOSUR (Protocolo de Colônia para a Promoção e a Proteção Recíproca de Investimentos no MERCOSUL), which covers intrazone investment. Brazil also signed the Buenos Aires Protocol for the Promotion and Protection of Investments originating from Nonmember States of MERCOSUR (Protocolo de Buenos Aires para a Promoção e Proteção de Investimentos provenientes de Estados não Partes do MERCOSUL). In addition to arbitration between the investor and host country, the protocols set forth rights and obligations similar to those of the BITs. These protocols were not ratified by Brazil either.

Brazil is not a signatory of the Washington Convention of 1965, which created the International Centre for the Settlement of Investment Disputes (ICSID), instituted under the auspices of the World Bank. On the other hand, Brazil is a party to the convention that created the Multilateral Investment Guaranty Agency (MIGA) in 1985. In any event, by virtue of the fact that Brazil has become an exporter of capital, it is possible that it will establish new treaties in the future, which will probably be based on the new generation of BITs. The new generation of BITs reconciles in a better way than the former BITs the interests of the host country with those of investors.

Publicly Held Companies—Capital Market Regulations

Publicly held companies are submitted to the legislation that disciplines the capital market and they, as well as the shares issued by them, must be registered with the Brazilian Securities Commission (Comissão de Valores Mobiliários or CVM). CVM is an independent administrative authority, in charge of regulating and overseeing the Brazilian capital market.

The shares of a publicly held company may be purchased directly on the capital market.

The foreign investor may invest in the same capital market modalities available to investors residing in Brazil. To this end, the investor should engage an institution to act as (i) legal representative, responsible for submitting all the registration information to the Brazilian authorities, (ii) fiscal representative, responsible for tax matters on behalf of the investor, with the Brazilian authorities, and (iii) custodian, responsible for keeping documents current and controlling all the assets of the foreign investor in segregated accounts, and also for supplying at any time information requested by the authorities or by the investor itself.

In the case of publicly held companies with disperse capital—that is, those that do not have controlling shareholders—the purchase of a relevant number of shares, or even that represent the control of the company, may be made through a series of private offerings for the purchase of securities (escalation), and also by a takeover bid, directed to the shareholders of the company, the terms and conditions of which are regulated by CVM.

The purchase of shares is formalized through the signing of a share purchase and sale agreement. However, the transfer operates differently, depending on the type of share: (i) if registered, it operates by means of transcription of the record in the transfer of registered shares book, signed by the assignor and assignee; and (ii) if book-entry, the transfer occurs by the entry made by the depositary institution in its books, debiting the seller's share account and crediting the purchaser's share account, against the presentation of the written order from the seller.

The direct or indirect acquisition of the control of publicly held companies generates an obligation for the acquirer to make a tender offer for the purchase of the voting shares owned by the other shareholders (tag along). Tender offers are regulated and supervised by CVM.

Alternate Investment Structures—Investment Funds

The constitution and operation of investment funds are regulated by the Brazilian Securities Commission (CVM). Among their various characteristics, investment funds are required to disclose their operations and appropriate operation through the disclosure and forwarding of various forms to the CVM at periods previously determined by prevailing legislation.

These funds do not have their own legal personality, and, therefore, are not subject to the payment of various taxes that are typical to legal entities. As in a condominium in which each participant is the owner of quotas, the investors are able to freely access and transfer the contributed capital, making a gain or loss by the amount paid at the time of the sale of the quotas—in comparison to the purchase price.

The most common investment funds are private equity funds (fundo de investimento em participações or FIP); multimarket investment funds (fundo de investimento multimercado); credit assignment investment fund (fundo de investimento em direitos creditórios or FIDC); and real estate investment fund (fundo de investimento imobiliário or FII).

OPERATIONAL LEGAL ENVIRONMENT

Tips on Negotiations in the Country

Brazil is a country of continental proportions with a population resulting primarily from eminently by miscegenation between different races and ethnic groups. These characteristics cause commercial negotiations to be guided by cultural aspects that vary from region to region in Brazil.

Whereas in the North and Northeast regions customs tend to be more informal, in the South and Southeast greater formalities are imposed. Situations in which the parties organize lunches or dinners during the negotiation process are frequent, in order to create a friendly and positive atmosphere for the conclusion of business. While this situation is frequent in private negotiations, the same cannot be said with respect to negotiations with members of government.

Brazil has sophisticated legislation concerning foreign corruption practices, which does not enable public authorities to carry out an enormous range of activities, directly or indirectly because of the positions that they hold in the government. Therefore, all meetings involving negotiations with public entities must be scheduled in advance, must occur at the headquarters of the government entity during working days and hours, and must rigidly observe all formalities. Any kind of gratuity or invitation, even if given or made in an innocent manner, should be avoided when involving relationships with public entities.

Lastly, punctuality is an essential element for a good business relationship, although small delays in regions of high population density (such as capitals, for example) are understood.

Foreign Exchange

In Brazil, the Central Bank of Brazil is responsible for controlling foreign capital and regulating the foreign exchange market, in compliance with the provisions and rules of the National Monetary Fund.

In March Desde 2005, the Central Bank unified the regulations pertaining to the foreign exchange market, adopting more flexible postures. As a result, remittances of funds should flow through one single foreign exchange market, regardless of the nature of the payments.

Foreign exchange transactions are regulated by the International Capital and Foreign Exchange Market Regulation (Regulamento do Mercado de Câmbio e Capitais Internacionais or RMCCI), instituted by Central Bank Circular 3,280, of March 9, 2005, which contains the following titles:

a) title 1—Foreign Exchange Market: disciplines foreign currency purchase and sale transactions, international transfers in reais and operations involving gold-foreign exchange instrument operations, as well as the necessary materials for its regular operation;

b) title 2—Brazilian Capital Abroad: regulates the values of any nature, the currency assets, and property and rights held outside of the Brazilian territory by individuals and legal entities resident, domiciled, or based in Brazil;

c) title 3—Foreign Capital in Brazil: regulates foreign capital in the country and its registration with the Central Bank of Brazil, dealing with foreign direct investment, financial operations, and other resources obtained abroad in accordance with prevailing legislation and regulations, including the capital.

Immigration and Visa Requirements

Brazilian legislation establishes seven different visa categories: transit, tourist, temporary, permanent, courtesy, official, and diplomatic.

Foreigners who intend to work, either temporarily or permanently, in Brazilian territory, under an employment contract, must obtain a temporary work visa. The conditions to obtain this visa and the requirements that the entity interested in foreign labor and the immigrant need to fulfill are established by normative resolutions of the Ministry of Labor and Employment, which regulate the law known as the Estatuto do Estrangeiro (Foreigners Law).

The temporary work visa is valid for two years and may be renewed for an equal period. At the end of four years, the foreigner may apply to have the temporary visa changed to a permanent visa.

For a non-Brazilian to be appointed as administrator of a Brazilian company he or she must have a permanent work visa. In this case, in addition to satisfying the necessary requirements for obtaining the temporary work visa, the Brazilian company must evidence a minimum investment of USD 200,000 per foreigner, or alternatively, an investment of, at least, USD 50,000, plus the generation of 10 new jobs, during the two subsequent years, for each foreigner.

The permanent visa can also be issued in the case of a family relationship of the foreigner (whether by marriage or steady union with a Brazilian or due to having a Brazilian child), in the case of a foreigner who has retired abroad but wishes to transfer his residence to Brazil and in the case of a foreign investor, who must evidence a minimum investment of USD 50,000 in a Brazilian company that either already exists or has been recently established.

Foreigners wishing to come to Brazil to participate in meetings, fairs, seminars, or conferences, to visit clients, or to conduct market research or any similar activities must obtain short-term business visit visas, which should be applied for at the Brazilian consulate in the foreigner's country of origin.

It is important to mention that issues concerning authorization for obtaining visas for permanent residence in Brazil reflect government policies and reciprocity of treatment, and may, therefore, vary in accordance with the domestic and international political scenario at the time of their application.

Lastly, Brazil's Federal Constitution adopts the principle of equality between Brazilians and foreigners residing in the country, guaranteeing them the same rights and obligations, though making some specific reservations, especially concerning certain political offices and the exploitation of certain economic sectors.

Import and Export Issues

The Brazilian Customs Regulation Decree[1] contains the main legal framework regarding the import and export of goods. The governmental body in charge of applying the aforesaid legislation is the Ministry of Development, Industry and Foreign Trade (MDIC) and the Foreign Trade System (SISCOMEX).

Generally, noncontrolled goods may be imported into and exported from Brazil without the need for licenses. Noncontrolled goods are those that are not specifically subject to import or export controls, as set out in relevant legislation, and all they need to enter the country is the registration of the Import Declaration at SISCOMEX.[2] The import and export of controlled goods[3] are subject to approval granted by the relevant authorities. These licenses may have to be granted prior to the dispatch of goods (nonautomatic licenses) or after dispatch but prior to arrival (automatic licenses). The import of used goods is not permitted in Brazil. However, there are some exceptions to this rule,[4] allowing for the import of used machines and other equipment when there is no domestic production of a similar product or when there is no local substitute capable of providing similar functions. Imports and exports of certain goods are also strictly prohibited in Brazil.[5]

Exports from Brazil are subject to less complex procedures than imports and a few products are subject to an export tax.

Taxation of Business and Cross-Border Transactions

Brazilian legislation establishes different taxes to be applied on business activities, at the federal, state, and municipal level.

Income Tax (Imposto de Renda). The taxable event of this federal tax on income and earnings of any nature is the acquisition of the economic or legal availability of (i) earnings, thus understood as the revenue gained from capital, labor, or the combination of both; and (ii) proceeds of any nature, thus understood as other increases in wealth.

Social Contribution on Net Profit (Contribuição Social sobre o Lucro Líquido or CSLL) is payable by legal entities and generally follows the same rules applicable to corporate income tax. Hence, it is imposed on the net profits of companies, at the rate of 9 percent.

PIS/COFINS Contributions (to the Social Integration Program for Funding of Social Welfare Programs) are levied monthly on the gross revenue of legal entities.

Excise Tax (Imposto sobre Produtos Industrializados or IPI) is due on operations involving manufactured products (submitted to any operation that changes its nature or purpose, or improves them for consumption) at variable rates in accordance with the essentiality of the product.

State VAT (Imposto sobre Operações Relativas à Circulação de Mercadorias e sobre Prestações de Serviços de Transporte Interestadual e Intermunicipal, e de Comunicação or ICMS) is a value added tax that is levied on (i) operations involving the circulation of goods; (ii) the provision of interstate and intermunicipal transport services; (iii) service rendered abroad; and (iv) the onerous provision of communication services. ICMS rates vary in accordance with the operation in question and depending on the states from which and to which the goods are transferred.

Service Tax (Imposto sobre Serviços de Qualquer Natureza or ISS) is a Municipal and Federal District tax and is imposed on the rendering of the services provided in law. The taxpayer is the provider of the service. ISS rates must be defined for each municipality up to the maximum rate of 5 percent.

International Taxation

Brazil is not a signatory member of OECD. It thus has its own rules established for purposes of international taxation. It is a signatory of agreements with various countries to avoid double taxation.

Thin Capitalization

As of 2010, legal entities with debts with related companies based abroad will be subject to a deductibility limit of the interest paid or credited, and they must meet certain requirements.

Transfer Pricing

Brazilian law establishes the market price as the objective parameter for the prices practiced between related companies, which can be obtained through the application of the methods defined in law. These methods generally use the following criteria: (i) independent prices; (ii) cost; or (iii) resale price.

Tax Havens

As of 2008, Brazilian legislation broadened the concept of a tax haven by defining that the jurisdictions that do not permit access to information concerning the corporate structures of companies and the assets or rights relating to the economic transactions effected thereby are also considered tax havens.

CFC Rules

Brazilian legislation provides for Controlled Foreign Companies (CFC) rules, according to which the profits made by a subsidiary or associated company abroad, for purposes of the determination of the tax base for the calculation of IRPJ and CSLL, are deemed to be made available to the parent or associated company in Brazil on the date of the balance sheet in which they have been computed, or on December 31 of the year following that in which the profits were computed.

Taxation of International Remittances

Amounts remitted abroad are normally subject to withholding at source at the rate of 15 percent, with the exception of remittances to countries that are considered to have favorable taxation, in which case the withholding is 25 percent.

Distribution of Dividends

The distribution of dividends, both to Brazilian residents and nonresidents, is exempt from Withholding Income Tax for profits computed as of 1996.

Interest on Equity

Interest on Equity (Juros sobre o Capital Próprio or JCP) is a means of remunerating the capital invested by the partners or shareholders in a company. This paid or credited interest is deductible for purposes of the determination of the Taxable Income of the Legal Entity and is subject to the levy of Withholding Income Tax (IRRF), at the rate of 15 percent. The remittance of JCP to nonresidents is subject to the imposition of Income Tax at Source at the rate of 15 percent.

Labor and Employment

Labor relations are rigidly regulated in Brazil, by constitutional and nonconstitutional laws, the most important being the Consolidation of Labor Laws (Consolidação das Leis do Trabalho or CLT). An employment contract may be entered into tacitly or expressly, and it is recommended that the contract be drawn up in writing with a clear definition of the rules that will be regulating the relationship between the parties. In any event, the contract should be registered in the Work and Social Security booklet (Carteira de Trabalho e Previdência Social or CTPS), which is an obligatory document for employees.

Although the parties may establish the clauses that will govern the employment contract, they are not allowed to transgress the minimum limits established by labor legislation and by the collective bargaining conventions and agreements made by the trade unions.

Employment agreements are normally made for an indeterminate period of time. Hiring for determinate periods is, however, permitted only in cases of (a) temporary services, the nature of which justifies predetermination of the period (such as the refurbishment of an office); (b) services related to activities of a temporary or seasonal nature (such as the sales activities of Christmas products); and (c) a probationary employment contract (contrato de experiência). In the first two cases, the contract may not exceed the period of two years but may be renewed once within this period. The probationary employment contract may be executed for a maximum period of 90 days, and is likewise renewable once only within this period.

There are minimum rights guaranteed to workers by Brazilian legislation. Other rights may be established by the parties, through the individual employment contract itself, or by the respective trade unions representing the blue-collar and white-collar workers, through collective bargaining agreements and conventions. In addition, the rights established by the International Labor Organization (ILO) Conventions that are ratified by National Congress apply to the employment contracts entered into in Brazil.

As a rule, the employment contract may be terminated at any time and by either of the parties, except when the employee has job stability, in which case his or her dismissal without cause is forbidden. The extinguishment of the employment contract may occur for various reasons, at which time the employer shall pay the employee the so-called termination amounts, which vary in accordance with the type of contractual termination.

Work hours cannot exceed eight hours a day, with a weekly 44-hour limit.

The Brazilian Social Security System is financed with monthly employee contributions (11 percent of the salary) that are withheld by the employer, as well as with monthly employer contributions (28 percent).

Antitrust and Competition Issues

The Brazilian Competition Act (Competition Act) is the main statute governing antitrust and competition issues in Brazil. It provides for merger control and penalties for violations of free competition and applies to all entities, individuals, and government authorities.

The main possible misbehaviors, under the Competition Act, are the cartel, price fixing and/or discrimination, bid rigging, and others. Competition issues may also give rise to civil and criminal liabilities. Affected parties may file private litigation cases to claim for damages to the parties that have violated the Competition Act. Private parties are allowed by the Competition Act to file judicial claims requesting: (i) a cease order to prevent the violator from continuing to act in a manner that is deemed to be illegal by the plaintiff; and (ii) indemnification for damages. There is no such thing as treble damages in Brazil, as there is in the United States.

The administrative sanction, among others, would be a pecuniary fine that varies between 1 percent and 30 percent of the pre-tax gross revenue of each defendant. The fines applied have been closer to the minimum for unilateral conducts, and to the maximum for cartel cases.

Moreover, there are criminal provisions for some violations of free competition, such as the cartel and bid rigging.

It is possible for one of the involved parties to claim immunity. Brazil has a leniency program that grants total administrative and criminal immunity to the applicant, if certain conditions are met. The leniency agreement would not, however, provide civil immunity.

On the subject of merger control, the Competition Act determines two different criteria to verify whether a mandatory merger-control filing is necessary, namely (a) the control of a market share equal to, or in excess of, 20 percent; or (b) that the parties posted gross revenues, in the previous fiscal year, equal to, or in excess of, R$400 million.[6] The Competition Law does not require a minimum effect within the Brazilian marketplace.

The Administrative Council for Economic Defense (CADE) is the administrative agency in charge of enforcing the Competition Act. Two secretariats assist CADE in this task: the Secretariat of Economic Law (SDE), linked to the Ministry of Justice, and the Secretariat of Economic Monitoring (SEAE), linked to the Ministry of Finance.

CADE's final decision, in all cases, may be the subject of judicial review. There is no administrative appeal to challenge CADE's final decision to a higher administrative authority. However, the Constitution of 1988, as well as the U.S. First Amendment, guarantees the right of petition and right of access to a judicial court.[7]

Environmental Issues

Brazil has a sophisticated legal environmental protection system. Even before the enactment of the Federal Constitution of 1988, several environmental laws had already been passed. The Federal Constitution of 1988 was then enacted, under which the environment was considered a constitutionally protected value for the first time in the Brazilian legal system. Since then, doctrine and jurisprudence in Brazil have unanimously recognized a healthy environment as a fundamental right. Moreover, "environmental defense" was also included as one of the principles that shall govern economic activity (article 170, item VI), and the use of private rural property, so that the latter may fulfill its social role (article 186, item II).

From a nonconstitutional standpoint, the following laws are relevant: Law 7,802/89 (Agrochemicals Law); Law 9,433/97 (National Water Resources Policy); Law 9,605/98 (providing for criminal and administrative sanctions resulting from behavior and activities that are harmful to the environment); Law 9,795/99 (National Environmental Education Policy); and Law 9,985/00 (establishing the National Preservation Unit System).

Additionally, several Brazilian state constitutions have included environmental protection provisions.

It can be noted that, in the Brazilian environmental law, liability is classified into three independent spheres: (i) civil; (ii) administrative; and (iii) criminal, if the act or omission practiced is considered a crime.

Consumer Protection and Product Liability

In the Private Law sphere, the Brazilian Consumer Protection Code (CDC), Law 8,078/90, provides for strict and objective civil liability (strict liability in tort) for manufacturing and service defects. The requirements for criminal liability are the ascertainment of the intention ("dolus") and/or lack of diligence ("culpa") of the agent. The liability of independent professionals likewise depends on negligence.

The CDC also determines the joint liability of all suppliers in the supply chain for damages caused to consumers. This means that when individuals are harmed by unsafe, defective, or dangerous products, they may have a cause of action against any company that is a member of said supply chain, which is jointly liable vis-à-vis consumers, pursuant to the CDC. Then, depending on the contractual terms, the supplier that was considered liable may have a right of recovery against the party of the supply chain that actually caused or was responsible for the damage.

Additionally, the CDC provides for the possibility of shifting the burden of proof to benefit the consumer when, at the discretion of the court, the consumer's claim is reasonable. A reasonable claim is one likely to be true, whether or not supported by evidence. In addition, it is possible to shift the burden of proof if the consumer is disadvantaged, or when there is both an economic and technical disparity between the litigants, making the consumer vulnerable.

Concerning the information and warnings required to be placed on products, these are sparsely determined in various regulations issued according to the product class and a failure to warn is a violation of law. In case of an anonymous, misidentified, or perishable product requiring special storage, the merchant can also be held liable because it becomes the apparent supplier.

The causes for exemption from civil liability are expressly and categorically provided by the Brazilian Consumer Protection Code, without prejudice to exemption from liability in the case of acts of God as defined in the Brazilian Civil Code. They are: failure to offer the product in the market, lack of defect in the product or service, and exclusive fault of the victim or third party.

Land Use and Real Estate

Land ownership in Brazil is generally freehold and is subject to registration with the official Land Registry where the land is situated. Since Brazil has a well-developed land register system, there is no title insurance system. There are no restrictions on foreign ownership and/or domain, except on large rural properties[8] or border areas, in which case prior governmental approval must be obtained.

The process of acquiring immovable property can be divided into three stages: (i) the pre-contractual stage, which normally involves initial negotiations, preliminary letters of intent, and a summary title investigation; (ii) the contractual stage, when detailed negotiations are normally completed and the contract is entered into; and (iii) the postcontractual or completion phase, involving the execution of the deed of conveyance with the notary public and registration of the deed at the Land Registry.

Chattel mortgages (alienação fiduciária em garantia) are the most commonly used security in relation to real estate ownership. The buyer remains in possession while the ownership title is transferred to the lender. The mortgage must cover a specific property and amount, and the underlying obligation guaranteed by the mortgage must also be certain and determined. Mortgages must be created by means of a public deed executed by the mortgagee and mortgagor before a notary public and then registered with the Land Registry in order to perfect the mortgage and produce effects against third parties. Foreclosure of the mortgage can be sought through special summary court proceedings, which provides for the sale of the property by public auction.

Urban lease provisions are generally of "public order" and cannot be altered by agreement of the parties. Urban leases need only be in writing, there being no notary or registration requirements. Urban leases of commercial property have a minimum term of three years whereas residential leases have a minimum term of two years. These minimum term requirements do not apply to certain types of leases such as tourism, parking spaces, and stalls at markets. Notwithstanding the minimum terms indicated above, after the first six months of the lease, the tenant has the legal right to terminate the lease by giving the landlord 60 days' prior notice. Lease agreements are subject to a maximum term of 10 years.

In general, the tenant shall be responsible for carrying out minor repairs and regular maintenance of the leased property and for those repairs caused by his fault. Any defects in the structure of the premises or more serious repair works are, however, the responsibility of the landlord.

Urban development in Brazil is basically governed by a federal development law and municipal zoning regulations and local building codes, which vary according to each jurisdiction.

Intellectual Property

Brazilian laws offer a gamut of rules that regulate and protect intellectual property rights. These rules can be found in the Brazilian Federal Constitution and in several federal laws and treaties signed by Brazil, such as the Agreement on Trade-Related Aspects of Intellectual Property Rights (TRIPS), the Berne Convention, the Paris Convention, and the Patent Cooperation Treaty (PCT).

Under Brazilian laws, the main intangible assets that are protected are trademarks, patents, industrial designs, trade secrets, geographical indications, mask works, copyrights, software, and domain names.

The Brazilian Industrial Property Act (IP Act) regulates trademark protection and registration with the Brazilian Patent and Trademark Office (BPTO). Visually perceptible and distinctive signs are subject to trademark protection in Brazil regardless of prior use in commerce; the Brazilian IP Act adopted the first-to-file system and will grant protection for the first applicant, except for well-known trademarks in their fields of activity. Certain signs are not susceptible to trademark protection in Brazil, such as words used to describe a product or service, advertising expressions, immoral or discriminatory signs, and others. BPTO will register three-dimensional trademarks, but olfactory and sound trademarks do not qualify for trademark protection in Brazil.

Trademark registrations in Brazil are valid for a 10-year term, renewable for successive 10-year periods. The Brazilian IP Act also grants special protection to famous trademarks, provided that BPTO acknowledges the trademark as famous; in this case, protection will cover all classes of products and services.

The Brazilian IP Act grants patent protection to inventions and utility models that meet the following conditions: (i) novelty (the invention must not be within the state of the art); (ii) inventive activity (the invention must be the result of an inventive activity and cannot result or derive from the state of the art in a manner evident or obvious to an expert); and (iii) industrial applicability (the invention must be usable or producible in an industry). Patent applications are filed at BPTO, and once BPTO grants the patent, it will be valid for a term of 20 years for inventions, or 15 years in the case of utility models.

According to the IP Act, certain inventions and utility models are not eligible for patent protection in Brazil, including living beings, in whole or in part, except for microorganisms that meet the patentability requirements.

Under the Brazilian IP Act, industrial designs that meet the requirements of novelty and originality and are registered with BPTO are eligible for intellectual property protection for a term of 10 years, renewable for three successive periods of five years each. Industrial designs are two-dimensional or three-dimensional representations that may be applied to a product, resulting in a new and original look in its external configuration, and that are suitable for industrial production.

There is no legal definition for the trade secret in the IP Act and its protection is afforded by the suppression of unfair competition acts. Thus, trade secrets are not subject to registration in Brazil. Generally speaking, trade secrets consist of secret knowledge or information that is not obvious to third parties and that gains economic value due to its secrecy. The protection of a trade secret will last for as long as it is kept secret, and the IP Act characterizes the unauthorized disclosure of a trade secret as an unfair competition crime.

The Brazilian IP Act grants protection to the following geographical indications, subject to registration with BPTO: (a) geographical names of countries, cities, or regions that became known as centers for extraction, production, or manufacture of a certain product or service rendering; or (b) geographical names used to designate the qualities and features of products or services due to the geographical environment. Only manufacturers or service providers that are headquartered or domiciled in the geographical area will be authorized to use the corresponding geographical indication.

Mask works or topographies of integrated circuits are eligible for protection for a term of 10 years, as of the date of application at BPTO or from the first use in commerce, whichever occurs first, provided that they are original, and therefore result from the creator's own intellectual effort, and are not obvious or generally known to experts in the same field of activity.

The Brazilian Copyright Act protects literary, artistic, and scientific works regardless of registration of the copyrights with any governmental entity. Nonetheless, registration of the work is optional. Copyright protection in Brazil covers creative expressions in any medium, including films, architectural designs, photography, paintings, books, designs, and sculptures, among others. Generally speaking, copyright protection is granted for a term of 70 years as of the author's death, or as of publication of the work (such as for audiovisual works or those of anonymous authorship).

The Brazilian Software Act grants software copyright protection, regardless of registration. Notwithstanding, registration of the computer program by the author is optional and may be applied for at the BPTO. Software protection lasts for a term of 50 years, as of January 1 of the year following the publication or creation of the software.

Domain names at the country level (".br") are registered by the Center of Information and Coordination (NIC), by delegation of the Brazilian Internet Steering Committee of the Ministries of Communication and Science and Technology. Several top-level domains correspond to certain types of activity, such as ".com.br" for commercial purposes, ".ind.br" for industries, ".org.br" for nonprofit organizations, and so on. The registration of ".br" domain names is conducted electronically. Any individual or entity may register an unlimited number of domain names at the same top-level domain. However, NIC sets forth additional requirements for foreign individuals or entities, such as the obligation of a foreign entity to initiate its activities and establish a local presence in Brazil within one year of the registration of the domain name.

Brazilian intellectual property laws and regulations provide for several remedies for the enforcement of intellectual property rights. These remedies include: (i) administrative appeals or forfeiture or annulment requests with the BPTO; (ii) preliminary search-and-seizure proceedings; (iii) civil lawsuits to discontinue any unauthorized use of intellectual property rights, seizure of infringing goods, and obtainment of indemnification; (iv) criminal prosecution for conducts defined as crimes; (v) border control; and (vi) suppression of unauthorized parallel imports.

Generally speaking, intellectual property rights may be licensed to third parties in Brazil or abroad. However, agreements for the licensing of trademarks, patents, and industrial designs, or the supply of technology and franchising must be registered with the BPTO to be enforceable vis-à-vis third parties. When involving an agreement with a foreign entity, registration with BPTO and the Central Bank of Brazil is also a condition precedent to enable the remittance of payments abroad and deductibility of payments by the Brazilian licensee/payor for Brazilian corporate income tax purposes.

Customs

The SISCOMEX system was developed to register and control foreign trade–related activities. Registration in the SISCOMEX operates under the authority of the Brazilian Internal Revenue Service (Secretaria da Receita Federal) (Normative Instruction 650/2006). SISCOMEX is in charge of enforcing legislation related to the import and export of goods, and the means and conditions under which said goods are carried.

Brazil has a specific regime for goods in transit.[9] This specific procedure, called the "Customs Transit Regime" (Regime de Trânsito Aduaneiro), establishes that goods may enter the country through a place located on the border and may be carried, without being nationalized, to a place of destination inland (usually a bonded warehouse). Following this procedure, the customs clearance and, consequently, the nationalization of the goods, are performed only at the final destination. This regime provides for the free transit of goods from the primary customs borders (airports, ports, train stations) to the secondary customs zone (bonded warehouses) and all taxes levied on the product are suspended.

Internet Regulations and E-Commerce

Brazil is the leading South American country in terms of Internet users and e-commerce transactions. It is also one of the countries with the greatest Internet growth potential. However, the majority of transactions entered into on the Internet in Brazil are not governed by specific rules, and civil, criminal, intellectual property, and consumer laws provide the general rules for business conducted on the Internet. Some specific aspects, however, such as the Brazilian Public Key Infrastructure, the domain name regulations, and electronic public bids, among others, have specific rules for the Internet.

Among the regulatory bodies that supervise the Internet, the National Telecommunications Agency (ANATEL) is the governmental entity responsible for the regulation of the telecom services that support access to the Internet. In addition, the Brazilian Internet Steering Committee (CGI) of the Ministries of Communication and Science and Technology is responsible for the registration of domain names. The Information Technology Institute, which is a government agency linked to the presidency, regulates and controls the Brazilian Public Key Infrastructure (PKI-Brazil). Moreover, competition and consumer protection agencies and other government entities deal with abusive practices of Internet service providers in a general manner.

In the litigation area, Brazilian courts will have jurisdiction over an Internet-related lawsuit when: (i) the defendant is domiciled in Brazil; (ii) the obligations are to be fulfilled in Brazil; and (iii) the lawsuit originates from an action or activity that occurred or was carried out in Brazil. As a general rule, in Brazil, the relevant authority to exercise jurisdiction will be the competent body in the defendant's place of domicile. However, the Consumer Protection Code (CPC) establishes that lawsuits claiming the liability of the supplier of products and services in consumer relationships may be brought in the plaintiff's domicile. If there is a consumer relationship, the Brazilian courts may be competent to judge the case, even if the service rendering does not occur in the country.

Although Brazil has no specific legislation that regulates advertising on the Internet, the guarantees and limitations set forth in the Federal Constitution regarding freedom of expression must always be observed. The Brazilian self-regulation code establishes ethical standards for the advertising industry and regulates specific advertising matters. The advertising of alcoholic beverages and firearms is restricted by the code in relation to advertising on the Internet to prevent access by minors, for instance.

Brazil has no specific legislation for the security of Internet transactions or encrypted communications. However, if the companies or ISPs cause any damage to users in an Internet transaction owing to lack of security, the company or ISP may be held liable for such damage. In addition, as Internet users are protected by the constitutional guarantee of privacy, ISPs and related companies must maintain a very efficient security system in order to protect all the sensitive data of their users. These entities may also be liable for damages in the event of any unauthorized access to personal data.

Financing Issues/Payments

Brazil's financial and banking sectors are regulated.

The National Financial System comprises (i) the National Monetary Council (Conselho Monetário Nacional or CMN), which is the maximum monetary authority responsible for the formulation of the monetary and credit policies, including relating to foreign exchange and the regulation of the operations of financial institutions in general; (ii) Central Bank of Brazil (Banco Central do Brasil or BACEN), which is responsible for ensuring that the regulations established by CMN are complied with and for implementing the obligations stipulated in prevailing legislation, such as the exercise of credit control over foreign capital, conducting rediscount and loan operations for bank financial institutions, and supervising all financial institutions, among others; (iii) Banco do Brasil S.A.; (iv) the Federal Development Bank (Banco Nacional de Desenvolvimento Econômico e Social or BNDES); and (v) other public or private financial institutions; full-service banks; investment, financing, and credit companies; investment banks; brokers; credit cooperatives; leasing companies; insurance companies; and other entities involved in the commercial banking business.

The federal and state governments still control certain financial institutions, especially those focused on fostering economic development, with greater emphasis on the agricultural and industrial sectors, in addition to commercial banking activities.

In Brazil, nonresidents are allowed to open accounts in reais, and bank balances derived from the sale of foreign exchange are freely transferrable abroad. Also, the following are authorized to maintain foreign currency accounts: institutions authorized to operate in the foreign exchange market, foreigners passing through the country, Brazilians residing abroad, and Brazilian international transport companies.

Foreign capital is defined as the goods and equipment brought into the country without foreign exchange cover or financial resources brought by a person or firms resident or domiciled abroad. With the exception of the foreign capital invested in share portfolios, foreign capital is classified either as a direct investment or loan, whether in the form of assets or cash, and includes reinvested profits.

All capital inflows require proof of registration with the Central Bank, which is a condition for the remittance of interest or principal, profits, dividends, or the repatriation of capital. Inflows in the way of assets without exchange cover require prior authorization from the Central Bank.

Secured Transactions

The following securities are subject to the Securities Act regime: (i) shares, debentures, and subscription warrants; (ii) coupons, rights, subscription receipts, and split certificates relating to the securities mentioned in this item; (iii) certificates of deposit of securities; (iv) debenture certificates; (v) shares of mutual funds investing in securities and shares of investment clubs in any types of assets; (vi) commercial papers; (vii) futures, options, and other derivatives agreements, whose underlying assets are securities; (viii) other derivatives agreements, regardless of the underlying assets; and (ix) when publicly offered, any other securities or collective investment instrument or agreement that creates the right to any participation on profits or remuneration, including as a result of the rendering of services, the profits that derive from the efforts of the entrepreneur or third parties.

Federal, state, or municipal government bonds, and negotiable instruments guaranteed by financial institutions (except debentures) are expressly excluded from the definition of securities and, consequently, are subject to the supervision of the Central Bank of Brazil.

Securities are distributed through offerings to the market. The public offering for the distribution of securities in Brazil is subject to the restrictions imposed by the Securities Act. The sale, promise of sale, and offer to sell or underwrite securities, as well as the acceptance of an order to sell or underwrite securities, when performed by the issuing corporation, its founders, or persons considered equivalent thereto are considered acts of public distribution and, thus, subject to prior registration with the Brazilian Securities Commission (CVM).

The obligation of the registration of the public distribution of securities is aimed at guaranteeing the adequate and accurate disclosure of information concerning the issuer and the securities that it wishes to sell. The registration, however, does not evaluate the risk of the issue.

On the other hand, the issue and distribution of debt securities abroad by Brazilian companies are not subject to registration at CVM.

Brazilian companies that desire to issue shares in the foreign capital market, with the purpose of obtaining resources, shall establish a program of Depositary Receipts (DRs), which are negotiable certificates evidencing shares or other securities related to shares issued by a publicly held Brazilian company. The implementation of this program requires the appointment of a depositary—that is, the foreign institution that will be issuing the DRs abroad, on the basis of the shares deposited in specific custody in its name in Brazil—and of a custodian institution in Brazil, which shall hold in custody the shares that back the DRs.

Foreign companies may also trade their securities in the Brazilian stock market, by means of the issue of certificates of deposit of securities or Brazilian Depositary Receipts (BDRs). BDRs are certificates representing shares issued by a publicly held or similar company, based abroad and issued by a depositary institution in Brazil.

Securities Laws Issues

The Brazilian Securities Commission (CVM) is the autonomous government agency responsible for the regulation of the Securities Act and other securities market regulations. The objective of CVM is to regulate and oversee the securities market, also managing (i) its general operation; (ii) public distribution rules; (iii) registration of securities in stock exchanges; (iv) disclosure requirements; (v) broker and dealer activities; (vi) types of securities traded; and (vii) types of companies that can be traded on the capital market.

CVM has signed memoranda of understanding with various countries, in connection with the sharing of information and legal assistance to securities regulators, including the United States (the Securities Exchange Commission and Commodities Future Trading Corporation), Argentina, Australia, Bolivia, Canada/Quebec, Chile, China, Ecuador, France, Germany, Greece, Hong Kong, Italy, Luxembourg, Malaysia, Mexico, Paraguay, Peru, Portugal, Romania, Singapore, South Africa, Spain, Taiwan, and Thailand.

Still, in this scenario, entities with self-regulation powers, typically stock exchanges and over-the-counter markets, operate as accessory institutions to the CVM, being subject to its supervision. These entities are responsible for supervising their members and ensuring compliance with the applicable rules and regulations.

The principal Brazilian stock exchange is Bolsa de Valores de São Paulo (Bovespa). At Bovespa, shares, commercial papers, debentures, fund quotas, and derivatives are regularly traded. The functions of stock exchanges include the organization, maintenance, registration, and supervision of securities operations. To this end, the stock exchanges may establish rules in addition to those issued by CVM.

Bovespa recently implemented a home-broker system, by means of which investors can deliver orders via the Internet to their brokers, who are connected to Bovespa's electronic systems. The custody and financial settlement of securities operations are conducted by a clearinghouse controlled by the stock exchanges. Currently Brazil has one clearinghouse, Companhia Brasileira de Liquidação e Custódia (CBLC), a private company with its headquarters in São Paulo, which carries out the custody and financial settlement of Bovespa and SOMA (entity of the organized over-the-counter market) operations.

The over-the-counter market includes business corporations or commercial companies, specifically incorporated with the purpose of trading securities, in accordance with the CVM rules and subject to its prior approval.

The nonorganized over-the-counter market is defined by article 3 of CVM Instruction 202 as the market that covers all trading conducted outside of the stock exchanges, with the mediation of members of the securities market. Shares that are traded on the stock exchanges cannot be traded on the over-the-counter market, except in cases of public distribution. Operations in the organized over-the-counter market are usually conducted by phone by brokers/dealers in their offices and are not coordinated by the CVM, although they are subject to its supervision.

Currently, the Asset Market Operator Company (Sociedade Operadora de Mercado de Ativos or SOMA) and Center of Custody and Financial Settlement of Securities (Central de Custódia e Liquidação Financeira de Títulos or CETIP) operate in the organized over-the-counter market.

Government Procurement

The Federal Constitution of 1988 establishes that, with the exception of the cases expressly provided in law, works, services, purchases, and sales shall be preceded by government procurements that guarantee equal opportunities and conditions among all participants and the contractor's right to the economic-financial balance of the contract.

The regulation of government purchases is provided by the General Law of Public Procurements and Administrative Contracts (Law 8,666/93), which establishes the administrative procedure for government procurement processes, and the general terms for administrative contracts. This law is also employed to regulate the selection processes of public utility concession and permit holders (Law 8,987/95), and the public-private partnerships entered into by the Brazilian state with private enterprise (Law 11,079/04). Complementarily, Law 10,520/02 created a specific modality of government procurement, called the reverse auction.

Thus, the Brazilian legal system contemplates six modalities of government procurement procedures: the public tender (concorrência); price survey (tomada de preços); invitation to tender (convite); competitive selection (concurso); auction (leilão)—the latter regulated by Law 8,666/93—and the reverse auction (pregão), regulated by Law 10,520/02. The factors that will determine the application of each government procurement modality are the contracting amount and the nature of the object of the contract.

Similarly, the legal system establishes situations in which Brazil's Public Administration may contract goods and services without a prior government procurement procedure. It can thus contract directly with private enterprise when it conclusively demonstrates that a competition between potentially interested parties is impracticable, or when the factual situations fall within the circumstances of article 24 of Law 8,666/93.

Liabilities of Company Directors and Officers

Members of the Board of Directors (Conselho de Administração) or Board of Executive Officers (Diretoria) of corporations, as well as managers of limited liability companies, are subject to the same duties and liabilities (board members, officers, and managers will be collectively referred to as "administrators").

As a general rule, the Brazilian Civil Code establishes that a company shall be bound by the acts performed by an administrator in strict observance with the limits established in the company's Articles of Association. This means that in such cases the company is liable on its own and may not bring a suit against an administrator in order to recover its losses.

The liability of administrators is regulated very broadly in the Civil Code, which, in contrast to the Corporation Law, does not provide for any specific conduct that could generate liabilities. Generally, a company may file a suit against its administrators whenever it incurs any liability or is adversely affected by an act performed by an administrator that is beyond the limits of such administrator's authority or that is contrary to the company's Articles of Association.

The Civil Code further determines that acts performed by administrators will validly bind the company before third parties, even when such acts exceed their corporate powers, unless (i) the limitation of said administrators' powers is duly indicated in the company's Articles of Association, (ii) the third party is aware of such limitation, or (iii) when the nature of the act performed is evidently unrelated to the company's corporate purpose.

Administrators are also jointly responsible before the company and third parties whenever they discharge their duties with negligence, fault, or willful misconduct.

The Corporation Law holds directors and officers equivalent for the purposes of establishing their liability. Officers and directors of Brazilian companies are not, in principle, personally liable for any obligations incurred on behalf of companies by virtue of regular management acts performed in the ordinary course of business.

Administrators may, however, be personally liable for the damages caused by their acts, whether performed: (i) within the limits of their authority, but in a fraudulent or negligent manner, or (ii) in violation of the law or of the company's bylaws.

Litigation/Dispute Resolution Systems

Court litigation and arbitration are the most commonly used dispute resolution mechanisms in Brazil. Mediation and other alternative dispute resolution methods are still not widely used.

Judicial proceedings in Brazil are complex and, due to the caseload, it usually takes a long time to obtain final judgments.

An important point to be highlighted is that Brazilian law does not acknowledge the parties' autonomy to choose the governing law of the contract. Although the parties' autonomy to choose the governing law in contractual relationships is defended by part of Brazil's legal scholars, this position is not supported by case law. Brazilian law clearly determines that obligations will be governed by the law of the country in which they are established. The criterion adopted by the Brazilian legal system to determine the governing law is the "place where the contract is formed." There is a default rule for distant contracts (that is, in cases where the parties to contract are not in direct and simultaneous contact), in which case the law of the offeree's domicile shall be adopted. Aware of this limitation on the parties' autonomy to choose the governing law, it is common for the parties to manipulate the place of the execution as a way of defining the governing law.

The use of choice of forum clauses is common in international transaction contracts, and parties expect their choice to be respected. In domestic contracts, choice of forum clauses—whenever a local court is chosen—are widely accepted. However, there is no settled case law with respect to the validity of choice of forum clauses in international contracts. Contradictory decisions have been issued especially when the choice of forum seeks to waive the jurisdiction of Brazilian courts in matters of concurrent jurisdiction of Brazilian judges.

For a foreign judgment to be effective in Brazil, it must be recognized by the Superior Court of Justice ("STJ"). The STJ president (or vice president) decides on whether to recognize and grant exequatur to foreign judgments, unless the other party to the proceedings or the respective public prosecutor objects to it. Objections can be raised based on lack of compliance with formal issues (for example, due process, sworn translations) or based on violation of national sovereignty, public policy (ordre public), or good morals. If there is an objection, the court assigns the proceedings to a reporting judge from the Special Court (a special panel within the STJ) to issue a decision. These proceedings usually last from 12 to 18 months.

Arbitration

The Brazilian Arbitration Act was enacted in 1996 and brought a drastic change in Brazil's position in relation to the validity and enforceability of arbitration clauses and the need to sign arbitration agreements (compromissos). Furthermore, the New York Convention on the Recognition and Enforcement of Foreign Arbitral Awards was ratified in 2002 by Decree 4311/2002.

A preference for the inclusion of arbitration clauses in international contracts can be verified. The main advantages of using arbitration to resolve disputes arising from such transactions are neutrality; celerity in comparison with the Brazilian judiciary; the possibility of conferring confidentiality to the procedure; and having the dispute resolved by specialized arbitrators with knowledge of these types of international transaction structures. Moreover, the Brazilian Arbitration Act (Law 9307/1996) expressly provides that the parties are free to choose the governing law, with the possibility of opting for judgment by equity, provided that there is no breach of public policy and good morals. Upon opting for arbitration, the parties gain considerable freedom to choose the governing law, venue, and language of the proceedings, and also to decide on whether the arbitration will be managed by an institution or held in an ad hoc manner.

Most arbitration proceedings involving Brazilian parties are managed by institutions. In addition to the main international arbitration institutions, such as the ICC, LCIA, and ICDR, some Brazilian institutions have a considerable number of proceedings in progress and maintain organized and reliable management structures. Examples include the Arbitration Center of the Brazil-Canada Chamber of Commerce (Centro de Arbitragem da Câmara de Comércio Brasil-Canadá) and the Chamber of Mediation and Arbitration of São Paulo (Câmara de Mediação e Arbitragem de São Paulo), among others.

The option for the arbitration seat in Brazil avoids the need of the recognition of the award rendered by a foreign arbitral tribunal before the Superior Federal Court (STJ). Arbitral awards rendered in Brazil have the same effects as a court judgment.

Mediation

As stated above, mediation is not widely used in Brazil to resolve disputes arising out of international transactions. In Brazil it is used more for family-related issues. In the legislative sphere, a bill proposing a law regarding mediation is currently pending in Congress (Bill 4827/1998). According to this bill, disputes involving freely negotiable rights could be settled by mediation. The bill also determines who can act as mediator and imposes the duties of impartiality, independence, competence, diligence, and secrecy. In addition, it provides that a settlement reached by mediation would be recognizable by the judiciary. However, there is no indication whatsoever as to if and when this mediation law will effectively be enacted.

CONTRACTS AND DOCUMENTS—FORMS AND ENFORCEABILITY

Brazilian law establishes that, for contracts or other legal transactions to be valid, (i) the parties must be legally capable, thus understood as individuals over the age of 18 and companies with their articles of incorporation/association regularly registered at a competent commercial registry office; (ii) the object must be legal, possible, determined, or determinable; and (iii) the form used must be the one prescribed or not prohibited by law. Concerning the last point, the general rule existing in Brazilian law is that of the freedom of form for contracts or other legal transactions. The requirement of a special form is the exception and depends on express provision in law. In accordance with Brazilian law, when a contract is about real rights, as is the case of the purchase and sale of real property or of a mortgage, the public deed is a formal requirement for its validity, its absence implying the nullification of the legal transactions.

If the three above requirements are not satisfied, the contract is considered void. Contracts and other legal transactions are also subject to annulment in cases of substantial error (mistake, inexact notion, or false idea of the reality); fraud or dolus (mistake induced by the malicious behavior of the other party); coercion (threat that compels a party to perform an act against its will); injury (disproportion of the established contractual obligations because of an urgent need or inexperience of the party); and fraud against creditors (malicious business practice to defalcate the patrimony of the insolvent debtor).

Private contracts or documents produced and signed by parties, or just signed by them—provided that they have free disposition and administration of their property—bind the parties to the contract and prove the obligations assumed, regardless of their value. In order for private contracts or documents to produce effects before third parties, they must be registered at the Commercial Registry.

As the official language in Brazil is Portuguese, public documents must be written in Portuguese. Private documents originating from foreign countries and written in foreign languages are binding on the parties to contract. However, for documents written in a foreign language to have legal force in Brazil, they must be translated into Portuguese, by a certified translator, in order to guarantee the credibility of the content of the document.

To produce effects in the federal, state, Federal District, and municipal departments or those of the territories, or in any degree of jurisdiction, court, or tribunal, foreign documents must be accompanied by their respective certified translations and must be registered at the Registry of Deeds and Documents.

In the case of powers of attorney, notarization (certification of the signature of the contracting party by a Public Notary) and consular legalization (verification by a Brazilian Consulate or Embassy that the notary's signature is genuine) are necessary. Only documents originating from France are exempt from consular legalization by virtue of a bilateral agreement signed with Brazil.

ENDING/RESTRUCTURING A BUSINESS PRESENCE

Dissolution/Liquidation

The termination of a company is preceded by a series of acts and procedures whereby the company is first dissolved by a decision of the partners or shareholders or by judicial decision. In limited liability companies or LTDAs, the decision to dissolve the company must be approved by partners representing at least 75 percent of the capital, and in corporations or SAs, by at least 50 percent of the voting capital. However, both the articles of association of an LTDA and the corporate bylaws of an SA may stipulate higher quorums for this type of decision.

The dissolution of the company marks the end of its business activities but does not bring about its immediate termination.

In this phase the company's assets are liquidated; that is, the company's assets are converted into cash for the payment of its liabilities. The realization of assets, in principle, includes the sale of the company's property, collection from its debtors, and the satisfaction of the liabilities and payment of creditors. When these objectives are accomplished, the remaining net worth is shared among the partners, as a rule according to the equity interest of each in the company capital. In the case of foreign quota holders, any surplus will be remitted through a specific procedure at the Central Bank of Brazil known as capital repatriation.

The company's management during the liquidation is performed by the liquidator, who is elected in the general or partners meeting that decides on the dissolution.

Once these three procedures (dissolution, liquidation, and apportionment of a possible surplus) have been concluded and the Foreign Investment Registration in SISBACEN (Brazilian Central Bank Information System)—if any—has been cancelled, the company may be considered extinct.

From a tax standpoint, the closedown of the activities of the Brazilian subsidiary will be possible only if it has no outstanding tax liabilities or accessory tax obligations.

The company must arrange for the cancellation of its federal, state, and municipal registrations. This process involves a great deal of red tape and implies a rigorous investigation of the company's tax regularity, the submission of income tax returns for the period in which the company remained open, and the payment of any taxes due.

Insolvency/Bankruptcy/Restructuring

Brazilian Congress enacted a new bankruptcy law, dated February 9, 2005, which took effect on June 9, 2005 (Lei de Recuperação Judicial e de Falência—11, 101, or LRF). The LRF distinguishes between (i) judicial reorganization; (ii) out-of-court reorganization (prepackaged); and (iii) bankruptcy. Both judicial and out-of-court reorganization are based on the submission of a reorganization plan. This document details the method of payment of the debts and various other pieces of information, as set forth by the law and negotiated with the creditors.

Judicial Reorganization

The filing must encompass all the existing claims and debts on the petition filing date, even if not overdue, including labor debts. After the reorganization plan has been approved, the court will determine its enforcement, and the novation of the claims pre-dating the petition will take effect. "Novation" in this case means that due to the approved reorganization plan the pre-reorganization claims are replaced by the ones provided for in the reorganization plan.

Out-of-Court Reorganization

Out-of-court reorganization basically consists of a proposed out-of-court reorganization plan negotiated directly between the specific classes of creditors and the debtor. The out-of-court reorganization plan cannot include tax or labor debts, and its scope is limited to the creditors indicated in the reorganization plan. Once the out-of-court reorganization plan is negotiated and its terms accepted by the creditors representing at least three-fifths of the total amount of the relevant class of creditors, a petition for ratification is presented to the court and once approved, all the creditors of that class are bound by court approval.

Liquidation

The declaration of liquidation determines chiefly the accelerated maturity of the debts of the debtor and of the unlimited and jointly and severally liable partners. In this case, the Judicial Trustee and Creditors' Committee shall thenceforth administer the assets of the debtor with the aim of determining the assets and the realization thereof for the purposes of the fulfillment of the debtor's obligations.

CONCLUSION

Brazil has a tradition of political, legal, and social stability. The country has no border, ethnic, or religious disputes, and no separatist movements or history of terrorism, extremism, or political assassinations. The country is a safe place to invest and is considered one of the best export platforms in the world. The country is also ready to act as an investor in other countries.

NOTES

1. Decree 6,759/1195, article 353, SRF Normative Instruction 285 of 2003 and 1013 of 2010.
2. Relevant legislation: SECEX Administrative Rule (*Portaria*) 10 of 2010.
3. Examples of controlled goods are used goods in general, certain foods, pharmaceuticals, chemical products, and wood articles and parts.
4. Article 22 of DECEX Administrative Rule 8 of 1991, with the changes introduced by MDIC Administrative Rule 235 of 2006.
5. A few examples are weapons, wild animals, drugs, pirated and counterfeited goods, any goods that threaten public order, and toys that simulate firearms.
6. Section 54, §3.
7. Item XXXV, of Section 5, of the Brazilian Federal Constitution of 1988.
8. Restrictions are set forth in Law 5,709, enacted on October 7, 1971.
9. Decree 6,759/1995.

CHAPTER 4

Chile

Marcos Ríos
Consuelo Raby
Paola Belan
Diego Peró
Carey y Cía Ltda.

COUNTRY OVERVIEW

Chile was founded as a Spanish colony during the sixteenth century. After more than 200 years of Spanish domination, independence was declared in 1818. Today, it is one of South America's most successful nations, with a gross domestic product (GDP) per capita of USD 14,700,[1] first in the region. Located in the southern part of the continent, Chile borders the South Pacific Ocean and neighboring Argentina, Bolivia, and Peru. It has a surface of 756,102 square kilometers,[2] and a total population of 16.7 million.[3]

The U.N. Human Development Index of 2009[4] ranked Chile at No. 44, top of the region. Life expectancy at birth is 78.5 years and the adult literacy rate is 96.5 percent.[5] The population ethnically is mostly white and white-Amerindian (95.4 percent), with Mapuche and other indigenous groups completing the remaining 4.6 percent.[6] Spanish is the official and main language spoken in the country.

A market-oriented economy, a high level of foreign trade, and strong legal and financial institutions have driven Chile's GDP annual growth rate to an average of 5 percent during the past 25 years. The International Monetary Fund projects that Chile's GDP will exceed the USD 200 billion milestone by 2011, reaching a size similar to Ireland, Israel, and Malaysia.[7] Chile's low level of public debt and its sound macroeconomic policies have given it the strongest sovereign bond rating in South America. According to the Risk Ranking published by the Economist Intelligence Unit in 2009,[8] Chile is one of the world's lowest-risk countries.

The country has 57 bilateral or regional trade agreements (more than any other country),[9] including treaties with approximately 80 percent of the world's GDP. Exports account for more than 25 percent of its GDP, with commodities making up around 75 percent of total exports.[10] Inflation in 2009 was at –1.4 percent and unemployment as of July 2010 was at 8.5 percent.[11] Chile is the top-ranked country in the region in the World Bank *Doing Business Report,*[12] the World Economic Forum *Global Competitiveness Report,*[13] and Transparency International's *Anti-Corruption Report.*[14]

Chile is a democratic republic with a presidential system. The president is the head of state and government and is elected for a fixed term of four years, with no immediate reelection. Congress is bicameral; representatives are elected for four-year terms and senators for eight-year terms, and both can be reelected indefinitely. Judicial power is vested in an independent Supreme Court and its subordinated courts.

The legal system is largely based on the civil law model of continental Europe and Latin America, with special emphasis on codified, statutory law. During the past decade, Chile has completely reformed its criminal justice system by implementing a new oral adversarial system.

ESTABLISHING A BUSINESS PRESENCE

Permanent Structures

Suitable Corporate Forms

The types of legal entities commonly used as business vehicles in Chile are limited liability companies (sociedades de responsabilidad limitada or SRLs); corporations (sociedades anónimas or SAs); stock companies (sociedades por acciones or SpAs); and branches (agencias or branches). Their main corporate differences refer to:

(a) *Organization.* SRLs and SpAs may be set up in a somewhat shorter time and require less bookkeeping than SAs. Typically, a legal entity may be set up in three to five weeks. Even though the creation of branches requires fewer formalities than SAs, their setup may take two to three months due to time delays in obtaining official translations of corporate documents when the foreign parent entity is incorporated in a non–Spanish-speaking country.

(b) *Amendments to Bylaws.* In an SRL, any material amendment to the bylaws (for example, capital increases, management, and withdrawal or entry of new members) must be unanimously agreed upon by its members. An amendment to the bylaws of an SA, however, generally requires the approval of a majority (and in some cases, such as mergers or transformations, a two-thirds majority) of its registered shareholders, adopted in a shareholder meeting, the minutes of which are then transcribed into a notarized document of public record. In the case of SpAs, an amendment to the bylaws may be adopted in the same manner as an SA or, alternatively, through unanimous shareholder consent in lieu of a meeting, provided that such consent is evidenced in a private notarized document. To amend any of the declarations and documentation included in the notarized public document required to form a branch, the Chilean agent will be required to comply with the same formalities required for the creation of the branch.

(c) *Management.* An SRL and an SpA are managed as agreed upon by their founding members or shareholders in their bylaws. Management of an SA, in contrast, is vested by statute in its board of directors, duly elected by a general shareholder meeting, and is otherwise more highly regulated. A branch is managed by an agent resident in Chile. Such agent must be empowered with broad authorities to act on behalf of the parent entity in Chile.

(d) *Transfers.* The sale of equity interests or quotas in an SRL requires the unanimous consent of all existing members and must be recorded as an amendment to its bylaws. In the case of SAs and SpAs, except as restricted by contract (shareholders' agreement or otherwise), shareholders are generally free to sell and assign their shares. A branch, however, cannot be sold separately from its parent entity, since the legal recognition of the branch is granted only because of the existence of its parent entity.

(e) *Profit Distributions.* Profits in an SRL and an SpA may be distributed among the entity's members or shareholders as determined in the respective bylaws, or as otherwise agreed upon by such members or shareholders. In SAs, however, dividends must always be distributed in accordance with the shareholding interest of the relevant shareholders. In addition, the shareholders of an SpA may agree that the entity shall pay only profits arising from one or more specifically identified business units or divisions. In the case of branches, the agent or the parent entity (as the case may be) will determine the distribution of profits to the parent entity.

(f) *Other requirements.* SAs and SpAs must fulfill certain statutory requirements not applicable to SRLs (for example, board approval, arm's-length criteria, or shareholder approval) for certain transactions, such as business dealings with their subsidiaries or granting of sureties or security interests in favor of third parties.

Wholly Owned Entities

SpAs may be incorporated by one or more individuals or legal entities (who do not need to be nationals or residents in Chile), thus allowing the incorporation of wholly owned subsidiaries that are exclusively controlled by a parent company and vested with full statutory legal capacity and limited liability (as opposed to branches, which are deemed to be the same legal entity as their foreign parent companies). SAs and SRLs, however, must be incorporated by and must continue to have at least two shareholders or members.

Joint Ventures

Chilean law affords substantial flexibility in the structuring and implementation of joint ventures. No major practical differences exist between Chile and many leading industrialized countries in the negotiation and implementation of cross-border joint venture deals. Commonly used transaction contracts include MoUs, letters of intent, joint venture agreements, shareholders' agreements, and stock purchase agreements.

While purely contractual joint ventures are legally possible, it is most common for joint venture partners to form a new legal entity or become members or shareholders in an existing one, and simultaneously enter into one or more contracts to further structure their relationship (for example, joint venture or shareholders' agreement). The types of legal entities commonly used in joint ventures are SAs, SRLs, and SpAs, all of which offer limited liability protection to their owners.

Investments in Mergers with Existing Entities

Major business transactions, investments, and mergers usually involve SAs (corporations). Corporate combinations can take the form of a merger or a purchase of assets or shares. Mergers, whether through the absorption of one company by another or through the creation of a new entity, need to be proposed by the board of directors and approved in a special shareholders meeting, by two-thirds of the issued voting stock. Certain sales of substantial assets (50 percent or more) of SAs or their subsidiaries, as well as certain changes of control, also require the approval of two-thirds of the issued voting stock. Approval of any of the foregoing matters confers dissenting shareholders the right to withdraw from the company by selling their shares to the company.

A purchase of shares in an SA can be structured either as a private transaction or as a tender offer. Unless a limited legal exemption is available, the way to gain control over an "open" or "publicly held" SA—that is, a corporation with shares registered in the National Securities Registry kept by the Securities and Insurance Superintendence (Superintendencia de Valores y Seguros or SVS)—is through a mandatory pro-rata tender offer, regulated by the Chilean Securities Law (Ley de Mercado de Valores or LMV).[15]

Agency, Reseller, Franchising, and Distribution Agreements

Agency, reseller, franchising, and distribution agreements are not specially regulated under Chilean law. As a consequence, freedom of contract will apply to the extent the relevant contractual provisions do not violate Chilean public policy laws, regulations, or rules (for example, antitrust laws, consumer laws, intellectual property laws, and certain contract law rules). In addition, because these types of agreements share various features with sales agreements, mandates, and commission agreements, certain Chilean civil and commercial law rules applicable to such contracts could apply where parties have been silent with regard to certain matters (for example, time of delivery of goods purchased under a distribution agreement).

Representative Offices and Other Nonpermanent Establishments

Chilean law does not contemplate the possibility of establishing a business presence through a permanent structure that does not entail the creation of a permanent establishment (PE) in the country. Except as provided in certain tax treaties entered into by Chile, Chilean tax law does not provide a specific definition for a PE. The Chilean tax authority (Servicio de Impuestos Internos or SII), however, has broadly stated that a PE is the extension of a foreign entity's activity, through an office that assumes complete representation of such foreign entity, having the authority to conclude contracts. As a general rule, a PE will be subject to the same taxation as an entity incorporated in Chile (for example, corporate tax and withholding tax).[16]

Approvals and Registrations

The creation of SAs, SRLs, SpAs, and branches requires certain formalities. Such formalities generally consist of the execution of a notarized document of public record or a notarized private document containing the articles of incorporation and bylaws of the company. An excerpt of such deed or document must then be registered in the relevant Commerce Registry and published in the Official Gazette. All entities carrying out activities in Chile must also apply for a taxpayer number (RUT) and report to the SII the commencement of their business activities. Shares of "open" or "publicly held" SAs must be registered with the Securities Registry kept by the SVS.

Further formalities, approvals, or registrations (for example, prior approval from a regulator) may be required if the company is a special SA (such as a commercial bank, insurance company, or fund manager), or for certain projects or activities (such as environmental approvals and construction and zoning permits).

Sensitive Economic Sectors/Restrictions on Foreign Ownership

Chilean constitutional and legal principles and rules afford foreign investors essentially the same rights as local investors. As a general rule, foreign nationals or entities may acquire any type of assets in Chile, with limited exceptions such as the purchase of real estate on or next to Chile's national borders. In addition, non-Chilean ownership in, or operation of, certain business sectors—such as air transportation, mass media, cabotage, fishing, banking, health care, pension fund, and insurance—is regulated and/or restricted and/or requires special approvals. Many of these regulations, however, involve only a requirement that the entity holding the relevant license or permit is a Chilean entity (even if owned by a foreign investor) and/or that it previously obtains a special license or governmental approval.

Political Risk and Related Issues

Chile has had a strong multiparty democracy for most of its existence as an independent nation. In addition, since 1990 Chile has enjoyed internationally recognized political and economic stability, with an overwhelming consensus across the political spectrum on most key political, economic, social, and legal matters. Such consensuses include the country's basic political and economic institutions (constitutional and civil rights, separation of powers, free and democratic elections, property rights, freedom of contract, and so on), other key issues such as the Central Bank's independence, and major legal reforms such as the new criminal justice system, three major capital markets reforms, and the creation of special tax courts. New elections to choose the successor of President Mr. Sebastián Piñera, member of the center-right coalition, will take place in December 2013.

INVESTMENTS ISSUES AND TAX INCENTIVES

Legal Treatment of Foreign Investment

Direct foreign investment and repatriation of capital and profits are essentially regulated by the Foreign Exchange Regulations of the Central Bank of Chile (Chapter XIV) and the Chilean Foreign Investment Statute, Decree Law No. 600 (DL 600). Chapter XIV and DL 600 are both efficient and straightforward mechanisms to enter foreign currency (and, in the case of DL 600, also certain in-kind investments) into Chile.

Under Chapter XIV, which is available for investments of USD 10,000 or more, investors may transfer the relevant funds into Chile without any prior governmental notice or authorization, provided that the Central Bank is given notice after the funds have entered the country. Under DL 600, available for investments of USD

5 million or more, investors file an application with the Foreign Investment Committee (FIC), which is usually preliminarily approved within 24 hours. Subsequent to the FIC's approval the investor must enter into a *foreign investment agreement* with the state of Chile, the contractual nature of which could arguably afford some greater degree of stability to the investment.

Other relevant differences between these regulations include a greater flexibility for repatriation of capital in the case of Chapter XIV (no waiting period as opposed to a one-year waiting period for DL 600 investments),[17] a certain tax rate stabilization option available for DL 600 investments (not available for Chapter XIV investments), and a special administrative remedy against undue discriminatory treatment (that is, contrary to the national treatment standard afforded to foreign investors) available under DL 600 and not under Chapter XIV.

Regarding the special tax regime option, foreign investors entering into a DL 600 foreign investment contract may choose to be taxed on their investment's income at an aggregate and fixed 42 percent income tax rate during a period of 10 years (instead of the lower rate that would usually apply under the regular tax regime). The tax stabilization starts upon commencement of the business activities and may be extended if certain conditions are met.

In general, there are no currency controls restricting the repatriation of capital, the repayment of debt, or the making of profit distributions or other payments to a non-Chilean shareholder, member, or partner of a local joint venture. The most salient exceptions are the aforementioned one-year waiting period for repatriation of capital, and the requirement that payment of applicable taxes be made and certified prior to any distribution of profits to a person or entity outside of Chile, both under DL 600.

Treaties on Foreign Investment Protection

In 1991, Chile became a signatory of the 1965 Washington Convention that created the International Center for Settlement of Investment Disputes (ICSID). Chile has since entered into multiple bilateral investment protection treaties committing itself to provide fair and equitable treatment to investments legally made in its territory by investors of the other contracting states, guaranteeing the free transfer of capital, profits, or interest generated by foreign investments. These treaties also provide dispute resolution mechanisms involving prior amicable discussions and, if no agreement is reached therein, domestic litigation within the host state or international investor arbitration against the relevant host state.[18]

Publicly Held Companies—Capital Market Regulations

If capital gains arise from the sale of shares of an "open" or "publicly held" SA, the seller may benefit from corporate tax[19] as a sole tax levying the transaction, provided certain requirements are met. In addition, in certain cases a tax-free treatment may benefit the seller of shares in "open" or "publicly held" SAs that are regularly traded.

Tax-free acquisitions through corporate reorganizations are also generally available for share acquisitions.[20]

Alternate Investment Structures—Investment Funds

An alternate investment structure that may afford tax benefits to foreign investors is the acquisition of quotas issued by a Chilean private investment fund (FIP). FIPs are an exception to ordinary taxation, since the profits earned or accrued by the FIP are not subject to corporate tax[21] until they are distributed. In the case of profit distributions from FIPs, the general rule is that its foreign contributors will have to pay withholding tax[22] at the time they receive the profits from the FIP. However, foreign investors would benefit from a tax-free treatment for FIP profit distributions if the FIP is backed at least 90 percent by foreign instruments, securities, or assets.

Another alternate investment structure is the investment in foreign capital investment funds and in foreign risk capital investment funds. The tax benefit to invest in these funds is that profit distributions made to foreign investors will be subject to a 10 percent tax rate, as a sole income tax, provided some specific conditions are met.

OPERATIONAL LEGAL ENVIRONMENT

Tips on Negotiations in Chile

The style of negotiations in Chile closely resembles that of the United States. Protocol is not of great importance, but a diplomatic behavior is always welcome. Though Chile's native language is Spanish, English is commonly used at business levels, and most Chilean executives conducting international negotiations can usually communicate adequately in English. With limited exceptions (for example, it is statutorily required that the execution of a notarized document of public record must be in Spanish), contracts may be executed in foreign languages.

Though quite lower than in other countries (including some developed nations), bureaucracy must be expected as a somewhat delaying factor, especially when dealing with registrars, regulating agencies, and other governmental entities. In addition, depending on the quality and sophistication of its Chilean advisors and counterparties, an investor could eventually have to deal with a certain "form-over-substance" approach to legal matters, a common trait in most Latin countries.

Foreign Exchange

Individuals and entities are free to engage in foreign currency transactions. The Central Bank's Compendium of Foreign Exchange Regulations provides, however, that all such transactions must be carried out in the Formal Exchange Market (FEM) and be informed to the Central Bank. The FEM is comprised of commercial banks operating in Chile and other entities expressly authorized by the Central Bank, such as exchange houses. The Central Bank daily reports the average USD exchange rate for the previous business day's foreign currency transactions between banks and companies. This is the official rate for payment of taxes and customs duties. Other publicly available USD exchange rates include (i) the *informal dollar:* exchange rate in connection to USD transactions within the FEM, published by the Santiago Stock Exchange; and (ii) the *interbank dollar,* which is the exchange rate established by the Central Bank on a daily basis for a limited number of transactions of its own.

Immigration and Visa Requirements

Two kinds of visas allow a foreign citizen to temporarily work in Chile for periods exceeding 90 days: a work contract visa (WCV) and a temporary residence visa (TRV). A temporary work permit allows a foreign national to perform any compensated activity for an initial period of 30 days, renewable for equal time periods up to a maximum of 90 days. A permanent residence visa allows a foreign national to live and work permanently in Chile.

A WCV may be granted to any foreign national employed by an employer with legal domicile in Chile. A WCV is granted for a maximum of two years, indefinitely renewable for identical time periods. The holder of a WCV may perform only the remunerated activities provided under the employment contract on which the visa is based and may apply for permanent residence after residing in Chile for two years.

A TRV may be granted to a foreign national who intends to live in Chile and evidences family ties or other interests in Chile, provided his or her residence is considered useful or advantageous to the country (for example, investors, businesspeople, scientists, and consultants). The holder of a TRV may develop any remunerated activity in Chile. The TRV is granted for a maximum of one year, and may be renewed only for one additional year. When the holder of a TRV completes one year of residence in Chile, he or she *may* request permanent residence; after two years, he or she *must* request permanent residence.

Import and Export Issues

Import and Export Regulations

Generally, goods and services can be freely imported into or exported from Chile without the need for special licenses. Importers and exporters must generally comply, however, with certain customs-related procedures (for example, submission of documents and information with the customs authorities) prior to carrying out an export or import operation. The import of certain controlled or regulated goods (such as firearms, ammunitions, explosives, chemical or flammable substances, vegetable products, and fertilizers and pesticides) will be subject to prior approval, certification, or control by other authorities (such as the Agricultural and Livestock Authority or the Health Authority), and the import of certain goods (asbestos of any kind, industrial toxic waste, and so on) will be strictly prohibited. Central Bank regulations impose certain obligations on importers and exporters, such as reporting obligations for importers and exporters having total annual import/export transactions equal to or exceeding USD 50 million on an FOB basis.

Goods imported into Chile are subject to a general 6 percent ad-valorem import duty rate on CIF value,[23] plus 19 percent value added tax (VAT). Other goods are subject to specific duties, and certain goods are subject to an additional tax levied over the ad-valorem duties. Exports are exempt from VAT and enjoy other tax benefits.

Trade Agreements

Since the early 1970s Chile has aggressively promoted international free trade, first by unilaterally reducing its import duties and eliminating its own domestic obstacles to international trade (such as unnecessary red tape and subsidy practices), and subsequently by seeking and entering into bilateral and multilateral free trade agreements (FTAs). Chile's FTAs and other commercial agreements include, among other matters, national treatment protection, most-favored-nation provisions, sales of goods and services, government procurement, protection of foreign investment, cross-border services, intellectual property protection, e-commerce, customs procedures, and dispute resolutions. As of this date, Chile has entered into FTAs with Australia, Panama, Japan, China, Canada, Mexico, the United States, South Korea, Central America (Costa Rica, El Salvador, Guatemala, and Nicaragua), the European Free Trade Association (Iceland, Norway, Switzerland, and Liechtenstein), the European Union (European Union Association Agreement), the Trans-Pacific SEP (New Zealand, Singapore, and Brunei), Peru, and Colombia.[24]

Taxation of Business and Cross-Border Transactions

Taxes

The main taxes commonly applicable to international businesses and cross-border transactions (in addition to customs duties[25] and personal income tax) include corporate tax, withholding tax, value added tax (VAT), stamp tax, and municipal license, substantially as follows:

(a) *Corporate Tax* is levied on net profits received or accrued by a legal entity (an SA, SpA, SRL), branch, or PE. As general rule, corporate tax is levied on income determined over regular accounting records, where income is defined as gross income less costs and expenses required for producing such income. However, taxpayers that meet certain requirements may be subject to a system based on presumed income. The current corporate tax rate is 20 percent. This rate was temporarily raised from 17 to 20 percent for the year 2011 and 18.5 percent for the year 2012, in order to partially finance the cost of reconstruction after the February 2010 earthquake. On dividend distributions, corporate tax paid by the distributing entity is creditable against the *personal income tax* payable by individuals who are resident or domiciled in Chile (at progressive rates), or against *withholding tax* payable on Chilean-source income obtained by individuals who are not resident or domiciled in Chile. Similar rules will generally apply to capital gains.

(b) *Withholding Tax* is levied at a 35 percent rate on profits distributed from a Chilean entity to a non-Chilean resident, with a credit for the corporate income tax (currently at a 20-percent tax rate) paid by the entity distributing the profits. Fees paid by Chilean entities to non-Chilean residents for certain types of services or rights are taxed at rates ranging from 15 percent to 30 percent. Interest payments on loans made by certain foreign qualified creditors or supplier credits in imported goods are subject to a 4 percent withholding tax. Thin capitalization rules may nevertheless apply, increasing this tax rate to 35 percent.

(c) *Value Added Tax* (VAT) is levied at a 19 percent rate on habitual sales of movable assets, of real estate totally or partially built by the seller, on imports, and on the provision of certain services. VAT is declared and paid on a monthly basis and its payable amount (if any) results from the difference between VAT *debits* (VAT charged on sales or services made by the taxpayer's business) and the VAT *credits* (VAT borne on goods or services purchased for the taxpayer's business). Excess VAT credits may be carried forward indefinitely. Exporters are exempt from VAT and are entitled to a refund of VAT borne on purchases of goods or services used as part of their export activity. VAT credits from the acquisition of certain fixed assets may be recovered in cash, provided certain requirements are met.

(d) *Stamp Tax* essentially applies to foreign loans (whether documented or not) made to Chilean entities, and to any document containing a "monetary credit transaction" (a transaction whereby one party delivers or undertakes to deliver an amount of money to another party who undertakes to repay such amount in the future). Stamp tax is levied on the principal of the relevant transaction, at the following rates: (i) for term loans, 0.05 percent per month for the duration of the loan, with a cap of 0.6 percent, or (ii) in the case of on-demand loans, 0.25 percent.

(e) A *Municipal License or Municipal Tax* on the relevant business's adjusted tax equity is payable by all persons or entities having business activities within the relevant municipality's jurisdiction. Commercial and industrial businesses are subject to a rate of 0.25 percent to 0.5 percent of their adjusted tax equity, capped at an approximate aggregate of USD 600,000[26] per year.

International Tax Treaties

Conventions for the Avoidance of Double Taxation, generally following the OECD Model, entered into by Chile and currently in force include those with Belgium, Brazil, Canada, Colombia, Croatia, Denmark, Ecuador, France, Ireland, Malaysia, Mexico, New Zealand, Norway, Paraguay, Peru, Poland, Portugal, South Korea, Spain, Sweden, Switzerland, Thailand, and the United Kingdom. A double-taxation treaty with Argentina is also in effect. Other treaties signed but not yet ratified by Chile include those with Australia, Russia and the United States. Chile has also concluded negotiations of a tax treaty with South Africa, and is negotiating other tax treaties with Austria, China, Cuba, the Czech Republic, Finland, Holland, Hungary, India, Italy, Kuwait, Uruguay, and Venezuela.

Labor and Employment

Like most jurisdictions in Latin America, Chile's labor and employment laws and courts are highly protective of employees. Whenever an employment relationship exists under Chilean law (that is, whenever an individual is rendering services with "subordination and dependence" to another person), an implied employment contract is deemed to exist. This employment relationship or implied contract should be put in writing, as otherwise (i) an implied written contract will nevertheless exist under applicable law, and (ii) labor courts will presume the accuracy of the employee's version of the terms of this implied contract, unless the employer brings substantial evidence to the contrary.

There is no employment or termination at will. Employers may terminate employees based only on the grounds set forth in the Chilean Labor Code, and a minimum legal severance shall be payable upon termination of an employee unless termination is based on one of the limited no-severance causes provided in the Labor Code.

All employees are required to make health care, pension fund, and unemployment insurance contributions. While these contributions are borne by the employees, the employer must withhold and make the relevant payments to the employee's pension and health care providers.

When outsourcing services, an entity is jointly and severally liable for the labor and social security obligations of the relevant contractor. Such joint and several liability may become an *alternate* liability if such entity requests from its contractor certain certificates proving the contractor's fulfillment of labor and employment obligations to its own employees.

In addition, several nonwaivable employment rights are mandated by law, such as a minimum wage, workers' compensation and workplace accident insurance benefits, a mandatory profit-sharing payable to employees, maximum daily and weekly working hours and mandatory overtime payments, minimum vacation time and rest periods, and the right to form unions and bargain collectively.

Finally, if a Chilean entity's payroll comprises more than 25 employees, a minimum of 85 percent of those employees must be Chilean nationals. This restriction may be relaxed in some cases, such as where foreign technicians or experts have skills otherwise unavailable in Chile.

Antitrust and Competition Issues

Chilean antitrust law seeks to promote and protect free market competition by prohibiting and penalizing any event, act, or agreement preventing, limiting, or hindering free competition. Some examples of anticompetitive practices under Chilean law include price-fixing agreements, abusive use of dominant position, and predatory or unfair competition practices. The Antitrust Court and the Economic Prosecutor's Office are the entities in charge of enforcing antitrust laws. Rulings by the Antitrust Court may be subject to a remedy before the Supreme Court.

Enforcement of antitrust laws has increased in strength and frequency, particularly during the past five years. With recent legal amendments including increased penalties and new enforcement tools (for example, a leniency plan to facilitate cartel detection and collusion practices), antitrust investigations and enforcement actions have increased substantially, as have the number of successful prosecutions, particularly in connection with cartel practices.

While no mandatory pre-acquisition or pre-merger notice or approval is required, the parties to any transaction may voluntarily request the Antitrust Court's prior approval thereof, by initiating a voluntary consultation procedure, as a means of obtaining a safe harbor protection for the relevant transaction. In 2006, the Economic Prosecutor's Office issued certain *internal* guidelines (that is, not legally binding on market participants) providing certain market concentration thresholds and other criteria based on which such agency would decide whether or not to engage in further analysis or investigation of the relevant transaction. This, together with the stricter enforcement of applicable laws in recent years, makes it highly advisable—particularly in the case of larger or high-profile transactions and/or transactions involving highly concentrated markets—to carefully review the potential effects of transactions on the relevant market in light of the aforementioned guidelines, in order to assess whether initiating a voluntary consultation procedure is appropriate or convenient.

Environmental Issues

Chilean environmental laws and regulations provide various environmental management tools, such as a well-established environmental impact assessment system, rules on emission and quality standards, prevention and decontamination plans for polluted areas, wildlife protection zones, and environmental liability actions (compensation actions and reparation actions) for damages caused by negligent or willful actions. Chile's environmental authorities and institutions, which included one national agency (Conama), various regional environmental agencies, and regional environmental directors, were replaced or complemented (as the case may be) with new environmental institutions and authorities created pursuant to a law enacted in January 2010. New environmental authorities include a Ministry of the Environment, a Ministers' Sustainability Council, an Environmental Assessment Service, and an Environmental Commission.[27]

Consumer Protection and Product Liability

Chilean consumer protection law regulates the basic rights granted to consumers in their purchases of products or services. These rights include, among others, no arbitrary discrimination, the right to receive truthful and timely information concerning prices and contract terms, and the right to bring contractual and negligence claims against suppliers. They also require certain duties and obligations of suppliers, such as honoring the terms, conditions, and specifications of offers, product liability, and certain statutory warranties. Some recent rules enacted to protect "small and medium-size businesses" made certain consumer law protections available to such small and medium-size businesses in their contractual relationships with their suppliers (for example, distribution agreements).

Consumers' rights provided under consumer law may not be waived in advance by the consumers, and are in addition to any remedies for compensation of damages for defective products or bad services. A collective action procedure, which may be initiated only through a claim filed by the government consumer agency, by a consumer association, or by a group of 50 or more affected consumers, further enhances enforcement of consumer protection law in cases of multiple and diffuse interests or claims.

Land Use and Real Estate

Chilean law distinguishes essentially between residential, agricultural, and industrial land use. Land use may be changed through a special permit. Zoning is reviewed at municipal and regional levels, with separate regional and municipal zoning plans. An "Industrial Classification" issued by the National Health Authority determines the "harmless," "bothersome," "dangerous," or "contaminating" nature of a certain industry, activity, or project. This can be a key legal document in land use change requests, as it may be required by environmental or other agencies, or by a municipality, as a precondition to granting certain permits. Changes in rural land from agricultural to nonagricultural (for example, to build an industrial project) require, among other permits and authorizations, a report from the Ministry of Housing and Urbanism's Committee on Agriculture, Urbanism, Tourism and National Assets.

Intellectual Property

Copyright

Copyright protection is granted to authors of creative works in the literary, artistic, and scientific fields. Unlike patrimonial (economic) rights, moral rights over a protected work cannot be waived. As general rule, copyrights last during the entire life of the author plus 70 years. An author is given protection over his or her work by the sole act of creating it. Registration of the work is not required in order to obtain legal protection. Assignments of rights over protected works must be registered, however, in order to be enforceable to third parties. Chile is a signatory of the Bern Copyright Convention, which protects copyrights of works created in countries that are members of the convention.

Industrial Property

The main types of recognized "industrial property" rights are trademarks; patents (inventions, utility models, and industrial designs); trade secrets; guarantees of origin; and business names. Unlike copyrights, industrial property requires registration in order to be protected. Trademark registration includes trademarks for products, services, businesses or industries, logos, and labels and slogans, and it grants exclusive use for 10 years, renewable for successive periods of 10 years. Inventions, utility models, and industrial designs are protected through the registration of a patent. An invention patent is granted for a term of 20 years from the application date. As an exception to the general registration system, trade secrets are given protection by the law without needing to be registered. Chilean law recognizes and protects those indications that identify certain products as coming from a certain country or region. Guarantees of origin are not applied for and registered. Instead, the Industrial Property Institute (IPI) keeps a list of recognized guarantees of origin. Applications for the recognition of guarantees of origin may be filed at the IPI. Once accepted by the IPI, a guarantee of origin has indefinite duration. Except in the case of SAs and SpAs, where the older entity may bring an action against the newly incorporated one in an attempt to stop the use of its name, there are no specific regulations protecting business names that are not registered as trademarks.

Customs

The National Customs Service (SNA) is the authority in charge of controlling the transit of products from and into Chilean territory and collecting all payments deriving from import transactions. Product importation is generally an efficient and straightforward process. Some of the most salient steps and features in the import process include:

> *Customs Destination or Regime:* A customs destination or regime (destinación aduanera) is determined through a statement by the products' owner or consignee regarding the customs regime that shall apply to the

relevant products once they arrive in Chile (for example, importation, temporary admission, and so on). Such statements must be made within 90 days from arrival of the products in Chile, by completing and filing a Statement of Custom Destination (*Declaración de Destinación Aduanera*). Prior to determining a customs regime, the importer may: (i) deposit the relevant products in privately operated warehouses under the SNA's jurisdiction for a maximum of 90 days; or (ii) enter and deposit the products in a Chilean free trade zone (FTZ) or the authorized extensions thereof without any time limitation, with prior posting of a bond securing payment of eventual import duties and taxes that may apply to the products.

Special Customs Regimes: In certain cases, an importer may subject imported products to a special customs regime. The main special customs regimes are (i) temporary admission (*admisión temporal*) and (ii) private warehousing (*almacenes particulares*). As applicable under these special customs regimes, if the relevant products are deemed "foreign" products (that is, not yet imported), otherwise applicable import duties and taxes are generally deferred.

Importation: In order to clear customs and import the products into Chile, the importer of record (which must be an in-country individual or entity) must record the relevant products as *imported* in the relevant Statement of Customs Destination. Custom duties and taxes will apply to the relevant import.[28] All customs proceedings (whether under special customs regimes or customs clearance for importation) of cargo exceeding an FOB value of USD 1,000, must be performed by an authorized customs broker (Agente de Aduana).

Internet Regulation and E-Commerce

Chilean law regulates certain specific aspects of the Internet and e-commerce, such as the registration of domain names, electronic signatures, the protection of consumer rights when involved in e-commerce, and Internet purchases by governmental entities. Domain names followed by the Chilean top-level domain ".cl" may be registered only by individuals or legal entities domiciled or resident in Chile, or authorized to conduct business in Chile. Registrations are filed with a specialized office in charge of domain name registrations. Domain names are effective for two years, and may be renewed for equal and successive periods. The Law on Electronic Signature (ESL) regulates electronic documents, their legal effects, and the use of electronic signatures. The ESL is based on the principles of technologic neutrality, international compatibility, and the equivalence between paper and electronic means. Pursuant to the governmental e-procurement system, most supply and service agreements entered into with government entities must be performed through the Internet. A special government agency controls and operates the government Internet system of acquisitions of the state.

Financing Issues/Payments

Chile's financial industry is an example of soundness and stability, and has a long-standing tradition as an active business venue. Its capitals market currently ranks third in Latin America, following Brazil and Mexico.[29] After a major financial crisis during the early 1980s, legal amendments restructured the banking market, setting the blueprint for the current success, insofar as the industry was not materially affected by the recent "sub-prime" crisis.

Banking rules follow the recommendations of the Basel Committee on Banking Supervision. Different bodies of law, such as the Banking Law, Central Bank Law, Securities Market Law, and the Corporations Law, govern financial entities, services providers, and products, under the supervision of regulatory bodies called "Superintendencias." The Banks and Financial Institutions Superintendence (BFIS) essentially oversees commercial banks and other financial institutions, such as leasing and factoring firms and foreign bank branches; the Securities and Insurance Superintendence (SVS) oversees stock and bond issuers, securities firms, stock exchanges, stockbrokers, hedge funds, and insurance companies; and the Pensions Authority regulates Chilean pension funds. Additionally, although most of the preparation, enactment, and enforcement of prudential and business conduct rules governing financial institutions is discharged by the BFIS, the Central Bank still plays a material role in the banking and financial system, with regard, for example, to the determination of interest rates and as a lender of last resort. While the relevant regulators often issue rules that benefit end-customers of financial services, they do not directly regulate consumer rights.[30]

Commercial banks are the most traditional means of financing in Chile.[31] Commercial banking is formed by some local banks (including one state-owned bank) and several major foreign banks that entered the market mostly by way of acquisition of or merger with existing local banks. Chilean banks also provide services in foreign currency (essentially USD and euros), thus allowing customers to open accounts, make payments, and carry out other transactions in such foreign currencies.[32] As in other jurisdictions, it is standard practice for banks to require collateral and/or guaranties in their lending activities.[33] In addition to local banks, lenders can always resort to foreign bank financing, which will enter the country under the Chapter XIV or DL 600 regimes, and will be subject to applicable taxes.[34]

Access to the local securities market is also a quite common means of financing and is available to domestic and foreign companies. Foreign issuers may also resort to authorized "off-shore markets" to place their securities.[35]

Securitization is also available in Chile.[36] Since 1999, legal amendments allowing the backing of securitization with assets other than mortgages boosted the market to unseen levels, and asset-backed securitization became increasingly common.[37] Mortgage-backed securities, however, still account for more than 50 percent of the securitization bonds in the market.[38]

Project finance has also been of great importance for large infrastructure and industrial projects. During the past three decades, multiple infrastructure projects have been developed and financed through project finance structures (for example, urban and interurban toll highways, power plants, mining facilities, oil and gas refineries, pipelines, chemical plants, subway system, ports and airports). An important element to promote and enable financing of infrastructure projects is the Chilean governmental concessions system governed by the Public Works Concessions Law, which provides an efficient and stable legal background for project sponsors to obtain adequate financing, both locally and internationally.

Secured Transactions

Chilean law provides different means for creditors to secure performance of obligations, whether present or future. The type of security interest and its means of creation, perfection, and enforcement will generally depend on the kind of collateral offered (for example, moveable assets, real estate, industrial assets, inventory, vehicles, and so on). The most common security interests on movable property are the pledge without conveyance, the commercial pledge, and the pledge on shares. Some special pledges may also apply to special assets, such as vehicles or money. Mortgages are available for real property.

While different bodies of law regulate each type of security interest, all securities are subject to certain statutory formalities for their creation and perfection (for example, creation by a contract contained in a notarized document of public record, or perfection through registration and/or publication). A secured creditor may enforce the relevant security agreement and foreclose on the collateral located in Chile only pursuant to a statutory procedure before a Chilean court, and no self-help mechanisms (such as repossession rights) are available.

Securities Laws Issues

Under Chilean law, a "public offering" is an offering addressed to the public in general or to certain categories or groups thereof. Otherwise, the offering is deemed to be a "private offering." Public offerings are subject to the LMV and to SVS regulations.

In addition to regulating the issuance and public offerings of equity and debt securities by Chilean corporations, the LMV regulates the offering of foreign securities in Chile. A public offering of foreign securities and certificates of securities deposit representing homogeneous transferable securities of a foreign issuer (certificados de depósito de valores or CDVs) may be conducted only if and when the relevant foreign securities or CDVs are registered in the Foreign Securities Registry (Registro de Valores Extranjeros or RVE) kept by the SVS, in compliance with the registration requirements issued by the SVS. If foreign securities are not registered in the RVE, however, they still may be sold in Chile, through or by local broker-dealers, subject to specific requirements set forth and enforced by the SVS, in the following cases: registered Chilean broker-dealers may (i) provide Chilean investors with Internet website link services with foreign intermediaries for the purchase and sale of foreign securities outside of Chile; (ii) act as agents (comisionistas) of Chilean customers in order to purchase or sell foreign securities through authorized foreign broker-dealers; or (iii) purchase and sell foreign securities for their own portfolio, subject to some stricter SVS requirements.

Government Procurement

Government procurement transactions are generally subject to an Internet tender process governed by the Public Procurement Act and its regulations (the PPA). The PPA guarantees fair and equal treatment to all offerors, and distinguishes three different tender processes: public bids, private bids, and direct trading.

Public bids (that is, those addressed to any potential offerors who can submit offers pursuant to the statutory rules and the relevant terms and conditions) are mandatory when the subject matter of the tender exceeds an estimated cost of approximately USD 75,000[39] or when it is not possible to estimate such cost. Private bids are those addressed to specific offerors who are usually registered in a special registry, and direct trading involves a direct negotiation with a particular offeror. When not obligated to call for a public bid, governmental entities must preferably call to a private bid, and may engage in direct trading only when and as permitted under the PPA.

The terms and conditions of government procurement tenders must at least include, among others, the basic requirements for acceptance of offers, the subject matter of the contract, terms and stages of the tender process, terms of payment and delivery, offer and performance bonds, and awarding criteria. Rights and obligations under the relevant contract are not assignable, although subcontracting is allowed with certain conditions.

Tenders under the PPA are subject to jurisdictional control by the Government Procurement Court. A party with a legitimate interest may appear before such court seeking relief on grounds that the awarding procedure was illegal or arbitrary, with a subsequent special remedy before the Court of Appeals.

Some special government procurements, such as those of the armed forces and/or involving sensitive products or services, are subject to special laws, regulations, and procedures.

Liabilities of Company's Directors and Officers

Directors and officers of an SA (corporation) or, as applicable, of an SpA (stock company)[40] generally owe fiduciary duties of care, loyalty, candor, and good faith to the company and its shareholders. The general standard of care is ordinary diligence. In discharging their duties, directors and officers may be held civilly liable for their negligent or willful actions or omissions causing damage to the corporation or its shareholders. If such liability is ascertained, they are jointly and severally liable to compensate for the damages they caused to the company and/or its shareholders.

As a general rule, directors and officers' liability is limited to compensating for damages caused to the company or its shareholders, and does not extend to third parties. Liability to third parties may arise, however, in certain specific cases where officers' and directors' culpability is presumed under applicable law, thereby shifting the burden of proof to the relevant director or officer (for example, not keeping accounting records, concealing corporate assets or simulating sales thereof, and causing damage to the corporation with undue interested director transactions).[41]

As to criminal liability, a director or officer may be held criminally liable if he or she has committed criminal conduct pursuant to applicable criminal law (for example, theft or fraud), or where, with regard to certain specific crimes that may be committed by legal entities (for example, financing of terrorism or active money laundering) they have personally participated in the relevant crime.

Litigation/Dispute Resolution Systems

Commercial legal disputes are largely resolved through civil court litigation or private arbitration, with mediation still at a very preliminary stage of development. The main mediation and arbitration institutions in Chile, both for domestic and international disputes, are the Arbitration and Mediation Center of the Santiago Chamber of Commerce, and the National Arbitration Center.

While the Chilean civil court system is well organized and comprised of an overwhelming majority of professional, independent, honest, and unbiased judges, litigation before Chilean civil courts tends to be overly slow and time-consuming. Commercial arbitration, on the other hand, tends to be more efficient, though more costly. As a consequence, parties involved in larger commercial disputes tend to resort to arbitration, while those having smaller business conflicts usually prefer the civil court system.

Civil litigation disputes are generally resolved by a trial court, the rulings and decisions of which may be reviewed on appeal by a Court of Appeals. The Supreme Court can review decisions through limited annulment or disciplinary remedies.

Arbitration has essentially two alternative legal regimes: one for purely domestic arbitration, governed by the Courts Code and the Code of Civil Procedure, and international commercial arbitration, governed by the International Commercial Arbitration Law, which is materially based on the UNCITRAL Model Arbitration Law.

In domestic arbitration, arbitrators may act *de jure* (following both the procedural and substantive rules provided by applicable law), *ex aequo et bono* (not bound by procedural or substantive law), or as *árbitro mixto* (bound by substantive law but with freedom to determine procedural matters). Unless expressly waived, the two main remedies available against a final award rendered in domestic arbitration are appeal and annulment. In addition, a nonwaivable disciplinary remedy is also available.

Under the International Commercial Arbitration Law, the parties to an international arbitration may agree on the procedural rules they deem appropriate, including noninstitutional rules (such as the UNCITRAL rules) or institutional rules (such as those of the International Chamber of Commerce, the American Arbitration Association, the London Court of International Arbitration, or the Santiago Chamber of Commerce). In addition, unlike domestic arbitration, an appeal remedy is not available to the parties under the International Commercial Arbitration Law, and the grounds for annulment of the award are more limited than in domestic arbitration.

Enforcement of foreign court decisions is conditioned by certain legal requirements (for example, existence of applicable international treaties, enforcement reciprocity by the country where the decision was rendered, and nonviolation of Chilean public policy), plus an exequatur proceeding before the Supreme Court. Once the exequatur approval is granted, a foreign court decision is enforceable as a domestic decision.

Foreign arbitral awards are fully enforceable in Chile. Chile has been a party to the New York Convention and the Inter-American Convention on International Commercial Arbitration (the Panama Convention) since the 1970s. In general, foreign arbitral awards are recognized and enforced in Chile, subject to a Supreme Court exequatur approval that is commonly granted if the legal requirements (as provided in the New York Convention or other applicable treaty or law) are met.

Investor-state disputes are generally resolved by either domestic litigation, or ICSID arbitration pursuant to the 1965 Washington Convention and the relevant bilateral investment protection treaties.[42]

CONTRACTS AND DOCUMENTS—
FORMS AND ENFORCEABILITY

As is consistent with Chile's free market economy and open commercial and trade policies, freedom of contract applies to the vast majority of contractual arrangements. Some important exceptions include regulated sectors (for example, telecommunications, energy, and water and sewage), public policy laws and regulations (for example, antitrust law, consumer protection law, and labor and employment law), and public policy rules (unenforceability of self-help mechanisms such as repossession rights).

While the validity of contractual arrangements generally does not require special formalities, as is the case in many Latin American jurisdictions, some types of contracts (such as the sale of real estate and the constitutional documents of a legal entity) require special notarized documents of public record which, among other formalities, must be executed in Spanish, executed before a notary public, and registered in the notary's public ledger.

As a general rule, Chilean law permits the choice of foreign law and jurisdiction on international commercial matters and contracts, and Chilean courts and arbitration tribunals will enforce such choice of foreign law. Some exceptions may apply, however, where Chilean law will govern irrespective of the contract's choice of law. Such is the case, for example, with the transfer of title and the creation and perfection of security interests on assets located in Chile.

ENDING /RESTRUCTURING A BUSINESS PRESENCE

Dissolution/Liquidation

While corporate law requirements for dissolution and liquidation of legal entities are straightforward and do not usually entail major legal risks, the tax implications of this process should be carefully reviewed prior to proceeding with a corporate dissolution. The dissolution of an SA must be agreed upon in a special shareholder meeting by at least two-thirds of the voting stock, and the minutes thereof must be converted into a notarized document of public record. The same rule applies to SpAs, unless otherwise agreed upon in the bylaws. SRLs and branches are generally dissolved through the execution by all members or the agent (as the case may be) of a notarized document of public record providing for such dissolution. Prior to such document's notarization, however, the SII (Chilean tax authority) must issue a certificate approving the dissolution document. For this purpose, the relevant entity must give the SII prior notice of its dissolution and request the cancellation of its taxpayer registration. This notice and request may (and frequently does) trigger a tax review or audit by the SII. Finally, an abstract of the respective notarized document must be registered in the Commerce Registry and published in the Official Gazette.

Following dissolution, the relevant legal entity must be liquidated. In SAs and SpAs, a special committee generally comprised of three members will conduct the liquidation process. In SRLs, the liquidator appointed in the notarized document of dissolution must perform the liquidation.

Insolvency/Bankruptcy/Restructuring

Insolvency/bankruptcy proceedings and restructurings are relatively frequent in Chile. The duration of judicial bankruptcy proceedings will depend on multiple variables, including the amount of assets and liabilities of the bankrupt estate, the type of liquidation procedure chosen, the existence or absence of claims and challenges, and the possibility of reaching a workout agreement.

The purpose of generally applicable insolvency and bankruptcy proceedings under the Chilean Bankruptcy Law[43] is to sell and liquidate, in one sole procedure, the assets of the bankrupt estate, in order to pay off its debts. These proceedings encompass all assets and liabilities of the debtor (even if not past due), except for assets and liabilities expressly excluded by law (such as mortgaged or pledged assets).

The Bankruptcy Law provides differential treatment between debtors engaged in commercial, industrial, mining, or farming activities (or "qualified" debtors) and other debtors (or "common" debtors). For example, qualified debtors are legally obligated to file a bankruptcy petition within 15 days from their default on any commercial commitment, an obligation that does not apply to common debtors.

Trustees are appointed by the relevant court and their role is, essentially, to represent the general interest of the creditors and of the bankrupt debtor to the extent beneficial to the estate, and to manage the assets of the estate.

Prior to a judicial bankruptcy declaration, the debtor and its creditors may agree on an out-of-court workout agreement, thus avoiding judicial bankruptcy. Court-sponsored workout agreements, whether proposed prior to or during the bankruptcy proceedings, are also available.

CONCLUSION

According to the United Nations Conference on Trade and Development (UNCTAD), Chile recently surpassed Brazil as Latin America's leading foreign direct investment receiver.[44] In 2009, Chile became the first South American country to become a member of the Organization for Economic Cooperation and Development (OECD). Multiple international surveys rank Chile at the top among South American countries in aspects such as transparency,[45] rule of law, regulatory quality, government effectiveness, accountability, political stability, and corruption control.[46]

Almost four decades of sound and effective legal protection of foreign investment, an extensive net of bilateral investment protection treaties and free trade agreements,[47] a consolidated democracy, a free and open economy, and sound public policies and regulatory regimes have helped Chile achieve this position as a regional leader. As a consequence of this political, economic, financial, and social stability, Chile is a preferred venue for foreign investors who want to benefit from a wide variety of local investment opportunities[48] and/or develop or grow their businesses in Latin America.

NOTES

1. Cent. Intelligence Agency, *The World Factbook: Chile,* https://www.cia.gov/library/publications/the-world-factbook/geos/ci.html.

2. *Id.*

3. *Id.*

4. UNDP (2009). Human Development Report 2009. Overcoming barriers: Human mobility and development, UNDP: United Nations Development Programme.

5. *Id* at 1.

6. *Id.*

7. *El Mercurio* (Chile), August 1, 2010.

8. *See* www.eiu.com.

9. *Id.* at 1.

10. *Id.*

11. *Id.*

12. *See* http://www.doingbusiness.org/Documents/CountryProfiles/CHL.pdf.

13. *See* http://www.weforum.org/pdf/Gcr/GCR_05_06_Executive_Summary.pdf.

14. *See* http://www.transparency.org/policy_research/surveys_indices/cpi/2009/cpi_2009 _table.

15. Law No. 18,045.

16. See the section on Taxation of Business and Cross-Border Transactions.

17. Under both Chapter XIV and DL 600, profits may be repatriated at any time and without any waiting period. DL 600 art. 4(2)(3).

18. For further information on international agreements *see* http://www.foreigninvestment .cl/english/regulaciones/acuerdos.asp, and on double taxation treaties *see* http://www .sii.cl/pagina/jurisprudencia/convenios.htm.

19. See the section on Taxation of Business and Cross-Border Transactions.

20. See the section on Financing Issues/Payments and the section on Securities Laws Issues.

21. See the section on Taxation of Business and Cross-Border Transactions.

22. See the section on Taxation of Business and Cross-Border Transactions.

23. Effective import duty rates are substantially lower than 6 percent—or even nonexistent—for many imports, due to the multiple free trade agreements entered into by Chile.

24. For further information on international agreements *see* http://www.foreigninvestment .cl/english/regulaciones/acuerdos.asp and http://rc.direcon.cl/.

25. See the section on Import and Export Issues.

26. Approximate equivalent of 8,000 monthly tax index units (unidades tributarias mensuales) as of September 2010.

27. As most of these amendments have yet to become effective, the former institutions will continue to operate until the transition and organization of the new authorities and institutions are completed.

28. See the section on Import and Export Issues for applicable duties and taxes.

29. *See* http://www.fiabnet.org/inf_mensuales/IM-May2010.pdf.

30. The current government sought to establish a financial services consumer protection agency, but later on it decided to empower the existing Consumer Protection Agency instead of creating a new agency for such purposes.

31. The banking financial market totaled USD 115,162 million for deposits during 2009, and equity capital and reserves (pursuant to IFRS rules) accounted for USD 13,584 million. Likewise, return on equity, after taxes, currently reached 20.24 percent. *See* http://www .sbif.cl/sbifweb/internet/archivos/Info_Fin_602_11323.pdf.

32. See the section Foreign Exchange (commercial banks as part of the formal exchange market).

33. See the section on Secured Transactions.

34. See the section on Legal Treatment of Foreign Investment and the section on Taxation of Business and Cross-Border Transactions regarding taxation of foreign loans, particularly the stamp tax (which will also apply to local loans).

35. See the section on Securities Laws Issues.

36. Chilean regulations required the SVS to authorize any entity to engage in securitization activities and to issue securitization bonds. Registration of the relevant bonds before the SVS is also required.

37. Asset-backed securities currently range from leasing and credit card debts, automobile loans, student loans, future cash flows of universities, infrastructure concessionaires, or timber industry companies, to government bonds and derivatives, among others.

38. To date, securitization bonds total approximately USD 5.9 billion in 110 issuances.

39. One thousand monthly tax index units (unidades tributarias mensuales) as of September 2010.

40. Only SAs have regulated officers and boards of directors. Directors or officers of SpAs may be subject to the same regulations as SAs unless otherwise provided in the relevant SpA's bylaws. See the section on Suitable Corporate Forms.

41. A manager or CEO of an SpA may also be held jointly and severally liable for damages caused to shareholders or third parties due to the lack of fidelity or validity of the information held in the company's shareholders' registry.

42. See the section on Treaties on Foreign Investment Protection.

43. Banks, financial institutions, and insurance companies are subject to certain special rules and regimes regarding insolvency and related oversight.

44. *See* http://www.unctad.org/sections/dite_dir/docs/wir10_fs_cl_en.pdf; http://www .unctad.org/sections/dite_dir/docs/wir10_fs_br_en.pdf; and http://www.foreigninvestment .cl/english/noticias/noticias_listado_detalle.asp?id=245.

45. In 2009, Chile continued to be ranked on top of all South American countries by the Corruption Perception Index (CPI) of Transparency International. According to the 2009 CPI report, Chile is among the top 25 countries worldwide, compared to others included in the index, with a score of 6.7. *See* http://www.transparency.org/policy_research/surveys _indices/cpi/2009/cpi_2009_ table.

46. *See,* e.g., http://info.worldbank.org/governance/wgi/mc_chart.asp.

47. *See* http://rc.direcon.cl/acuerdo/list and Treaties on Foreign Investment Protection, *supra.*

48. *See* http://www.foreigninvestment.cl/english/home.asp.

CHAPTER 5

Colombia

Carlos Urrutia Valenzuela*
Tomás Holguín*
Brigard & Urrutia

*The following additional members of Brigard & Urrutia have contributed to this chapter: Laura Carreño (corporate); María Fernanda Castellanos (intellectual property and IT); María Catalina Jaramillo (tax); Pilar López (labor and employment); Valeria Herrán (regulatory and government procurement); María Camila Bagés (insolvency and litigation); Francisco Uribe (real estate); Richard Galindo (corporate); Andrés Umaña (Internet regulation); Alejandro García (antitrust); Giovanni Acosta (products liability); Felipe Mendoza (banking/financing); Laura Villaveces (exchange stock regulations); and Eduardo José del Valle (environmental).

COUNTRY OVERVIEW

Colombia is organized as a centralized republic. Its political system is based upon strong democratic institutions. They include the election by popular vote of a president for a four-year term, with possible re-election for an additional term, and a Congress composed of two chambers, the Senate and the House of Representatives. Colombia's Constitution was the subject of a major reform enacted in 1991 by a Constitutional Assembly with the participation of all the major parties, including representatives from the former guerilla group M19. The new Constitution places significant emphasis on the civil rights of citizens, as well as on the social role of the state. Although historically Colombia operated as a two-party system composed of the Liberal and the Conservative parties, the 1991 Constitution afforded participation by minorities and new political movements. As a result, Colombia is today a multiparty system where the traditional political movements control less than 50 percent of the members of Congress and for the past three terms, the president did not originate from either one of the traditional parties.

Colombia has approximately 44 million people distributed among 32 departments. Bogota is the capital city with over 7 million inhabitants. Spanish is the official language, but various indigenous communities still maintain their aboriginal languages.

Over 90 percent of the population belongs to the Roman Catholic Church. However, the Constitution provides for freedom of religion, and the state has no religious affiliation.

The Constitution assigns an important role to private enterprise and respects the principle of private property. Since the 1990s, the state has retreated from sectors that had historically been in the hands of government, including power generation and distribution, telecommunications, and water and sewer services. Many of the government-owned entities that until recently had absolute control of their respective markets have been privatized, and new players actively participate in an environment of free competition. As a result, the role of government is now that of a regulator that supervises and brings order to the markets.

Until the early 1990s, Colombia's economy was heavily dependent upon exports of coffee. However, with the advent of the 1991 Constitution, the Colombian economy was liberalized and opened to trade in the global scenario. Colombia is an active member of the World Trade Organization and maintains dynamic relations with the major economies of Europe, Asia, the Americas, and, to a lesser extent, Africa. Colombia's economy has diversified significantly, to the point that coffee is no longer the leading export product. Indeed, today Colombia's main export products originate from natural resources, mainly coal (production in excess of 72 million tons for 2009) and oil (production of almost one million barrels per day for 2010).

The Colombian currency is the peso. The exchange rate varies daily in accordance with supply and demand in the exchange market. At present, one U.S. dollar is equivalent to 1,850 pesos.

Colombia is located in the northwest tip of South America. It occupies 1,138,910 square kilometers and is the largest country with a Caribbean coastline. Colombia's territory borders Venezuela, Brazil, Peru, Ecuador, and Panama. Additionally, Colombia has over 1,500 kilometers of coastline on each of the Atlantic (Caribbean Sea) and the Pacific oceans. Colombia's territory also includes the San Andres and Providencia archipelago of islands located in the Caribbean Sea, as well as the Gorgona and Malpelo islands in the Pacific.

In light of the importance that the world community attaches to the environment, it is worth mentioning that due to Colombia's position as a land bridge between North America and South America, nearly 14 percent of the species of flora and fauna accounted for by scientists on a global scale are found in Colombia, which makes it the second-most biologically diverse country in the world. The country ranks fourth with 2.2 percent of the world's total water supply, including 1,200 permanent rivers, 1,640 lagoons and lakes, and 1,940 swamps. Furthermore, Colombia's 46 national natural parks, wildlife sanctuaries, and other reserves occupy over 10 million hectares, equivalent to 10 percent of the country's landmass.

ESTABLISHING A BUSINESS PRESENCE IN COLOMBIA

Permanent Structures

Colombia has improved in reducing the requirements to formalize the incorporation of companies in the country. It is important to point out that Colombian law
provides a regulation regarding "permanent businesses," for cases in which foreign
entities undertake business directly in Colombia. Thus, the Commercial Code lists
some of the most common activities that are considered and qualify as permanent.
This list is not exhaustive and, therefore, other activities may be considered permanent as well, analyzed on a case-by-case basis. The Colombian Commercial Code
considers the following activities to be permanent:

- the opening of a local establishment or a business office in the country. The
  law specifically mentions that these include technical or consultancy offices;
- participating as contractor in the construction industry or in the rendering
  of services;
- obtaining a governmental concession or its assignment thereto, or participating in any way in the exploitation of natural resources.

Colombian law affords different options for the incorporation of a local entity in
the country: (1) subsidiary companies, such as a limited liability company, corporation, and simplified stock company, and (2) the branch of a foreign company.

Corporations

The capital of a corporation is divided into shares, which are freely negotiable
by endorsement, unless the bylaws provide for a right of first refusal in favor
of the remaining shareholders. The corporation requires that there be at least
five shareholders, none of whom can directly own more than 94.99 percent of
the outstanding shares of the corporation. There is no limit to the number of
shareholders of the corporation. The corporation requires a board of directors
composed of at least three principal members and their respective alternates. The
powers of the board of directors typically include (i) the appointment of general
managers and officers of the corporation, (ii) the authority to issue shares subject
to pre-emptive rights in favor of the remaining shareholders, and (iii) the power
to approve certain acts of the general managers as provided for in the bylaws of
the corporation.

Limited Liability Company

The limited liability company (LLC) requires at least two partners and may not have
more than 25 partners. The capital of an LLC is divided into quotas. The transfer
of quotas implies an amendment of the bylaws of the LLC and must be executed as
a public deed before a local notary public.

    In an LLC the partners are, as a general rule, liable only to the extent of their
equity contributions to the company, with the exception of taxes, where the partners

are jointly and severally liable with the company for taxes not paid by it, and moneys owed to employees and not paid by the company (such as salaries, fringe benefits, vacations, and indemnities).

Simplified Stock Company

A simplified stock company (sociedad por acciones simplificada or SAS) can be formed by one or more shareholders. There is no maximum limit as to the number of shareholders. The capital of an SAS is divided into shares that are, in general, freely negotiable by endorsement, unless the bylaws provide for rights of first refusal in favor of the remaining shareholders. The shareholders are liable to the extent of their contribution. An SAS does not require a board of directors. However, the shareholders may create this corporate body in the bylaws of the company. The board of directors may be formed by any number of individuals with or without alternates, appointed by the shareholders assembly or by the sole shareholder. The powers of the board of directors should be specified by the shareholders in the bylaws.

Branch of a Foreign Company

The branch of a foreign company shares the legal personality of its parent company; thus it does not have partners or shareholders but (1) an assigned capital, (2) a defined corporate purpose, and (3) its own managers and fiscal auditors.

In order to formalize the incorporation of a branch of a foreign company, the following documents must be submitted before a notary public at the domicile of the branch: (i) founding charter documents of the parent company (foreign company); (ii) bylaws of the parent company; (iii) a resolution of incorporation of the branch issued by the competent body of the parent company (such as the board of directors), approving the incorporation of the branch in Colombia; (iv) documents evidencing the existence of the foreign company; and (v) documents evidencing the authority of the officers of the foreign company.

Restrictions on Foreign Ownership

As a general rule foreign investors are welcome to invest in all sectors of the economy, with the exception of materials or radioactive substances not produced within the country.

There are percentage limits on foreign investment participation in some sectors of the economy, such as the telecommunications sector, and authorizations can be required for certain sensitive sectors, such as finance. Namely, the Constitution establishes some business restrictions,[1] some of which are related to the development of financial activities that involve the receipt of money, such as brokerage and insurance companies and banks. In these activities, the law establishes some specific requirements that companies wishing to engage in such businesses must fulfill in order to obtain the necessary license to operate in Colombia.

Nonpermanent Establishments

Agency Agreements

Colombia has only one kind of agency agreement, governed by articles 1317 to 1331 of the Code of Commerce. Pursuant to article 1328 of the Code of Commerce, an agency agreement performed in Colombian is governed by Colombian law and any provision to the contrary is illegal, unenforceable, and otherwise void.

Upon termination of an agency agreement, regardless of whether the termination occurs with or without cause, under the Code of Commerce the principal must pay to the agent a severance compensation equivalent to one-twelfth of the average commission received by the agent during the last three years of the agreement, multiplied by the number of years of duration of the agreement. In addition, if the principal terminates the contract without cause or the agent terminates the contract due to a breach attributable to the principal, the agent is entitled to be paid an equitable compensation for its promoting efforts within the territory.

Distribution Agreements

Generally, distribution agreements are governed by the rules of supply agreements set forth in the Code of Commerce. Special rules apply also to the supply of water, gas, waste, energy, or telecommunications services by local utilities. In addition, other regulations have effects on agreements, including consumer protection, technical standards, and antitrust regulations.

The parties to a distribution contract are free to agree upon its terms, so long as they do not violate public policy rules. However, in the absence of provisions on quantities, price, payment, duration, and termination, the Code of Commerce sets forth rules that apply by default. Unlike the rules governing agency agreements, the Code of Commerce does not provide for special compensation or indemnification rights in favor of the distributor upon the termination of distribution agreements. Accordingly, distribution agreements are governed by the general rules of contractual liability under which the plaintiff may recover any actual damages or losses that are demonstrated to have been suffered, so long as such losses are direct and foreseeable.

Franchising Agreements

There are no special rules for franchises in Colombia. Franchise contracts must abide by general regulations on contracts and intellectual property law, among others.

Representative Offices

The Code of Commerce does not contemplate the possibility of establishing representative offices by foreign companies interested in undertaking activities in Colombia. In fact, as mentioned earlier, in accordance with the rules provided by the Code of Commerce, if a foreign company wishes to undertake activities deemed to be permanent in Colombia, the company must either set up a branch or incorporate a subsidiary.

However, there is one exception: the Colombian Financial Statute provides that foreign financial institutions (banks, investment banks, and so on) and broker-dealers can market their financial products, as well as their securities products, to Colombian residents so long as the institution establishes a representative office in Colombia. Such an office is not a legal person and is nothing more than a vehicle to promote the off-shore services of the foreign institution.

The opening of the office, as well as the appointment of the person who is to act as representative, is subject to the prior approval of the Superintendence of Finance.

INVESTMENT ISSUES

Pursuant to the Colombian Constitution and Decree 2080 of 2000, foreign investors will have the same rights as Colombian nationals. Therefore, a foreign investor has the right to purchase real estate properties in Colombia subject to the same imperative laws and public policy rules that apply to all Colombian citizens, provided, however, that the sovereign right of the Republic of Colombia upon its territory is not affected. Per Colombian law, foreign entities or individuals are not entitled to acquire ownership of real estate properties located on the national coastline or in the boundaries set forth with neighboring countries. Said real estate properties may be acquired only by Colombian nationals.[2]

Treaties on Foreign Investment Protection

Since the 1990s, Colombia has pursued a policy of entering into reciprocal investment protection treaties with other countries. At present, Colombia has reciprocal foreign investment protection undertakings with México, Perú, Spain, Switzerland, Chile, Guatemala, El Salvador, and Honduras.

The following chart shows those investment protection undertakings:

Agreement	Effective Date
FTA G2 (México and Colombia)	1995
BIT Peru	2003
BIT Spain	September 22, 2007
FTA Chile	May 8, 2009
BIT Switzerland	October 6, 2009
FTA Northern Triangle (Guatemala, El Salvador, and Honduras)	Guatemala: November 12, 2009 Salvador: February 1, 2010 Honduras: March 27, 2010

Although the specific wording may differ among these treaties, they all include the usual elements of modern bilateral investment treaties such as: (i) a broad concept of investment, (ii) most-favored-nation and national treatment principles, (iii) rules on direct and indirect expropriation, (iv) rules on compensation upon expropriation, and (v) dispute resolution mechanisms. Notably, Colombia is a signatory to the Convention on the Settlement of Investment Disputes between States and Nationals of Other States (ICSID), which came into force for Colombia in 1997.

In addition, Colombia is currently a member of the World Trade Organization as well as the Latin American Integration Association and the Andean Community. The country has negotiated free trade agreements with the United States, Canada, and the EFTA states (Iceland, Liechtenstein, Norway, and Switzerland), which are on the final ratification proceeding by each state. At the same time, Colombia has been negotiating FTAs with Panama and South Korea and the European Union.

OPERATIONAL LEGAL ENVIRONMENT

Foreign Exchange Regulations

Foreign exchange regulations, including foreign investment matters, are aspects to consider when incorporating a company in Colombia. Decree 2080 of 2000 states that any contribution in the capital of a Colombian company, a provisional investment in trust, acquisition of real estate, a contribution in kind, and an investment in the assigned capital of a local branch of a foreign company, among others, qualifies as a direct foreign investment (DFI).

Pursuant to Decree 2080 of 2000, the following are the rights and benefits of registering a DFI before the Colombian Central Bank: (i) to remit abroad or repatriate proven net profits generated by the relevant investment; (ii) to reinvest profits or retain them as surplus undistributed profits; (iii) to capitalize amounts with remittance rights and further remit them abroad; and (iv) to remit any income received from purchasing the investment in Colombia, from liquidating the company receiving the investment, or from reducing its capital.

Colombian regulations in force provide for the application of a foreign exchange regime in Colombia for transactions formalized and operations undertaken in foreign currency by Colombian residents. According to Decree 1735 of 1993, the following are considered Colombian residents for foreign exchange purposes: (i) all individuals who live in the national territory; (ii) civil service entities and corporations including nonprofit corporations that have their domicile in Colombia; and (iii) branches of foreign corporations duly incorporated in Colombia. People who have not spent more than six continuous months in Colombia within the previous year are not considered Colombian residents.

Immigration

According to Colombian immigration laws, a foreigner who intends to enter the country must obtain either a visa or an entry and permanence permit in order to enter Colombia as an immigrant in good standing. A visa is the authorization issued by the Ministry of Foreign Affairs that grants a foreigner entry into Colombia. An entry and permanence permit is the authorization issued by the DAS to a foreigner who does not require a visa, for entry into Colombia as a tourist or a visitor.

Except for citizens of countries for which a visa is not required, entry of non-nationals into Colombian territory must be authorized by a visa. Citizens of countries for which a visa is not required may enter the country as tourists or visitors without a visitor's visa (tourist, temporal, or technical), but with an entry and permanence permit. Exit permits are not required. However, foreigners must present their passport and valid visa or entry and permanence permit at the moment of departure.

Import Issues

The general rule is that any entity may import goods freely without previous registration. The exception to this rule is the requirement of registration and import licenses for certain goods that the Colombian government considers dangerous, inconvenient, or sensitive for the country, or when they need to comply with technical rules.

When the merchandise to be imported has an FOB value exceeding USD 10,000, the import proceeding must be carried out by an authorized agent called a customs agent, unless the importer may act by itself in certain specific cases. Customs agents are specialized in customs proceedings and are responsible before the customs authorities for the veracity and accuracy of the information included in the import documents. The customs agent is also responsible for declaring the corresponding import duties, which as a general rule are applicable tariff and VAT. Should there be applicable antidumping duties or compensatory rights, they would also be charged on a case-by-case basis.

Every import into Colombia triggers the payment of customs duties (tariff and VAT) of the relevant merchandise customs value.

Notwithstanding the above, certain goods are exempt from tariff when imported for particular purposes or when their use in Colombia is related to sensitive areas of the economy, such as the oil and gas sectors, or the publishing of cultural books or magazines.

According to Colombian Customs Law, machinery and equipment can be imported through a temporary import type, which allows for the suspension of customs duties on certain merchandise that will be re-exported within an established term.

There are two kinds of temporary imports for re-exportation of goods in the same condition as they were imported: short-term and long-term. For example, both might be used when importing under a leasing agreement.

The Colombian customs regulations have developed special programs and legal schemes that are entitled to have customs duties or taxes, including the following:

- Special Import-Export Programs (Plan Vallejo): Through these programs, the import of certain raw materials and machinery is exempt from customs duties or deferred payment when they are to be used in the production of goods or in rendering services to be exported.
- VAT exclusion for the following imports: Temporary import of heavy machinery for basic industry when the corresponding merchandise is not produced in Colombia, and import of machinery devoted to recycling and processing waste.
- Colombian companies registered as International Trading are allowed to buy such products in the national market exempt from VAT.
- Colombian importers and exporters qualified as permanent customs users or high export users have the prerogative of acting directly before the Colombian customs authorities without using a customs agent.

Export Issues

Export of goods is not subject to duties. The export of services is VAT-exempted when the corresponding services are used exclusively abroad.

Free Trade Zones

Free trade zones are areas in the Colombian territory that are considered outside the Colombian customs territory and, therefore, a legal fiction of extraterritoriality applies over them. Based on such legal fiction, the merchandise that enters the free trade zones from abroad does not trigger customs duties, and the merchandise that enters the Colombian customs territory from a free trade zone is deemed to be an import for customs purposes.

The industrial users of free trade zones have the following tax benefits: (i) a special income tax rate of 15 percent (instead of the general 33 percent rate), and (ii) the exemption from VAT on the sale of goods, raw materials, and supplies. The Colombian free trade zone regime includes free trade zones for multiple users as well as single enterprise free trade zones that allow for a single company to perform industrial activities in a specific area declared a free trade zone and access the benefits mentioned above. In order to be declared a free trade zone, the petitioner must commit to an investment project that includes not only new investments but also the creation of new jobs.

Taxation and Tax Treaties

Personal Income Tax

Income tax is a national tax levied on the basis of ordinary and extraordinary income obtained during a taxable year, at rates that vary between 0 percent and 33 percent. Foreign nonresident individuals and companies are taxed solely on their Colombian source income.

Income tax rates for individuals taxed on their worldwide income vary depending on each individual's taxable income.

Corporate Tax

The corporate income tax rate is 33 percent[3] on taxable income. Although considered a single tax, income tax has two components: (i) income tax and (ii) the tax on capital gains. While income tax is levied on the basis of ordinary income, capital gains taxes are levied on occasional income obtained by taxpayers. They are both included in an annual income tax return and are subject to the same 33 percent rate, but each is determined separately, so that ordinary costs, deductions, and net operating losses are applied exclusively to ordinary income, and occasional costs, deductions, and losses are applied to capital gains.

Presumptive Income

For income tax purposes, it is presumed that the taxpayer's net income is at least 3 percent of the net assets held the last day of the immediately preceding taxable year (the percentage was 6 percent until 2006). As a result, if the taxpayer's net income is lower than 3 percent, income tax will apply over the latter.[4]

The Colombian Tax Code states that the net value of assets related to enterprises in unproductive periods will be deducted from the presumptive income base.

Nevertheless, Article 188 of the Colombian Tax Code provided that the excess of presumptive income over ordinary net income could be offset with the net income determined within the following five years.

General Rules on Deductions

As a general rule, deductible expenses are costs and expenses incurred with regard to the income-generating activity, provided that they are necessary and proportional to such activity and that they are accrued or paid in the fiscal year in which they are claimed as deductions.[5]

In accordance with the above, any expense that meets the foregoing requirements may be claimed as a deduction. However, certain special deductions are worth highlighting:

- Amounts paid by affiliates, branches, subsidiaries, or agencies in Colombia to their home offices or offices abroad for administrative or management

expenses, royalties, and exploitation or acquisition of intangibles, provided the corresponding tax withholdings have been made at the source.[6]
- The total of the amounts paid for industry and commerce tax (a municipal and property tax) during the fiscal year, provided that said expenses have a direct relationship with the activity of the taxpayer.[7]
- One-quarter of debit tax paid by the taxpayer.
- Fixed assets (other than land) are depreciable in accordance with their useful lives, as follows:[8]

Type of Asset	Useful Life
Computers and vehicles	5 years
Machinery and equipment	10 years
Real estate (e.g., pipelines and buildings)	20 years

A different useful life can be used if proper authorization is given by the Colombian Tax Office (DIAN), provided that the request is filed by the taxpayer no less than three months prior to the initiation of the tax year in which the new useful life will be used.

- Depreciation may be done using the straight-line method, the declining balance method, or any other approved method of recognized technical value. All these methods would follow international accounting principles.
- Amortization of investments, such as feasibility studies, installation and organization, development and research, business assignment premiums, and purchase of intangibles.[9]
- Salaries paid to employees, if the corresponding payroll taxes and social security contributions have been duly paid.[10]
- Bad debt provisions.[11]
- Voluntary investments in environmental control or improvement, up to 20 percent of the taxpayer's net income.[12]
- Deduction for investments in scientific and technological developments.
- Special allowance for investment in productive real fixed assets.[13] Colombian law provides for a special 30 percent deduction over investments in the acquisition of productive real fixed assets. This deduction is in addition to the depreciation of the assets acquired by the taxpayer. Productive real fixed assets are goods and property, bought to become part of the net worth or capital, that play a direct and permanent role in the taxpayer's income-generating activity, and that are depreciated or amortized for tax purposes (such as infrastructure construction costs).

Dividends

Dividends distributed to shareholders of a Colombian company are not taxable income or capital gains, insofar as the profits from which they are derived have been taxed at the corporate level.

Notwithstanding the above, Colombian companies that pay dividends to foreign shareholders must apply a 33 percent withholding tax on the amount of untaxed book profits.

Goods and Services Tax (Value Added Tax or VAT)

VAT is a national tax levied on the sale of tangible movable goods and the provision of services within Colombian territory, as well as on the import of tangible movable goods, unless expressly excluded from said tax.

Being a tax over added value, it allows taxpayers to credit input VAT against output VAT, provided that the former was levied on goods and services used in the production or manufacture of taxable goods and services.[14]

In some cases, imported services (services executed abroad and used in Colombia) are subject to VAT in Colombia, provided that the recipient of the services is located in Colombia. Examples of said services would be (i) licenses and authorizations to use intangible assets; (ii) consulting, advisory, and audit services; (iii) rental of corporate movable assets; and (iv) insurance and reinsurance services.

Exported services are exempt from VAT if the service is executed in Colombia but used exclusively by a non-Colombian resident, under a written agreement. It is mandatory that the provider of services is registered with the National Exporter Register and that the foregoing agreement be registered with the Ministry of Commerce, Industry and Tourism.

VAT is generally levied at 16 percent but admits different rates over specific goods and services if the law so dictates. Sometimes goods or services can be taxed at 0 percent (in which case they will be exempt from VAT).

Double Taxation Treaties and Their Key Elements

Aware of the importance of stimulating foreign investment in Colombia, the Colombian government is committed to strengthening its network of treaties to avoid double taxation with non–tax-haven jurisdictions.

To date, the following treaties have been negotiated:

Tax Jurisdiction	Double Taxation Treaty with Colombia	Domestic Law Document	Constitutionality Decision
Spain	Enforceable	Law 1082 of 2006	C-383 of 2008
Chile	Enforceable	Law 1261 of 2008	C-577 of 2009

Tax Jurisdiction	Double Taxation Treaty with Colombia	Domestic Law Document	Constitutionality Decision
Switzerland	Ratified	Law 1344 of 2009	C-460 of 2010
Mexico	Signed	Pending	
Canada	Signed	Pending	
Korea	Signed	Pending	

The tax treaties with Spain and Switzerland are based on the OECD model and provide the following main benefits:

- *Capital Gains Tax:* As a general rule, capital gains obtained by foreign investors from the sale of shares of Colombian companies are subject to a 33 percent capital gains tax. The taxable base is the difference between the sale price and the tax basis of the shares.
- Under OECD-based treaties, the sale of the shares would be considered a taxable event in Colombia, only if 50 percent or more of the assets underlying the shares in a Colombian company consists of real estate located in Colombia. Otherwise, the gain on the sale would be taxable in the residence country only (Spain or Switzerland).
- *Dividends:* Under Colombian law there is no tax on dividends, to the extent that they are paid out of profits that were taxed at the corporate level, as stated above. This local rule applies regardless of the country of domicile of the shareholder.

The treaty with Spain sets forth a 0 percent withholding tax for any shareholders domiciled in Spain holding at least 20 percent of the shares of a Colombian company (provided that dividends were previously taxed at the corporate level).

Even though it has not yet entered into effect, the rule regarding dividends in the treaty with Switzerland may be more beneficial than the Spanish rule. According to the Swiss treaty, dividends are not taxed at the shareholder level regardless of whether or not such dividends are paid out of profits that were not taxed at the corporate level.

Labor and Employment

Labor relationships in Colombia have been governed since 1965 by the Labor Code (hereinafter referred to as the CST), which has been amended by a series of subsequent laws, the most important of which are Law 50 of 1990, Law 789 of 2002, Law 100 of 1993, Law 797 of 2003, and Law 1122 of 2007.

Colombian law governs any labor relationship carried out in Colombia. According to the CST, labor law applies throughout the territory and to all inhabitants, irrespective of their nationality. Most employee rights are statute-based and mandatory, regardless of whether the law of another jurisdiction is chosen to govern the employment contract (such laws are not enforceable in Colombia).

Colombian labor legislation assumes that every personal work relation is governed by an employment contract. For the purposes of declaring that a contract exists, the following elements must concur:

- the personal activity of the employee;
- continued subordination or dependency of the employee with respect to the employer;
- a salary that remunerates the service.

Once these requirements have been met, it is deemed that an employment contract exists, regardless of the name assigned to it. Labor contracts may be classified in four types, according to their duration: (i) fixed term; (ii) indefinite term; (iii) occasional, accidental, or transitory; and (iv) for the duration of the work.

Salary

The salary is the main and direct compensation that the employer provides to the employee for his or her services. It consists of two types of direct compensations: (i) ordinary compensation (periodically paid) that may be fixed or variable, and (ii) extraordinary compensation (overtime work, commissions, additional salaries, regular bonuses, permanent travel expenses, and in general any payment made as a direct compensation of the employees' work).

Labor law provides that employers and employees may define in the labor contract which sums or payments are deemed to be excluded from the employee's salary base. However, all payments made as a *direct* retribution of the employee's work will be deemed to be part of the employee's salary without exception.

Minimum Legal Salary

No worker can earn a salary lower than the monthly minimum legal salary, which was COP$515,000 (USD $278) for 2010.

Integral Salary

Integral salary is a sole sum that, in addition to compensating for the ordinary work, remunerates the value of all surcharges, benefits, and legal fringe benefits other than vacations. The employee receives only a monthly sum of money and is not paid separately any additional legal fringe benefits. For 2010, the minimum amount of integral salary was COP$6,695,000 (approximately USD 3,618). The agreement to remunerate the employee based upon integral salary must be in writing.

Fringe Benefits

Under Colombian labor law, the employer must recognize and pay to all of its employees who earn ordinary salaries (not integral salaries) certain benefits, in addition to their salaries, which are known as legal fringe benefits. These benefits are transport aid, footwear and dress, severance, interest on severance, and service bonus.

Vacations

All employees have the right to enjoy 15 working days of remunerated rest for every year of service and proportionally for a fraction thereof, which can be accumulated only for up to two years. However, in certain special cases, the employee can accumulate up to four years of vacation time.

Payroll Fees

Employers are required by law to make some additional payments, calculated as percentages of the total value of the company's payroll. The total percentage is 9 percent.

Social Security

The General Social Security System comprises the General Pensions System, the General Health Social Security System, and the General Professional Risks System. Pursuant to Law 100 of 1993, every employer must affiliate its employees with the three systems. Each system contemplates certain contingencies that are covered and some allowances or benefits to be complied with that the respective administrative entity must grant.

Trial Period

Pursuant to the Labor Code, an employee's trial period may not exceed two months in the case of indefinite term contracts and no more than one-fifth of the total term of fixed term contracts. During the trial period, an employee may be dismissed by the employer without the payment of the legal indemnification, and likewise the employee may decide to leave his or her work, without having to pay a legal indemnification.

Termination of Individual Employment Contracts

Every employment agreement entails the resolutory condition for breach, which, in turn, requires the responsible party to indemnify the other for damages.

Labor agreements may be terminated without previous notice by either party. If the contract is terminated by the employer, the effects of the termination will vary depending on the type of contract and whether the contract is terminated with or without just cause.

In termination by the employer without just cause, the employer must pay the legal indemnification provided by the Labor Code, which varies depending on the salary and the employee's time of service.

Unions

The right to incorporate labor unions is protected by the Constitution, and union officials have special legal protection that prevents them from being dismissed and, in some cases, permits them to devote most of their time to union matters while being paid by the employer.

Strikes are recognized as a legal instrument in order to obtain improved working conditions. However, strikes are illegal in certain sectors considered essential public services (such as the Central Bank).

Antitrust and Competition Issues

Colombian antitrust laws and regulations have been enacted and issued in furtherance of article 333 of the Constitution. Pursuant to said article, the government is required to intervene in the Colombian economy in order to prevent unfair competition and anticompetitive conduct, and to ensure free and fair competition in all the local markets.

The legal framework governing antitrust matters in Colombia has two main sets of rules: (i) Law 155 of 1959 sets forth the basic principles governing the Colombian antitrust and competition regime; and (ii) Decree 2153 of 1992 determines the basic structure, scope of authority, and powers of the competition authority and sets specific rules governing anticompetitive conduct.

Law 155 of 1959 and Decree 2153 of 1992 were recently amended by Law 1340 of 2009, which was enacted in order to update certain aspects of the existing framework and improve the ability of the Superintendence of Industry and Commerce (SIC) to enforce the existing laws and regulations.

Merger Control

Under Colombian antitrust law, all entities that carry out the same manufacturing, distribution, or consumption activity or are part of the same value chain in the production of certain products, raw materials, or goods or services, must file a report with the SIC in connection with any transaction that implies the merger, consolidation, acquisition of control, or economic integration in Colombia. For purposes of the analysis of a given merger, the SIC has indicated, via different opinions, that any kind of legal agreement or economic transaction that results in the combination of two or more business units under a common interest is regarded as an integration.

Under the current regulations, a merger needs to be cleared in advance by the SIC whenever three conditions are met: (i) local overlap; (ii) revenue or assets are equal to or exceed certain defined thresholds; and (iii) market share exceeds 20 percent. No filing is required in transactions in which the following two conditions are met: (i) when the combined annual operational income of the parties (including all other related companies within the Colombian territory) as of December 31 of the year immediately preceding the transaction is below the relevant threshold; and (ii) when the value of the combined assets of the parties (including all other related companies within the Colombian territory) as of December 31 of the year immediately preceding the transaction is below the relevant threshold.

Anticompetitive Conduct

Pursuant to Decree 2153 of 1992, any behavior that affects or restricts free competition is forbidden and is considered to have an illicit purpose. Three different groups of conduct are deemed to restrict competition: (i) anticompetitive agreements, (ii) anticompetitive conduct, and (iii) abuse of dominant position. Colombian law prohibits any agreement reached by competitors in a given market with an anticompetitive purpose or effect.

Environmental Issues

In 1991, Colombia incorporated into its Constitution international principles for environmental protection. It is said that the Constitution of 1991 qualifies as a "green constitution" due to the degree and importance of its references concerning environmental principles and the rights given to nationals seeking to protect the environment. For instance, the Constitution expressly states that a healthy environment is considered a fundamental right; citizens may seek protection of this right by means of class actions and *acción de tutela,* a summary proceeding to protect constitutional rights.

Those principles included in the Constitution gave rise to a proliferation of environmental regulations in the decade following its enactment. Among those regulations, Law 99 of 1993 introduced the most significant changes to the environmental laws then in effect, such as the creation of the Ministry of Environment as the maximum authority in these matters. Decree 2820 of 2010 introduced the concept of Environmental License, and Law 1333 of 2009 regulates the liability arising from violations or other actions against the environment.

Controls—Competent Authorities and Types of Control

In Colombia, the use of renewable natural resources or the performance of any activity that may affect the environment is subject to strict controls. Consequently, subjects, nationals, and citizens must apply for environmental licenses, concessions, permits, and/or authorizations before the environmental authorities prior to the execution of certain activities and projects. The Environmental License is the main administrative mechanism to control the use and exploitation of environmental and natural resources. As a general rule, the Environmental License is required to undertake any project, operation, or activity that may involve environmental impact. The Environmental License is granted by different governmental entities, depending on the location and magnitude of the projects. Those governmental authorities are (i) the Ministry of Environment and (ii) the Regional Environmental Authorities (CAR). Activities that require an Environmental License include the exploration and exploitation of mines, transport and storage of oil, projects that affect natural parks, exploration and exploitation of hydrocarbons, and construction of international airports.

It is important to note that in situations in which the location of the project, operation, or activity creates a controversy as to which CAR should issue the Environmental License, the Ministry of Environment has the power to solve such a controversy; and if the competent authority, whether it is the CAR or the Ministry of Environment, denies the Environmental License, the petitioner may appeal the decision before the administrative courts.

Permits and Authorizations Applicable to Each Natural Resource

The authorizations or permits required in order to perform an activity bearing environmental impact are classified according to the natural resource that is to be used or exploited or that may be affected. Accordingly, different regulations apply to the discharge of atmospheric emissions, liquid waste and water use, and noise.

Main Environmental International Treaties Ratified by Colombia

International treaties entered into by Colombia include the Agreement on Biological Diversity; the Ramsar Convention; Convention about International Trade of Threatened Species of Wild Fauna and Flora; Montreal Protocol on Substances That Deplete the Ozone Layer; the Vienna Agreement for the Protection of the Ozone Layer; the Basel Convention on the Control of Transboundary Movements of Hazardous Wastes and Their Disposal; the Basel Protocol on Liability and Compensation; and the Cartagena Protocol on Biosafety.

Sanctions

Several persuasive methods are available to governmental authorities to secure compliance with environmental laws. Among these instruments, the environmental authorities may impose sanctions, penalties, or fines for breach of the conditions set forth in the Environmental License or any other violation of environmental regulations, permits, or authorizations including commencing activities without the required environmental license, permit, or authorization. Furthermore, certain violations of environmental laws are considered criminal offenses, such as illicit holding or handling of hazardous substances, illicit use of biological natural resources, and illicit exploration and/or exploitation of mines.

In the event of breaches to environmental obligations and/or environmental damages attributable to a citizen or company, the culpable party may be exposed to environmental administrative proceedings in which the environmental authority may impose one of the following preventive measures: (a) written admonition; (b) confiscation of all the products and elements used to commit the infraction; (c) apprehension of all animal and plant species, products, and subproducts; (d) suspension of the works or activities when they may produce any damages upon the environment, natural resources, the landscape, or human health; as well as one or more of the following sanctions: (i) daily fines up to COP$5,000 minimum legal monthly wages (USD 1,391,891); (ii) temporary or permanent closing of the work or activity; (iii) revocation of the environmental license, permits, or authorizations granted to develop the work or activity; (iv) demolition of the work or activity; (v) confiscation of all the plant and animal species, products, or subproducts used to commit the infraction; (vi) restitution of the plant and animal species; and (vii) communitarian work in the conditions determined. Additionally, if a citizen or company is sanctioned, it will be listed in the Environmental Infractors Lists.

Consumer Protection and Products Liability

In Colombia the main regulation on consumer protection is set forth by Decree 3466 of 1982, also known as the Consumer Protection Statute (CPS). The most important features of the CPS are related to the rules applicable to the information provided to consumers and to the implied guaranty of products and services. It is important to mention that such rules are binding to both manufacturers and distributors.

Regarding the information provided to consumers, the CPS sets forth that any information about the products or services offered to the public must be truthful and sufficient. Therefore, advertisements that contain false, misleading, deceptive, or insufficient information are forbidden.

In the case of warranties, the CPS states that all purchase and services agreements are deemed to contain the minimum presumptive warranty, according to which all producers must guarantee the quality and workmanship provided for a given product or service. Such quality and/or workmanship must in certain cases be recorded with the SIC, which must comply with the applicable official technical standard.

As far as product liability is concerned, according to Colombian consumer protection regulations, all participants in a distribution chain (for example, manufacturers and distributors) must warn consumers about any dangers associated with a product that may affect the safety or health of the consumer. In addition, certain products must adhere to minimum safety standards, the breach of which results in product liability. In some cases, producers may be exempted from liability (for example, where the damage resulted from misuse of a product).

Under provisions in both consumer protection regulations and the Code of Commerce, the manufacturer and distributor of goods can be held liable for breach of implied warranties or hidden defects.

Real Estate and Property

Prior to a transaction investors must (i) perform a due diligence of the property; (ii) execute agreements in order to acquire a property; and (iii) register such public deed before the Office of the Public Registry. Pursuant to Colombian Law, purchase agreements of real estate properties shall have the solemnity to be formalized in a public deed. In addition, the ownership right is consolidated only with the registration of the Public Registry.

For real estate, an investor should conduct due diligence by reviewing the property titles of the past 20 years, the certificate of land conveyance, and tax certificates and land use.

Prior to the execution of the public deed of purchase, it is common to enter a promise of purchase and sale agreement. The final purchase agreement must be formalized in a public deed. The notary public charges fees of approximately 0.28 percent of the value of the sale. The public deed of purchase must be filed before the Office of Registration of Public Instruments in order to obtain the registration of the document in the certificate of conveyance. This proceeding requires payment of a registration tax of 1 percent of the value of the sale and registration rights of 0.5 percent of the value of the sale.

Intellectual Property

The protection of intellectual property is governed by regulations issued by the Council of the Andean Community, formed by Colombia, Ecuador, Bolivia, and Peru. Even though the regulations are common for all member countries, each country has independent agencies, independent Industrial Property Registries, and discretionary criteria for applying the common regulations. Thus, registration on a country-by-country basis is required.

As regards copyrights, IP protection is governed simultaneously by regulations from the Andean Community and internal regulations.

In general terms, intellectual property rights may be enforced through civil infringement actions, unfair competition actions, and criminal actions.

Trademarks and Distinctive Signs

The Colombian trademark system is a registration-based system. Thus, no rights arise from the mere use of a trademark in commerce. Registration with the competent agency (the Office of the Superintendent of Industry and Commerce) is required to secure exclusive rights and the prerogative to prevent third parties from using the same trademark or a similar one, where likelihood of confusion arises.

The proceeding for registering a trademark includes a publication and opposition stage, and may last from eight to 12 months, provided that no oppositions are filed by third parties. Protection is awarded for a renewable 10-year term. A trademark registration may be canceled by the competent agency, as per the request of any interested party, if the owner does not prove effective use of the trademark in commerce during a three-year term.

Colombia recently approved its adherence to the Trademark Law Treaty (TLT), which allows applications in multiple classes of the International Nice Classification. However, the treaty has not yet entered into effect, since the regulation for implementing the treaty has not been issued. It is expected that the TLT will enter into effect during 2011. In the meantime, each trademark application must comprise just one class of the International Nice Classification.

Patents

Patents are granted to inventions that are novel, inventive, and have industrial application. The patent owner has the exclusive right, for a 20-year term from the date of the application, to exploit the invention as described in the claims thereof, and to prevent third parties from exploiting the invention.

Under Colombian law, the following are not deemed to be inventions (and are therefore not patentable):

- Discoveries, scientific theories, or mathematic methodologies.
- Biological proceedings, live forms, genoma.
- Works that are granted protection under copyright regulations.
- Business methods, games, or intellectual activities.
- Software.
- Ways of displaying information.

Also, second-use patents are not permitted in Colombia. Colombia is a party to the Patent Cooperation Treaty, which is currently in force.

Copyrights

Copyright protection is awarded to intellectual creations in the fields of art, literature (including software), and science. The protection is awarded only to the formal expression of the intellectual creations, not to the ideas that underlie said expression.

Please note that Colombia has a *droit d'auter regime*, derived from the country's civil law tradition, as opposed to a copyright regime, found in common law countries. Thus, Colombian regulations award protection to authors; that is, individuals who have created a protected work have both moral and patrimonial rights.

Moral rights are defined as nonrenounceable, nonassignable rights to claim paternity of the work, and the right to prevent third parties from modifying the work in any way that may affect the author's good name and reputation.

Moreover, authors are granted patrimonial rights, which are the rights to use and commercially exploit their works, and to prevent any third party from doing so without authorization. Patrimonial rights are assignable; prior compliance of legal formalities are necessary for the validity and enforceability of the assignment.

No registration of the protected works is required to be awarded protection. However, registration is prima facie evidence of ownership of a given work. Also, all agreements regarding protected works must be registered with the copyright office to be enforceable vis-à-vis third parties.

Even though special provisions apply in certain cases (namely, audiovisual works, collective works, and works created under a services contract), Colombian law does not expressly provide that patrimonial rights over works created under a labor relationship are deemed to be owned by the employer; thus particular measures must be adopted to secure ownership of the employer over these works.

Internet Regulation

Notwithstanding Law 1341 of 2009, which dictates the telecommunications regime and establishes the general conditions for the provision of services and networks, there is no specific regulation regarding Internet practices or content, other than the ones established regarding personal data and customer protection.

Law 1266 of 2008 (the Privacy Act) sets forth the general legal framework applicable to privacy matters and the management of personal information stored in databases. However, the Constitutional Court reduced the scope of the Privacy Act's provisions to apply only to financial, credit, commercial, and services information (and to information of the same characteristics coming from abroad) that is vulnerable to financial risk and credit risk.

According to Law 1273 of 2009, it is a crime to unlawfully or without authorization obtain, compile, subtract, offer, sell, exchange, send, buy, intercept, publish, modify, or use personal codes or data. This crime is punishable by a prison term of 48 to 96 months and a fine of USD 23,000 to USD 230,000.

E-Commerce

Law 527 of August 1999 (Law 527) and Decree 1747 of 2000 (Decree 1747) regulate e-commerce. Law 527 follows the 1996 UNCITRAL Model Law on Electronic Commerce and regulates the access and use of data messages, electronic commerce, electronic signatures, and bodies certifying electronic signatures.

The SIC authorizes certification entities, carries out inspections, and imposes penalties for failure to comply with the law. Decree 1929 regulates electronic invoices, allowing the use of electronic means to issue and store invoices, as long as the mechanisms used comply with the authenticity and reliability requirements imposed by Law 527. Article 2 of Law 1231 of 2008 allows the treatment of electronic invoices as negotiable instruments, pending a regulation by the government that has not been issued to date.

Securities and Securitization

The Colombian Constitution sets forth that Congress has the duty of issuing the general laws by which the government must abide to regulate banking, securities, and insurance activities, and, in general, any other activity related to the use, management, and investment of funds raised from the general public. In this context, Congress enacted Law 964 of 2005 (Law 964), which sets forth the general principles of the Colombian capital markets and the guidelines that the Ministry of Finance must follow to regulate the securities market. In general, the objectives of Law 964 are to (i) promote the development and efficiency of the securities market; (ii) protect investor rights; (iii) prevent and control systemic risk in the securities market; and (iv) preserve the functioning, transparency, discipline, and integrity of the securities market. Practically all of the regulations that govern the securities market in Colombia were recently compiled by the Ministry of Finance into Decree 2555 of 2010 (Decree 2555), which also contains regulations in connection with the banking and insurance sectors.

Supervision of the Securities Market

The entity in charge of conducting the inspection, supervision, and control of the securities market in Colombia is the Superintendence of Finance, a technical entity linked to the Ministry of Finance that is vested with financial and administrative autonomy with respect to the central government.

Furthermore, Colombia also has a self-regulatory organization created pursuant to Law 964 known as the Autorregulador del Mercado de Valores (AMV). As set forth in Law 964, self-regulatory organizations are charged with regulating and supervising the activities of securities intermediaries and brokers.

Public Offerings and Private Placements

Pursuant to Decree 2555, a public offering in Colombia is that which is addressed to the public at large or to 100 or more specific investors, with the purpose of subscribing, selling, or acquiring massively issued securities. Securities that are to be offered publicly must be registered with the National Registry of Securities and Issuers maintained by the Superintendence. Also, a public offering of securities is subject to the prior approval of the Superintendence. Accordingly, an offer placed with less than 100 investors, which was nonetheless marketed to 100 or more investors, would be deemed a public offer. Moreover, if the issuer plans to launch the offer through the Colombian Stock Market, the securities must also be listed in the stock exchange.

On the other hand, any offer that is not a public offering is deemed to be a private placement. Private placements of debt and equity securities are not subject to any specific rules and are not subject to approval by the Superintendence.

Secondary Market Transactions

Secondary market transactions of publicly traded shares are governed by two principles.

First, whenever a stock transaction exceeds an amount of USD 6,620, it must generally be settled through the Colombian Stock Exchange, either through the exchange's automated trading system or through special mechanisms such as tender offers or auctions. Second, whenever an investor or group of investors that constitutes the same beneficial owner intends to acquire, either directly or indirectly, 25 percent or more of the outstanding shares of a listed company, or when such investor or group already owns 25 percent or more of the outstanding shares of a listed company, and intends to increase its holdings, directly or indirectly, by 5 percent or more of the outstanding shares of the target company, the purchaser is required to launch a tender offer in the secondary market.

Investment Funds

Decree 2555 of 2010 regulates investment funds, which do not qualify as legal entities. They consist of a separate patrimony managed either by (i) a trust company, (ii) a brokerage firm, or (iii) an investment management company, which acts as the managing company and represents the relevant investment fund. Pursuant to Decree 2555 there are three different types of funds:

- Closed pooled funds are those characterized because any redemption of shares may be done only at the end of the duration period of the relevant fund, and the fund may receive subscriptions only for a limited period of time established on the relevant placement terms (reglamento). Private equity funds (PEFs) are included as a subtype of closed pooled funds, although they are regulated by certain additional provisions and rules.
- Staggered funds (carteras colectivas escalonadas) are those characterized by a certain period of time running successively for as long as the fund's duration period. Any redemption may be made only after the respective period of time set forth for such purpose in the placement terms has ended. The minimum period may not be less than 30 days.
- Open funds are those for which both subscriptions and redemptions may be made at any time. However, the fund's placement terms may establish a minimum term for redemption, which, if breached, would subject investors to a penalty.

In addition, there are different categories of investment funds such as real estate funds, hedge funds, and securities funds, among others, including the equivalent of exchange traded funds (ETFs), which are comprised of some or all of the securities that make up an international or national index and aim to replicate such index. Decree 2555 does not, however, preclude the establishment of funds structured with other characteristics, if authorized by the SFC.

Public Procurement

The legal framework for public procurement is mainly regulated in Law 80 of 1993 and Law 1150 of 2007. Pursuant to said legal framework, the Government is required to apply the principles of economy, efficiency, and transparency.

In general terms, the execution of any kind of agreement (including concession contracts) by a public entity and a private entity must be formalized subject to a competitive bidding process whereby detailed requests for proposals must be issued and complied with.

In addition, there are procedures applicable for public procurement such as abbreviated selection, merit-based selection, and direct contracting. The latter is the exception to the general rule, whereby the public entity is entitled to contract without a bid and can be used exclusively in the following cases: (a) emergency circumstances (such as natural disasters) that require the acquisition of goods or services on an urgent basis; (b) to contract loans; (c) in agreements among public entities; (d) for the acquisition of goods or services related to national security; (e) for contracts for the development of scientific and technological activities; (f) to contact a trust fund; (g) when there are not multiple suppliers; and (h) to lease or to buy real estate.

Liability of Company Directors

In line with contemporary corporate law, Law 222 of 1995 (Law 222) adopted a regime based on fiduciary duties that was, to a certain extent, inspired by the U.S. experience.

Article 24 of Law 222 provides that directors and officers are jointly and severally liable without limitation for damages willfully or negligently caused to the company, its shareholders, or third parties.

Law 222 does not explain the concept or characteristics of a "manager," but rather provides the following exhaustive list of persons who are deemed to be (i) the legal representative; (ii) the liquidator (officer in liquidation management proceedings); (iii) the manager of an ongoing concern; (iv) the members of the board of directors; and (v) whoever performs or is vested with said functions according to the company bylaws.

Law 222 also establishes three different general duties and certain specific obligations applicable to managers, as follows: (a) duty of good faith; (b) duty of care; and (c) duty of loyalty. In the event of breach of said general duties, the company or the offended person is entitled to initiate a lawsuit against the member of management.

According to general rules of civil liability and based on Article 200 of the Commercial Code, to bring an action against members of management, plaintiffs must argue and demonstrate: (i) the director's breach of an obligation; (ii) the level of scienter in the conduct (negligence or willful misconduct); (iii) the existence of losses or damages; and (iv) causation between the defendant's act and the plaintiff's losses or damages.

Litigation and Dispute Resolution

Pursuant to article 116 of the Constitution of Colombia, the administration of justice in Colombia is divided into five equal supreme judicial entities:

- The Constitutional Court (Corte Constitucional) guards the integrity and supremacy of the Constitution, and rules on the constitutionality of laws and international treaties. The judges of the Constitutional Court are nominated by the president, selected by the Senate and may serve one eight-year term;
- The Supreme Court of Justice (Corte Suprema de Justicia) is the highest court for criminal, labor, civil, and commercial law. The judges of the Supreme Court are selected from the nominees of the Higher Council of Justice and may serve one eight-year term;
- The Council of State (Consejo de Estado) is the highest court of administrative law. The judges of the Council of State are selected from the nominees of the Higher Council Justice and serve one eight-year term;
- The Higher Council of Justice (Consejo Superior de la Judicatura), which administers and disciplines the civil judiciary; members of the disciplinary chamber resolve jurisdictional conflicts arising between other courts. The members of the disciplinary chamber of the Higher Council of Justice are elected by the Congress for one eight-year term and the six members of the administrative chamber are elected by the Supreme Court of Justice (two), the Constitutional Court (one), and the Council of State (three); and
- The Office of the Attorney General (Fiscal General de la Nación), which is the highest criminal office. The Attorney General is elected by the Supreme Court of Justice for a four-year term.

Alternative Dispute Resolution in Colombia

ADR mechanisms and techniques are the fastest and most effective way to resolve conflicts, taking into account the time and costs associated with litigation before the courts. In Colombia, ADR mechanisms are regulated by Decree 1818 of 1998.

These include conciliation, *ex aequo et bono arbitration*, and arbitration that has been classified into legal, institutional, or independent arbitration. Despite its classification as an ADR mechanism, the procedure adopted by each of the afore-mentioned categories of arbitration is quite similar to the existing civil procedure in Colombian law.

In the case of international ADR, Colombia is a party to the 1958 New York Convention on the Recognition and Enforcement of Foreign Arbitral Awards, as well as to the 1975 Inter-American Convention on International Commercial Arbitration, and the 1965 Washington Convention for the Settlement of Disputes between States and Nationals of Other States. In addition, based upon the UNCI-TRAL Model Law on International Commercial Arbitration, the Congress approved Law 315 of 1996, which regulates International Commercial Arbitration.

CONTRACTS AND DOCUMENTS—FORMS AND ENFORCEABILITY

Generally, a contract may be made orally, in writing, or by a course of conduct. However, certain contracts must be in writing, such as the promise to enter into a contract in the future. Other contracts need to be made through public deeds, such as those concerning real estate transactions. Finally, certain contracts are made by delivering goods, such as the deposit contract. A valid contract is created if the following requirements are met: (1) mutual assent (meeting of minds); (2) legal capacity of the parties; (3) legality of subject-matter; (4) legality of purpose; (5) lack of defects in the assent; and (6) compliance with formalities (if applicable).

Challenges to the Validity or Enforceability of Contracts

- *Incapacity.* Contracts entered into with minors (persons under the age of 18), mentally incapacitated persons, and deaf-mute persons unable to communicate in writing are void. Acts of a company beyond the scope of its corporate purpose (ultra vires) are voidable as they exceed the corporate capacity.
- *Lack of Essential Elements.* If the applicable regulation foresees that a given contract requires the inclusion of "essential elements," the absence of mutual assent in connection with such essential elements prevents the formation of the contract if there is no default rule to fill the gap left by the parties. For example, the absence of agreement by the parties as to the price of goods being sold will prevent the formation of the contract as the law foresees that price is an essential element of a sale of goods contract.
- *Misrepresentation.* A contract may be declared null by a court on the grounds of misrepresentation where a party makes a false statement of

material fact or uses any fraudulent practice intended to induce the other party to enter into the contract.

- *Duress*. A contract may also be declared null by a court on the grounds of duress when a party has been induced by the other contracting party to enter into a contract by means of illegal and unfair physical force or psychological intimidation.
- *Mistake*. A court may declare that a contract is null where one party has made a mistake as to a material fact related to the terms of the contract or the identity of the other party. Mistakes as to legal issues are not a basis for challenging the validity of the contract. Where there is mutual mistake (or no "meeting of minds") there is no contract at all if such mistake relates to an essential element.
- *Illegality*. A contract is deemed null due to illegality, whenever such illegality relates either to the subject matter of the contract or to the motive that has led the parties to make it. This is the only event of nullity that may not be ratified by subsequent agreement between the parties.
- *Lack of Formalities*. Lastly, a contract may be set aside if it fails to comply with a formality that the law classifies as necessary for its formation. Typical examples of these types of formalities are contracts on real estate property, which shall be made through public deeds executed before a notary public.

ENDING/RESTRUCTURING A BUSINESS PRESENCE IN COLOMBIA

Insolvency Proceedings

Insolvency proceedings are governed by Law 1116 of 2006 (Law 1116), which establishes permanent rules that regulate the reorganization and the liquidation of insolvent debtors. Law 1116 also regulates cross-border insolvency proceedings based on the model of the United Nations Commission for the International Commercial Development, which has aimed to protect the creditors when the assets, the creditors, or the debtors are in different countries, in order to satisfy the needs of a global economy and international business.

Insolvency proceedings seek to protect the credit, the recovery, and the conservation of the companies as an economic production unit and as a source of employment, through reorganization proceedings and judicial liquidation. The reorganization proceedings aim to preserve feasible companies and to standardize their commercial and credit relations through their operational and administrative restructuring, as well as that of their assets and liabilities. The insolvency regime also applies to individuals who are merchants and to legal entities not excluded from its application.

As a general rule, the Superintendence of Companies acts as bankruptcy court. The purpose of reorganization proceedings is to arrive at an agreement between the debtor and its creditors and to promote the viability and the stability of the credits through the restructuring of the assets and the liabilities of the debtor. If it is not possible to arrive at an agreement, the assets of the debtor are liquidated and the proceeds from the liquidation of the debtor's estate are distributed among its creditors in accordance with the applicable rules of priority of payment.

NOTES

1. Colombian Constitution, article 334.
2. See Decree 1415 of 1940, article 5.
3. The corporate income tax rate was 35 percent in 2006, 34 percent in 2007, and 33 percent in 2008. Individuals are taxed at progressive rates depending on their taxable income.
4. As regards the mining sector, section 189 of the Colombian Tax Code establishes that the net value of assets directly linked to enterprises exclusively dedicated to mining activities (other than the exploitation of gas and liquid hydrocarbons) will not be part of the basis for the calculation of the presumptive income.
5. Colombian Tax Code, Article 107.
6. CTC, Article 124.
7. CTC, Article 115.
8. CTC, Article 128.
9. CTC, Article 142.
10. CTC, Article 108.
11. CTC, Articles 145, 146.
12. CTC, Article 158-2.
13. CTC, Article 158-3.
14. CTC, Article 485.

CHAPTER 6

Ecuador

Bruce Horowitz
PAZ HOROWITZ, Abogados

COUNTRY OVERVIEW

Taken over from the Inca Empire by the Spanish Empire in 1535, the territory that currently comprises the Republic of Ecuador was a part of the Republic of Gran Colombia that existed for a few years following the liberation from Spain of the Andean Region of South America. In 1830, Ecuador became a separate republic.

Ecuador is a founding member of the Andean Community of Nations (CAN), a free trade zone, whose other members are now Peru, Colombia, and Bolivia. The CAN has supranational legal control of a number of commerce-related areas, including, among others, trade, intellectual property, sanitary controls, and anti-trust. The supranational laws of the CAN are called "decisiones."

Ecuador's main trading partners are the United States, Peru, Chile, China, Colombia, Brazil, Venezuela, and Panama.[1] The United States has long been Ecuador's main trading partner. The Andean Community members have a very strong trading and political relationship with Ecuador. In recent years, Canada has become a close trading and investment partner. In order to expand its trading network and lower its political and strategic dependence on the United States, the present government has sought stronger trade, investment, and political ties

---

Co-authors Bruce Horowitz, David Benalcazar, Paola Gachet, Leopoldo Gonzalez, Maria Edith Jativa, Megan Parker-Johnson, Jorge Paz Durini, and Gabriela Villalobos also contributed to this chapter.

with other countries, including China, and to a lesser extent, India. As part of its attempt to gain commercial and political independence, the present government has placed a high priority on its relationship with Iran.

Since March 2000, Ecuador's currency has been the U.S. dollar.

Under the present government, Ecuador has been limiting and terminating its existing bilateral investment treaties, but it is looking for stronger trading and investment ties in particular with China, India, Brazil, Argentina, Venezuela, and Chile.

Ecuador is a member of the Organization of American States (OAS) and is a founding member of the recently organized Union of South America Nations (UNASUR) (www.pptunasur.com).

ESTABLISHING A BUSINESS PRESENCE IN ECUADOR

Permanent Structures

Suitable Corporate Forms

There are two types of companies in Ecuador: a business association (regulated by Corporate Law) and a civil corporation (regulated by the Civil Code). Business associations are incorporated to conduct only "commerce acts" as characterized by the law, and civil corporations are incorporated to conduct other activities.

Corporate Law recognizes the following business associations:

- A general partnership
- A limited partnership, divided by stocks
- A limited liability corporation
- A corporation
- A mixed economy company and
- An incidental company or "cuentas en participación."

The corporate forms depend upon the particular needs of the individuals who constitute the business presence; nevertheless, the suitable corporate forms for the business presence's legal and commercial use are the corporation, the limited liability corporation, and the civil corporation. Alternatively, for foreign investors it may also be appropriate and useful to establish a local branch of the foreign company in Ecuador.

   a)   *Corporation.* The main characteristics of this type of company are:

- It is under the control of the Superintendency of Companies.
- It requires a minimum of two persons as the incorporators.
- It is an open corporation that will issue shares in direct relation to its paid-in capital.
- The minimum subscribed capital is USD 800, out of which at least 25 percent must be paid in at the time of incorporation, with the other 75 percent required to be paid in within 24 months of its incorporation.

- Liabilities of the shareholders are limited to their paid-in capital.
- There is freedom to transfer shares.
- The only restriction on foreign ownership is that the foreign owner must hold "registered shares."
- The shareholders must hold at least one shareholder meeting per year (actual shareholder presence is not required).
- The company should have at least two officers (president and general manager, or any other name for these positions).

b) *The Limited Liability Corporation.* The main characteristics of this type of company are:

- It is under the control of the Superintendency of Companies.
- It requires a minimum of two persons for the incorporation.
- It is prohibited from operating with more than 15 shareholders; if this happens, the company has to be transformed into another type of company or it has to be dissolved.
- The shares are issued in direct relation to its paid-in capital.
- The minimum subscribed capital is USD 400, out of which at least 50 percent must be paid in at the time of incorporation, and the rest must be paid in within 12 months of incorporation.
- Liabilities of the shareholders are limited to the amount of their paid-in capital.
- The shares may not be freely negotiated. The transfer must be done by means of a notarized document, and all of the shareholders must approve it.
- In this type of company the shareholders cannot be banks, insurance companies, capitalization and saving companies, or international stock companies or foreign companies with bearer shares.
- The shareholders must hold at least one shareholder meeting per year (which does not require the actual presence of shareholders).
- The company should have at least two officers (president and general manager or any other name for these positions).

c) *Civil Corporation.* According to the Civil Code, there are three types of civil corporations: a partnership company, a limited partnership, and a civil and commercial corporation. In practice, the civil and commercial corporation form is the only one in use.

The main characteristics of the civil and commercial corporation are:

- No specific regulations exist for this type of company. Therefore, they are regulated as corporations (business associations). This type of civil corporation requires a minimum of two persons for the incorporation. The minimum subscribed capital is USD 800, the liabilities of the shareholders are limited to their paid-in capital, and there is freedom to transfer shares.
- In practice they are known as "civil and commerce corporations."

- They are not controlled by any public entity.

  d) ***Branch of a Foreign Company.*** The main characteristics of this type of company are the following:

- It is under the control of the Superintendency of Companies.
- The company's shareholder structure does not need to be reported to Ecuadorian authorities or to third parties; this information therefore remains confidential.
- The minimum operating capital is USD 2,000, and capital must be registered as a foreign investment.
- The company should have an attorney-in-fact in Ecuador. (This attorney-in-fact should be an Ecuadorian national or a foreigner holding an Ecuadorian resident's visa.)

Wholly Owned Entities

In 2006, the Corporate Law was amended and the single-member limited liability company was created. This type of limited liability company belongs to a single individual called a "manager-owner." There is no co-ownership in this type of company, except in the case of succession upon death.

The above-mentioned amendment also stipulates that if corporations and limited liability companies do not have at least two partners or shareholders, they must be transformed into single-member limited liability companies; if they do not comply with this stipulation they may be officially dissolved.

The denomination of this company should have the name or at least the initials of the name of the "manager-owner" plus the corporate form. This name cannot be similar or identical to one previously registered.

The capital assigned to single-member limited liability companies must not be less than the product of the multiplication of the minimum wage of the general employee times 10 (this is currently valued at USD 2,400).

The owner of this type of company may incorporate several "one-person limited liability companies," but the corporate purpose (a single activity) must be different in each one, and their corporate names must not cause the public to confuse them. Nevertheless, these companies are not permitted to contract or negotiate between themselves, or with people whose family ties with them are within the fourth degree of consanguinity or second degree of affinity, as defined in the Civil Code.

The liabilities of the manager-owner are limited to the amount of their paid-in capital.

Joint Ventures

Ecuadorian law does not recognize the joint venture as a legal business structure; it is treated as an association contract subscribed to by two or more parties to carry out specific projects or a particular business activity. There is no obligation to register a joint venture with any public entity.

The rights and duties of the associates are regulated by the terms of the contract entered into by the parties. There is no limited liability, which means that the associates are liable to third parties with their own assets.

Investments in and Mergers with Existing Entities

According to Ecuadorian Corporate Law, companies are allowed to merge for the following reasons:

a) When two or more companies merge to form a new company.
b) When one or more companies are absorbed by another company, which acquires all of the absorbed companies' assets and continues to exist.

A merger may be completed only between Ecuadorian companies. Therefore, if a foreign investor is interested in investing by conducting a corporate merger, the investor should incorporate a domestic company first.

Agency, Reseller, Distribution Networks, and Franchising

Agency

It is called a "commissioned agency" when foreign companies select and hire Ecuadorian individuals or legal entities that have infrastructure and experience in product sales in order to accomplish the marketing of products in Ecuador. The foreign company pays a commission to the agent for the sale of products. To achieve this kind of business, the foreign company usually uses a local company, that is, a company established in Ecuador.

Reseller

It is called "resale" when the agents buy import products strictly using their own funds and resell the products at a higher price, directly assuming responsibility for the business and usefulness of the business, as well as the declaration and payment of taxes. Local companies, meaning Ecuadorian companies, are usually used for this kind of business transaction.

Distribution Networks

A network distributor is an individual or legal entity based in Ecuador that buys and imports large quantities of products owned by foreign companies and then sells them wholesale within the country. The distributor is characterized by maintaining a stock of inventories of products within the company to meet the needs of a particular sector of the country's population. There are two types of distribution agreements in Ecuador, namely: (a) free distribution, which allows the distributor to maintain independence from the manufacturer or producer, thus assuming the management and associated responsibilities of the business itself, and reporting only to the foreign company; and (b) integrated distribution, that is, assuming the discipline and conditions of the manufacturer, thereby losing a certain amount of autonomy but receiving as a benefit the exclusive distribution of products.

The agency, resale, and distribution are business structures that are regulated by a general legal framework, namely the Commercial Code and Civil Code, in which no specific provisions for these types of contracts are contained. The lack of provisions in the Commercial Code and Civil Code causes the contract or agreement between the parties to have particular importance, as it is in that document that the rights and obligations of the signatories are described.

However, it is important to note that with respect to those contracts that relate to the business structures mentioned above and that were entered into prior to September 19, 1997, these contracts and relationships were regulated by the Law on Protection Agents, Representatives, and Distributors of Foreign Enterprises (Supreme Decree 1038-A, RO 245, 31-XII-76 and its interpretative law Act 125, RO 982, 5-VII-96); these laws and supreme decrees particularly regulated the issue of compensation in the case of unilateral termination. However, that law was repealed by Law 22, which was announced in Official Gazette No. 156, of September 19, 1997. Only relationships that began before September 19, 1997, may still be regulated by Supreme Decree 1038-A.

Franchising

The use of franchise agreements in Ecuador has increased over the past decade, which is easy to verify when one sees chain restaurants, shops, and products that previously could not be found in the country. Hence, franchises found in Ecuador are those that legal doctrine defines as "business format" and "product distribution" franchises. In the first case, it is the obligation of the franchisor to provide the franchisee with technical assistance and business know-how. In the second case, an additional obligation is added—the obligation of the franchisor or its suppliers to provide the products.

There is no specific franchise legislation in Ecuador. As a result, the principal source of franchise obligations arises from the text of the contract entered into by the franchisor and the franchisee.

As a result, franchise agreements are subject to general rules and obligations that are consistent with the Commercial Code and Civil Code. In addition to these rules, the following requirements must be met: (a) those relating to the establishment of the business that will operate the franchise, usually a local company, which is subject to the tax rules; (b) those that involve marks and intellectual property of the franchise; and (c) those that involve anticompetitive and monopolistic contract stipulations.

Representative Offices and Other Nonpermanent Establishments

Regarding representative offices and other nonpermanent establishments, Article 9, paragraph 3 of the Regulation for the Implementation of the Organic Law on Internal Taxation refers to them as follows:

3. The term "permanent establishment" does not cover:

- The use of facilities solely for the purpose of exhibiting goods or merchandise belonging to the business entity;
- The maintenance of a location, the sole purpose of which is collecting and providing information for the company; and
- The development of activities through a broker, general commissioning agent, representative, distributor, or any other agent of an independent status, provided that such persons are acting within the ordinary course of their professional activities, and even when, to comply with the Companies Act, they have been granted power, without limiting the personal tax liability of said broker, general commission agent, representative, distributor, or mediator.

Nevertheless, the representatives of the respective companies that use the abovementioned locations must register themselves with the National Register of Taxpayers, provided that such use is for a period exceeding one month and without having the obligation to submit declarations or withhold tax payments. As a result of this legal reference, such representative offices and permanent establishments are not liable to income tax. The professionals that work in representative offices and other nonpermanent establishments, because they are not particularly regulated by Ecuadorian law, are subject to the general conditions of the obligations stipulated in the Civil Code and conditions that are more specific when occurring between traders.

Finally, all of these businesspeople or entities are subject to Article 6 of the Companies Act, which states, "Any domestic or foreign company that negotiates or enters into commitments in Ecuador must have an agent or representative available within the Republic/country to answer demands and fulfill the respective obligations."

Approvals and Registrations

The Business Association

The Superintendency of Companies is the authority that controls business associations (corporations, limited liability corporations, and branches of foreign companies). The incorporation procedure involves the following steps:

- The company's name must be approved. It cannot be similar to that of an existing company. However, in the case of a local branch of a foreign company, it must use the same name as the parent office even if another company with the same name already exists in Ecuador.
- A provisional bank account for the company must be opened.
- The deed of incorporation with the bylaws and provisional account certificate must be submitted to the Superintendency of Companies. In the case of a local branch of a foreign company, a power of attorney should also be submitted.
- Corporate documents are reviewed and approved by the Superintendency of Companies.
- The registration process takes place at the municipality and the Mercantile Register.
- Shareholders have their first meeting, to approve the process and appoint the first officers. This does not apply to a local branch of a foreign company.
- Registration of the officer's appointments is made at the Mercantile Registrar.
- A tax ID number for the company (RUC) and number to import goods (if required) should be obtained.
- The initial deposit of the paid-in capital should be collected.
- Registration of foreign investment is made in the case of a branch of a foreign company or if the new shareholder of the domestic company is a foreign person.

The incorporation process takes approximately three to four weeks, after which the company is fully operative.

The Civil Corporation

There is no public entity that controls this type of corporation. The incorporation procedure involves the following steps:

- Submission of the deed of incorporation with the bylaws to the Civil Court in the company's domicile jurisdiction.
- Review and approval of the corporate documents by the Civil Judge.
- Registration process (municipality and Mercantile Registrar).
- First meeting of shareholders, approving the process and appointing the first administrators.
- Registration of appointments of the corporate administrators.
- Obtainment of a tax ID number for the company (RUC) and a number to import goods (if required).

Once incorporated, and regardless of its legal form, the company must declare taxes each month, and once a year the company must declare its annual income.

Additionally, in the case of the business association, it must pay the Superintendency of Companies an annual rate that is determined by the corporation's assets, and it must annually submit the following documents to the Superintendency of Companies: financial statements; general balance sheet; profit and loss statement; earnings distribution report; income tax return; lists of managers, legal representatives, and partners or shareholders; general manager's or legal representative's report; and other relevant information.

Sensitive Economic Sectors/Restrictions on Foreign Ownership

The Ecuadorian Constitution states that foreigners who find themselves in Ecuadorian territory have the same rights and responsibilities as Ecuadorians. Therefore, foreign individuals or legal entities may invest in Ecuador in all economic sectors, with some regulations.

The Law of Companies describes foreign companies as branches or subsidiaries of companies established outside of the country. However, branches of foreign companies are not considered to be national companies with foreign capital.

Companies or other foreign businesses organized as legal entities that will perform public works, offer public services, exploit natural resources, or habitually exercise their activities in the country, should set up a domicile for the foreign company in Ecuador in order to comply with the Law of Companies.

Foreign companies and local companies that have foreign capital should register their investment with the Central Bank. If this is not done within 45 days (from the date of the legalization of the investment), the company must pay a fine of at least USD 20. The registration with the Central Bank is for statistical purposes.

Foreigners and foreign legal entities can be shareholders in national public limited companies and corporations (sociedades anónimas or SAs). Foreign legal entities cannot be partners in limited liability companies (compañías limitadas or Cía. Ltda.).

Companies that are based in Ecuador and national companies that maintain foreign capital from legal entities must annually submit to the Superintendency of Companies a power of attorney (so that they are represented in Ecuador), a list of the shareholders in the foreign company, and a certificate that proves the legal existence of the foreign company.

In certain cases, in order to obtain a concession of permission to operate (in Ecuador), an Ecuadorian company is required to maintain 51 percent of the shares in the name of an Ecuadorian individual or legal entity.

With regard to sensitive economic sectors such as mining, chemicals, hydrocarbons, and petroleum, there may soon be increased fiscal and environmental control, along with increased participation on the part of the state relative to the utilities and royalties that these companies generate.

Political Risk and Related Issues

In 1979, Ecuador was the first South American country to pull itself out of the dictatorship model that had plagued South American politics and geopolitics since the mid-1960s. Ever since then, Ecuador has been a political democracy, and more recently a social-political democracy, with obligatory suffrage for adults. Since the Constitution of 2008, 16-year-olds and permanent-resident foreigners with more than five years of residency can also vote in all elections.

The present government has outlasted several previous governments, and continues to have relatively high levels of acceptance. This means that the president is likely to last the full term of elected office and may be re-elected for another four-year term until 2017. The governing model is left-populist, with a strong drawing in of powers to the central government, and a drawing in of those central government powers to the Office of the presidency.

Risks

Present and foreseeable political risks include:

- *Press and media freedoms.* The government has sought and received legislation that limits the rights of the media and increases government control over news coverage.
- *Land ownership.* The 2008 Constitution has placed restrictions on land ownership by foreigners in border, shore, and national security areas, and has placed potential limits or prohibitions on foreign ownership of land around water sources. It is also requesting laws that will provide greater discretion to the government in determining what lands may be expropriated if social goals are not met by the present property owners.
- *Government contracts.* The government has shown that it is a hard bargainer over terminations and renewals of these contracts.
- *Bilateral guarantees.* The government is seeking the termination of a number of bilateral trade and investment treaties, which could place contracts and relationships at a disadvantage for investors from those countries.

Improvements

- The relationship between Ecuador and Colombia has improved.
- The relationship between Ecuador and Peru remains stable and friendly.
- The relationship between Ecuador and Brazil has improved.

INVESTMENT ISSUES AND TAX INCENTIVES

Legal Treatment of Foreign Investment

The Ecuadorian legal system gives equal treatment to foreign investment, as if it were national. The Law and Regulations on Promotion and Guarantee of Investments[2] and the Foreign Trade and Investment Law are the main legal instruments governing income and the protection of foreign investment in Ecuador. In the framework of the Andean Community, Ecuador has adopted Decisions 291 and 292.[3]

As such, the Law on Promotion and Guarantee of Investments indicates that foreign investment can be made under the same conditions as those enjoyed by investments of Ecuadorian individuals or legal entities. This means that foreign investments are not subject to prior authorization by the government of Ecuador. However, the cited law allows for discrimination between foreign and domestic investors in "strategic" areas, including fisheries, mining, and hydrocarbons.

The current Ecuadorian Constitution grants certain exclusive rights to the state regarding the provision of public services, and the use and management of strategic sectors such as energy, telecommunications, nonrenewable natural resources, the transportation and refining of hydrocarbons, biodiversity, genetic heritage, and the radio-electric sector.[4] Therefore, private investment in these areas is subject to permits, concessions, or other restrictions that apply to both nationals and foreign investors.

The Ecuadorian regulatory framework extends to any kind of capital transfer to Ecuador from abroad, carried out by foreign individuals or legal entities, for the production of goods and services.[5] This definition includes financial resources in freely convertible currency, and other tangible and intangible assets, including trademarks and industrial designs.[6]

The Central Bank of Ecuador is the entity that records foreign investment in Ecuador. Once notified by the investor, the Central Bank creates a registration record after each investment has been realized.[7] According to authorities, this record is kept for statistical purposes. Domestic investments do not need to be registered with the Central Bank. The investor may delegate the management of the registration to a representative. According to the type of investment, one or more of the following documents are required in order to complete the registration: a copy of the deed, a proof of sale of foreign currency, the importation document, and the documents authorizing the transfer of shares. Registration is a simple process, provided that one fulfills all of the formal requirements.

In principle, there are no restrictions on the methods of investment through which foreign investors can be established in Ecuador. However, investors in the oil sector, both domestic and foreign, are bound by a contract with the state oil company.

Treaties of Foreign Investment Protection

The Law on Promotion and Guarantee of Investments and Decision 291 of the Andean Community guarantee foreign investors the right to transfer the profits generated by their investments to locations abroad. Investors may also freely transfer resources abroad that they obtain through the liquidation and sale of stocks, shares, or rights.

Ecuador has signed bilateral investment agreements with several countries, and has made agreements to avoid double taxation with respect to income tax in Belgium, Brazil, Chile, France, Germany, Italy, Mexico, Romania, Spain, and Switzerland.

There is also a system to avoid double taxation between the countries in the Andean Community.[8]

The Ministry of Industry and Productivity and COMEXI CORPEI are the entities responsible for implementing policies to promote and encourage foreign investment. Created in 1997 by means of the Foreign Trade and Investment Law, CORPEI is a private nonprofit organization recognized by the state as the official agency dedicated to the promotion of exports and investments. To fulfill its mission, CORPEI conducts outreach programs and outreach opportunities for investment in Ecuador's image abroad and organizes investment missions. Other institutions working with CORPEI to stimulate investment are the commercial and foreign services of Ecuador, the chambers of industry, and the provincial commissions dedicated to the promotion of exports and investments, among others.

Publicly Held Companies—Capital Market Regulations

In the past four years, Ecuadorian entrepreneurs have changed their mentality, replacing the previous use of the financial system with that of the stock exchange as a new source of funding, with enormous benefits in terms of time and conditions. As the characteristics of the commercial paper are created to suit the needs of the issuing companies, payment of return has been made more flexible, so that the issuance of bonds, securitization, and trading of commercial papers are now the mechanisms through which additional resources are obtained to finance and plan the expansion of a business or investment in working capital. Additionally, companies have found that local capital markets are an important mechanism for achieving greater visibility and competitiveness in the market.

It has become easier to find issuers or public sector investors, as there is an aggressive public institutions plan with excess cash flow to acquire the securities traded on the stock market.[9] Furthermore, private investors and investment funds administrators now actively participate in the acquisition of securities, and it currently takes between 15 days and one month to place or sell 100 percent of a securities issue, both in the private and public sector.

The supervision and control of the securities market in Ecuador have worked quite well. The securities market is primarily regulated by the Securities Market Law, the General Rules of the Securities Market Law, and resolutions issued by the National Securities Council.[10] The National Securities Council is the institution responsible for establishing the general policy of the market and for regulating the operations of the entities participating in the market, as well as the operation of the market itself. The National Securities Council is part of the Superintendency of Companies.[11]

Ecuador has two stock exchanges actively engaged in intermediation: the Stock Exchange of Quito and the Stock Exchange of Guayaquil.[12] By law, these stock exchanges have self-regulatory power over their activities.[13] Also, the only broker-dealers authorized by law are the brokerage houses, legal entities that can negotiate on behalf of third parties or on their own behalf, both in the stock market and in transactions that are not connected to the stock market. The existence of rating agencies is of fundamental importance. These agencies are subject to the control and vigilance of the National Securities Council; they provide their opinions on the solvency and ability to make payments of companies that are issuing securities or intend to do so.[14]

Securities are traded on stock exchanges, which provide two systems of trading, or "ruedas de bolsa" (market rounds).

The rueda de piso consists of physical attendance on the part of the securities dealers, but currently this system is very rarely used. The rueda electronica, which is used more often, is an interconnected system in which supply, demand, and closures operations are performed through a computer network. Currently, the stock exchanges use high-quality technology, allowing flexibility in the negotiations of dematerialized securities, which are electronically negotiated securities accepted by Ecuadorian legislation.

The Ecuadorian securities market has the following advantages.

- The Ecuadorian market is an organized, integrated, and transparent market in which securities intermediation is competitive, orderly, and continuous as a result of accurate, complete, and timely information.
- It promotes the generation of savings, which aids investment.
- It generates an important and continuous flow of resources for short-term and long-term financing.

Alternative Investment Structures—Investment Funds

In Ecuador, the Securities Market Law regulates three types of investment funds, all managed by companies of Administrators of Investment Funds and Trusts: (i) *Managed Investment Funds* are authorized to capture and invest public resources under the parameters set forth in the Securities Market Law, in which investors will be the owners of participation units and have the power to enter and exit the fund at will. (ii) *Collective Funds* are created to invest in productive projects or securities of medium liquidity. Their constitution is by public bid and contributions are freely negotiable through the stock exchanges of the country. (iii) *International Funds* are mutual funds incorporated in Ecuador that are limited to foreign investments, or whose liquid assets will be invested in securities both domestically and internationally, or funds established abroad by nationals or foreigners—which may operate in the domestic market and which are established by contributions from Ecuadorians or foreigners.[15]

In the market, investment and trust fund administration companies have a variety of managed funds in which the investor can deposit money, according to the terms and levels of risk and return. They can be classified as follows.

Equity funds: Some or all of the fund is invested in stocks of companies with
    very strong cash flows.

Fixed income funds: These funds are invested in securities such as promissory notes, guarantees, bills of exchange, and Central Bank securities.
    In accordance with their term, they can be divided into short-term (with
    maturities less than 180 days), medium-term (with maturities greater than
    180 days but less than three years), and long-term (with maturities greater
    than three years).

Each fund has its own internal regulation that indicates the commission
charged for its services, minimum entry participation, the cost of exiting the fund,
the minimum stay, and other conditions.

At the beginning, each fund has assets or net assets, which are divided into
shares or participation units. The fund is administered by specialized technicians
who invest the money on a daily basis, basing their decisions on their perception of
the best options within and outside the stock market.

The amount invested will generate a return that will reflect daily on the value
of the share or unit of participation, indicating the number acquired upon entering
and the dollar sales value when exiting the fund.

OPERATIONAL LEGAL ENVIRONMENT

Tips on Negotiating in Ecuador

While there are a number of business negotiation styles in Ecuador, all business
agreements should be put in writing, and in many cases, those written agreements
should be notarized as public documents or deeds (escrituras).

Individual Worker Negotiations

At the individual level of work and payment negotiations with domestic employees
(for example, nannies, maids, drivers, gardeners, assistants, factotums, and cooks),
beware of agreements that do not strictly follow the law. Even if the worker offers
to forego social security payments, there is at least an 80 percent chance that at
the termination of employment, the worker or the worker's family will bring labor,
tax, and social security claims that can overwhelm whatever savings the worker
may initially have suggested. This is true of business employees up to and including
negotiations with general managers and attorneys-in-fact. Furthermore, vehicle,
home, and land purchases and leases should be negotiated very carefully and with
the assistance of a lawyer from the time of any serious offer.

Formalities

In business negotiations, preliminary formalities and small talk are still important,
but they are not as lengthy as they once were. Knowing about and asking about

family members and business associates is still a worthwhile method of creating an initially secure negotiating atmosphere. Invitations to lunch and dinner, and more recently, breakfast, are expected as part of the negotiating process. However, overly expensive hospitality is not necessary, and in some situations it can even be counterproductive for businesspeople who are looking for serious business partners.

Negotiating Government Contracts

Whether or not it actually occurs, be prepared for undue payment requests from government functionaries at all levels of the pre- and postcontract negotiations. In Ecuador, government contracts can be won without the payment of bribes. Make it clear from the beginning that you must comply with both your company rules and your country's laws prohibiting the payment of bribes; use lawyers, accountants, and other agents with reputations for refusing to pay bribes. Make sure that you and all of your agents treat government functionaries as worthwhile human beings. Be trustworthy yourself. The negotiation of bribes should not be confused with the negotiation of government contracts. Like the hostage-situation negotiator, you may repeatedly have to let the other party know that its bribe demand is not negotiable, but look for legitimate benefits that you can provide as part of the real negotiation on the government contract. You should also make other parties aware of the real punishment that they could suffer in losing visa rights, losing face in the community, losing future business opportunities, and losing sleep over whether the next morning their names will appear on the news in a corruption exposé.

Eye Contact, Nose Angle, and Voice Level

Maintain comfortable, but not constant, eye contact. Ecuadorian negotiators are not intimidated or put off by eye contact, but they find it natural for themselves and others to sometimes look down or away, as part of the thought process. Try to keep your nose level. As in most Western societies, tilting your nose up is a sign that you are trying to make the other party feel inferior. Voices are modulated and rarely loud, even at dinner.

Foreign Exchange

The U.S. Dollar

The U.S. dollar is the national currency of Ecuador. Paper currency is purchased by the Ecuadorian government directly from the U.S. government. U.S. coins are used in circulation. In particular, U.S. 50-cent and U.S. dollar coins are in general circulation in Ecuador, even though they are not generally circulated in the United States. Ecuador also has its own fractional dollar currency coins.

Transfer Tax

There are no limitations on repatriation or movement of money across borders. However, there is presently a 2 percent tax on the sending of money outside of

Ecuador. This is true of currency, coins, checks, and electronic credit and payment transfers, and whether the transfer is done through banks, other credit institutions, by courier, or by mail.

Foreign Exchange Market

Prior to the dollarization of Ecuador's currency, there was a thriving, open, and legal foreign exchange market. However, since dollarization, foreign exchange dealers have largely closed their doors due to lack of business.

Large Exchanges between ALBA Member Countries

The members of the incipient **Bolivian Alliance of the Americas (ALBA) are** presently attempting to use a supranational credit value for significant intercountry value exchanges. This exchange value currency is called **Sistema Unitario de Compensación Regional (the Regional Unified Compensation System), or "the Sucre,"** in remembrance of Ecuador's previous currency of the same name.

Immigration and Visa Requirements

General Information

A valid passport with at least six months of remaining validity is required to enter Ecuador. Tourists must also provide evidence of return or onward travel. Ecuador has a policy of open frontiers; therefore, citizens of most countries in the world do not need a visa if they intend to stay for 90 days or less.

Foreigners who remain in Ecuador past the expiration dates on their visas (or past approved periods of extended stay with a valid passport) are barred from re-entering Ecuador for 12 consecutive months, starting from the date of departure.

Individuals intending to work or to live in Ecuador must obtain a visa allowing them to work in the country. Ecuadorian Immigration Law distinguishes two different categories of visas: immigrant visas and nonimmigrant visas.

Immigrant Visas

Immigrant visas are granted to foreigners intending to live permanently in Ecuador. Immigrant visas are granted for an indefinite term. However, there is a limitation on the amount of time that residents (or immigrant visa holders) are allowed to leave and remain outside of Ecuador. In the first two years of residency, one may not remain outside of Ecuador for more than 90 days per year. After the second year, this maximum period of time increases to 18 consecutive months.

Immigrant visas can be obtained within Ecuador if the foreigner holds a valid prior visa, or at the Ecuadorian consulate if the visa was previously approved by the Foreigners Bureau (Dirección de Extranjería), and if the Consul receives prior authorization from the Ministry of Foreign Affairs to stamp the visa. There are seven types of immigrant visas.

Nonimmigrant Visas

Nonimmigrant visas are temporary visas, which allow multiple entries to foreigners during the term of the visa. Nonimmigrant visas are granted for periods from 90 days up to two years, with the possibility of renewing the visa or obtaining a visa in a different visa category while remaining in Ecuador.

Nonimmigrant visas can be applied for and obtained in Ecuador, or at the closest Ecuadorian consulate with jurisdiction over a foreigner's area of residence.

If a foreigner has all of the proper documentation, visas will be granted in Ecuador within approximately seven business days, and within one to five business days at the Ecuadorian consulates, depending on each consulate's procedures. There are 11 types of nonimmigrant visas.

Import and Export Issues

Imports

All Ecuadorian or foreign persons or corporations with domicile in Ecuador may import goods to Ecuador. In order to import any goods, the importers must obtain a tax number, register themselves as importers on the Customs Agency's web page, and register their signature, or the signature of the representative of the importer, with the Interactive System for Customs Operation (SICE).

In addition to import duties, all imports are subject to a 12 percent value added tax, 0.5 percent children's development fund tax, and 2 percent remittance tax. In addition, some luxury products are subject to a special consumption tax. Many products, however, enter the market without paying normally required tariffs and taxes, if certain conditions are met.

A wide range of products must comply with Ecuadorian standards (INEN). In addition, before being imported to Ecuador some products must obtain a prior authorization from various government agencies (such as sanitary registrations).

Ecuador maintains a ban on the import of some products such as used motor vehicles, used tires, and used clothing.

In December 2008, the Ecuadorian Quality Council (CONCAL) changed labeling compliance requirements for some specific items; it also imposed specific requirements on certain imported goods. An authorized customs agent must manage all import procedures.

Exports

All exporters must obtain a tax number and register themselves as exporters on the Customs Agency's web page.

Exporters can recover any VAT paid for the production of the exported goods. The Ecuadorian Internal Revenue Service (SRI) administers the refund. A special procedure must be followed in order to obtain a refund.

General Information

It is important to note that Ecuador is a member of the WTO and is part of the Andean Community Region and the ALADI (Asociación Latinoamericana de Integración).

Taxation of Business and Other Cross-Border Transactions

Personal Income Tax

In Ecuador, taxation of Ecuadorian residents is based on the "worldwide source" principle, where all income received from anywhere by a resident is subject to income tax. A "resident" under the Ecuadorian Tax Law is a person who has been in Ecuador for more than 183 days in a given fiscal year (January 1 to December 31).

Taxable income includes business profit, salaries, interest, rental income, dividends, and other income. It is important to note that all foreign income previously subject to any type of tax in the foreign/source country is considered "exempt income" for income tax purposes. However, Ecuadorian law treats income received from a tax haven or low taxation jurisdiction differently. Therefore, if a resident's income comes from one of these countries or jurisdictions, further analysis will have to be performed.

The current income tax rate for individuals can be up to 35 percent. Every resident has the right to deduct certain personal expenses under the Ecuadorian Tax Law.

Corporate Tax

Ecuadorian companies, and foreign companies with local branches in Ecuador, are subject to Ecuadorian income tax. The current corporate income tax rate is 25 percent, but it can be lowered to 15 percent if the corporation increases its capital with the revenue obtained in the fiscal year and uses it to acquire new equipment, machinery, or software.

Dividends

Dividends are subject to income tax if (a) they are paid to shareholders located in countries considered to be tax havens or countries with low taxation rates, in which case dividends will be subject to a 10 percent withholding; (b) they are paid to Ecuadorian residents (individuals), in which case they will be subject to a withholding of from 1 percent to 10 percent depending on the amount of the dividend.

Dividends paid to shareholders that are Ecuadorian corporations, foreign corporations, or individuals who do not meet the conditions described above will not be subject to any withholding.

Withholdings for Income Tax Purposes

Nonresidents (individuals or legal entities) will be subject to a flat 25 percent income tax withholding for services subject to income tax. The only circumstance where withholdings will not apply is if a Treaty to Avoid Double Taxation exists.

Exceptions include payments for imported goods and payment of credits properly registered with the Ecuadorian Central Bank; for this last case, certain conditions must be met.

Treaties to Avoid Double Taxation

Ecuador has signed Treaties to Avoid Double Taxation with more than 20 countries; special conditions for certain types of income are detailed in each treaty. The scope of each treaty is limited to residents of the signatory countries and to the matter of income tax.

Value Added Tax

Value added tax (VAT) is applicable to the transfer or importation of goods and services, or to the payment of any intellectual property fee. Exceptions are provided in the Ecuadorian Tax Regime Law for certain transfers or importation of goods and services. For example, export of goods and services is subject to a VAT of 0 percent.

Exporters have the right to recover the VAT paid in the production of the exported goods, which includes tourist activities, when certain conditions are met.

Remittance Tax

Cross-border money operations and transactions, with or without the intervention of the financial system, beginning January 1, 2010, are subject to a 2 percent tax on the amount remitted. If the transfer is made by the financial system, the financial institution as a retention agent, at the time of the transfer, will collect the tax. If the transfer is not made through the financial system, the taxpayer must file a return and pay the tax.

All payments for importations will be subject to this tax, even in cases where the payment was made from outside of Ecuador. Ecuadorians, as well as foreign travelers leaving Ecuador with an amount up to USD 8,910, are exempt from the 2 percent tax.

Special Consumption Tax

This tax is applied to local and imported cigarettes, beer, beverages, liquor, and luxury items in general. Items subject to this tax and its exceptions are listed in Ecuadorian Tax Law.

Extraordinary Income Tax

This is an annual tax applied to the income earned by companies that have signed contracts with the government for the exploration and exploitation of nonrenewable resources. The tariff is 70 percent of the total amount of extraordinary income.

This tax is considered a deductible expense for income tax purposes.

Property Tax

There is an annual tax on rural properties over 25 hectares. The tariff is USD 8.91 per hectare. There are specific exemptions if certain conditions are met.

In addition to this tax, the municipalities charge a property tax on rural and urban properties. The tariff is up to 2 percent of the value of the property.

Labor and Employment

According to Ecuadorian Law there are two possible ways to hire someone's services: through a civil relationship agreement, or through a labor agreement.

Private sector entities or persons may hire services through civil agreements only when the services to be performed are not part of the regular and habitual activities of the hiring party, and when the service provider has total independence and infrastructure to perform the services.

Concerning labor relationships, Ecuadorian labor law favors employees and is very protective of their rights.

Ecuadorian Law permits several kinds of labor contracts. The following are the most common ones: probationary contracts as part of a fixed-term contract for up to 90 days; fixed-term contracts for one year (renewable for one additional year); indefinite contracts; piece-work contracts; contracts for specific work; temporary contracts; occasional contracts; seasonal contracts; apprentice contracts, and part-time employment contracts. Labor contracts by the hour are no longer permitted in Ecuador, and outsourcing is also forbidden.

Ecuadorian Labor Law states that employees are to perform their services five days per week (Monday to Friday, unless expressly authorized by the Ministry of Labor), and for up to eight hours per day. Overtime payments are applicable to work that exceeds the regular eight hours per day, to work on Saturdays and Sundays, and to night-shift work.

The Ecuadorian government annually fixes the minimum wage applicable for a regular employee. For the year 2010, the minimum wage for an employee working eight hours per day was USD 240 per month (proportional part applicable to part-time contracts). In the course of a labor relationship, in addition to the monthly salary, the following costs are also applicable:

	Description of the Cost	Regular Payment Period	Recipient Payee	Applicable Amount
1	Salary	Monthly Basis	Employee	
2	Thirteenth Salary	Annual Basis	Employee	The value of the salary earned during the year (from December 1 to November 30 of the following year) divided by 12
3	Fourteenth Salary	Annual Basis	Employee	One month's minimum wage (USD 240 for year 2010) paid as a bonus once a year
4	Vacation	Annual Basis	Employee	15 days of paid vacation, or a monetary compensation of one-twenty-fourth of the employee's income for the year
5	Mandatory Contribution to the Social Security	Monthly Basis	National Social Security Institute (IESS)	9.35 percent of the employee's salary to be paid by the employee; 12.15 percent to be paid by the employer
6	Reserve Funds	Annual Basis, but starting from the second year	National Social Security Institute (IESS)	8.33 percent of the employee's salary
7	Profit Sharing	Annual Basis	Employee	15 percent of the employer's profits, distributed among the employees

Antitrust and Competition Issues

Present Status

In the absence of a national antitrust law, the Andean Community Decision 608, Norms for the Protection and Promotion of Free Competition in the Andean Community, became the law of the Republic of Ecuador, and the first Administrative Resolutions were handed down in 2010. Currently, the governmental authority charged with this area is the Sub-Secretary of Competition and Consumer Defense of the Ministry of Industries and Productivity.

So far, three cases have been decided by the Ministry of Industry after administrative review by the Sub-Secretary of Competition. These cases included:

- Pricing on government-required mandatory car insurance for personal injury medical costs;
- Two cases concerning predatory pricing claims in the airline industry

In 2010, more than a dozen cases were presented before the Competition Sub-Secretary.

At present, a pre-bill on antitrust and competition is being passed around the Ministry of Industry, which will soon be presented to the president, who is expected to send it to the National Assembly within the next year.

Prior Antitrust and Unfair Competition Laws

Under both supranational Andean Community law and Ecuadorian modernization laws, certain monopolistic practices, such as "tie-in" arrangements, have been illegal for many years. Unfair competition prohibitions were written into the Ecuadorian Intellectual Property Law, No. 83, in May of 1998. That law was related only to unfair competition in the IP area, and it was rarely used on its own.

It appears that the proposed antitrust and free competition bill will remove IP "unfair competition" jurisdiction to the future governmental body that controls the wider array of competition matters.

Environmental Issues

Ecuador is known for its mega-biodiversity. In recent years a series of laws and regulations have been enacted in order to protect the environment. The first significant legislation (1999) required that any new project with a potential significant impact to the environment would need an environmental license prior to initiation.

Conflicts over which governmental entity was in charge became a bit clearer only in 2010. The national authority in charge of granting environmental licenses is currently the Ministry of Environment. The exception to this rule lies in the authority given to the municipalities in relation to the activities within the respective municipal jurisdictions.

It is not always clear which business activities require a prior environmental license; however, most activities that might have an impact on a community or on the environment should be understood to require an environmental license. Within the list of activities that require a license we find the following: all mining, oil, and gas; all major construction activities, including the building of roads and dams; all power generation projects; all new industrial projects, including the building of any industrial plant; all forestry and flower projects; and new tourism operations, including the introduction of new vessels in the Galapagos. A number of other activities should require an environmental license but presently lack sufficient enforcement, such as new farming activities, major developments, and real estate projects, especially outside the city limits, and smaller industrial projects that may have the potential to impact the community or the environment.

As to the process of obtaining the license, the general regulations require the approval of the terms of reference (TDR) for the preparation of an environmental impact assessment (EIA), which normally must include the possible social and environmental effects as well as mitigation measures. A diffusion process for the EIA includes risk assessment and the mitigation measures. After an evaluation by the authority, a license could be granted. The diffusion process is not currently being enforced by the majority of municipalities, although the law does not provide any exception to this requirement for the municipalities.

At the national level, very few licenses have been granted to the private sector, and there is a backlog at the level of the Ministry of Environment that is significantly delaying investment projects, especially in mining and power generation.

Under the 2010 regulations, public diffusion of the proposed projects should be carried out by the government authorities; it should not be carried out directly by the interested party. However, the process has not yet been implemented. Although the opinion of the community has no binding effect, the competent authority should carefully consider and evaluate the position of the community when issuing a license.

The length of time it takes to obtain a license is estimated at about one year for large national private projects, and approximately four months for municipal projects.

Consumer Protection and Products Liability

Ecuadorian Law treats consumer protection matters very seriously. The Constitution establishes several provisions regarding the rights of consumers. According to such provisions, a fundamental principle of consumer protection is that every person not only has the right of access to high-quality goods and services, but also has the right to freely choose among these goods and services.

Provisions regarding public information and advertisements are also included in the Constitution to protect consumer rights. One of these provisions states that, in order for consumers to be able to fulfill their rights, the producers and services providers must provide information about the contents and characteristics of every product and service; and furthermore that listed prices must include all applicable taxes and surcharges.

Fraudulent information, misleading advertisements, or product adulteration can lead to civil or criminal liability for the producer or service provider.

According to Ecuadorian Law, if a product or service has caused any kind of damage to a consumer, then all producers, manufactures, importers, distributors, traders, or any other persons that have intervened in the manufacturing or distribution and sales process of that product or service could be held *jointly* responsible for those damages.

The Organic Law for Consumer Protection declares that, in case there are any doubts about contractual provisions or legal regulations, those doubts should always be interpreted in favor of the consumer. Moreover, if producers or service providers try to avoid their responsibility through contractual provisions, these provisions could be declared null and void.

If a producer or service provider has violated the rights of any consumer, then the affected consumer may initiate legal actions based on that violation. The Organic Law for Consumer Protection also provides some alternative compensation measures for consumers who have had a negative consumer experience. These alternative compensation measures include the right to the free repair of the defective product, the exchange of the product for a similar one, or even a full refund of the purchase price. Fines and indemnity payments can also be charged against the infringing producer or service provider.

In Ecuador, these kinds of rights must be claimed individually. The legal system does not allow class actions or collective claims.

Arbitration is possible between consumers and producers/providers. Nevertheless, in the case of preprinted contracts, additional evidence of the consumer's confirmation of accepting arbitration is required, in order to impose the arbitration process on the consumer.

Preprinted contracts are considered to be "adhesion contracts," which must follow certain rules in order to be valid.

Land Use and Real Estate

In order to have the legal right to use and control a piece of a real estate in Ecuador, an acquisition process is necessary. Therefore, it is important for a future owner to consider a variety of matters under Ecuadorian Law.

In the acquisition of a piece of real estate by means of "tradición," the title of control is transferred by means of a purchase agreement. The Civil Code and the Registry Law regulate the transfer process.

A purchase agreement will not be valid and effective unless the following conditions are met:

- The purchase agreement must be completed through the signing, notarization, and recording of a public deed.
- The agreement must clearly establish the agreed-upon real estate property object and purchase price.
- In order to protect the transferred rights to the property, and in order for any improvements to be made to the property, the agreement must be registered at the Land Registry Office in the municipality where the piece of real estate is located.

There are four required steps in the purchase and sale of a piece of real estate:

1. **Legal Review and Analysis.** The lawyers should compile all the documentation related to the purchase and sale process, analyze the documents, and advise whether there is any impediment that would negatively affect sale and transfer of the property rights.
2. **Local Land Registry.** Subsequently, the transfer process is taken to the municipality in the corresponding town to record the change of ownership in the land registry system. In addition, the buyer and the seller are required to pay taxes on the real estate transfer. These taxes consist of (a) "Alcabala" (1 percent of the real estate value), generally paid by the buyer; and (b) capital gains tax (10 percent of the difference between the last purchase price and the new sales price of the piece of real estate), generally paid by the seller. In certain cities like Quito, an extra tax is paid to the Provincial Council; it can be up to 0.11 percent of the total value of the new sales price of the piece of real estate.
3. **Notary Closure.** As soon as the taxes are paid, the transfer documents and the tax receipts are presented to the corresponding notary, who prepares and formalizes the respective public deed. The notary receives approximately 0.3 percent for the sales value of the property shown in the deed.
4. **Inscription in the Land Registry.** Lastly, the purchase and sale process is filed for revision and inscription in the corresponding Land Registry, which completes the sale and transfer process. This last step includes a fee to the Land Registry of approximately 0.5 percent of the deed value, up to a maximum of USD 560.

The purchase and sale process in Ecuador takes about 20 to 30 business days.

Intellectual Property

In addition to its own Intellectual Property Law No. 83 of May 8, 1998 (www.wipo .int/clea/en/details.jsp?id=1205&tab=2), Ecuadorian intellectual property matters are controlled by the supranational law of the Andean Community of Nations:

- Common Industrial Property System (Decision 486) (http://www .comunidadandina.org/ingles/normativa/D486e.htm);
- The Common Regime on Copyright and Related Rights (Decision 351) (http://www.comunidadandina.org/ingles/normativa/D351e.htm);
- Protection of the Rights of Obtainers of Plant Varieties (Decision 345) (http://www.comunidadandina.org/ingles/normativa/D345e.htm);
- Common Regime on Access to Genetic Resources (Decision 391) (http:// www.comunidadandina.org/ingles/normativa/D391e.htm).

Intellectual property matters are also controlled by the judicial determinations (*sentencias and interpretaciones prejudiciales*) and resolutions of the Andean Community of Nations.

At a time when Ecuador had advanced further in international IP law than many other countries in Latin American, its Law No. 83 of 1998 became the legal blueprint for the later Andean Decision 486 of 2000.

In general, the levels of enforcement are highest for trademarks, trade names, commercial slogans, and geographic indications; followed by the protection of registered patents; followed by the protection of copyrights. An important exception to enforcement concerns music and video entertainment products, which are well protected on paper but tend not to be protected on the street.

Prosecution Time Lines

Trademarks generally take five to eight months to register; oppositions take about 12 months; cancellation and nullification actions take about three years. Nonpharmaceutical patent applications take about two to three years. Pharmaceutical patent registrations are relatively difficult to obtain at the present time. Ecuador is a member of the PCT (Patent Cooperation Treaty) but not a member of the Madrid System.

Obligatory Licensing of Pharmaceutical Patents is now available by presidential decree. The first Obligatory License was granted in April 2010.

Intellectual Property Application forms can be found at www.iepi.gob.ec/ index.php?option=com_content&view=article&id=54&Itemid=62.

Ecuador was the first country in the world to register a tactile trademark, the crinkled-glass bottle texture for Diageo's traditional OLD PARR whiskey.

Customs

Please see the section above titled Import and Export Issues.

Internet Regulations and E-Commerce

Given the importance of new communications technologies that have appeared in Ecuador since 2002, the Ecuadorian government believes that there is a great need to regulate the use of information systems, electronic networks, and especially Internet services in the country. For this purpose, the Congress issued the Electronic Commerce, Electronic Signatures, and Data Messages Law of 2002.

The above law regulates the following fields:

- Data messages
- Electronic signatures
- Certification services
- Electronic and telematics (data transmission) contracting
- Electronic services assistance
- Electronic commerce
- User protection in each of the fields mentioned above

Electronic data, correspondence, and signatures are now accepted as evidence in most administrative and judicial proceedings.

The Electronic Commerce, Electronic Signatures, and Data Messages Law of 2002 has helped manage technological issues in thousands of cases in the judicial system. This law also offers legal protection to all users of the diverse electronic systems and services that are part of society. It is important to emphasize that this law helped identify certain infractions in information technology, and created criminal penalties for those individuals who commit crimes or offenses in the area of information technology.

The Civil Procedure Code and the Consumer Protection Organic Law are the regulations that support the above-mentioned law.

Financing Issues/Payments

The Ecuadorian financial system could be characterized as one of universal banking, where the banks are the most important entities in the financing of businesses and they fulfill a wide variety of functions, from the issuance of credit cards to commercial leases. Private banks specialize in intermediation/brokerage, as the majority of their operations are realized by means of concession of credit, having a relatively smaller involvement in investment securities.

Following the generalized regional banking crisis of 1999, the Ecuadorian banking system maintains solid indicators for solvency, liquidity, capital gains, and income.

Between the months of December 2008 and December 2009, the banks reported a 10 percent overall growth in assets, reaching USD 1.869 billion. Likewise, the solvency index increased from 13 percent to 13.8 percent in the year 2009, which is 4.8 points above the currently required 9 percent standard.

The positive evolution of this indicator relates to the banking industry's effective application of capital and credit policies, and the constant supervision and control by the Superintendency of Banks. There is no deterioration in the overall levels of solvency of these institutions; on the contrary, it is evident that they have the capacity to respond to the liabilities and other obligations that banks have relative to their customers.

As evidence of the stability of the financial system, there are currently 25 banks in Ecuador, of which 16 (including the largest banks, in terms of assets) registered improved solvency. By virtue of this, deposits in Ecuadorian banks had increased by 6.5 percent as of December 2009.

This indicates that in Ecuador, the measures taken by the national government have successfully fulfilled the goal of slowing and reversing the decline in deposits. The client base has broadened and deposits have increased, allowing local banks to better position themselves in order to deal with the after-effects of the international financial crisis that hit the major markets worldwide.

Bank credit has declined from USD 9.653 billion to USD 9.463 billion, mirroring behavior similar to that of the banks in the region that, given the uncertainty about the scope of the international financial crisis and the reduction in consumer confidence, chose to moderate the expansion of domestic credit that had been recorded in recent years.

Public banks, meanwhile, injected USD 2.131 billion in loans during 2009, compared to USD 1.521 billion in the previous year, which greatly energized the financial market.

Available bank funds in Ecuador increased from USD 3.865 billion to USD 4.400 billion, which demonstrates that they have sufficient resources to meet the requirements of their clients.

The Superintendency of Banks, as the controlling entity of the national financial system, maintains a permanent integrated system of supervision and of evaluation of Ecuadorian banks. This system has produced good results, which are reflected in terms of trust and security of the users of the Ecuadorian banking system.

Secured Transactions

In accordance with the regulations of the Ecuadorian Financial System and its controlling entity, the Superintendency of Banks, the financial system may receive as adequate guarantees for financial operations the guarantees that are mentioned below. It is important to note that some of these guarantees may be used by businesses that are independent of the financial system, depending on the level of acceptance of these guarantees in those different business areas.

The following are considered adequate security guarantees:

- The pledging of cash deposits and other financial investments made in the same financial institution or in other institutions of the country, or titles issued under guarantee from the state or from the Central Bank of Ecuador (these last items are used in transactions that involve the Ecuadorian state). Certificates of deposit of easily realized commodities issued by bonded warehouses that specify the quality and quantity of the deposited commodity are also considered adequate guarantees.

- The guarantees that are most commonly used in business transactions between private institutions or with the finance sector are mortgages related to real estate, including those that are for accession; that is to say, all constructions and improvements joined to the principal piece of real estate. Ships and planes may also be mortgaged.
- Commercial, agricultural, and industrial guarantees are considered adequate security interests and are used very frequently. These security interests are provided on or encumber inventory, agricultural machinery, and industrial machinery, respectively.

In general, the process involved in creating guarantees and mortgages is very simple and does not last very long. The terms and conditions of this type of guarantee, duly accepted by the parties in a contract (in the case of a mortgage, this same document should be elevated to the level of a public deed), should conclude (both for guarantees and mortgages) with the registration of the guarantee and the corresponding ban on the sale or alienation of the good registered in the Public Registry of the province where the piece of real estate can be found.

Currently, the "business credit guarantee trust" is widely used as a security interest, involving the transfer or assignment of goods, monies, and securities to an authorized institution in order to realize operations of the business credit guarantee trust. The purpose of this kind of trust is to ensure that these assignments guarantee the obligations incurred on behalf of an institution that is part of the financial system or on behalf of a third-party beneficiary.

Ecuadorian legislation also accepts the following as adequate security guarantees out of the country:

- The pledging of cash deposits and financial investments in financial institutions operating outside of Ecuador, whose solvency will be accredited internationally.
- Mortgages on real estate located outside of Ecuador, for example, bonds issued by companies incorporated outside of the country, whose solvency is accredited internationally. These types of guarantees are accepted provided that the document is signed on behalf of the creditor financial institution that commits itself to the unconditional and irrevocable payment of the debtor's overdue obligations upon request of the creditor.
- Irrevocable letters of credit, letters of exchange, and additional letters of credit issued by operative banks and financial institutions outside of Ecuador (with recognized international solvency) that guarantee financing loans for exportation, and "standby" letters of credit issued by operative banks outside of Ecuador whose solvency has been accredited internationally.
- Bills of lading on the shipment of oil, as long as they refer to previously negotiated (sold) purchases of oil by the client of the financial entity.

The conditions for the acceptance of guarantees/securities, mortgages, and business credit guarantee trusts consist of the appraisal of the goods carried out by an expert evaluator, certified by the financial institution. The good, or piece of real estate, must have an insurance policy that covers all risk, duly endorsed by or on behalf of the creditor institution.

In order to appraise the goods accepted as an adequate guarantee/security interest, the commercial value of goods with similar characteristics, as well as the market conditions where the goods may be sold, must be taken into account.

With respect to guarantees established via financial instruments that are quoted on the stock market, in order to realize the appraisal of these goods, the average quotation price over the three immediately preceding months must be taken into account at the time of the appraisal.

In the case of shares that are not quoted on the stock market, their value should be calculated on the basis of the solvency and liquidity of the issuing company.

In accordance with the General Law of Institutions of the Financial System, the value of the granted credit should never be more than the value of the guarantee. Moreover, as a general rule, the adequate guarantee must have a value that is no less than 120 percent of the guaranteed obligation.

Securities Laws Issues

Please see the section above titled Alternative Investment Structures—Investment Funds.

Government Procurement

Ecuador's Public Contracting Law regulates public contracting for acquisitions, rent, public works, and professional and consulting services. Contracts for exploration and exploitation of natural resources and purchases of goods necessary for national defense are not subject to this law.

All suppliers must be registered in the Unique Registry for Suppliers (RUP). Registration is a mandatory procedure completed via the Internet that allows the person to participate in any public contracting process.

In order for a corporation (Ecuadorian or foreign company), joint venture, or branch to qualify as a supplier or a bidder, it must submit a list of shareholders until an individual can be determined to be the person interested in the bidding process. If any of the shareholders or affiliates is a corporate entity domiciled in a tax haven country, the bidder or supplier will not be allowed to participate in the bidding process, and if it does so it will be immediately disqualified from any bidding process. Branches must present a list of their headquarters' shareholders.

If a corporation or entity signs a contract with the Ecuadorian government (subject to the Public Contracting Law), before transferring any shares, interest, or rights in companies, the entity must comply with the following in order to avoid the termination of its contract by the public entity:

1. If the transfer is less than 25 percent of the capital of the entity, the private contracting party must notify the public entity within five business days.
2. If the transfer is more than 25 percent of the capital of the entity, the private contracting party must obtain prior authorization from the public entity.
3. If the private contracting party wants to engage in a capitalization, merger, or conversion that represents 25 percent or more of the private contracting party or consortium's capital, the private contracting party must obtain prior authorization from the public entity.

The law also establishes different procurement systems, from the traditional bidding process (licitación), to the new "catalog purchases" and inverse bid system (under which any contractor can lower the offer to provide a specific product to a public institution).

Public entities now sign contracts after the award of the contract and the delivery of the guarantees, without any further approval by any other authority.

The Ecuadorian government intends to promote transparency in procurement procedures; therefore all bidding procedures are published on the website www.compraspublicas.gov.ec and on the websites of the contracting agencies.

Liabilities of Company's Directors and Officers

In compliance with the Law of Companies, the administrators will have responsibility derived from the obligations that the law and the company charter dictate. However, all stipulations that tend to absolve or limit the statutory obligations of the administrators are null.

The administrators do not assume any personal obligations for the business transactions of the company due to their administrative duties; however, if it can be proven that the administrator committed a crime or is found guilty of wrongdoing, the responsibility can be personal or even criminal. The legal consequences could be criminal, for example, in the case of tax evasion, or when an administrator provides false information relative to the payment of guarantees or pledges in order to legalize the decrease in capital, when an administrator submits false balances and inventories, or when he or she hides company assets.

The administrators become exempt from responsibility (a) when the balances have been approved at a general shareholders meeting, unless they were approved because they included false information; (b) when the administrators acted in accordance with agreements made at a general shareholders meeting, unless those agreements were notoriously illegal; or (c) when there is a memorial of their opposition with regard to a decision or action requested at a general shareholders meeting. While an administrator is working for a company he or she may not go into business independently, or for someone else, in the same type of business that constitutes the company's corporate purpose unless they have expressly been given the authorization at a general shareholders meeting. "Self-contracting," or "one party acting on behalf of both parties," is prohibited.

When the company's administration entrusts itself to a group of individuals, these individuals constitute an advisory board, who will act through a president. In the company charter, it is possible to confer on the advisory board special attributes, which, according to the law, are not exclusive to the shareholders.

Litigation/Dispute Resolution Systems

Unless there is a prior ADR arrangement, the Ecuadorian public courts are the deciders of all litigation. The public courts are organized according to the subject-matter of the litigation; for example, there are civil courts, labor courts, tax courts, criminal courts, and so on.

In most circumstances, Ecuadorian Law provides for an appeal after the trial judge hands down a judgment in a case. Please bear in mind that under a current provision of the Constitution due process requires that any process must be reviewed by a higher-level court. In consequence, even those cases in which appeal is legally prohibited are being reviewed in order to determine whether that is unconstitutional. These appeals are acknowledged and reviewed by the provincial courts of the country (there is one in every province of Ecuador). Further motions for cassation (appeals on issues of law) are also possible. If these motions are granted, the case will be heard by the National Court (formerly Supreme Court).

Ecuadorian Law has established that every person has the right to free access to justice. Consequently, no public fees are to be paid in the case of litigation heard by public courts. The Ecuadorian Constitution also provides for a broad range of rights in order to guarantee due process for the parties involved in the litigation.

Arbitration, mediation, and other alternative methods of dispute resolution are legally recognized and allowed in Ecuador. Of these alternative methods, arbitration is very popular, especially in business disputes, and there are several registered Arbitration Centers throughout Ecuador. As Arbitration Centers are private entities, regular fees for arbitration apply, depending on the amount of money involved in the case in litigation.

Even though arbitration is generally permitted, a favorable pronouncement from the Attorney General of Ecuador must be obtained in order for public sector entities to enter into arbitration.

The Ecuadorian Arbitration and Mediation Law recognizes the possibility of international arbitration whenever any of the following occurs:

a. When the parties, at the time of accepting the arbitration clause, are domiciled in different countries.
b. When the place of fulfillment of a relevant part of the obligations of the contract, or the place in which the possible litigation has a closer nexus, is located outside the country. One of the parties must be domiciled in this foreign location as well.
c. When the main issue involves an international trade operation that does not affect Ecuadorian national or collective interests.

Under the present Ecuadorian Constitution, Ecuador must not enter into international treaties when the treaty implies international arbitration in the case of commercial or contractual litigation between the Ecuadorian state and other persons or entities. There are only two exceptions to this limitation: (i) international arbitration is possible when the litigation is between Ecuador and another Latin American country or the citizens of another Latin American country, provided that the Arbitration Tribunal is from a Regional Center; and (ii) when litigation is related to a foreign debt acquired by Ecuador.

Due to the previously mentioned provision of the Constitution, Ecuadorian courts have started to conduct special reviews of international treaties on the protection of foreign investments that are currently signed. An example of this is the case of the treaty between Ecuador and China in which the Constitutional Court of Ecuador has decided that Ecuador must denounce this treaty because it is in conflict with the Constitution.

CONTRACTS AND DOCUMENTS—FORMS AND ENFORCEABILITY

Ecuador follows the civil law system with similar principles to those of all civil law countries. The Ecuadorian Civil Code provides the principles of contract formation, requirements, consent, breach, and so on.

The purpose of contracts is to fulfill the will of the parties, except in circumstances that subject the parties to specific statutory provisions. In private commercial practice there are almost no restrictions on the free will of the parties, while in contracts involving government participation (public contracts) there are often statutory conditions imposed on the parties.

Private Commercial Contracts

International business terms are commonly used and applied, especially in relation to terms of payment, responsibility for the goods, warranties, and formalities. Terms of payment depend on whether it is an international contract or a local contract. For international contracts, wire transfers and letters of credit issued by banks are quite common. Payments made through escrow agents, even though possible, are not used very often.

Local contracts payments are commonly done by wire transfer, local letters of credit, or checks. Cash payments tend to be limited to smaller transactions. By law, all payments in excess of USD 5,000 must be made through the financial system.

In relation to the responsibility about the goods, ICOTERMS and other international standards are commonly used and recognized by local legislation as well. Therefore, terms such as CIF and FAS are used frequently in all international transactions, but not much in internal transactions.

The guarantees applicable to the products often create points of discussion, especially when one of the parties is from a common-law system. The meaning and scope of express and implied warranties vary substantially from one system to the other; therefore, when entering into a contract the person who wants to limit its warranty must clearly state those limitations in the contract.

In general, private commercial contracts do not require any formality; however, certain contracts, such as real estate documents, may require public notarization, and without such formality they may be null and void.

Alternative dispute resolution is open for negotiation, which may include international arbitration. Furthermore, parties may subject themselves to foreign law for the interpretation of the contract.

Public Contracts

Unlike private contracts, those entered into with any public institution are heavily regulated. Quite often, there is very little space for negotiation, pre-approved formats are the common rule, and warranty payment forms and many other conditions are normally imposed prior to the bidding process. Arbitration alternatives for dispute resolution are quite limited, and governmental entities require prior authorization from the Attorney General to include arbitration as an alternative form to resolve disputes. International arbitration is even more difficult or impossible to include in government contacts.

The law of public contracting determines most of the terms and conditions for contract formation, termination, payments, and so on. If a contract fails to include these terms and conditions, then it will be null and void. Public contracts are often biased in favor of the government, and it is sometimes difficult for private parties to enforce them.

General Forms

Forms are often used in day-to-day commercial practice and are widely accepted, with the only requirement in relation to the forms being the size of the type, which must be 10-point or larger. There is no major legislation in relation to oppressive clauses.

Enforceability

Enforcing private commercial contracts may be easier if they contain local arbitration clauses. Public contracts and any other contracts that require judicial resolution will face lengthy and time-consuming procedures, plus enforcement difficulties.

International arbitration awards are difficult to enforce locally regardless of whether the issue is with a private or public counterpart, to the point that national arbitration is recommended over international arbitration if the award will have to be enforced in Ecuador. However, securing local enforcement of foreign judicial awards is even more difficult.

ENDING OR RESTRUCTURING A BUSINESS PRESENCE

Dissolution/Liquidation

The winding up of a company is a long and complex process that is greatly affected by the profits or losses that result from the termination of the relationships that the company has acquired over the years of its existence.

The winding up or cancellation of a limited liability company or corporation happens in two phases: the first phase is the dissolution of the company, and the second phase is the liquidation and termination of the company.

Dissolution of a Company

Dissolution is a process that occurs prior to the liquidation of a company in which legal ties established between the company, third parties, and the partners of the company are resolved.

Companies can be dissolved by lawsuits or in their own right, at the will of the partners or shareholders, or by other means. In Ecuador the legal grounds for dissolution are the following:

a.   Due to the expiration of the stated life of the corporate entity;
b.   As a result of a move of the principal location (of the company) to a foreign country;
c.   Due to legally declared and court-decreed bankruptcy.

Other grounds for the dissolution of a company are:

a.   Agreement by the shareholders;
b.   Fulfillment of the company's activities or the impossibility of accomplishing the corporate purpose;
c.   A loss of 50 percent or more of the corporate capital;
d.   A merger;
e.   A reduction in the number of partners, below the minimum required number;

      f.   Failure to meet the requirements of the Superintentency of Companies for a period of five years;

      g.   Failure to increase the corporate capital to the legally established minimum;

      h.   A failure to comply with, or a violation of, the law, regulations, and/or statutes that impedes the normal corporation operation or harms the interests of the shareholders, partners, or third parties;

      i.   For obstructing or making the job of control and surveillance by the Superintendency of Companies more difficult, or for failure to comply with the resolutions of the Superintendency of Companies.

A company may begin the process of dissolution for any of these reasons, setting in motion a series of actions that lead to the liquidation of the company, while protecting the interests of third parties that have dealt with the company over the course of its existence.

Liquidation

Once a company has been dissolved it must begin the liquidation process, which constitutes the final process in the winding up of the company. Several legal actions terminate the relationships that the company has with third parties and with its partners: collection of pending accounts, payment of debts, sale of the assets of the company, and distribution of the corporate capital. The liquidation culminates with the cancellation of the resolution issued by the Superintendency of Companies. It is performed in compliance with the regulations contained in the Law of Companies, and in the resolution correspondingly issued by the Superintendency of Companies.

The resolution requires that the company name a liquidator. This person can be an outside individual or a legal representative of the company. The liquidator should be named by resolution of a general meeting of shareholders, and that resolution should be recorded in the Mercantile Registry. Liquidators are responsible for their own actions. During liquidation, once the remainder of the outstanding share capital debt has been paid, the company then will be able to complete the distribution of what remains of the company's corporate assets, or share of the liquidation, between the partners. This must be done in compliance with the established regulations for each type of company.

In Ecuador, when a company finds itself up-to-date on all of its obligations to the state (that is, the company does not have pending debts with third parties and it has completed its activities), it can dissolve itself, liquidate itself, and terminate itself in one single act.

In order to accomplish this, at a general meeting, the shareholders or partners approve the dissolution, liquidation, and cancellation of the company. They also approve a final balance of operations, in which the final remainder of the corporate assets (if it exists) is distributed. These approvals are then memorialized and recorded as a public record, and the Superintendency of Companies issues a summary or statement of that recording that must be published in a widely circulated newspaper. In this statement, a formal notice to third parties of their right to file an opposition is published, so that if, within a period of 30 days, no one has filed an opposition to this process, the Superintendency of Companies will issue a resolution approving the process and will order the cancellation of company's registration in the Mercantile Registry. With this recording, the company is canceled and no longer exists.

Reactivation of the Company

Companies engaged in the process of liquidation may reactivate themselves up until the registration of the cancellation in the Mercantile Registry. Reactivation is possible as long as the company has overcome the problem or situation that was the basis for beginning the process.

The reactivation of the company is authorized by a public document written by the company's legal representative or by the liquidator. The company's shareholders in a general meeting decide which individual will assume the company's legal representation.

The Superintendency of Companies will approve the reactivation of the company by issuing a resolution. This institution will also order the company to register itself with the Mercantile Registry.

Insolvency/Bankruptcy/Restructuring

Please see the section above titled Dissolution/Liquidation.

CONCLUSION

Since the 2008 Constitution entered into effect, Ecuador has been undergoing significant changes in its internal laws and regulations. Reforms increasingly provide the government with more control over certain strategic sectors such as mining, oil, and the media. The Ecuadorian economy will soon be adapting to changes in the hydrocarbons law, production and investments regulations (a new code to regulate production is currently under review by the government), and other structural modifications, which are currently under review either by the National Assembly (former Congress), in the first case, and within the government and private sectors. If the production code is approved, it should encourage new investments, and investors should contact Ecuadorian legal counsel to keep up with developments and take correct actions when opportunities appear.

Even with the changes introduced by the current government, there has recently been an increase of confidence in the private sector.

The currency regulations and the use of the U.S. dollar as the country's currency provide Ecuador with more certainty and control over transactions, which have led to increased business stability.

Opportunities to raise capital by investors, through direct capitalization or credit (such as factoring or creation of commercial papers sold through the stock markets) have become a good alternative for local corporations to obtain capital.

Legal matters can take a significant amount of time to reach a conclusion within the Ecuadorian judicial system; however, in recent years, alternative solutions for conflicts such as mediation and arbitration have received more recognition and are becoming a popular way to promptly and efficiently resolve conflicts.

Ecuador offers many excellent opportunities for business (especially in natural resources) with a free transfer of currency and products, but considering all the existing bureaucratic procedures, limitations on labor contracts and labor protections laws, tax changes, and the like, it highly advisable to consult with a local expert when making business decisions.

NOTES

1. CIA FACT BOOK, https://www.cia.gov/library/publications/the-world-factbook/geos/ec.html.

2. Law No. 46, Official Register 219, December 19, 1997.

3. Decisions 291 and 292 of the Andean Community, March 21, 1991.

4. Article 313, Political Constitution of the Republic of Ecuador, 2010.

5. Article 12, Law of Promotion and Guarantee of Investments.

6. Article 14, Law of Promotion and Guarantee of Investments.

7. Article 15, Law of Promotion and Guarantee of Investments, and Article 3 of Decision 291 of the Andean Community.

8. Decision 578 of the Andean Community Commission, May 4, 2004.

9. Article 37, Law of the Securities Market.

10. Article 5, Law of the Securities Market.

11. Article 9, Law of the Securities Market.

12. Chapter 1, Subtitle IV, Codification of the Resolutions of the National Securities Council.

13. Article 43, Law of the Securities Market.

14. Chapter III of the Resolutions of the National Securities Council.

15. Chapter I, Title IV, Codification of the Resolutions of the National Securities Council.

CHAPTER 7

Paraguay

Alejandro Guanes Mersan
Guanes, Heisecke & Piera, Abogados

COUNTRY OVERVIEW

Officially the Republic of Paraguay (in Spanish, República del Paraguay, and in Guaraní, Tetã Paraguái), Paraguay is known as the "Heart of the Americas." It is a landlocked country located in the heart of South America, and it is bordered by Argentina to the south and southwest, Brazil to the east and northeast, and Bolivia to the northwest. It lies 800 kilometers (497.1 miles) from the Pacific Ocean and 600 kilometers (372.8 miles) from the Atlantic Ocean. Its area covers 406,752 square kilometers or 252,744 square miles.[1]

The Paraguay River splits the territory into two clearly defined regions: the western or Chaco and the eastern sectors. The Chaco area covers 61 percent of the national territory, and comprises 2 percent of the population. The eastern region covers 39.3 percent of the total land and comprises almost all the population of the country. In terms of political division, Paraguay has 17 departments, 14 of which are located in the Oriental or eastern region and three of which are in the Occidental or western region.[2]

As of 2009 the population was estimated at 6.3 million. The capital and largest city is Asunción, which is ranked among the world's least expensive cities in which to live for the fifth year running. Paraguay differentiates itself from its neighbors with its culture and its deeply rooted traditions. The official languages are Spanish and Guaraní, both of which are widely spoken in the country.

Despite being landlocked and despite the relatively small size of its economy, Paraguay benefits from its location at the confluence of an important river system, formed by the Paraguay and Paraná rivers, both of which directly affect its territory; and the crossroads of two oceans, a situation that offers the potential for uniting the major ports and markets of South America. Because of its geographic location, Paraguay plays an important role in the future of two regional development projects. The first, called Hidrovia, includes the construction of ports and improvements to the navigability of the Paraguay River designed to make the transportation of economic products from the heart of Brazil and Paraguay easier and safer. In the bioceanic corridor, the government has initiated a project to improve the roads along the whole country, especially in the western area. The project is intended to increase the volume of trade that crosses the country from the Atlantic to the Pacific and vice versa.[3]

The Paraguayan economy can be characterized as small and open, with wide dependence on international trade and commerce. Paraguay's economy is based on the production and export of a few primary agricultural products and meat, as well as on commerce associated with the import and re-export of consumer products. Its external trade represented 61.6 percent of the gross domestic product (GDP) in 2006, and 47.1 percent on average during the past decade. Because it is landlocked, Paraguay's economy is very dependent on Brazil and Argentina, its major trade partners. Roughly 38 percent of the GDP derives from trade and exports to Brazil and Argentina.[4]

The structure of the Paraguayan economy reflects the comparative advantage of agriculture and agro-industries. Paraguay's primary economic activities are cattle farming and agriculture, accounting for more than 25 percent of the country's production. The agricultural sector is characterized by the split between the traditional, labor-intensive sector of cotton cultivation, and the modern sector, related to soybean production. Soybean cultivation represents more than 30 percent of the gross value of all agricultural production. Paraguay is ranked sixth in the world in soybean production and fourth in volume of soybean exports.[5]

Industrial production is concentrated primarily in the processing of local raw materials. There is little value added in the production process at present, with primary products or those with a low grade of processing representing more than 90 percent of the exports in this sector. Food, beverages, and wood are the principal industrial products, which are mostly produced by small and medium-sized businesses using raw materials. Small businesses represent 80 percent of the total of all industries but account for only 14 percent of total production. Large companies constitute only 2 percent of the total number of companies but generate 48 percent of the GDP in this sector. The food sector is the most important single category, accounting for approximately 33 percent of gross production in the industrial sector, followed by textiles and clothing manufacturing (16.4 percent); beverages and tobacco (13 percent); nonmetallic mineral products (8.5 percent); manufactured products (5.9 percent); wood industries (4.3 percent); metallic products (3.6 percent); leather products (3.9 percent); chemical and pharmaceutical products (3.3 percent); and paper industries (3.2 percent). The services sector contributes more than 45 percent of the GDP, reflecting this area's growing importance.[6]

Banks are the main financial institutions inside the Paraguayan financial system, and they are the main source for financing business activity. The stock market is still very small, but more recently a group of local enterprises decided to use bonds to finance their growth, an interesting alternative for investment in either dollars or guaranies.[7] The state has limited participation in business activities, giving private initiative a more important role in investment and economic growth. Paraguay offers important opportunities for private investment in industries aimed at producing for the local and export markets in the areas of metal castings, textiles, vegetable oils, dairy and meat products, leather and hides, and assembly of electronic appliances, as well as wood and other products. Rural development and commercially viable programs for the protection of the environment are ongoing objectives.[8]

Through various treaties, Paraguay has been granted free ports in Argentina, Uruguay, and Brazil, through which it sends its exports. The most important of these free ports is on the Brazilian Atlantic coast at Paranaguá. The Friendship Bridge that spans the Paraná River between Ciudad del Este and the Brazilian city of Foz do Iguaçu permits about 40,000 travelers to commute daily between both cities, and allows Paraguay land access to Paranaguá. A vibrant economy has developed in Ciudad del Este and Foz do Iguaçu mostly based on international commerce and shopping trips by Brazilian buyers.[9]

Together with Argentina, Brazil, and Uruguay, Paraguay is a member of MERCOSUR, a common market of more than 215 million consumers established in 1991, whose objective is to integrate the economies of the aforementioned countries by achieving the free movement of goods, services, and production inputs throughout the four-country area.[10]

Taxes in Paraguay are the lowest in MERCOSUR and among the lowest in the world. The low tax rates are the result, among other things, of the fact that Paraguay has proportionately fewer taxes than other countries.[11]

Paraguay's highly centralized government was fundamentally changed by the 1992 constitution, which reinforced a division of powers that in the previous two Constitutions existed mostly on paper. Nowadays Paraguay is a democratic republic with a multiparty system and separation of powers in three branches. Executive power is exercised solely by the president, who is both head of state and head of government. Legislative power is vested in the two chambers of the National Congress (Congreso Nacional): the Chamber of Deputies (Cámara de Diputados) and the Chamber of Senators (Cámara de Senadores). The judiciary is vested in tribunals and courts of civil, juvenile, criminal, labor, administrative, and exchequer law, all of which are independent of the executive and the legislative branches. Paraguay's highest court is the Supreme Court of Justice.[12]

Paraguay is a member of the United Nations and several of its specialized agencies. It also belongs to the World Trade Organization (WTO), the Organization of American States (OAS), the Latin American Integration Association (ALADI), and the Rio Group, among other multilateral organizations.[13]

ESTABLISHING A BUSINESS PRESENCE

Permanent Structures

A foreign company has mainly two ways to develop commercial activities in Paraguay: (a) the first choice would be to open a branch of the foreign company in Paraguay; (b) the second option would be to set up a commercial company (as a subsidiary), in which the principal shareholder will be the foreign company or one of its related businesses.

In order to set up a branch in Paraguay, the foreign company's board of directors, through its minutes, will have to formalize the decision to proceed with the establishment of the company's branch. Besides specifying the decision of setting up a branch, the board of director's minutes will have to indicate the following: (a) term of duration; (b) designation of the branch's name; (c) designation of a registered address; (d) determination of the main purpose or activity; and (e) assignation of the branch's capital stock (Paraguayan legislation doesn't have a requirement for a minimum amount of capital stock). The branch's constitution necessarily implies the designation of a Paraguayan or foreign legal representative resident in Paraguay, who may or may not be a lawyer. Besides designating a legal representative, the board of directors' minutes must determine the powers that it will grant to the legal representative. The minutes that settle the branch's constitution must be notarized by a notary public and legalized by the Paraguayan consulate located at the headquarters' country.

For establishing a commercial company, the two most common types are the limited liability company (sociedad de responsabilidad limitada or SRL) and the corporation (sociedad anónima or SA).

Both types of companies must have at least two members. There are no restrictions regarding the number of foreign members or the percentage of participation in the company, except with regard to some specific sectors such as commercial air transportation. However, the General Office of Public Registry (DGRP) generally does not accept the record of companies with foreign directory members or managers that don't have permanent or temporary residence in Paraguay. Even though there is no separate legal prohibition, the DGRP and Treasury Department look to migrations' laws forbidding nonresident foreigners to practice remunerated activities.

In order to establish an SA or SRL in Paraguay, the foreign legal entity, through its board of directors or managers, according to the applicable national legislation or its statutes, must document that decision and also grant power of attorney to a local representative. If it refers to individuals who would integrate as members of a local business, they could either designate local representatives in order to constitute the company or if those intended representatives are currently in Paraguay they could go to a notary public to sign a memorandum of association and grant power of attorney allowing them to conduct the establishment proceedings. Power of attorney—in either of the cases mentioned above—will have to contain basic dispositions that are included in the statutes, such as the name of the company, its objective, duration, percent of shareholding or shares, assigned capital, and subscribed capital, as well as the faculty to designate members of the board of directors or general managers.

The proceedings for a branch's establishment are:

a. Translation of documents into Spanish (if written in another language) by a public translator registered at the Supreme Court of Justice of the Republic of Paraguay and completion of the legalization process of the foreign documentation.

b. Recording the power of attorney granted by the headquarters to the person who will be empowered to establish the foreign company's branch at the power of attorney section of the General Direction of Public Registry, which is under the aegis of the judicial branch.

c. The legal representative and a local notary public must formalize the branch's constitution. Then the public deed must be presented at the Treasury Department from the Ministry of Treasury, where a favorable ruling must be granted in order to record the public deed at the Public Registry.

d. With the favorable ruling granted by the Treasury Department, the memorandum of association's public deed has to be registered at the Public Registry of Commerce and at the Registry of Legal Entities and Associations, both of which are under the General Direction of Public Registry. Once the public deed is registered, an extract of the memorandum of association has to be published in a local newspaper.

The proceedings for establishing a local company (subsidiary or otherwise, of a foreign company) are:

a. Formalize the constitution through a public deed notarized by a notary public. The public deed must include the name of the company, its objective, duration, percent of shareholding or shares, assigned capital, determination of who will represent the company, and the designation of members of the board of directors, general managers, and other representatives.

b. The public deed must be presented at the Treasury Department from the Ministry of Treasury, where a favorable ruling must be granted in order to inscribe it at the Public Registry.

c. With the favorable ruling granted by the Treasury Department, the company will acquire legal personality only when it is inscribed at the Public Registry, meaning at both the Public Registry of Commerce and the Registry of Legal Entities and Associations.

d. Once the public deed is registered, either as an SA or as an SRL, it has the legal obligation to publish an extract of the constitutive act in a publication with national circulation.

The above procedure for establishing a company takes approximately 25 to 40 days.

After documenting the company's registration at the Public Registry, there are other requirements in order to finish the formalization of the business:

- Registration at the Unified Taxpayer Registry of the Ministry of Treasury
- Registration at the Institute of Social Prevision (IPS)
- Registration at the Ministry of Justice and Work (MJT)
- Obtaining a License and Municipal Permit for commercial activities
- Registration at the National Direction of Customs (DNA) (only for importers and exporters)
- Rubric or signature of company and accounting books.

Agency, Reseller, Franchising, and Distribution Agreements

In Paraguay Law No. 194/93[14] regulates the promotion, sale, or placing of goods or services in the country by manufacturers and foreign firms through their representatives, agents, or distributors in Paraguay.

According to this law the foreign party can cancel the contractual relationship (without the obligation to indemnify the local party) only if is proved in a judicial court that there is a fair cause for it. Fair cause is understood as fraud or trust abuse and conflict of interests. The foreign party is in charge of the burden of proof. Otherwise, the unjustified contractual rescission is presumed, giving the local party the right to claim the payment of compensation in an amount determined according to the criteria established by law.

Even if there is a fair cause, the foreign party must grant the local business 120 days to resolve the deemed cause. Once the specified period has elapsed the foreign party can request, through the court, cancellation of the contract. Otherwise, unjustified cancellation is presumed.

According to Law No. 194/93 the foreign firm and the local party must have a contract specifying the relations among the representatives, agency, and/or the distributor. This is a public order law; therefore, the stipulations established between the parties cannot be infringed upon.

Law No. 194/93 grants to the parties the possibility of submitting their controversies through arbitration, either before or after a lawsuit is presented at the ordinary justice, as long as a definite sentence was not sanctioned.[15] Even though Law 194/93 recognizes the principle of independent judgment by establishing that "parties can freely regulate their rights through contracts abided by dispositions from the Civil Code," this recognition has its limits that granted rights are inalienable.[16]

INVESTMENT ISSUES AND TAX INCENTIVES

Legal Treatment of Foreign Investment

Article 109 of the National Constitution[17] guarantees private property and consecrates that it is inviolable. No one may be deprived of their property except by virtue of a judicial decision. Expropriation for reasons of public use or social interest will be allowed. According to these constitutional guarantees, special laws have been sanctioned to establish a legal framework for foreign investments.

Law No. 117/1991[18] has been sanctioned with the objective to guarantee equal conditions for local and foreign investments. This law grants foreign companies the same guarantees, rights, and obligations that the law grants to Paraguayan investors.

A regime of free currency exchange without restrictions for income and outcome of capital, repatriation of profits, interests, commissions, royalties from technology transfer, and other concepts are guaranteed. All trade, remissions, or transfer operations are subject to taxes established by law.

A regime of free trade is guaranteed covering: (a) free trade of production and commercialization of goods and services in general, as well as free price setting, excluding goods and services for which production and commercialization are established by law; and (b) free importation and exportation of goods and services except the ones prohibited by law.

Any person (individual or legal entity, public or private) that reaches an agreement with a foreign investor could agree to solve any differences by submitting them for arbitration, either national or international.

In tax matters, national and foreign investments are subject to the same tax regime.

Natural citizens and foreigners, established legal entities located or represented in Paraguay, and governmental entities, including public law entities, can associate through a joint venture contract for allowed activities.

Law No. 60/90[19] establishes "The Fiscal Regime to Incentive National and Foreign Capital Investment" to promote and increase national and/or foreign investments. The law grants tax benefits to individuals and legal entities settled in the country, whose investments are realized in concordance with the national government's economic and social policies, and those who have the following objectives:

a. Increasing the production of goods and services
b. Creation of permanent work sources
c. Promotion of exportation and substitution of importation
d. Incorporation of technologies that increase productive effectiveness and facilitate better utilization of national raw materials, skilled labor, and national energy resources.
e. Investment and reinvestment of capital goods and utilities.

Investments protected by this law enjoy the following fiscal and municipal benefits:

a. Total exoneration of fiscal and municipal taxes that applies the constitution, inscription, and registration of societies and companies;
b. Total exoneration of customs obligations and other equivalent effects, including internal taxes of specific application on importation of capital goods, raw materials, and supplies destined to local industry, stated in the investment project;
c. Release of any requirement of any kind of bank reserves or special deposits for importation of capital goods;
d. When the amount comes from foreign financing and the benefited activity is at least USD 5 million, tax charges of remittances and payments to the exterior for interest, commissions, and capital for a fixed period will be released as long as the borrower is a company indicated in Article 10, inc. (g) of Law 125;
e. Total tax exoneration that affects the utilities and dividends arising from approved investment projects from up to 10 years, counted from project initiation, when the investment is at least USD 5 million and the tax of utilities and dividends is not a credit tax of the investor in the country the investment is from;

Individuals or legal entities that invest net utilities of their business subject to the income tax will have the right to a 50 percent reduction of it, corresponding to the net utility to invest in the previous exercise of the investment.

In order to have the right to this incentive, the investment has to be reflected in the increase of at least 30 percent of the integrated capital, in accordance with the approved investment project.

Law No. 1.064/97[20] was sanctioned with the purpose to promote the establishment of maquila companies that are devoted totally or partially to carry out industrial or service processes, by incorporating local work force and other national resources aimed to the transformation, elaboration, repairing or assembling of goods of foreign origin, imported temporarily for their later re-exportation, in execution of the contract signed with the foreign company.

The maquila contract and the activities performed for its execution are applied by a single tax of 1 percent on the added value in the national territory or on the value of the bill issued by account and order of the head office, whichever rises higher. The sub-maquila contract applies a single tax of 1 percent of the added value in the national territory, in terms of income tax.

The added value in national territory is equal to the sum of:

a. Goods acquired to fulfill the maquila and sub-maquila contracts,
b. Hired services and the salaries paid in the country for the same purpose as set out in the previous clause.

Taxes will be settled by sworn declaration in the manner, terms, and conditions established by the Ministry of Finance. The maquila contract and the activities carried out in the performance of it are exempt from all other national, departmental, or municipal taxes.

This exoneration is extended to:

a. Importation of goods established in the maquila contract, whose authorization is agreed upon,
b. Re-exportation of imported goods under said contract,
c. Re-exportation of transformed, elaborated, repaired, or assembled goods under said contract.

Maquila exportation will be exonerated from value added tax (IVA).

Treaties on Foreign Investment Protection

In the scope of MERCOSUR, Paraguay has ratified and internalized the "Protocol on Promotion and Protection of Investments Coming from States Not Part of MERCOSUR," with the sanction of the Law No. 593/95.[21] The "Protocol of Colony for the Promotion and Reciprocal Protection of Investments in MERCOSUR" is currently pending ratification from Paraguay.[22]

Paraguay has signed an important number of "bilateral treaties" in the matter of promotion and protection of investments, according to the following chart:

No.	Treaty (Document Name)	Signed with	Signature Place
1	Commerce and Investments Treaty	Brazil	Asuncion
2	Agreement on Investment and Industrial Complementation	Argentina	Buenos Aires
3	Agreement on Economic Cooperation and Investment	South Africa	Pretoria
4	Agreement on Commercial Trade, Industrial Complementation and Investment	Uruguay	Montevideo
5	Agreement on Reciprocal Promotion and Protection of Investments	France	Asuncion
6	Agreement on Reversal Notes Related to Obligations of Investors in the Republic of Paraguay	France	Asuncion
7	Agreement on Protection and Promotion of Investments	United Kingdom and Northern Ireland	London
8	Agreement on Reversal Notes Related to the Adoption of a New Version of the Text in Spanish of the Agreement on Promotion and Protection of Investments signed on June 4, 1981	United Kingdom and Northern Ireland	Asuncion
9	Agreement on Reciprocal Promotion and Protection of Investments	Switzerland	Berne
10	Agreement on Mutual Guarantee of Investments	Taiwan	Taipei
11	Agreement on Incentive for Investments	United States	Asuncion
12	Agreement on Reciprocal Promotion and Protection of Investments	Belgium	Brussels
13	Agreement on Reciprocal Promotion and Protection of Investments	Luxembourg	Brussels
14	Agreement on Reciprocal Promotion and Protection of Investments	Netherlands	The Hague

Signature Date	Ratified Law Number	Date	Date It Became Effective
Oct. 27, 1956	127	March 9,1957	Sept. 6, 1957
July 20, 1967	18	Oct. 22, 1968	Oct. 3, 1969
April 3, 1974	443	Aug. 9, 1974	Aug. 16, 1974
March 25, 1976	575	June 11, 1976	July 1, 1976
Nov. 30, 1978	804	Aug. 19, 1980	Dec. 1, 1980
Nov. 30, 1978	804	Nov. 11, 1980	Jan. 12, 1980
June 4, 1981	92	Dec. 20, 1991	Dec. 20, 1991
June 17, 1993	798	Dec. 27, 1995	Dec. 27, 1995
Jan. 31, 1992	17	July 31, 1992	Sept. 28, 1992
April 6, 1992	29	Sept. 11, 1992	May 25, 2001
Sept. 24, 1992	155	May 3, 1993	May 19, 1993
Oct. 6, 1992	200	July 7, 1993	Jan. 9, 2004
Oct. 6, 1992	200	July 7, 1993	Jan 9, 2004
Oct. 29, 1992	349	June 8, 1994	Aug. 1, 1994

No.	Treaty (Document Name)	Signed with	Signature Place
15	Agreement on Protection and Promotion of Investments	Korea	Asuncion
16	Agreement on Reversal Notes That Modifies the Agreement on Promotion and Protection of Investments	United Kingdom	Asuncion
17	Agreement on Reciprocal Promotion and Protection of Investments	Hungary	Asuncion
18	Treaty on Promotion and Reciprocal Protection of Capital Investments	Germany	Asuncion
19	Agreement on Protection and Promotion of Investments	Austria	Asuncion
20	Agreement on Reciprocal Promotion and Protection of Investments	Spain	Asuncion
21	Agreement on Reciprocal Promotion and Protection of Investments	Ecuador	Quito
22	Agreement on Reciprocal Promotion and Protection of Investments	Peru	Lima
23	Agreement on Promotion and Reciprocal Protection of Investments and Its Interpretative Protocol	Romania	Asuncion
24	Agreement on the Exchange of Diplomatic Notes Related to the Clarification of Article IV, Paragraph II of the Treaty on Promotion and Reciprocal Protection of Capital Investments	Germany	Asuncion
25	Agreement on Reciprocal Promotion and Protection of Investments	Chile	Asuncion
26	Agreement on Reciprocal Promotion and Protection of Investments	Venezuela	Asuncion

Signature Date	Ratified Law Number	Date	Date It Became Effective
Dec. 22, 1992	225	July 19, 1993	Aug. 6, 1993
June 17, 1993	798	June 13, 1997	June 13, 1997
Aug. 11, 1993	467	Nov. 14, 1994	Feb. 1, 1995
Aug. 11, 1993	612	June 3, 1995	July 3, 1998
Aug. 13, 1993	1180	Dec. 2, 1997	Dec. 1, 1999
Oct. 11, 1993	461	Oct. 21, 1994	Nov. 22, 1996
Jan. 28, 1994	469	Nov. 14, 1994	Sept. 18, 1995
Jan. 31, 1994	468	Nov. 14, 1994	Dec. 13, 1994
May 21, 1994	527	Dec. 30, 1994	April 3, 1995
July 14, 1994	Pending		March 7, 1998
Aug. 7, 1995	897	Aug. 4, 1996	Dec. 17, 1997
Sept. 5, 1996	1058	June 16, 1997	Nov. 14, 1997

No.	Treaty (Document Name)	Signed with	Signature Place
27	Agreement on Reversal Notes Related to the Interpretation of Certain Terms of the 1993 Agreement on Promotion and Protection of Investments	Austria	Asuncion
28	Agreement on Reciprocal Promotion and Protection of Investments	El Salvador	San Salvador
29	Agreement on Reciprocal Promotion and Protection of Investments	Czech Republic	Asuncion
30	Agreement on Reciprocal Promotion and Protection of Investments	Costa Rica	San Jose
31	Agreement on Reciprocal Promotion and Protection of Investments and Its Protocol	Italy	Rome
32	Agreement for Reciprocal Promotion and Protection of Investments and Its Protocol	Portugal	Lisbon
33	Agreement on Reciprocal Promotion and Protection of Investments	Cuba	Havana
34	Agreement on Reciprocal Promotion and Protection of Investments	Bolivia	Asuncion

Capital Market Regulations

The securities market is one of the subsystems of the Paraguayan financial system. In this market, securities, known as negotiable securities or financial activities, are publicly commercialized.

The securities market has basically the following components:

1. *Securities and Exchange Commission (CNV):* the regulator entity of the securities market is related to the executive branch through the Ministry of Industry and Commerce;
2. *Products and Stock Exchange of Asuncion S.A. (BVPASA):* a nonprofit organization (determined by law and its statutes) that grants its intermediaries an organizational and technological infrastructure to make negotiable securities viable to trade among them.

Signature Date	Ratified Law Number	Date	Date It Became Effective
July 4, 1997	Pending		Jan. 12, 1999
Jan. 30, 1998	1316	Sept. 15, 1998	Nov. 8, 1998
Oct. 21, 1998	1472	Sept 13, 1999	March 4, 2000
Jan. 29, 1998	1319	Sept. 14, 1998	May 25, 2001
July 15, 1999	Pending		
Nov. 25, 1999	1722	June 28, 2001	Nov. 3, 2001
Nov. 21, 2000	1900	May 31, 2002	Dec. 6, 2002
May 4, 2001	1891	May 24, 2002	Nov. 4, 2003

3. *Brokerage Houses*: the financial intermediaries of the securities market and the only authorized society to operate on its own risk, order risk, and customers' risk.
4. *Issuing Businesses:* legal entities that grant securities to the market to capture financial resources to execute investments in fixed assets or current assets.
5. *Investors:* individuals or legal entities that purchase or sell securities to obtain better financial yields for resources.

Law No. 1284/98[23] of the securities market regulates public offerings of securities and their issuers, stock exchanges, brokerage houses, and in general, all the securities market participants as well as the Securities and Exchange Commission (CNV).

Every public offering of securities requires previous authorization from the CNV. Securities must be negotiable, and will be represented in securities. A public offering could also be executed with securities that represent credit rights, subscription, property, participation, and others.

The law allows a public offering of securities to be granted by the state, governments, municipalities, centralized and decentralized public institutions, and the Paraguayan Central Bank.

Foreign legal entities that intend to make a public offering of securities in the country will have to abide by dispositions established by this law and to other market securities' dispositions. In any case, the commission's authorization is subordinated to the foreign country's reciprocal treatment. Foreign issuing securities made in Paraguay by issuing businesses of country members of the Treaty of Asuncion (MERCOSUR) or of other associated countries will have regulations established on the protocols subscribed to by member countries. These issuings will be documented at the Registry and must be in accord with the rules applicable to local issuers.

Law establishes that public offerings of securities representative of debts will be executed through bonuses. The emission of bonuses can be executed through guarantees established by the Civil Code. Such emissions also could be guaranteed through bank guarantee, bank deposits, bank certificates in foreign currency deposited in a financial entity in the country, insurance caution policies, and others established by the commission through dispositions of general character. Bonuses converted to assets can be issued only by the decision of the shareholder's meeting, which has to determine bases and conversion modalities and will agree to increase the capital as necessary.

Besides bonuses, promissory notes, bills of exchange, and other values determined by the commission could be used as representative instruments of debt.

Corporations of open capital conduct the public offering of assets according to law and must include in their denomination the expression "corporations of open capital" (SAECA). Corporations of open capital must obtain the registration from the Registry and must have an integrated social capital not less than the amount set by the commission through a general character resolution, and social capital must be represented by nominative actions.

Alternate Investment Structures—Investment Funds

Law No. 811/96 that creates the "Administration of Patrimonial Funds of Investment" regulates mutual funds, investment funds, and foreign investment funds. This last one is the patrimony made with foreign contributions from individuals, legal entities, or collective entities for securities investments of public offerings, a condition of which is that shares issued from fund participation are not redeemed. Set funds and administrating companies will be regulated by this law and elaborated management regulations, which must be previously approved by the Securities and Exchange Commission (CNV).

Fund operations will be carried out by the administrating society under the name of the fund, which will be the owner of representative instruments of investments and goods acquired in its case, which for all legal effects, will be considered as a legal entity and the administrator will act as the legal representative.[24] The administrating society will be equally forced to hire external auditors for the supervision and control of operations made with its own funds and resources administrated by it.[25]

Administrating companies and their directors, managers, or administrators, directly or through individuals or legal entities, cannot acquire financial instruments or securities from their administrated funds or patrimony, or transfer their own funds to these funds, nor can they loan money from these funds.[26]

In Paraguay, diversification of fund investments of foreign capital has certain regulations and limitations,[27] including the following:

- Stock investments of issuing companies of open capital whose main objective is the exploitation of industrial, agro-industrial, agricultural, mining industry, and reforestation projects cannot exceed 70 percent of the patrimony of administrated funds.
- Stock investments of issuing societies of open capital whose objective is banking and financial activities, in compliance with all the requirements of the General Law of Banks, finance entities, and other credit entities, cannot exceed 5 percent of the total of stocks subscribed by each entity of the finance system. Likewise, the total investment of the entities' funds cannot exceed 10 percent of the total of the administrated funds' patrimony.
- By the end of the first year, the fund will have to have at least 5 percent of its active investment in stocks from issuing companies of open capital.

Before the fund's investment of foreign capital, the following requirements will have to be fulfilled before the Securities and Exchange Commission:[28]

a. The fund's constitution must be documented by public deed or its equivalent;
b. The Paraguayan limited liability company's individualization in charge of the investment's administration in the foreign country must enclose antecedents that accredit its legal constitution;
c. When entering the country through the fund, the patrimony's value cannot be less than USD 1 million;
d. The fund's term of duration must be documented;
e. The fund's operation must be internally regulated.

When the fund's constitution is written in a foreign language, it has to be translated to Spanish, certified by the fund's legal representative. The commission must accredit that the entity is current and legally constituted according to the country of origin's law. These documents will be registered at the commission and from its registration date will be considered authentic instruments for all legal effects.

When investments are made through investment funds of foreign capital under Law No. 60/90 (mentioned above), they will have all the releasing, franchise, and benefits according to this law.[29]

Every consignment utility that doesn't correspond to invested capital or that does come from investments regulated by Law No. 60/90 will be set with a 10 percent tax rate. This tax will be retained by the administrator's company by the time the consignment is executed. This tax will be the only one that affects general rents by the fund's operations during its permanence in the country. Before making the utilities' consignment, the administrator's company will have to obtain an authorization from the National Commission of Securities.

Fund operations in Paraguay will be subject to the Paraguayan laws and the jurisdiction and competence of Paraguayan courts.[30]

OPERATIONAL LEGAL ENVIRONMENT

Immigration and Visa Requirements

For admission and entry into the country, foreigners must present a valid passport and a visa granted by the Paraguayan consulate, except when there are valid international agreements or dispositions given by competent authorities that establish other documental requirements and/or foreign releases of the visa requirement. Passports, visas, and other documents that authorize entrance into the country are subject to an established consular fee for each case.

The admission, entrance, permanence, and departure of foreigners in the Paraguayan territory are regulated by Law No. 978/96.[31] According to this law, foreigners can enter the country under two categories: resident or nonresident. Nonresidents are foreigners who enter the country without the intention to remain in it. Under this concept are included—among others—tourists, passengers in transit, accredited reporters for a special event, people who enter the country to undergo medical treatment, and investors who come to verify some aspect related to their eventual investment. Once nonresidents enter the country, they cannot perform remunerated or lucrative jobs, either on their own or for a company. Residents are foreigners who enter the country with the intention to remain in it. Residence can be granted as temporary or permanent.

Temporary residence is granted to foreigners who have the intention to remain temporarily in the country while their determined activities last, which will be taken into account for their admittance in the country. In this category are scientists; investigators; professionals; academics; technicians; teachers and their assistants; scholarship holders; specialized personnel hired for public or private entities and national or foreign companies; those who develop activities in Paraguay to do their specialized work; businesspeople, directors, managers, and administrative personnel of national or foreign companies relocated to fulfill specific charges in those companies; and members of churches, religious orders, or congregations recognized in the country who come to develop activities related to their beliefs.

Regarding permanent residence, legislation demands that foreigners intend to develop activities "of interest" for national development. Such activites would include the incorporation of qualified human resources and new technologies, the creation of new jobs for Paraguayan workers, the reduction of importations, the increase of exportation, the increase of population in regions where it is low, and expansion of the farming frontier. Activities that foreigners come to develop in Paraguay will be considered by authorities with the power to grant their settlement. However, permanent residents can conduct any kind of legal activity in the country, except when the entry authorization is subordinated to specific activities for a given period of time.

Foreigners who want to enter the country as permanent residents can do so as: (i) "spontaneous immigrants" assuming on their own the translation and installation expenses; (ii) "assisted immigrants" when the entry has been promoted by public or private organizations and when the state participates either directly or indirectly in translation and installation expenses; (iii) "immigrants with capital" who contribute their own goods to realize activities considered of interest for national development; (iv) "investors" when investments and/or transfer of financial and technological resources are realized; and (v) retirees, pensioners, and renters who can prove that they receive a regular and permanent income of external sources that allows them to live in the country without being a social burden for the state. In order to obtain permanent residence in any of the subcategories mentioned above, besides the documentation required for both categories (permanent or temporary), the interested party must fulfill the requirements and particular proceedings established by law for each case.

Foreigners who obtain their permanent settlement in the country, known as "permanent residents," will have the same rights and obligations as Paraguayan citizens, except certain limitations established by laws and the National Constitution, such as the right of access to public charges and the right to vote in the national elections. The foreigner who has obtained the permanent residence will be able to enter and depart the country at will. However, the resident foreigner cannot be absent from the country unjustifiably for over three years.

Law prohibits entrance to the country in a resident character—either permanent or temporary—by foreigners who have infectious or contagious diseases that could be considered a risk for public health; people with mental disabilities; people with physical or mental congenital or acquired defects; people with chronic diseases that prevent them from working; people who have been sentenced to more than two years of jail time; people who have serious criminal records; people who practice or profit with prostitution; drug addicts; people who don't have a profession, job, industry, or art; beggars; alcoholics; and people who have been expelled, with entrance to the country prohibited through sentences dictated by a competent judicial order.

Diplomatic and consular employees, representatives, and members from international organizations, accredited and/or recognized by the Paraguayan government, as well as administrative and technical employees in a mission of service are excluded from the legal migratory regime.

Procedures to obtain permanent or temporary residence could be implemented from abroad before the competent Paraguayan consulate or directly before the General Migrations Office (DGM) in Paraguay. In the first case, the Paraguayan consulate will remit the antecedents to the DGM in Paraguay. Basic documents required to begin the settlement procedures for either permanent or temporary residence are the following: (i) identification document or passport granted by the country of origin; (ii) birth certificate, and/or marital certificate or divorce certificate showing marital status; (iii) certificate of judicial or criminal record issued by the country of origin or residence certificate of the past five years (this is not a requirement for minors under 14 years old); (iv) certificate of criminal records for foreigners granted by the information department of the national police; (v) certificate of INTERPOL; (vi) certificate of health granted by an authorized doctor and legalized by the Ministry of Health establishing physical and mental health and that the interested party is free of an infectious or contagious disease; (vii) life and residence certificate granted by the jurisdictional police or peace judge; (viii) certificate of entrance and permanence in the country; and (ix) two ID photos (size 2.5 x 2.5 cm). All the documents must be originals with two authenticated photocopies by a notary public. Documents from the country of origin or residence from the interested person must be legalized by the Paraguayan consulate and by the Ministry of Exterior Relations of Paraguay. Documents written in a foreign language (such as Portuguese) must be translated to Spanish by a translator registered at the Paraguayan Supreme Court.

Taxation of Business and Cross-Border Transactions

Although it is important that countries establish agreements to avoid double taxation and prevent tax evasion, it is also important that state parties have an internal regulation to support the effective application of those agreements. In that respect, Paraguay does not yet have specific legislation regarding transfer price or information exchange with third countries, even though countries do tend to participate in regional integration agreements and at the same time to face up to the tax rules of those agreements, which shows the great need to balance the efficiency and efficacy of tax administrations.

Double taxation can be avoided or at least reduced through two different mechanisms: unilateral measures and those established through international treaties. In that sense, Paraguay's National Constitution establishes that it can't be the object of double taxation of the same taxable event of the tax obligation. In international relations, the state could establish agreements to avoid double taxation based on reciprocity.[32] Paraguay has agreements to avoid double taxation in matters of air-freight, fluvial, and ground transportation; but the only agreement in force is the one with Chile to avoid international double taxation in matters of income tax and property tax.

The tax reform was sanctioned by Law No. 125/91[33] and established a new tax regime divided by types of taxes: income tax (Book 1); capital tax (Book 2); consumption tax (Book 3); and other taxes (Book 4). This law was modified, most meaningfully by Law No. 2421/04.

The effect of taxes in business and international transactions is mainly given by two taxes: Income Tax of Commercial Activities, Industry or Services (IRACIS) (an income tax) and the Value Added Tax (IVA) (a consumption tax).

IRACIS imposes taxes on commercial activities, industry, and services from Paraguayan sources that are not of a personal nature. As a general rule the tax imposes the rent obtained by unipersonal businesses, companies with or without legal personality, associations, corporations, public businesses, self-sufficient entities, decentralized entities, and mixed economy societies.

Corporations, limited liability companies, and their branches, agencies, or establishments of people addressed or established abroad are comprehended in the IRACIS. Paraguayan tax is based on the source criteria. In this way the country applies unilateral methods to avoid double taxation by establishing the exemption of national taxable income to all or part of the income or patrimony located in a foreign territory, by establishing that the tax will be imposed on all Paraguayan source incomes.

Is important to clarify that Paraguayan source incomes are considered incomes that come from developed activities, located goods, or economically used rights in the country, independently of the nationality, address, or residence of whoever participates in the activities. Namely the general rule of imposition is the criteria of territory source except in cases of interest, commissions, yields, or capital profits located abroad, as well as trade differences of Paraguayan sources when the investor or entity is established in Paraguay, applying taxable principles to "global income."

Technical and service businesses are also considered of Paraguayan source when they are used in the country. Transfer of goods and rights of use are of Paraguayan source if they are used in the national territory, even partially. International freight will be 50 percent of Paraguayan source when used between Paraguay and Argentina, Bolivia, Brazil, and Uruguay; and will be 30 percent of Paraguayan source when used between Paraguay and any other country.

As for international incomes, the law establishes that individuals or entities settled abroad, with or without a branch, agency, or establishment in Paraguay, will determine their net profits of Paraguayan source, without admission on the contrary, using the criteria established in the law for activities of insurance and re-insurance, ticket operations, radiograms, phone calls, audio and video transmission services, data emission and reception through the Internet's protocol, and other similar services used from Paraguay to foreign countries, as well as those operations and services provided from abroad to Paraguay, including international freight and production and distribution of cinematographic or television movies, magnetic tapes, and any other similar kind of projection.

Is important to mention that branches, agencies, and establishments of individuals or entities based abroad will determine net profits considering their separated accounting and deductible expenses of branches, agencies, or individuals based abroad; interests in capital, loan, or any other kind of investment from the head office, branches, or agencies abroad; and payments for royalties and technical assistance as long as those expenses represent taxes for the beneficiary abroad.

As mentioned before, Paraguayan regulations do not have specific normative rules that regulate the imputation of price transfer between entities in the country with associated entities abroad. However, Paraguayan regulations have some dispositions that for certain types of operations use the logic of the arms'-length principle (of the normal price of the open market) by establishing, for example, that operations will be conducted with market prices. Therefore, in imports operations it is presumed, unless the contrary is proved, that costs of goods introduced in the country cannot be superior to the price of the current wholesale level in the place of origin plus the transport and insurance expenses to Paraguay; therefore the difference will constitute fixed interests. On the other side, income will be determined in exportation cases in which the price has not been set or when the declared price is inferior to the wholesale price in the country plus transport and insurance expenses to the place of destiny.

As can be seen, the legal text doesn't request or specify that the operations have been realized between associated businesses, nor does it establish any presumption of its entailment. As for taxes or applied aliquots, the general tax is 10 percent. Payment and distribution of dividends to partners or shareholders (corporations) or investors (limited liability companies) are imposed with an additional tax of 5 percent. Profits and accredited dividends (abroad money remittance) by local entities (subsidiaries), local agencies, or commercial establishments to the head offices of their partners or shareholders domiciled abroad are imposed with a tax of 15 percent. This is applicable when the money transfer (abroad remittance) is coordinated using a retention system. When foreign entities act directly in the country without the intervention of local subsidiaries or branches, a tax of 30 percent is applied (provided by the sum of taxes of 10 percent + 5 percent + 15 percent).

Like other Latin American countries, Paraguay applies a principal tax of consumption called value added tax (IVA) with an aliquot part of 10 percent for most goods and/or services. IVA is imposed on the sale of goods and provision of services, excluding personal services and importation of certain goods.

Current positive legislation regarding IVA applies territorial criteria in matters of importation from the country of origin. The article related to territoriality states that "the sale and provision of services rendered in the national territory will be imposed, independently of the place where the contract was celebrated, address, residence or nationality of whoever takes part on operations, as well as whoever receives it and place of payment."

As well as in the IRACIS, technical and services assistance is considered rendered in national territory when used in the country. Transference of use of goods and rights is considered to be from a Paraguayan source when they have been used, even only partially, in Paraguay.

Finally, Law No. 125/91 establishes in its book of general dispositions of General Application articles about fiscal address, stating that contributors are obligated to establish a fiscal address in the country. As for a natural or legal entity, it's presumed that its address in the country is (1) the place of its regular residence when it remains there for over 120 days a year; (2) the place where it develops civil or commercial activities in case there is not a place of regular residence in the country; (3) its representative's address; (4) the address of the person with rights in case there is more than one address. In case it is not possible to determine the address, it will be the place where the taxable event takes place.

The address of an entity established in the country is presumed to be (1) the place of its address or administration; (2) the place of its main activity, in case its address or administration does not exist or is unknown; (3) the one that the person with rights chooses in case there are doubts of it. In case it is not possible to determine the address, it will be the place where the taxable event takes place.

Regarding entities established abroad, if they have a permanent establishment in the country the above dispositions will be applied; otherwise the address of the representative will be applied, which will have to meet the above criteria; and if it is not possible to determine the address in the country, it will be considered the place where the taxable event takes place.

Labor and Employment

Law No. 213/93 of the Labor Code[34] establishes the relationship between workers and employers regarding the subordinated labor activity.

The following persons are subjected to the dispositions established by the Labor Code: (a) intellectual, manual, or technical workers and their employers; (b) private institution teachers and those who practice sports and professional activities; (c) employer's syndicate workers and workers from the private sector; and (d) workers from state-owned companies and municipal companies who produce goods and services. Rules for other state workers, either from the central administration, municipalities, or departments, are established by special Law No. 1626/00.[35]

Rights recognized by labor law cannot be renounced, changed, or limited. Any pact against dispositions established on the Labor Code is null.

Paraguayan labor legislation establishes a maximum workday of eight hours per day or 48 hours per week for daytime work (from 6:00 am to 8:00 pm); and of seven hours per day or 42 hours per week for night-shift work (from 20:00 to

06:00 hours). When the workday period exceeds the maximum period established in the law, the excess is considered overtime hours for purposes of remuneration, for which the law establishes rules.

According to the law, every worker has the right to an uninterrupted daily recess of at least 10 hours after finishing the workday period and has the right to a weekly day of rest, which is normally on Sundays.

The law also recognizes workers' rights to a period of remunerated vacations after each continued year of work, annual durations of which are as follows: (a) 12 working days for workers with less than five years of seniority; (b) 18 working days for workers with more than five years and less than 10 years of seniority; and (c) 30 working days for workers with more than 10 years of seniority.

Regarding remuneration, the Labor Code establishes that the salary can be freely arranged between the parties but in any case cannot be less than the minimum salary established by law. The regulation of the types of minimum wage is established according to the nature of the job and is handled by the Minimum Wage Council, under the Administrative Authority of Labor, which periodically evaluates the workers' socio-economic conditions in order to make adjustments to their salaries.

The law also gives workers the right to receive a complementary annual remuneration or Christmas bonus equivalent to one-twelfth of the worker's accrued remunerations in a calendar year, which has to be paid before December 31 or at the moment the labor relationship ends if that occurs sooner. It also establishes the payment of a monthly family assignation equivalent to 5 percent of the salary for each son or daughter younger than 17 years old, or without age limitation for a physically or mentally disabled son or daughter. The worker's right to a family assignation requires certain conditions established by law, and it is automatically extinguished when those conditions are not met or when the worker's salary exceeds 200 percent of legal minimum wage.

On the other hand, Paraguayan labor legislation has a special regulation for labor relations in regard to education, work by minors and women, home-based work, domestic work, rural work, and ground transportation work.

The Labor Code also establishes rights and obligations for employers and workers, as well as justified reasons to end the labor relationship for any of the parties. It establishes a test period at the initial stage of the labor relationship, which can be finished without incurring responsibility.

For cases in which the employer decides to end the labor relationship without a reasonable cause of dismissal, once the test period is accomplished, labor legislation establishes the payment of compensation in favor of the worker. Labor legislation establishes that none of the parties can end the labor relationship without giving previous notice to the other party; such notice varies between 30 and 90 days according to the worker's seniority.

Likewise, law establishes that the worker has job stability and the relationship cannot be terminated when the worker has reached 10 uninterrupted years of service with the same employer. In this situation the employer can end the labor relationship only in the following ways: (a) the employer must previously prove the existence of a justified legal cause of dismissal attributed to the worker; (b) a reassigned worker decides to accept compensation instead; and (c) a worker has chosen to retire.

In matters of social security, wage-earning workers who bring services or execute a piece of work according to a work contract, additional and decentralized state personnel, and mixed company workers are mandatorily included in the social security regime (Instituto de Previsión Social or IPS). The IPS was created by law decree No. 18071/43, and subsequently modified by law decree No. 1860/50, which is currently valid with modifications made over the years.

Social security according to law covers nonprofessional risks of disease, maternity, accidents during work, professional disease, disabilities, old age, and death of workers.

The social security law establishes a contribution in the concept of social security and retirement of 25.5 percent. The amount of 16.5 percent has to be contributed by the employer, and the other 9 percent contributed by the employee. This means that the 16.5 percent paid by the employer is calculated from the worker's gross salary, and the other 9 percent paid by the employee is deducted from the assigned salary.

Finally, the Labor Code establishes pecuniary sanctions if the employer does not comply with labor laws. The sanctions are summarily imparted by the competent Administrative Authority. Previous administrative instances at the Ministry of Justice and Labor discuss labor conflicts derived from the employer's breach. Likewise, national labor legislation is very protective of employees. In the case of judicial disputes, legal presumptions established by law are all in favor of the worker.

Consumer Protection and Products Liability

Consumer protection matters are governed by public order law, which recognizes rights that cannot be waived, subject to transaction or conventional limitation, and cannot prevail upon any other legal regulation, use, custom, practice, or stipulation unless otherwise specified.[36]

All acts between providers and consumers relative to the distribution, sale, purchase, or any other commercial transaction of goods and services are subject to the law,[37] as long as the consumer acquires, uses, or enjoys the goods or services as the end-consumer[38] in a process of consumption understood to be established between the person who provides the product or service and the person who acquires or uses it as an end-consumer.[39]

Basic consumer rights include (a) free election of the goods or services; (b) protection of life, health, and security against the risks caused by the provision of goods and services considered harmful or dangerous; (c) clear information on products and services; (d) suitable protection against misleading publicity and abusive contractual clauses; and (e) effective prevention and reparation of patrimonial and moral damages.[40] This law has a chapter establishing certain rules applicable to companies that supply public services, especially for residential services.

Regarding contracts of adhesion, their validity is allowed, as long as they don't have abusive clauses. A contract of adhesion is understood as one unilaterally drafted by the provider without the possibility that the consumer could discuss or substantially modify the content at the moment of signature.[41] Abusive clauses or agreements are considered ones that: (a) remove or restrict damage responsibility; (b) allow the provider to unilaterally modify the price or other conditions; or (c) impose unfair contracting conditions exaggeratedly burdensome for the consumer, among others.[42] In this matter, contractual terms or clauses will be interpreted in favor of the consumer.[43]

The law establishes the prohibition of any misleading publicity (defined as publicity that contains information that is entirely or partially false or that is capable of inducing the consumer to make an error).[44] The law also prohibits abusive publicity (considered as publicity that is discriminatory by nature or that incites violence, instills fear, or takes advantage of children's lack of maturity).[45] Comparative publicity is forbidden when, through negligent actions, general or discriminative declarations induce the consumer to establish the superiority of a product or service in regard to others.[46]

The law also recognizes that upon request of an interested party, a judge can (a) forbid the exhibition, circulation, transport, and commercialization of products that infringe on the law; (b) order the products confiscated when they are dangerous or harmful for health; (c) order the temporal closing of an establishment; and (d) apply fees in proportion to economic wealth.[47]

Subsequently, by Decree No. 2.348/99,[48] the General Direction of Defense of the Consumer (DGDC) was created under the Ministry of Industry and Commerce. The DGDC is authorized to understand and receive claims related to facts that violate the law in consumer protection matters; train and sustain administrative summaries and recommend respective resolution; decide controversies through arbitration; and promote conciliation, among other actions.[49] Approved agreements in controversy matters or resolutions emitted by the authority of application have the value of legally settled matters and are to be executed according to the administrative resolution, or they could be promoted to contentious administrative proceedings before the judicial Administrative Court.[50] Finally, the filing of complaints considered "malicious" is sanctioned with a fee of up to the maximum allowed.[51]

In the MERCOSUR context, no common regulation specifically regulates subject matter. Resolution No. 126/1994 sanctioned by the Common Market Group

(GMC) recognizes the need for a common regulation; it establishes that until a common regulation is approved "each State part will apply its legislation of consumer protection and technical regulations to products and services commercialized in its territory."[52] The only product of the legislative activity of MERCOSUR with dispositions that could be applied to consumer protection is the "Protocol of Cooperation and Jurisdictional Assistance in Civil, Commercial, Administrative, and Labor Matters" known as The Las Leñas Protocol.[53] Consumer protection in MERCOSUR is treated in a specific way only in the "Santa Maria Protocol of International Jurisdiction of Consumer Relations Matters," signed in December 1996, but it has not yet come into force.

Land Use and Real Estate

In Paraguay, real estate can be acquired through a contract of sale and purchase, which has to be undertaken according to legal forms established in the Paraguayan Civil Code. In that sense, Article 669 states that: "Those interested could freely establish their rights through contracts complying with law's imperative regulations, in particular, the ones established in this title relative to juridical acts."

Likewise, Article 673 states that: the essential requirements of a contract are: (a) consent or agreement between parties; (b) object; and (c) form, when it is stated in the law under penalty of absolute nullity.

According to the Paraguayan legislation, the required form for acquisition of real estate is public deed. In that sense, Article 700 states that real estate transactions and arbitral agreements shall be conducted under the form of a public deed. A public deed is a public instrument that can be granted only by a notary public registered at the Supreme Court of Justice.

When someone decides to acquire real estate, the person should meet with a notary public to begin procedures establishing the parties' intention to register a public deed, and to consequently register it at the appropriate Registry Office. On this subject, article 389 of the Civil Code states that public acts and deeds can be authorized only by a registered notary public. Peace judges will be authorized in places where there are no notaries public. The notary public will personally receive declarations from interested parties and will be responsible for their redaction and the content's accuracy, even if it was written by its dependents.

Deeds have to be written in the official language of the Republic of Paraguay, which means in Spanish, without prejudice that one of the undersigned (buyer or real estate's seller) doesn't understand the language, then minutes have to be documented in the language of the person who doesn't understand Spanish, which then must be translated by a public translator registered at the Supreme Court of Justice. The minutes must be attached to the public deed and registered at the Public Registry.

Paraguayan legislation has certain requirements for the validity of public deeds, without which they will be null. These requirements are set forth in article 396 of

Civil Code, which states that public deeds are considered null if they don't specify one of the following requirements: (a) the date and place in which they will be granted; (b) the names of the parties or representatives in the case, and witnesses if required; (c) the object and nature of the act; (d) the mention that powers and documents are in the protocol of an authorized notary; (e) the notary's attestation to the parties' identification or statement that the parties justified their identities according to the required form; (f) verification personally received granting party's declaration and witnessed handling, that the deed was made according to law, as well as verification that the deed was read to interested parties and instrumental witnesses, if any; (g) the parties' signature in the prescribed form, with any indication of one of the parties' impediment or request regarding signature if applicable; (h) signature of notary public and witnesses, if any. The deed will be null if one of the witnesses is considered legally incapacitated, or if it is not stated in the established deed's page according to its chronological order.

Real estate transactions can be conducted through a private contract between parties. In this case, the parties are obligated to subsequently subscribe the correspondent public deed, under conditions mentioned in the above paragraph. If the obligation is not fulfilled, the other party can initiate a trial before the Civil and Commercial Court of First Instance from the jurisdiction of the subject of the action in order to request that the obligation be fulfilled. As long as the contract is not formalized through public deed, it will be valid only between the parties and not before third parties.

Regarding forms for real estate acquisition, article 747 of Civil Code states that real estate sales can be conducted (a) without designating the extension, and for only one price; (b) not indicating the area, but the unity; (c) expressing the area under a certain number of measures to be determined in a larger field; (d) mentioning the area, by the price of each unity, with the total fixed or not; (e) area designation by a single price and not as much by the measure; and (f) the area under the clause does not guarantee the content, and that the difference more or less won't produce any effects.

Intellectual Property

In Paraguay, intellectual property rights are recognized at the constitutional level, according to the law established in Article 110 of the National Constitution.[54]

Positive legislation in matters of intellectual property rights has been updated according to standards set by the Agreement on Trade-Related Aspects of Intellectual Property Rights (TRIPS) of GATT. In fact, since the approval of TRIPS by Law No. 444 of November 10, 1994, Paraguay has sanctioned the following laws: Law No. 1.294 on trademarks (August 6, 1998) and its respective Regulatory Decree No. 22365 (August 14, 1998); Law No. 1.328 on copyright and related rights (October 15, 1998) and its respective Regulatory Decree No. 5.159 (September 13, 1999); and Law No. 1.630 on patents (November 29, 2000) and its respective Regulatory Decree No. 14201 (August 2, 2001). Updating of the industrial models and designs law is still pending.

Regarding Paraguay's adhesion to international treaties, Paraguay has ratified such agreements as the Paris Convention for the Protection of Industrial Property, and its revisions and amendments;[55] the Agreement on Trade-Related Aspects of Intellectual Property Rights (DPIC), previously mentioned; the Berne Convention for the Protection of Literary and Artistic Works;[56] the Universal Copyright Convention;[57] the Rome Convention for the Protection of Performers, Producers of Phonograms and Broadcasting Organizations;[58] and the Geneva Convention for the Protection of Producers of Phonograms against unauthorized duplication of their phonograms.[59] Recently, Paraguay has ratified new treaties with the World Intellectual Property Organization (WIPO) on authors' rights[60] and a Treaty on Interpretation or Execution and Phonograms.[61] Paraguay, as a member country of the MERCOSUR, has ratified the protocol on harmonization of norms on intellectual property in MERCOSUR in matters of trademarks, indications of sources, and appellations of origin.[62]

Paraguay has not joined systems of international registration of marks and/or patents as established, for example, by the Madrid Agreement concerning the international registration of marks or the Patent Cooperation Treaty. Paraguay doesn't have specific legislation in matters of protection to layout designs (topographies) of integrated circuits.

As for specific legislation regarding the observance of intellectual property rights, Law No. 3440/08[63] has recently been sanctioned, which partially modifies the Penal Code, widening the categorization of criminal acts relative to the violation of copyrighted works, trademark and industrial property law, and industrial models and industrial designs law, establishing a deprivation punishment or fee to offenders.

Trademark Law

- Trademark law establishes an "attributive" system of rights, which means that exclusive rights are effective from the time the registration of the trademark is granted.
- Among the susceptible signs that can be registered as trademarks are shapes, labels, containers, wrappings, and presentations or conditioning of products or of their containers or wrappings. Sound trademarks are not included. An isolated color cannot be registered as a trademark.
- The law adopts the international trademark classification of NIZA and a "one class trademark" filing system.
- A special protection is established for well-known trademarks.
- The registration of a trademark shall have a validity of 10 years and may be extended indefinitely for like periods.

Copyright Law

- Copyright law establishes a "declaratory" system of rights, which means that a previous registration is not required for the recognition of rights and use of copyrights.
- The quality of "author" is recognized only for individuals. In favor of the author the following rights are recognized: "moral" (publishing, paternity, and integrity rights) and "patrimonial" (reproduction, public communication, public distribution, importation, translation, adaptation, and transformation). An author's patrimonial rights are protected for a term consisting of the life of the author plus 70 years after death.
- Computer programs are protected in the same terms as literary works.

Patent Law and Inventions

- Products and processes are considered patentable subject matter, provided that they: (i) are new, (ii) involve an inventive activity, and (iii) are capable of industrial application.
- Excluded patentable subject matter includes "isolated" computer programs considered outlines, plans, economic methods, principles, advertisements, or publicity; and diagnostic, therapeutic, and surgical methods for the treatment of humans or animals.
- The duration of the patent is 20 nonextendable years, beginning from the application's presentation date in the country. To maintain the patent's validity, an annuity fee has to be paid.
- The law recognizes the possibility of obtaining mandatory exploitation licenses for the nonexploitation of a patent when there exists sanitary emergency situations, national security, socio-economical and technological development of certain strategic sectors, or when exceptional situations could affect national interests.
- Protection of utility models is equally recognized through patent concessions, which have a validity of 10 years.

Internet Regulations and E-Commerce

Domain Names

The registration of domain names in Paraguay is handled by the NIC.PY, under which two institutions are responsible for the administration of Internet domain names corresponding to a superior domain level in Paraguayan code. The National Computer Center (CNC) is responsible for the administration and operation of servers DNS, and the Digital Electronic Lab (LED) is responsible for the approval of applications for domain registrations.

The domain name registration policy that NIC-PY follows gives the priority for registration to whoever applies first. This system is known as "first come, first served." Applications to register domain names that are identical to others already registered or in the process of registration, subject to confirmation, will be rejected by NIC-PY. However, no rules exist for "typo-piracy" cases, which occur when a requested domain name is confusedly similar to a registered trademark or to another domain name previously registered by other owners. An example of typo-piracy is the kind of misspelling case that occurs when a registered domain name is a deliberately incorrectly written denomination, with the intention of redirecting a competitor's customers who inadvertently misspell the competitor's domain name.

One of the principal deficiencies of the Paraguayan system is the lack of a controversy solution system for situations that arise between the owners' rights (especially trademark rights and commercial names) and the domain name owners. NIC.PY adopts a "clean hands" position in the sense that it won't interfere in conflicts between domain name owners and/or applicants and third parties regarding the domain name registration or use. NIC.PY defines itself as a "coordinating organization" that doesn't perform as a mediator or as an arbitrator in such conflicts. NIC.PY exonerates itself of all kinds of responsibility and has a clause that declares that all applicants recognize they have no right to pursue legal action against the NIC.PY.

NIC.PY also has no jurisdictional power. In another words, if any type of conflict arises, the parties will have to appeal to an ordinary court to solve their differences, except when they agree to solve their controversies through an alternative system (such as mediation or arbitration). In this sense, NIC.PY will accept any decision emanating from a competent judge, including the suspension of a registry application, cancellation of a domain name registration, or any other pertinent order. Although NIC.PY doesn't expressly acknowledge that a competent judge could order the transfer of a domain name from one person to another, NIC.PY would have to comply with such a measure.

Electronic Documents and Signatures

In 2009, submitted before the Chamber of Deputies was a draft bill of law titled "The legal validity of digital signatures, text messages and electronic files."[64] In the general account of the referred bill of law, its editors declare that the object of the law is to recognize the validity of electronic text messages data as well as establishing a mechanism that would allow a digital signature to be used in an electronic commercial transaction. They add that interactions using the new electronic method must be regulated taking into account basic principles applied to all electronic fields and securing technological neutrality. The language states that "digital signature is a mechanism developed with the purpose to facilitate electronic commercial transactions and give a legal certainty to the parties involved in those transactions."

The draft bill is a unified synopsis of certain dispositions inspired by the Model Law of Electronic Commerce (LMCE) and the Model Law of Electronic Signatures (LMFE). In fact, Title II has dispositions relative to the legal value of text messages; the use of text messages in the formation of contracts; conservation of data messages; and sending and reception of text messages (return receipt, time, and place); whereas Title III has regulations on electronic signatures (owner's obligation, effect of the use of an electronic signature, legal validity, and revocation), and finally it has rules about the digital signature. On section II relative to digital signatures are articles about the legal validity of digital signatures, exclusions,[65] requirements for the validity of digital signatures, effects of the use of digital signatures, and revocation of digital signatures.

The whole section III under the Third Title is about certification of service providers, establishing a procedure for habilitation, determining obligations and responsibilities, and offering guidance for provision of services. An innovation that the bill of law brings refers to the "electronic file,"[66] which establishes in the fifth and last title that the Ministry of Industry and Commerce has authority over its application.

The referred bill of law was approved by the Chamber of Deputies on July 16, 2009. It was then approved by the Chamber of Senators on October 22, 2009, with modifications made, and adopting, wisely, the denomination of law on "Juridical Value of Electronic Signature, Digital Signature, Text Messages and Electronic File." On July 15, 2010, the bill was vetoed by the executive branch and it is currently being studied at the national Congress.

Data Protection

The right to access to information is granted in the National Constitution. In fact, Article 137 consecrates the institution of "habeas data" to grant that any persons can access information and data about themselves or their assets, documented in official or private registry of public character, as well as to learn how that information will be used. Any person could request before a competent judge the actualization, rectification, or destruction of wrongful information.

Law No. 1682, regulating information of a private character, was sanctioned in 2000. This law established the protection of "sensible data" of individuals, such as data referring to their racial and ethnic origins, political preferences, health information, religious beliefs, sexual intimacy, and in general all types of information that could affect privacy.[67] Law 1682 was modified by Law No. 1969/2002, which regulates in a much more detailed way the publication or diffusion of data on individuals or legal entities that reveals, describes, or estimates their patrimonial situation, economic solvency, or fulfillment of their commercial and financial obligations.

In the National Constitution other dispositions complement the protection of personal data, such as the right of inviolability of documental assets and private communications.[68] In addition, Paraguay has ratified international instruments such as the Universal Declaration of Human Rights[69] and the Pact of San José, Costa Rica,[70] which have general principles of privacy protection.

Finally, the Penal Code has a chapter dedicated to "crime against the life and the intimacy of a person."[71]

International Framework

At the MERCOSUR level, the Subgroup of Work No. 13 is in charge of the study of topics related to the development and promotion of electronic commerce within the block. Resolution No. 21/04 concerns "the right to information of the Consumer and Commercial Transactions effectuated through the Internet." Resolution No. 22/04 concerns "The Use of Digital Signature in the Secretariat of Mercosur."[72] Resolution No. 34/06 concerns "Directions for the celebration of agreements of mutual recognition of advanced digital signature in Mercosur." And Resolution No. 37/06 concerns "Recognition of legal efficiency of the electronic document, electronic signature and advanced electronic signature in Mercosur."[73]

Government Procurement

Law No. 2051/03[74] has been a very important tool in regulating public contracts in Paraguay, since they have been identified as one of the areas most vulnerable to corruption.

Law No. 2051/03 establishes a standard contracting system for the public sector and its main object is to regulate actions of planning, organization, budgeting, contracting, execution, expenses, and control of acquisitions and rentals of all kinds of goods, contracting of services in general, consultancy and public works, and services related to it. It does so by (a) organizations of the central administration of the state, integrated by the legislative, executive, and judicial branches, such as the National Comptroller's Office, the Ombudsman's Office, the Public Prosecution Office, the Council of Magistracy, the Magistracy Jury of Procedure, and state organizations of the same nature; (b) governmental offices; national universities; self-sufficient, autonomous, regulatory, and superintendence's entities; public entities of social security; public and mixed entities; limited liability companies in which the state is the major shareholder; official finance entities; and the state's national banks and decentralized public administration entities; and (c) municipalities.

On the other side, Law No. 2051/03 expressly establishes that the following contracts are excluded: (a) personal services regulated by the Law of Public Function; (b) concessions and public services and the granting of permissions, licenses, or authorizations for the use and exploitation of goods of public domain; (c) contracts executed according to established international treaties that Paraguay is part of and those financed by funds from multilateral organizations of credit; (d) acts, agreements, and contracts executed between and among organizations, entities, and municipalities; (e) contracts affected by operations of public credit, currency, financial and exchange rate fluctuation control, and in general, financial operations; and (f) international and internal correspondence transportation.

Originally the authority allowed to dictate administrative dispositions for the better performance of the law was the Normative and Technical Central Unit (UCNT), under the Sub-Secretary of Financial Administration of the Treasury Department. Subsequently, according to modifications introduced by Law No. 3439/07,[75] the National Directorate of Public Contracting (DNCP) was created under the executive branch in lieu of the UCNT, as an institution of control and verification of bids from Law 2051/03.

Law No. 2051/03 establishes an annual program of bids, whose main objective is to organize and plan the annual purchases in which interested parties will have access to the needs of the public sector so that all competitors will have the opportunity to give relevant bids.

According to the tender proceedings, the convener (entities established by law) will have to carry out the public tender through some of the following proceedings established by law: (a) public tender, either national or international; (b) tender bid; (c) direct contracting; and (d) contracting with reserved funds. Established proceedings vary according to the bid's amount.[76]

Notwithstanding the foregoing, the regulation anticipates alternate scenarios in which the convener could incorporate the ordinary proceedings, such as (a) pre-classification modalities; (b) financed bid; and (c) a bid with two or more evaluation stages, or a stop-out price.

The law and the regulations clearly establish formalities for each type of proceeding, which has to be fulfilled for all cases and in the period set by the legislation, concluding each type of proceeding with the award to the best offer. It also regulates periods and conditions for the formalization of contracts, the rights and obligations of the parties, and the modalities of the contract. The law also establishes an information system for public contracting (SICP) that makes public the tender process, adjudications, cancellations, modifications, and any other information related to it, including adjudicated contracts, independently of the type of tender.

The law and its regulations contain numerous dispositions relative to electronics use either by regular citizens or as part of the National Directorate of Public Contracting in the different methods of public contracting. This law is considered cutting-edge in matters of the use of the electronic signature in Paraguay, since it recognizes the possibility of using "means of electronic identification," either to send offers or to present complaints recognizing full legal value by establishing that those media replace the written signature and produce the same effects. The creation of a certification signature system is also expected, in order to exert control and safeguard information confidentiality transmitted by electronic methods. Although the law introduces these measures, they are not yet widely applied.[77]

Finally, the law contemplates the infringements and sanctions if providers, contractors, or public employees do not fulfill their obligations, establishing qualifications and proceedings to set the sanction. Mechanisms for complaints and dispute resolution are in place so that interested people can file their complaints when they believe an act violates the dispositions set by the law. The complaint must be written or filed through an electronic communication within the period established by the law.

Liability of Company's Directors and Officers

In matters of civil law, Paraguay's Civil Code adopts a general principle that a legal entity is "subject of rights, different from its members and independent from its patrimony."[78] However, referring to directors and administrators, the law applies the criteria that "acts from legal entities are considered as of their organisms."[79] Therefore, "legal entities respond for the damage that the acts from their organisms had caused to third parties, either by an action or omission even if it is an offense, when those acts were executed in the exercise of their jobs and in benefit of the legal entity."[80] These acts personally obligate directors and administrators in relationship with the legal entity.[81] Directors and administrators are responsible for the legal entity regarding rules of mandate. Those who have not participated in the act that has caused the damage will be exempt from responsibility, except if they had knowledge that the act was going to be performed but didn't manifest their dissent.[82]

In matters of corporations (SAs) in particular, the civil code has dispositions of responsibilities for directors and administrators. In this sense, is important to know that company administration will be in charge of one or more directors.[83]

The administrator who has interest in a determined operation on its own or through third parties, and is in conflict with the company, has to inform the other administrators and trustees in order to abstain from deliberations relative to that operation. In case of inobservance of these legal regulations the administrator will be responsible for the loss derivative to the company in fulfillment of the operation.[84]

The directors are unlimitedly liable and are jointly and severally liable before the company, shareholders, and third parties for the nonexecution or wrongdoing of the mandate, as well as for violating the law or its statutes, and for any other damage caused by a fraudulent action, abuse of their faculties, or gross negligence. The director's responsibility is exempt in cases in which he or she did not participate in the deliberation or resolution and expressed his or her discomfort in writing to the trustees before any responsibility was assigned to him or her.[85]

Directors won't be responsible before the company in cases where they proceeded according to the assembly's resolutions that weren't against the law or its statutes. They won't be responsible either when their acts were approved by the assembly or if it declined the action, as long as the responsibility doesn't deviate from the violation of a law or its statutes, and in case there are no oppositions from the shareholders that represent at least 20 percent of the capital.[86]

When discussing a balance, the decision relative to administrators' responsibility could be adopted even if it doesn't figure in the agenda, if it is a direct consequence of the resolution of a matter. The resolution that declares responsibility will produce the dismissal of the affected director or board of directors and will force their replacement.

Administrators respond before social creditors given the inobservance of obligations inherent to the conservation of the integrity of the social patrimony.[87]

The code also recognizes the right of indemnification of damages to a shareholder or third party that has been directly affected by fraudulent acts of the administrators.[88]

In matters of penal law, the Penal Code[89] establishes the general principle of personal responsibility for the commission of an offense against an individual who acts as the representative of a legal entity or as a member of its organization, as a representative partner of a company of people, or as a legal representative.[90]

The Penal Code also has dispositions regarding offenses against patrimonial rights that establish responsibility when one removes, hides, destroys, or damages books or papers of commerce that a trader has a legal obligation to keep or save; elaborates or modifies balances to obscure real financial liability; or in the mercantile system uses fake or distorted information on the real liability of the business or its patrimony.[91]

Litigation/Dispute Resolution Systems

The classic division of the government is exercised by the judicial, legislative and executive branches through a system in which the three branches of government are kept independent, balanced, and coordinated, and have reciprocal control.[92]

As for the judicial branch, article 248 of the National Constitution establishes that the independence of the judicial branch is guaranteed. Only the judicial branch may hear and decide cases. In no case will members of other branches of government or other officials claim to have judicial powers other than those expressly established by the Constitution, nor can they reopen closed cases, interrupt existing ones, or interfere in any way with ongoing court cases. Acts of this nature are completely null. The law does not preclude, however, solutions through arbitration on cases falling within the framework of private law, following the procedures established by law to ensure the right to defense and equitable solutions. It provides that those who threaten the independence of the judicial branch and its judges shall be ineligible to hold any public post for five consecutive years, in addition to any other punishments established by law.[93]

The judicial branch is the custodian of the Constitution, which it interprets, carries out, and enforces laws. The administration of justice is entrusted to the judicial branch, exercised by the Supreme Court, by the courts of appeals, and by the trial courts in the manner established by this Constitution and by law.[94]

Between the alternative methods of dispute resolution, arbitration has a constitutional rank, as article 248 mentions. Law No. 1879 on arbitration and mediation, sanctioned in 2002, is a modern legislation based on the Model Law on International Commercial Arbitration of the United Nations Commission of International Trade Law (UNCITRAL).

In matters of international agreements regarding recognition and execution of sentences and awards, Paraguay has ratified the 1958 New York Convention by Law No. 948/06, which acknowledges and executes foreign arbitration sentences. The 1979 Interamerican Convention on Extraterritorial Validity of Foreign Judgments and Arbitral Awards, subscribed in Montevideo, was ratified by Law No. 3303/07. The 1992[95] Protocol on Judicial Cooperation and Assistance in Civil, Commercial, Labor and Administrative Matters guarantees that nationals and permanent residents of any of the states' parties shall have free access to the courts of the other states for the defense of their rights and interests. Finally, the 1994 Buenos Aires Protocol on International Jurisdiction in Contractual Matters[96] applies to the administrative contentious jurisdiction relative to international contracts concerning civil or commercial matters between individuals or legal entities.

ENDING/RESTRUCTURING A BUSINESS PRESENCE

A company can be initially constituted as a specific type of business organization and subsequently transformed into another type established in the Civil Code without having to be dissolved or affecting its current members' rights and obligations. In that sense, Article 1187 of Civil Code states that a company's transformation does not release limited liability members from the liability held prior to the restructuring, if not all members gave their consent for the transformation. Consent is presumed if the decision to restructure was authentically communicated to members and consent was not denied within 30 days of their having received that communication. Silence is considered consent.

Likewise, Article 1188 establishes that "if during the company's transformation some members assume unlimited liability, it extends to preexistent social obligations."

Article 1189 of Paraguayan Civil Code enumerates the following requirements for a company's transformation: (a) unanimous agreement between members, unless otherwise stipulated, notwithstanding dispositions stated in the code for certain societies; (b) a special balance has to be approved by members, which will be placed for 30 days at the creditor's disposal; (c) the executive branch's approval of modified statutes when the law requires it; (d) publication of the company's transformation for five days; (e) granting of the transformation by the transformed company's competent authority, with evidence of retired members' assent, represented capital, aggregation of a signed copy of the special balance, and formalities' fulfillment for the new type of society; and (f) instrument's registration with a copy of the signed balance, at the correspondent registry according to the type of company, nature of goods integrated in its patrimony, and encumbrances.

A merger is the combination of two or more business entities into a single entity; in an acquisition, one of them takes over the other and dissolves it without liquidating it. At the moment of formalization of the merger agreement, the new company or the merging business assumes the rights and obligations of the dissolved one.

Article 1193 of the Civil Code states the requirements for a company's merger as follows:

a. The merger agreement must be granted by the company's legal representative with requirements fulfilled for the early dissolution. Each company will prepare an updated balance sheet for company members and creditors.

b. Required publicity for the transformation of commerce establishments must be made. Creditors can oppose the merger, which will not proceed if it is not paid or duly guaranteed.

c. The merger's definite agreement that will be granted when the previous requirements are met should contain proof of the interested company's approval, a partner nominee list showing the right of recess and represented capital, and opponent creditors' nominee list and amount of credits.

d. The agreement's execution, according to regulations for each company's dissolution, must include actions required of the dissolved company's partners and prescribed balances. Definite instruments must be registered in the same terms for the company's transformation.

Likewise, Civil Code states that when the merger is produced by the companies' dissolution, a new one will be constituted according to the correspondent regulations. Acquisition cases must fulfill regulations regarding statutory reforms.

On the other side, regarding legal representation of the new company or the acquired one, the legal code sets forth that it will necessarily represent the dissolved ones, with the liquidator's liability and without prejudice of its own. The dissolved company's administration will end with the new company's constitution or acquisition. Companies of either type could be disbanded for: (a) expiration of their term; (b) fulfillment of their social purpose; (c) the inability to reach the social purpose or bankruptcy; (d) partner's unanimous agreement; and (e) other causes established in their social agreements.[97] Companies can dissolve by either partners' request, by death or renunciation of a partner whose assistance is necessary to continue the transfer; and when the company has an unlimited term, among other causes.[98]

Assets liquidation will begin once the company is dissolved. During the liquidation process the company will conclude pending matters, and administrate, maintain, and realize its social patrimony.[99] The liquidation process will be handled by the liquidators who have to realize all the necessary proceedings for the liquidation.[100]

For limited liability companies, is important to mention that the merger, transformation, and dissolution of the company, as well as the designation of the liquidators, is under the authority of the Extraordinary Assembly of Creditors.[101]

CONCLUSION

Paraguay is a democratic republic, with a juridical civil law tradition. According to the National Constitution, international treaties approved and ratified by Paraguay take precedence over its own national laws. International treaties and laws mentioned in this chapter are part of the appropriate and favorable framework for foreign investments.

Paraguay has a privileged geographical position that benefits investments in the region. Within the past five years, Paraguay has had positive economic growth and has strengthened its democracy with the government's transition in 2008 to new political sectors.

Likewise, Paraguay offers a wide variety of competitive and comparative advantages for the eradication of foreign investments, such as (i) wide extensions of lands; (ii) a majority of people willing to work; (iii) competitive levels of salaries; (iv) low tax pressure; (v) legal regime of incentives for investors; (vi) and favorable conditions for the exploitation and industrialization of raw materials.

Culturally, Paraguay offers a friendly and receptive atmosphere to foreigners.

NOTES

1. The Paraguayan American Chamber of Commerce, http://www.pamcham.com.py/ and Paraguay according to Wikipedia, http://en.wikipedia.org/wiki/Paraguay#Administrative_subdivisions (last visited October 13, 2010).
2. *Id.*
3. *Id.*
4. Investors and exportations network, http://www.rediex.gov.py/. Paraguayan national chamber of commerce and services, http://www.paraguayy.com/paraguay-paraguay/camara-nacional-de-comercio-y-servicios-del-paraguay%E2%80%93-cncsp.html?pagina=13 (last visited October 13, 2010).
5. *Id.*
6. *Id.*
7. Ministry of Industry and Commerce, http://www.mic.gov.py/. Paraguayan Central Bank, http://www.bcp.gov.py/ (last visited October 13, 2010).
8. *Id.*

9. Treasury Department, http://www.hacienda.gov.py/web-hacienda/index.php (last visited October 13, 2010).

10. Paraguay according to Wikipedia, http://en.wikipedia.org/wiki/Paraguay#Administrative_ subdivisions (last visited October 13, 2010).

11. Treasury Department, http://www.hacienda.gov.py/web-hacienda/index.php (last visited October 13, 2010).

12. Paraguay according to Wikipedia, http://en.wikipedia.org/wiki/Paraguay#Administrative_ subdivisions (last visited October 13, 2010).

13. *Id.*

14. Law No. 194 of July 6, 1993 approves the modification of Decree No. 7 on March 27, 1991, which establishes the Legal Regime of Contractual Relations between Manufacturers and Foreign Firms, Individuals, or Legal Entities located in Paraguay."

15. *Id.*

16. *Id.* art. 9.

17. PARA. CONST. art. 109.

18. Foreign Investment Law No. 117 of December 6, 1991.

19. Law No. 60 of December 13, 1990 [Law No. 60/90].

20. The Maquila Export Industry Law No. 1.064 of December 20, 1997.

21. Law No. 593 of June 15, 1995. http://www.mre.gov.py/dependencias/tratados/mercosur/ registro%20mercosur/Acuerdos/1994/español/6.%20Protocolo%20de%20Promoción%20 y%20Protección%20de%20Inversiones(portugués).pdf (last visited on October 13, 2010).

22. http://www.mre.gov.py/dependencias/tratados/mercosur/registro%20mercosur/Acuerdos /1994/español/5.%20Protocolo%20de%20Colonia.pdf (last visited on October 13, 2010).

23. Securities Market Law No. 1284 of July 28, 1998. Law No. 811 of December 13, 1996 [Law No. 811/96] creates the "Administration of Patrimonial Funds of Investment." Art. 5.

24. *Id.*

25. Law No. 811/96. Art. 8.

26. Law No. 811/96. Art. 29.

27. Law No. 811/96. Art. 52.

28. Law No. 811/96. Art. 61.

29. Law No. 811/96. Art. 62.

30. Law No. 811/96. Art. 63.

31. Migrations Law No. 978 of November 8, 1996 and its Regulatory Decree No. 18295/97.

32. PARA. CONST. art. 180.

33. Tax Law 125 of January 9, 1992. Modified by Law No. 2421/04.

34. Labor Code Law No. 213 of October 29, 1993.

35. Public Function Law No. 1626 of December 27, 2000.

36. Consumer and User Protection Law No. 1.334 of October 27, 1998 [Law No. 1334/98] art. 2.

37. Law No. 1334/98 art. 3.

38. Law No. 1334/98 art. 4a.

39. Law No. 1334/98 art. 5.

40. Law No. 1334/98 art. 6.

41. Law No. 1334/98 art. 24.

42. Law No. 1334/98 art. 28.

43. Law No. 1334/98 art. 27.

44. Law No. 1334/98 art. 35.

45. Law No. 1334/98 art. 37.

46. Law No. 1334/98 art. 36.

47. Law No. 1334/98 art. 51.

48. Decree No. 2.348 of April 6, 1999, sanctioned by the executive branch, created the General Direction of Defense of the Consumer (DGDC).

49. Resolution No. 197 on April 27, 1999.

50. Law No. 1334/98 art. 29.

51. Law No. 1334/98 art. 31.

52. Resolution No. 126 (1994) sanctioned by the Common Market Group (GMC). art. 2.

53. Las Leñas Protocol of May 27, 1992.

54. PARA. CONST. art. 110 states that every author, inventor, producer, or trader has exclusive property of his work, invention, trademark, or commercial name, according to the law.

55. Law No. 300 of January 10, 1994.

56. Law No. 12 of June 26, 1991.

57. Law No. 777 of May 17, 1962.

58. Law No. 138 of October 9, 1969.

59. Law No. 703 of July 27, 1978.

60. Law No. 1582 of August 8, 2000.

61. Law No. 1583 of August 8, 2000.

62. Law No. 912 of June 26, 1996.

63. Law No. 3440 of July 16, 2008.

64. See Draft Bill, The Legal Validity of Digital Signatures, Text Messages, and Electronic Files [Draft Bill].

65. Draft Bill. art. 21, subarticle c) the dispositions on this law are not applicable to acts that they should be implemented under the requirement or formalities incompatible with the use of digital signature, either as a consequence of legal dispositions or an agreement between parts.

66. Draft Bill. art. 2 defines the "electronic file" as the orderly serial of public documents registered by the Internet, tending to the formation of the administrative will in a determinate manner.

67. Data Protection Law No. 1682 of December 28, 2000, art. 4.

68. PARA. CONST. art. 36.

69. American Declaration of Human Rights or Pact of San Jose, Costa Rica [Pact of San Jose] Art. 12.

70. Pact of San Jose art. 11 (2).

71. Penal Code art. 141 classifies invasion of private property and says it will be punished with a sentence of up to two years or a fee; article 143 classifies the invasion of privacy and sanctions it with a fee. It directly refers to the public exposition of the privacy of a person, his or her private life, sexual life, and health; article 144 classifies injury of the right of communication and image and sanctions it with a sentence of up to one year or a fee; article 148 classifies revelation of private secrets by employers or people with a special obligation and sanctions it with a sentence of up to three years or a fee.

72. These resolutions were adopted in the marc of the LV Plenary Meeting of the Common Market Group, fulfilled in Brasilia from October 6 to Oct. 8, 2004, Minute No. 03/04.

73. These resolutions were adopted in the XXXI Extraordinary Meeting of the Common Market Group, in Cordoba, on July 18, 2006, Minute No. 01/06. Information referring to the resolutions of the Sub-Group of Work No. 13 was obtained from the official page of the MERCOSUR: http://www.mercosur.int/msweb/portal%20intermediario/es/index.htm.

74.Public Hiring Law No. 2051 of 2003 [Public Hiring Law] and Regulation of Public Hiring Law, Decree No. 21.909/2003.

75. Law No. 3439 of December 31, 2007.

76. A minimum wage is approximately equivalent to USD 12 for the year 2010.

77. Public Hiring Law art. 1.

78. Civil Code art. 94.

79. Civil Code art. 97.
80. Civil Code art. 98.
81. *Id.*
82. Civil Code art. 99.
83. Civil Code art. 1102.
84. Civil Code art. 1109.
85. Civil Code art. 1111.
86. Civil Code art. 1112.
87. Civil Code art. 1115.
88. Civil Code art. 1116.
89. Law No. 1160 of November 26, 1997 [Law No. 1160/97].
90. Law No. 1160/97 art. 16.
91. Law No. 1160/97 art. 179.
92. PARA. CONST. art. 3.
93. Law. No. 595 of May 23, 1995 [Law. No. 595/95].
94. PARA. CONST. art. 247.
95. Law. No. 270/1995. This protocol is an amendment that was approved in Paraguay by Law 3541/08.
96. Law. No. 595/95.
97. Civil Code art. 1003.
98. Civil Code art. 1004.
99. Civil Code art. 1006.
100. Civil Code art. 1009.
101. Civil Code art. 1080.

CHAPTER 8

Peru

Jean Paul Chabaneix
Mariano Fuentes
Rodrigo, Elias & Medrano Abogados

COUNTRY OVERVIEW

Starting in the early 1990s, Peru undertook a comprehensive modernization process that included establishing a reliable legal framework geared toward maintaining the stability required for boosting private business activity, investment, and privatization. As a result, the country has attracted substantial capital investment, which has allowed for sustained economic growth.

The development of the agribusiness, fishing, mining, and telecommunications sectors, as well as the completion of major infrastructure projects primarily in the fields of energy, gas, and transportation, contributed to increased internal consumption and expanded international trade, thereby making Peru one of South America's most attractive countries for investment opportunities. In this context, the country continues to negotiate and enter into free trade agreements while strengthening its commercial ties with nations throughout the Pacific Basin, including the United States.

This chapter briefly describes the legal framework that applies to any person or entity interested in doing business in Peru. Regulations regarding foreign investment, alternative corporate structures, and other relevant provisions are summarized in order to explain the legal means available for conducting business in Peru.

Of course, the most favorable structure for any business must be determined on a case-by-case basis and, therefore, this chapter is not a substitute for appropriate legal advice.

ESTABLISHING A BUSINESS PRESENCE IN PERU

Permanent Structures

In general, Peruvian regulations regarding corporations are similar to those found in other jurisdictions.

The corporation is a capital stock company with capital represented by shares; it grants its shareholders the rights set forth in the General Corporations Law and in the respective corporate bylaws. Different kinds of stock may exist. The difference may be found in the rights granted to shareholders, the obligations incurred by owners, or both. All shares of a single class of stock will enjoy the same rights and will be subject to the same obligations.

The corporation may issue nonvoting stock, which shall provide for the right to receive preferred dividends as per the terms established in the bylaws. If there are distributable profits, the corporation is required to pay the aforementioned preferred dividends to nonvoting stock shareholders.

Incorporation

Corporations require at least two founding shareholders to file a public document that must include the articles of incorporation and bylaws stating, among other things, the names of the shareholders, their addresses, the corporation's legal name, its corporate purpose, capital stock, corporate form, and appointment of the initial directors.

The notarized incorporation documents must be filed with the Corporate Register where the corporation is located.

Shareholder Liability

Regardless of the type of corporation used, shareholder liability for corporate debts is limited to the amount of the shareholders' contributions.

Capital

As a general rule, the General Corporations Law does not require a minimum amount of capital for incorporation. In some cases, however, the law does require that corporations be formed with a minimum amount of capital based on the nature of their activities (for example, companies in the national financial system, companies managing pension funds, and employment outsourcing companies).

In all cases, shares making up a corporation's stock must be fully subscripted and at least 25 percent of the value of each share must be paid in.

Increases and decreases of capital stock and the corresponding amendments to corporate bylaws are relevant resolutions that must be adopted by a majority of the voting members at a general shareholders meeting. These resolutions must be set forth in a public document and filed with the Corporate Registry for Juridical Persons.

Governance and Administration

The bodies governing corporations are the general shareholders meeting, the board of directors, and the management.

The general shareholders meeting is the corporation's highest governing body. At a general shareholders meeting that is duly convened and at which a legal quorum is present, matters under its jurisdiction are decided by majority vote (as established by law and by the corporate bylaws). The general meeting must be held at least once a year, within three months of the end of the fiscal year (December 31 of each year), in order to approve the corporation's management, its economic performance during the previous fiscal year, and the application of profits (if any), among other matters.

A corporation is managed by a board of directors, which is elected by the general shareholders meeting. In the case of closed corporations, the existence of a board of directors as the governing body is optional. A board of directors must have a minimum of three directors. The members of the board of directors may be Peruvians or foreigners, domiciled or nondomiciled. It is not necessary to be a shareholder in order to serve as a board member, unless so stated in the bylaws. Directors may be removed at any time.

The board of directors must provide shareholders and the public with information that is timely, reliable, and sufficient, as determined by law, regarding the company's legal, operational, and financial conditions. The board of directors is responsible for carrying out resolutions passed by the general assembly, unless the latter decides otherwise in particular cases.

A corporation is also managed by one or more managers. If a closed corporation has no board of directors, the general manager will be responsible for managing and legally representing the corporation. The manager may be removed at any time by the general shareholders' meeting or by the board of directors, depending on the body making the appointment.

Unless otherwise stated in the bylaws or by a special resolution of the general shareholders meeting, it is presumed that the general manager has, inter alia, the power to enter into and execute ordinary acts and contracts related to the corporate purpose, and to represent the corporation.

Distribution of Profits

Profits are distributed to the shareholders in proportion to their capital contributions, unless otherwise stated in the articles of incorporation or bylaws.

Corporations are required to set aside a minimum of 10 percent of their after-tax profits during each fiscal year for the creation or increase of a reserve fund, until an amount is reached that is equal to one-fifth of the capital stock. The reserve fund is used to compensate for losses in a given fiscal year if there are no other reserves or accumulated profits.

Dividends must be paid in cash up to an amount equal to one-half of the distributable profits during each fiscal year, after subtracting the amount that must be set aside for the reserve fund, if so requested by shareholders representing at least 20 percent of the total voting stock. This request may be made only with respect to profits from the immediately preceding fiscal year.

Financial Statements

The board of directors or, in its absence, the general manager, must prepare the annual report, financial statements, and proposal for use of profits (if any), at the end of each fiscal year in order to submit them for consideration at the annual shareholders meeting.

Financial statements are prepared and submitted in accordance with the law and with generally accepted accounting principles.

In the case of ordinary corporations, annual independent audits may be provided by the articles of incorporation, bylaws, or a resolution of the general shareholders adopted by 10 percent of the voting shares. In the case of closed corporations, the resolution must be adopted by 50 percent of the voting shares. Open corporations are required by law to have annual independent audits performed by auditors who are currently listed on the Peruvian National Register of Auditors' Associations and to submit quarterly financial statements to CONASEV.

Transfer of Stock

Shareholders may transfer, mortgage, or freely encumber their stock, unless the law, corporate bylaws, or a shareholders' agreement duly registered with the company limits such transfer, mortgage, or encumbrance. This limitation may not be understood as an absolute prohibition on all transfers, mortgages, or encumbrances of corporate stock.

A temporary ban on transfers, mortgages, or other means of encumbering stock is valid when so established by the bylaws or articles of incorporation, so agreed to by the bearer of the corresponding shares of stock, or so resolved by the general shareholders meeting. The ban must be for a certain period and may not exceed 10 years. It may be extended before it expires for periods no greater than 10 years.

In ordinary corporations, the transfer of stock is limited by the other shareholders' right of first refusal, solely when that right is expressly set forth in the bylaws. In the case of closed corporations, the general rule is that shareholders have the right of first refusal unless the bylaws state otherwise. Additionally, it may be established in the bylaws of closed corporations that the transfer of stock must be approved by the corporation and/or that the shareholders may act as substitute heirs in the acquisition *mortis causa* of the deceased shareholder's stock.

The following are not permitted in open corporations: limitations on the free transfer of capital stock; any type of restriction on negotiating shares; or preferential shareholder rights in the event of stock transfers.

Minority Shareholders

The General Company Law establishes different measures for protecting minority shareholders. For example, shareholders representing no less than 20 percent of the voting stock have the right to request that the board of directors convene a general shareholders meeting. If a meeting is not convened, such shareholders may request a judge to issue a judicial summons for the meeting. In an open corporation, shareholders representing 5 percent of the voting stock have this right.

In certain cases, the General Company Law grants the right of withdrawal to those shareholders who have made their opposition known at a general meeting, to absent shareholders, to those who may have been illegally deprived of their vote, or to owners of nonvoting shares. Exercising the right of withdrawal obligates the corporation to reimburse whoever may withdraw for the value of his or her stock.

Although different types of company structures may be used to do business in Peru, investors generally choose those types that limit shareholder liability.

Suitable Corporate Forms

The corporation and the limited liability company are the most important and most frequently used types of companies regulated by the General Corporations Law (Ley General de Sociedades, or General Company Law), which has been in effect since January 1, 1998. Foreign investors may also establish a branch office in Peru.

Corporation Types

Peru's legislation recognizes and regulates three types of corporations: (a) ordinary corporations; (b) closed corporations; and (c) open corporations. All three types have the essential features of any corporation, meaning that they issue capital stock, their ownership is divided into shares of stock, and they enjoy limited liability.

Specific regulations dealing with closed corporations include features that are characteristic of partnerships, without failing to recognize their essential nature as a capital stock corporation. They seek to provide a suitable corporate structure for a limited number of shareholders who are usually involved in managing the company. The closed corporation may not have more than 20 shareholders, and given the importance of personal factors in owning and managing capital, its shares may not be listed on the Lima Stock Exchange or publicly traded on the securities market, unlike most open corporations.

On the other hand, the open corporation satisfies one or more of the following conditions: (i) it has made an initial public offering of stock or of corporate obligations convertible into stock; (ii) it has over 750 shareholders; (iii) over 35 percent of its capital stock is held by 175 or more shareholders; (iv) it is incorporated as such; or (v) all voting shareholders unanimously approve the motion to adopt such a system. The open corporation must publicly register its stock in the Public Registry of Securities, meaning that its stock may not be limited regarding its free transfer and negotiation. This type of corporation is subject to the supervision of Peruvian Securities and Exchange Commission (Comisión Nacional Supervisora de Empresas y Valores or CONASEV).

Agreements between shareholders or between shareholders and third parties are valid in all types of corporations and are enforceable in all matters concerning the corporation, from the moment they are duly recorded with the company. If any discrepancy exists between any stipulation in the shareholders' agreements and the company's articles of incorporation or bylaws, the latter shall prevail without prejudice to the relationship established by the agreement between the parties thereto.

The General Corporations Law also applies to banks, financial and insurance entities, and companies managing pension funds, among others, as these entities must (in accordance with special regulatory law) take the form of corporations and must also satisfy specific requirements, such as obtaining prior authorization from the corresponding regulatory body before being incorporated or initiating their operations.

Limited Liability Company

On the other hand, regulation of the limited liability company (also known as an SRL) is similar to that of the closed corporation, given the importance of personal factors involved in this type of company, which the General Company Law tries to preserve. This is a company whose capital is represented by nonstock shares (participaciones). A limited liability company may not have more than 20 stockholders.

Incorporation

Limited liability companies are incorporated by a minimum of two founding partners by filing a public document containing the articles of incorporation and the bylaws, which must include the names of the partners, their identification documents, their addresses, the legal name of the corporation, the corporate purpose, the mailing address of the corporation, and the appointment of the management officers, among other things.

The notarized incorporation document must be filed with the Corporate Register where the corporation has its domicile.

1. *Liability.* Partners are not personally liable for corporate obligations.

2. *Capital.* At the time of incorporation, partners' contributions must be subscribed in full and at least 25 percent of each share must be paid in. As is the case with corporations, no minimum amount of capital is required for incorporation. The corporate bylaws must contain rules regarding formalities that must be observed for increasing and decreasing capital stock, including partners' right of first refusal, and those cases in which stock may be offered to nonpartners if the partners refuse.

3. *Governance and Administration.* The general partners' meeting is the limited liability company's highest governing body. Its actions are subject to the norms that apply to the general partners' meeting as regards compliance with the General Company Law. The company is managed by one or more managers, whether shareholders or not, who represent it in all matters related to its corporate purpose. Managers may not participate personally or through a third party in any line of business that falls under the company's purpose.

4. *Distribution of Profits.* Profits are distributed to partners in proportion to the amount of shares owned, unless otherwise stated in the bylaws.

5. *Financial Statements.* Rules regarding the preparation and approval of financial statements must be included in the corporate bylaws. Financial statements are prepared and submitted in accordance with the law and with generally accepted accounting principles.

6. *Transfer of Stock.* Whoever is listed as the owner of one or more shares in the records of the company shall be considered as such. Transfers are carried out on the basis of a public deed signed by the transferring party and the purchasing party. In the event of a transfer of shares to nonpartners, the other partners shall have the right of first refusal. The bylaws may establish agreements and conditions for the transfer of shares and criteria for evaluating their value in such cases, but in no case may resolutions totally prohibit transfers.

7. *Minority Partners.* A general meeting must be held when requested by partners representing at least 20 percent of the capital stock.

Wholly Owned Entities

Wholly owned entities are considered branches of foreign companies, which are secondary establishments that do not possess a corporate status separate from the parent company, and are the entities through which foreign corporations carry out certain activities included in their corporate objectives. Accordingly, the principal is fully liable for all of its Peruvian branch obligations.

Branches are deemed to have permanent legal representation and enjoy procedural autonomy in the sphere of activities assigned to them by the parent company, in accordance with the powers granted to their representatives.

Establishment

Branches of foreign corporations are established through a public document prepared by a Peruvian notary public, in which the following information (among other items) must be provided: (1) the working capital assigned to the branch for its activities undertaken in the country; (2) the activities of the branch and a declaration stating that such activities are a part of the parent company's corporate purpose; (3) the branch address; and (4) the appointment of at least one permanent legal representative in the country.

In addition, the following must be inserted into the public document establishing the branch: (1) a certificate of good standing for the parent company in its country of origin, certifying that neither its articles of incorporation nor bylaws prohibit the establishment of foreign branches; (2) a copy of the articles of incorporation and bylaws of the parent company and of any other equivalent instruments in its country of origin; and (3) the resolution issued by the parent company's governing body in order to establish the branch in Peru.

The aforementioned original documents and copies must be legalized by the Peruvian consulate in the country in which the parent company is located.

Liability

The parent company is liable for all obligations incurred by the branch; any agreement exempting responsibility is consider null and void.

Capital

The total amount of assets assigned by the parent company to undertake the branch's activities is known as "assigned capital."

Administration

Branches are required to have a permanent legal representative in Peru who is authorized to enter into contracts on behalf of the parent company.

Remittance of Profits

There are no limitations on the remittance of profits by a branch to its parent company.

Joint Ventures

Peruvian law establishes two different types of joint ventures: the consortium and the participation association contract. This is not a closed list, so other associative contracts such as partnerships, shared risk, or joint ventures are also permitted under Peruvian law, albeit no specific regulation exists in respect thereof.

The General Company Law defines the participation contract as an agreement in which an individual or company grants to a person or persons (whether individuals or entities) a participation in the profits of the business that it carries out with third parties. In exchange, the participating partner usually provides some kind of contribution to the venture. In this type of contract, the participating party remains hidden in front of third parties with whom its partner may undertake business activities.

The consortium is defined as a contract in which two individuals or entities join together in order to participate in a certain business to share profits and reduce their transaction costs.

Consortia do not generate a separate independent entity from their partners.

Investments in and Mergers with Existing Entities

There are no restrictions for investments made by foreign companies in Peruvian companies. Foreign investments are awarded equal treatment with local Peruvian investments.

Mergers between companies are permitted and must comply with the applicable requisites and formalities provided for in the General Company Law.

Agency, Reseller, Franchising, and Distribution Networks

Peruvian law does not have any specific provisions about the establishment, requisites, or the treatment of agency, reseller, franchising, or distribution networks. Likewise, no agent or distributor protection regulations exist. Accordingly, any agency, reseller, franchising, or distribution agreements undertaken with Peruvian entities shall be ruled by the provisions of any contract entered into between the parties.

Foreign companies that wish to enter into contracts involving operations in Peru must assure that the person who runs the agency, reseller, franchising, or distribution network has enough powers of attorney to sign contracts and to enter into operations to develop activities in Peru.

Franchising agreements must be registered before the National Institute for the Defense of Competition and the Protection of the Intellectual Property (INDECOPI) (Peruvian competent authority in charge of the registration of trademarks), in order to use the marks involved in such agreements.

Representative Offices and Other Nonpermanent Establishments

Foreign companies can establish offices and nonpermanent establishments without the need for any registry or approval, except in certain regulated industries such as banks and insurance companies. As a requirement, this type of establishment must have enough powers of attorney so the agreements signed are enforceable according to the Peruvian law.

Approvals and Registrations

The undertaking of certain business activities requires prior approval from applicable authorities. This is the case, for instance, with banking and financial activities, insurance activities, and telecommunications, among others. Likewise, any activities involving natural resources, renewable or nonrenewable, require prior authorization or concession.

Sensitive Economic Sectors and Restrictions on Foreign Ownership

Peruvian law does not provide restrictions on undertaking any business activity or owning property in Peru, except for the ownership of land within 50 kilometers of the borders with other countries, which requires prior authorization.

Political Risk and Related Issues

Peru has offered a stable legal and business environment for the past 20 years. As a result, the country recently has been considered investment grade by major risk assessment entities. Provided they comply with certain minimum requirements, foreign investors are entitled to enter into the so-called "legal stability agreements," which ensure stability for a 10-year term in respect to income tax as well as foreign exchange and with no discrimination provisions regarding investments.

INVESTMENT ISSUES AND TAX INCENTIVES

Legal Treatment of Foreign Investment

Peru is governed by a general regime that promotes and ensures foreign investments. In addition, specific laws regarding mining, hydrocarbons, telecommunications, agriculture, and fishing (among other areas) further regulate foreign investment in those sectors.

The most important elements regarding foreign investment are as follows:

1. Investments by foreigners enjoy the same treatment as investments by Peruvians, which means that foreign investors and Peruvian investors have the same rights and obligations (neither group receives better treatment than the other).
2. Foreign investors may invest in any sector of the economy.
3. According to the law, foreign investment is deemed to be any investment from outside of the country that produces income in any of the following ways:

    a. Capital contributions to a new or existing business formed in any of the ways established by the Peruvian General Company Law (Ley General de Sociedades), either in freely convertible currency or in the form of tangible or intangible assets. Capital surplus is also considered to be a type of foreign investment;

    b. Investments made in Peruvian currency resulting from resources that may be remitted abroad;

    c. Conversion of private foreign obligations into shares;

    d. Reinvestments;

    e. Investments in property located in Peru;

    f. Intangible technological contributions, such as trademarks, industrial models, technical assistance, and patented or unpatented technical knowledge, which could be submitted as intangible assets, technical documents, or instructions (know-how);

    g. Investments used to purchase securities, financial documents, and commercial paper trading on the stock exchange, or bank certificates of deposit, either in Peruvian or foreign currency;

    h. Resources used to enter into partnership investment agreements or similar contracts; and

    i. Any other type of foreign investment contributing to Peru's development.

4. The government's prior express authorization is not required for foreign investments. Once undertaken, the investment should be registered with the Peruvian agency known as PROINVERSION (Agencia de Promoción de la Inversión Privada).

5. There are no exchange controls and the use, convertibility, and remittance of foreign currency are free.

Treaties on Foreign Investment Protection

Parties may avail themselves of Peru's legal stability regime by entering into contracts known as legal stability agreements (convenios de estabilidad jurídica), based on which the government provides certain guarantees to investors and to the companies in which they invest for a period of 10 years, including: (i) income taxes on investors and companies; (ii) free exchange of foreign currency and the remittance of capital and profits (only for investors); (iii) hiring of workers (only for companies); and (iv) export promotion measures, including drawback (only for companies receiving investments). In addition, concession agreements entered into regarding infrastructure projects and/or public services in which investors hold an interest may obtain legal stability for the same period of duration of the concession granted.

Article 62 of the Constitution of Peru provides that contracts shall have force of law, meaning that the parties thereto (including the government) must abide by them. In particular, the government may not unilaterally modify them by passing a law or otherwise leaving them without effect.

Contracts may be entered into before, or within 12 months of, the making of the investment.

Investors must qualify under any of the scenarios set forth below in order to receive the aforementioned protections under the legal stability regime:

    a.   Within two years of entering into a legal stability agreement, capital contributions of at least USD 10 million for the mining or hydrocarbon sectors or USD 5 million for the other sectors are made to the capital of a company in Peru. The term for investors making investments in concessionary companies undertaking infrastructure projects and/or public services is based on that which has been established in the relevant concession agreement.

    b.   Undertake investments involving risk with third parties (for example, joint ventures) for the amounts and based on the terms and conditions referenced in the preceding subparagraph (a).

    c.   Shares are acquired from companies that are directly or indirectly owned by the government (via privatization), as long as over 50 percent of the shares are in the amounts, for the periods, and based on the conditions referenced in subparagraph (a).

    d.   A foreign investment may also be guaranteed through an agreement, that is, the capitalized portion of the monetary contributions made by foreign investors as capital surplus, if undertaken in the amounts, periods, and conditions referenced in subparagraph (a).

    e.   Capitalization of private obligations abroad (loan capitalization) may be considered a foreign investment capable of being guaranteed through an agreement, as long as it is done in the amounts and for the time periods referenced in the foregoing subparagraph (a).

In the aforementioned cases, investors must channel their investment through an entity of the Peruvian financial system.

Companies receiving investments may also enter into an agreement with the Peruvian government if they receive investments from at least one investor meeting the requirements set forth above.

Companies fulfilling this requirement may receive the benefits associated with the hiring of workers, export promotion, and taxation, as long as they meet the basis for one of the following:

a. New investments must be made in an amount exceeding 50 percent of their capital and reserves and must be used to increase productive capacity or improve technology, meaning that such investments must be carried out through a capital increase.

b. New investments must entail the acquisition of over 50 percent of the shares of a company that is directly or indirectly owned by the government (as in privatizations).

Investors entering into agreements are guaranteed certain rights. Agreements provide foreign investors with legal security in the following areas:

a. Income taxes: Dividends and any other form of profit-sharing to which foreign investors are entitled will not be affected by any tax resulting in a greater tax burden than that which was in effect as of the date on which the contract was signed;

b. Freely convertible currency;

c. The right to freely remit all capital, profits, dividends, and royalties, without any limitations or restrictions;

d. The right to make use of the best exchange rate available on the market.

e. The right to nondiscrimination, meaning that no government company or entity (either on the national, regional, or local level) may provide different treatment based on nationality, sector, type of economic activity, or geographic location as regards investments, currency exchange, prices, nontariff duties or fees, type of company (including natural or juridical person), and any other equivalent reason.

Companies receiving investments are also guaranteed certain rights. Agreements provide companies receiving investments with legal security in the following areas:

a. Income taxes: As long as the agreement remains in effect, the income tax regime cannot be modified. Similarly, taxable income shall be calculated based on the same rates, deductions, and scale as set forth in legislation in effect at the time of signing the agreement. This protection exists regardless of whether such modifications prove favorable or not to the company. As mentioned previously, only those companies meeting the criteria set forth in the second point qualify for such protection.

b. Hiring of employees: For the duration of the agreement, these companies may hire workers in any way established by the labor laws in effect at the time of execution of the agreement.

   c.   Export promotion, as established by the General Customs Law (temporary admission, drawback and repositioning of merchandise based on exemption of duties), as well as favoring the exporter as set forth in the General Sales Tax Law.

The main characteristics of these agreements and their durations are as follows:

   a.   They are legally binding on parties and may not be unilaterally modified.

   b.   They are governed by the provisions of the private contract law (Civil Code) and not by the government's exclusive administrative rights.

   c.   They have a maximum period of duration of 10 years starting on the date of execution, except in the case of agreements entered into by concessionaires engaged in infrastructure and public service projects, in which case the period of duration is extended so as to remain in effect while the respective concessionary or contract is in effect.

   d.   They may be waived by investors and companies receiving investment, in which case common legislation shall apply, starting on the date on which the waiver is submitted.

   e.   The investor may assign his contractual rights to another investor, subject to authorization by the competent entity. Although assignment is prohibited in the case of companies receiving investments, the law allows in the case of corporate reorganization (mergers or divestitures) for contractually granted benefits to be assigned to one of the parties participating in such reorganization, as long as the competent entity expressly authorizes it after having received an opinion from the Peruvian tax authorities.

   f.   Any amendments agreed upon by the parties may not refer to the period of duration, to the extension of the two-year period for making the investment, or to a reduction in the amount of the investment below the limits established by law (USD 10 million in the mining and hydrocarbon sectors, or USD 5 million in other sectors). If the amendment provides for an increase in the amount of the investment, such increase may also be included in the legal stability regime by receiving authorization from the competent entity.

   g.   Agreements may be legally terminated in the following cases: (a) failure by investors or companies to undertake or receive contributions or purchases, respectively, to which they have agreed within the allotted time frame; and (b) failure by investors to obtain prior authorization for assigning their contractual rights and obligations.

Capital increases brought about as a result of capitalizing a revaluation surplus or adjustment for inflation may be included in the legal stability regime, as long as notice of such capitalization is given to PROINVERSION within 30 days of such increases having been undertaken.

PROINVERSION is the national entity that is responsible for representing the government when contracts are signed with foreign investors.

Contracts entered into by companies receiving foreign investments are signed jointly by PROINVERSION and by the ministry of the sector in which the investment will be made or by the person appointed by such ministry. If Peruvian and foreign investors wish to invest in the same company and submit their requests jointly, PROINVERSION shall be the competent entity.

OPERATIONAL LEGAL ENVIRONMENT

Foreign Exchange

Peruvian law does not have any restrictions or limitations concerning foreign exchange. There are no foreign exchange controls, registrations, approvals, or other similar restrictions regarding the remittance of foreign currency to or from Peru. There is no need to have an approval to undertake foreign exchange transactions or to carry foreign currency. Any currency can be exchanged for Peruvian new sols and may be used in every transaction in Peru provided that the parties agree to do so.

Bank accounts of any kind can be opened in U.S. dollars and other currencies as long as the referred bank offers that kind of product. Also, credit facilities may be agreed to in U.S. dollars or other currencies without any special conditions.

Immigration and Visa Requirements

Business Visa

Under Peruvian immigration law, business visas are issued to persons who enter the country without the intent of residency. While such persons may not receive income from a Peruvian source, they may sign contracts and engage in transactions.

A business visa does not confer the right to render services (either as an employee or independent contractor) to entities domiciled in Peru, even when such services are performed on behalf of a nonresident entity. Because business visas are temporary in nature, foreign workers must leave the country when their visa expires and then reenter with another business visa, unless a multiple-exit visa has been issued, which allows travel into and outside of the country for the period of its duration.

Foreign Workers from a Nonresident Company

Such immigration status is granted to those foreign workers who are sent to Peru by their nonresident employers in order to render contractual services on the employer's behalf.

Both companies must enter into a service agreement based on which the company domiciled abroad agrees to provide a certain type of service to the company domiciled in Peru. Upon executing this service contract, the company domiciled abroad transfers some of its workers to Peru.

A foreign citizen who obtains this immigration status shall have the right to reside legally for as long as he or she needs to be in Peru and may work in the country.

Worker Immigration Status

Foreign workers who seek to work and reside in Peru are required to obtain resident worker immigration status.

In order to do so, they must enter into a foreign employment contract, which is approved by the Peruvian Administrative Work Authority once it is confirmed (based on the documents submitted) that all legal requirements are met and that foreign worker percentage quotas are complied with.

Subsequently, a request must be submitted to the Peruvian Immigration Office, which then issues an identification card for the foreigner allowing him or her to work for an employer in the country.

Import and Export Issues

Import

The General Law of Customs (Ley General de Aduanas) established different regimes for the admission of goods into Peru, depending on whether their import is definitive or temporary.

Except for those restrictions based on sanitary, security, or other specific circumstances, there is no restriction for the import of any goods into the country. Although there is no legal requirement in this respect, as a matter of practice only domiciled entities or individuals can act as importers or exporters of goods.

Import operations are subject to three different kinds of payments that formed the tax debt: 1) customs duties; 2) internal taxes; and 3) customs clearance fees.

Customs Duties

Ad-valorem duties apply to the importation of goods at the rates of 0 percent, 4 percent, 9 percent, or 17 percent of the CIF value of the imported merchandise, in accordance with the approved list of goods (which follows international classification). Exports are exempted from customs duties.

Internal Taxes

Import operations are taxed with the value added tax (IGV) at the rate of 19 percent, as well as with a luxury tax (ISC) if the merchandise is considered luxury goods in accordance with the provisions regulating this tax.

Customs Clearance Fees

All taxes and rates must be paid before the merchandise is withdrawn from Customs so the Customs Authority can issue approval for using imported merchandise and consider it national or nationalized. If the importer can fully pay the tax debt, he or she can constitute a custom guaranty until the owed amount is paid.

Export

The General Law of Customs considers exportation as the exit of nationalized merchandise from the country. Export operations are tax free and are subject to tax benefits, as will be explained in the following section.

Taxation of Business and Cross-Border Transactions

In accordance with the Peruvian Constitution, taxes may be levied, amended, or repealed only by Congressional legislation or, in the event that legislative power is delegated to the executive branch, by executive order. However, import tariffs are regulated solely by presidential decree.

Regional and local governments may levy, amend, and eliminate taxes and fees in their jurisdictions, within legally established limits. When exercising its power of taxation, the government must respect the principles of statutory reserve, equality, and fundamental human rights. Similarly, the Constitution expressly establishes that no tax may be confiscatory in nature.

The main taxes established in Peruvian legislation are described next.

Income Tax

Assessment Criteria

The assessment criteria used for levying income tax in Peru are *domicile* (residence) and *source*. The following persons are considered "residents" for income tax purposes: Peruvian and foreign individuals who reside in the country, corporations incorporated in Peru, and permanent establishments in Peru operated by foreign entities.

Income taxes are levied on individuals or corporations that are residents of the country, and are based on their income from "worldwide sources." In the case of nonresident taxpayers, as well as branches, agencies, and other local establishments permanently operated by nonresident individuals or corporations, taxes are levied solely on income from Peruvian sources.

The term "income from Peruvian sources" includes, among other things, that which is generated and/or produced by real estate, loans, capital investments, technical assistance used for economic gain inside the country, royalties and property located in or used for economic benefit inside the country, and personal work undertaken inside the country as well as that which is derived from civil, commercial, business, or other activities conducted in Peruvian territory.

Resident Companies

(a) *Tax Rate*. Income earned by companies "domiciled" in Peru is subject to an income tax rate of 30 percent. Dividends paid to individuals (whether residents or nonresidents) and to nonresident corporations are subject to income tax at the rate of 4.1 percent.

(b) *Expenses*. In the specific case of resident companies, as a general rule, deductions are allowed for all business- and production-related expenses, as long as such expenses are used to generate taxable income. However, the law sets limitations and restrictions on deductions of certain expenses. For example, in the case of loans between related parties, interest is proportionally deductible on amounts of indebtedness not exceeding three times the net worth of the debtor (otherwise, the debtor would be legally insolvent).

(c) *Banking Regulations*. Since 2004, companies domiciled in Peru are required to meet certain formalities when fulfilling payment obligations to third parties. One formality thus established requires that payments be made through the Peruvian banking system when such amounts are greater than 3,500 PEN (Peruvian new sols) or USD 1,000 (depending on the currency in which the obligation was contracted), in order to document expenses, costs, and/or tax credits for tax effects.

(d) *Depreciation*. As a general rule, resident companies in Peru may make deductions for depreciation of capital assets used in the conduct of their business (20 percent in the case of machinery and equipment used for mining, petroleum, and construction activities; 25 percent in the case of data-processing equipment; 5 percent in the case of buildings and construction; and 10 percent in the case of other fixed assets).

(e) *Fair Market Value*. In the case of sales and other transfers of title, as well as of services rendered and other types of transactions, regardless of the value placed on the transaction by the parties, it is understood for tax purposes that all operations have been undertaken at fair market value. If the value placed on the transaction by the contracting parties differs from fair market value as a result of overvaluation or undervaluation, the Tax Administration Agency will adjust it for the receiving party as well as for the transferring party. For transactions between related parties or with corporations established in offshore territories, the respective fair market value is established by the regulations on transfer pricing.

(f) *Carrying Over Losses*. Resident companies may carry over at least a part of their tax losses from previous fiscal years in order to offset future profit. In order to do so, companies must choose one of the following methods: the first allows for carrying over a tax loss incurred during a fiscal year over the next four fiscal years; and the second allows for the indefinite carryover of tax losses from prior fiscal years, but may be used to offset only 50 percent of the net income earned during the following fiscal years.

(g) *Partial Payments.* Resident companies are required to make monthly income tax payments, based on the amount of net income earned in the month. A percentage or coefficient must be applied to this income, in accordance with legally accepted procedures. Partial payments are credited against the annual principal account.

Resident Individuals

Income earned by resident individuals is subject to income tax based on two groups of tax rates: (i) Capital incomes, formed by incomes of the first and second category; and (ii) Work incomes, formed by incomes of the fourth and fifth category.

Capital incomes are subject to income tax based on a tax rate of 5 percent, except for dividends paid to individuals, which are subject to a tax rate of 4.1 percent.

Work incomes are subject to income tax based on the following progressive rates:

Tax Rate	Annual Total Net Income
15%	Up to 27 UITs* (approximately USD 27,000)
21%	Over 27 UITs and up to 54 UITs (approximately USD 27,000 USD to USD 54,000)
30%	Over 54 UITs (approximately USD 54,000)

Note: *The UIT (unidad impositiva tributaria or taxable income unit) is set annually.

Nonresident Taxpayers

As a general rule, nonresident taxpayers are subject to a tax rate of 30 percent on their income from Peruvian sources. Taxes must be withheld by the payer of the income.

There are special tax rates for the transfer of shares and securities. The tax rate for these operations is 5 percent, as long as such shares or securities are listed in the Lima Stock Exchange and the transaction is undertaken through the stock exchange.

Also, special treatment is given in the case of foreign interest payments made by Peruvian companies on loans from nonresident entities with which they have no legal association. Such interest payments are subject to a tax rate of 4.99 percent, as long as certain requirements are met.

Withholdings may be reduced if an agreement to avoid double taxation exists between Peru and the country in which the creditor resides (for example, treaties signed by Peru with Chile and Canada provide for a maximum withholding rate of

15 percent in the case of interest paid by debtors who are residents of Peru to creditors who reside in Chile or Canada).

At present time, Peru has subscribed to double taxation agreements with Chile, Canada, and Brazil. Similar taxation agreements exist with Ecuador, Bolivia, and Colombia.

Provisional Net Assets Tax (Impuesto Temporal a los Activos Netos or ITAN)

ITAN is a provisional tax on the value of a company's net assets as of December 31 of the previous fiscal year.

ITAN must be paid only by those companies that have initiated commercial operations on or before December 31 of the preceding fiscal year. The regulatory norm set forth in the ITAN law has determined that a company is understood to have initiated "commercial operations" when it performs the first transfer of goods or rendering of services.

ITAN tax rates for the year 2009 were as follows:

Tax Rate	Net Assets
0%	Up to 1 million PEN (approximately USD 300,000)
0.4%	Over 1 million PEN

ITAN declarations must be filed with tax authorities within the first 12 business days of the month of April. ITAN may be paid in cash or in installments of up to nine monthly payments between the months of April and December.

Companies have the option of considering the amount actually paid in cash for ITAN (i) as a deductible expense, or (ii) as a credit against payments on account and as an income tax correction for the corresponding fiscal year.

At the end of the fiscal year, if the amount paid for ITAN is greater than income tax during the same period, companies may submit a request to tax authorities for a refund of the excess amount paid. (A refund must be issued within a maximum of 60 business days from the income tax filing date for the corresponding period.)

Value Added Tax (Impuesto General a las Ventas or IGV)

VAT taxes apply to the following operations at a rate of 19 percent: (i) the sale of personal property inside the country; (ii) the rendering or use of services inside the country; (iii) construction contracts; (iv) the first sale of real estate property by builders; and (v) the importation of goods.

The IGV paid on the acquisition of goods and services can be used as a tax credit against any sales and rendering of services. IGV must be declared and paid monthly.

Export operations are not subject to this tax. By meeting certain requirements, however, exporters may recover IGV tax credits monthly, up to a limit that is the equivalent of 19 percent of the FOB value of monthly exports. To this effect, exporters may do the following: credit this amount against other taxes (such as income tax) and, if there is a balance, request a return in the form of a negotiable bank note or check.

Negotiable bank notes may be used to pay other taxes, or may be freely transferred by endorsing them to third parties in exchange for cash.

Luxury Tax (Impuesto Selectivo al Consumo or ISC)

This is a tax on the importation and local sale of certain goods considered to be luxury items, such as vehicles, cigarettes, cigars, liquor, beer, and fuel. Depending on the nature of the item, the tax is determined on the basis of three systems: (1) value (for example, 30 percent in the case of used vehicles produced for mass transport); (2) fixed amount (for example, 1.50 PEN per liter of the Peruvian alcohol known as *pisco*); and (3) value according to the retail sales price (for example, 27.8 percent in the case of beer).

Labor and Employment

Labor Contracts

Individual Labor Agreements

Labor laws provide that all employees must be hired for an indefinite period. Contracts for a fixed term are available only in certain cases provided they meet the requirements established by law.

The most important cases in which the law allows for a worker to be hired for a fixed term are as follows: (i) starting or increasing operations (contract arising from the initiation of a new business activity); (ii) market needs (contract entered into in order to meet business production increases); (iii) substitution (contract entered into in order to temporarily substitute for a permanent employee of the company); and (iv) a certain project or specific service (contract with a previously established purpose and a specific duration).

Each term-based labor contract has a maximum period based on its type. However, none may exceed five years. Contracts must be entered into in writing and the Labor Authority [Autoridad Administrativa de Trabajo] must be notified for the corresponding registration thereof.

Collective Agreements

Collective agreements are entered into by one or more employers and one or more unions or workers' representatives in order to regulate the rights of workers and their relationship with their employer, as well as any matters affecting such relationship.

In Peru, the law establishes the procedure that must be followed by workers and employers when signing collective agreements. If the parties do not reach an agreement, the law provides for various means of resolving conflicts, such as conciliation, mediation, and arbitration.

Special Agreements

Given the special characteristics of activities involved in rendering services, special regimes exist for contracting labor regarding mining, agriculture, civil construction, foreign employees, and micro and small business employees, among others. Each regime is governed by special legislation establishing its characteristics and specifications.

Nonlabor Agreements

Trainee contracts do not qualify as labor relations as their purpose is to train the workforce (ideally young people) who have not yet joined the labor market. The types of contracts regarding training include apprenticeship contracts, internship contracts, youth trainee contracts, clerkships, and labor re-insertion. Persons rendering such types of services are not entitled to legal benefits arising from work contracts.

Service and project contracts may be used only in the case of independent services, where the party rendering the service is under no type of subordination or control exercised on the part of whoever benefits from such work. Persons contracted under these systems are not entitled to benefits that are routinely a part of work contracts.

Worker Age

The Child and Adolescent Code provides for specific minimum ages in order for a legal minor to be authorized to perform a job under a work contract. The minimum age depends on the activity performed, although generally it must not be below the age of 14.

On the other hand, retirement age is 65 for men and 60 for women, at which age workers may choose to apply for a retirement pension, as long as they satisfy the corresponding requirement for longevity of contributions.

Similarly, Peru's laws provide for compulsory and automatic worker retirement at age 70, as long as the worker is entitled to a retirement pension, although the parties may reach an agreement to the contrary.

Worker Nationality

The Foreign Worker Hiring Law provides that Peruvian or foreign companies may hire foreign workers, as long as the latter do not exceed 20 percent of the total number of their workers. Similarly, it provides that total payments to foreign workers may not exceed 30 percent of the value of the total payroll.

Notwithstanding the foregoing, there are cases in which the aforementioned percentage limits do not apply, as in the case of a foreigner whose spouse is Peruvian or a foreigner with an immigrant visa. Similarly, there are cases of foreign workers who are exempt from such percentages because they perform work involving specialized, managerial, or leadership tasks.

Work Shift

The ordinary workday is eight hours, or a maximum of 48 hours per week. Work performed after the end of the workday must be treated as overtime. Overtime work is voluntary on the part of the worker. Overtime pay for the first two hours may not be less than 25 percent above the pay scale per hour, based on the pay received by the worker. A percentage of 35 percent above the pay scale is applied to any additional hours.

Employers must keep an "Electronic Register" in order to document information on workers, pension workers, and third-party services. This "Electronic Register" must be presented to the Administrative Labor Authority and the Tax Administration.

Paid Vacation Time

Workers are entitled to a 24-hour weekly rest period. This day of rest should preferably be taken on Sunday. However, because of the nature of company activities, it may be taken on another day.

Workers are entitled to 30 calendar days of paid vacation for each full year of service. Vacation time must be taken in the year following the year in which it was accrued.

Maternity Leave and Benefits

Female workers are entitled to 45 days of prenatal leave and 45 days of postnatal leave. The prenatal leave can be added to the postnatal, at the worker's choice. In the event of multiple births, there shall be an additional 30 days of postnatal leave. Similarly, at the end of the postnatal period, the mother is entitled to a daily one-hour nursing leave until the child is one year old.

Remuneration

Peruvian legislation considers remuneration to be the total amount received by workers for their services, whether in cash or in kind, provided it may be used freely by workers. However, other legal concepts exist such as special bonuses, profit sharing, and value of work conditions, among others.

The form in which payment is made is established by mutual agreement between the worker and the employer. It is also possible for employers to establish a total annual payment with those workers who receive monthly payments greater than two taxable income units (unidades impositivas tributarias or UITs), which corresponds to approximately USD 2,300. This amount includes all legal and conventional benefits to which the company is subject, with the exception of profit-sharing.

Workers are entitled to the following benefits, among others:

1. *Minimum Living Wage*. Workers shall receive a minimum monthly income of approximately USD 196.18.

2. *Profit-Sharing.* Legislative Decrees 677 and 892 establish a system of profit-sharing for personnel at private companies. The workers' share is not based on employer earnings, but rather on annual income calculated in accordance with income tax regulations. The percentage that must be distributed by the employer to the workers depends on the employer's activity.

3. *Seniority Pay.* All workers are entitled to seniority pay, as long as they work a minimum of four hours a day. This benefit is deposited semi-annually in the banking or financial institution of the worker's choice. The amount of each deposit is equal to one-twelfth of the computed monthly pay for the months worked. Computed pay is the total amount that the worker regularly receives as compensation for his or her work, whether in cash or in kind. This amount must be deposited in the bank that the worker chooses.

4. *Legal Bonuses.* Workers are entitled to two bonuses a year, one in the month of July (Independence Day) and another in the month of December (Christmas). The amount of each bonus is equal to one month's pay.

Social Security Health Insurance

The social security health system offers its beneficiaries the following benefits: prevention, awareness, recovery, and subsidies for health care, social welfare, and work and professional illnesses. This system is administered by a public entity known as the Social Security Health Institute (Seguro Social de Salud or ESSALUD) and is supplemented by health plans and programs provided by employers in their own contracts or contracted through private health-care providers (entidades prestadoras de salud or EPS), which in certain circumstances may act in the place of ESSALUD.

Termination of Work Relations

Peruvian legislation basically provides for three possible scenarios in which an employer may dismiss individual workers.

In the first scenario, the employer dismisses the worker for a serious breach, following the procedure established by law. In this case, the worker is not entitled to any severance pay whatsoever as a result of his or her dismissal.

In the second scenario, the employer dismisses the worker unfairly and directly pays him or her the aforementioned severance pay, which in the case of workers contracted on a permanent basis amounts to one and a half months' pay for every full year of service, with a cap of 12 months' pay. In the case of workers contracted for a fixed period of time, severance pay amounts to one and a half months' pay for each month in which work was not performed until expiration of the contract.

Finally, in the third scenario, the employer dismisses the worker based on an illegal reason (that is, a discriminatory motive such as the worker's union affiliation; status as a candidate to represent workers; discrimination on the basis of race, sex, or religion; or other things). In this final case, the worker is entitled to be reinstated in his or her employment and to be compensated for the pay he or she stopped receiving as a result of the dismissal.

There are two possible scenarios in which an employer may dismiss workers collectively.

The first scenario is the reduction of personnel. In this case, the employer may reduce personnel for economic, technological, organizational, or similar reasons, as long as the termination of work contracts based on such causes pertains to a number of workers not greater than 10 percent of the company's total personnel. To this end, an administrative procedure must be carried out before the Administrative Work Authority. In such cases, workers are not entitled to seek any severance pay whatsoever for being laid off.

The second scenario arises from the dissolution and liquidation of the employer. Employers may agree to their dissolution or liquidation at any time, without the need for prior authorization or any cause or reason to justify their decision. Dissolution of a corporation in Peru does not result in any type of employer liability toward workers. Upon dissolution of the corporation based on a resolution passed at the general shareholders meeting, the liquidator is authorized to terminate labor relations with the workers. In such cases, workers are not entitled to seek any type of severance pay whatsoever for the termination of their work relationships.

Outsourcing and Third-Party Services

Outsourcing is permitted only when there is a need for temporary, supplementary, or specialized services. The law clearly states that transferred workers hired under this scheme may not render services that entail the ongoing performance of the employer's main activity.

The law establishes that the number of workers that may be transferred to a user firm may not exceed 20 percent of the user firm's total workforce. This percentage will not be applied to supplementary or specialized services, as long as the service provider assumes full technical autonomy and responsibility for carrying out its activities.

Third-party services implies the hiring of companies of services to develop specialized activities, as long as they carry out the contracted assignments on their behalf and at their own risk; have their own financial, technical, and material resources; and have workers who are under their exclusive control. The use of these types of contracts doesn't restrict the individual and collective rights of the workers.

Peru's legislation has established that the following do constitute third-party services: management contracts; project contracts; contracts for the purpose of placing a third party in charge of an integral part of a company's production; and services rendered by contracting and subcontracting firms, as long as they carry out the contracted assignments on their behalf and at their risk; have their own financial, technical, and material resources; and have workers who are under their exclusive control.

The company that hires the services company is jointly liable with the latter for workers' payment.

Unions

The main function of unions is to represent workers in a particular industry in conflicts or complaints of a collective nature, and to enter into labor contracts with their employers.

Formation of a union depends on the industry or the level on which workers intend to negotiate with their employer or employers. If the workers are going to negotiate solely on a company level, they will need to form a company union, for which a minimum of 20 persons is needed. On the other hand, if they intend to negotiate with several employers, they will have to form a trade union, for which a minimum of 50 workers must join together.

More than one union may coexist in a company. However, only a union with a majority of affiliated workers may negotiate on such a level. Union affiliation is free and voluntary for workers and is offered based on the union's bylaws.

Pension Systems

Peru has two pension systems. In both cases the worker must be at least 65 years old in order to apply for retirement pension, and the worker also must have contributed for the minimum number of years. In special cases, both the retirement age and the longevity requirement may be reduced as a result of high-risk activities performed by workers, who may then receive their retirement pension at an earlier age.

1. *National Pension System.* The National Pension System is a system administered by the government through the Office of Pensions. All workers subject to labor regulations in the private sector must adhere to this system, unless they are affiliated with the private pension system.
2. *Private Pension System.* Workers subject to labor regulations in the private sector may choose to be affiliated with the private pension system administered by private pension fund managers.

Taxes on Compensation

The main taxes on compensation received by workers are as follows:

1. *Social Security Health Insurance.* A sum of 9 percent of the monthly salary is paid into social security health insurance and is charged to the employer.

2. *National and Private Pension System.* In the case of the national pension system the contribution amounts to 13 percent of compensation. In the case of the private pension system, the contribution amounts can be up to 14 percent. In both cases, the worker is responsible for payment.

3. *Income Tax.* This tax is levied on all work-related income. It is charged to the worker but must be withheld and paid by the employer. For resident workers in the country, the tax is based on a progressive scale applied to net income (total payments received in the year minus 7 UITs, that is to say, approximately USD 7,345). For nonresident workers in the country, a general rate of 30 percent is applied to total gross income without any deductions being made.

Antitrust and Competition Issues

Peruvian legislation promotes and protects free competition. Conduct against free competition is forbidden and sanctioned by the Legislative Decree 1034, Law of Repression of Anticompetitive Conducts. Sanctions are determined and executed by INDECOPI (the Peruvian National Institute for the Defense of Competition and Protection of Intellectual Property) regarding each case that is presented before it.

Two main conducts are sanctioned by the competition regulations: (i) abuse of dominant position, and (ii) concerted practices.

The conduct of abuse of dominant position is defined as the performing of acts or the undertaking of transactions or agreements by a person who has a dominant position in the market, in order to obtain anticompetitive benefits. A person or company is considered to have a dominant position when it can alter supply and demand conditions because of its participation quota in the market. Each case of abuse of dominant position is reviewed by INDECOPI in order to establish the existence of the conduct and the respective sanction.

Concerted practices involve the entering into or performing of agreements, decisions, recommendations, or practices between persons or companies in order to limit or restrict free competition such as price fixing, supply limitations, or client distributions.

Other conduct can be considered anticompetitive according to the general criteria established by INDECOPI.

Environmental Issues

Enactment of the Environmental and Natural Resources Code (Código del Medio Ambiente y de los Recursos Naturales or CMARN) in 1990 was the first attempt at systematizing Peruvian environmental legislation. The 1993 Peruvian Constitution also established a series of governing principles in the area of environmental policy, such as the government's role in setting national environmental policy and its role in promoting the sustainable use of natural resources.

Furthermore, Legislative Decree 757, the Law for the Promotion of Private Investment (Ley Marco para el Crecimiento de la Inversión Privada), modified CMARN and established the competent environmental authority.

In this respect, Peruvian environmental legislation has undergone significant development aimed at (among other objectives) creating a less bureaucratic environment in which companies undertaking activities with a potential environmental impact may conduct business without facing administrative obstacles, unnecessary costs, and possible social conflicts.

Accordingly, various legal norms have been implemented in recent years in order to provide for efficient and coordinated actions by each state entity, thereby establishing the principles for environmental legislation and laying the groundwork for national environmental policy while (most importantly) setting guidelines for the elimination of overlapping authorities.

Similarly, the General Environmental Law (Ley General del Ambiente or LGA), which repealed CMARN, seeks to harmonize the conduct of governmental operations and business activity in order to achieve sustainable development in the country. It also establishes clear rules for economic development and introduces mechanisms for promoting economic activities. A clear example of the intent to foster the creation of "clean policies" that go hand in hand with the proper development of economic activity is the establishment of the groundwork for granting tax incentives.

Finally, LGA introduces innovative changes, including the following: strengthening the National Environmental Council (Consejo Nacional del Ambiente), which is the highest national authority on environmental affairs; establishing a National Comprehensive Code for Sanctions, to which other codes providing for sanctions and violations in each economic sector must be adapted; introducing the new concept of "environmental responsibility," the objective of which is to provide compensation for possible damage generated by negative environmental impacts; and, finally, creating a system for assigning environmental responsibility.

Consumer Protection and Products Liability

A new Code of Protection and Defense of the Consumer (Código de Protección y Defensa del Consumidor) has been recently approved. According to this code, consumers shall have access to suitable products and services and all effective mechanisms for their protection. The new code has established several criteria to reduce the information asymmetry in favor of the consumer. The Consumer Protection Commission of INDECOPI (Comisión de Protección al Consumidor) is in charge of reviewing claims for violation of any of the code's regulations.

The Consumer Code is applicable to all consumer relations that are entered into or performed in Peru.

Land Use and Real Estate

Peruvian law protects private property. Property rights can be affected only in case of public necessity declared by law or domestic security, provided that adequate indemnification is previously paid to the owner.

Property ownership rules apply equally to nationals and foreigners, except that foreigners cannot own or possess, whether individually or through a legal entity, mines, land, woods, domestic waters, fuels, or energy sources within 50 kilometers of Peruvian boundaries. Land and real estate in general can be mortgaged as a guaranty.

Intellectual Property

Trademarks

In Peru, the right to exclusively use a trademark is acquired upon registration thereof with INDECOPI. Any mark that may be graphically represented and that is suitable for distinguishing products or services in the marketplace may be registered as a trademark.

Names and commercial slogans, collective marks, certification marks, and denominations of origin are also considered to be distinctive marks capable of being registered.

If the filed application for registration satisfies all legal requirements without opposition, the procedure takes approximately four months. If there is opposition, the procedure takes approximately one and a half years.

Registration is granted for 10 years from the date of authorization and may be renewed indefinitely for successive 10-year periods. For this purpose, a registration renewal request must be filed within six months of the registration's expiration date. No proof of usage is required for renewal of a trademark.

Trademark registrations may be canceled at any interested party's request if they have not been used in one of the member countries of the Andean Community (Bolivia, Colombia, Ecuador, Peru, and Venezuela) for three years prior to the date on which the request for cancellation was filed. The legal owner of the trademark has the burden of proof in respect to use of the trademark.

Transfers, licenses, mergers, name changes, and, in general, any acts in respect to trademarks must be registered with INDECOPI in order to be enforceable vis-à-vis third parties.

Inventions

In Peru, patents are issued for inventions of products or procedures in all technological fields, as long as they are new, novel, and capable of industrial application.

If the filed patent application satisfies all legal requirements and there is no opposition, the registration procedure takes approximately three years. If there is opposition, registration takes approximately five years.

Patents for inventions are granted for 20 years starting on the application filing date.

Annual fees established by the INDECOPI Office of Inventions and New Technologies must be paid in order for an existing patent or pending patent application to remain in effect.

Protection may also be obtained for utility models, industrial designs, and integrated circuit drawings by registering them before the INDECOPI Office of Inventions and New Technologies.

Utility models are protected by patents. Registration of a utility model is granted for 10 years starting on the date the application is filed.

New industrial designs may be registered. Registration of an industrial design is granted for 10 years starting on the dated the application is filed before the INDECOPI office.

A drawing will be protected if it is original. Registration is granted for 10 years starting from the last day of the year in which the first commercial use of the drawing was made anywhere in the world, or from the date the application is filed before INDECOPI. In either case, protection of a registered drawing will expire in 15 years, starting from the last day of the year in which the drawing was created.

Transfers, licenses, mergers, name changes, and, in general, any acts involving any of the above-mentioned rights must be registered before the INDECOPI Office of Inventions and New Technologies in order to be enforceable vis-à-vis third parties.

Copyrights

Copyright protection covers all literary or artistic works of human creation, regardless of genre, form of expression, merit, or purpose. Copyrights require no formal registration in order to be protected.

The author retains original ownership of an exclusive copyright that is enforceable vis-à-vis third parties.

Internet Regulations/E-Commerce

At present, Peruvian legislation does not include any rules about Internet transactions and e-commerce. Accordingly, any such relationship will be ruled by whatever conditions the parties agree to in connection with the undertaking of transactions through electronic means.

Financing Issues/Payments

The entering into of financing agreements with foreign financial entities is not subject to any restriction and does not require any prior authorization or registration with the Central Bank of Peru or any other authority. Payment of debt abroad under such agreements is equally free of authorizations or restrictions, provided that payment is made for applicable income tax withholdings on any interest paid.

Financial leasing activities are restricted to Peruvian authorized entities.

Securities Laws Issues

Securities are mainly regulated by the Securities Market Law. This law applies to securities that are widely issued, are freely negotiable, and give their holder credit rights over the capital, patrimony, or profits, as is the case with stock shares, debt instruments, bonds, short-term instruments, or any other similar values. Securities may be offered publicly or privately. All securities publicly offered must be previously recorded with the Capital Market Public Register held by the Peruvian Securities and Exchange Commission (Comisión Nacional Supervisora de Empresas y Valores or CONASEV).

The Securities Market Law, along with other regulations issued by CONASEV, establishes certain standards such as transparency and timely availability of information. All information provided to CONASEV or the stock exchange must be truthful, sufficient, and timely so that it can be made available to the public. The information contained in the register of CONASEV is freely accessible unless it is determined as private by law.

Capital market regulations establish different kinds of public offerings according to the securities to be offered.

Public Offerings

Peru's legislation regards a public offering as any offer that is directed to the general public or to a determined segment of noninstitutional investors for the purchase, sale, or placement of securities. Every offer is presumed public unless the offer is directed to institutional investors or the lowest unitary value of the offered security is 250,000 PEN (Peruvian new sols).

Initial Public Offering

An initial offering is the public offering of newly issued securities. Securities that are subject to this kind of offer shall be registered in the register of CONASEV, along with the Information Memorandum and the financial statements from the previous two years.

The Information Memorandum must contain all characteristics, rights, and obligations to be granted to the buyer, all relevant clauses of the issuance contract and the company's bylaws, risk assessments, the entity in charge of the structuring of the transaction, all financial statements, and the placement procedure. CONASEV may determine any additional information that shall be made available.

The placement of securities under this kind of offer cannot last more than 18 months from the date of inscription in the register.

Secondary Public Offering

This kind of offering is directed to all securities that have previously been issued and placed, such the Public Offer of Acquisition (Oferta Pública de Adquisición or OPA), also known the tender offer.

The rules for the OPA establish that if a person or company intends to acquire or increase, directly or indirectly, a significant participation (defined as any acquisition of 25 percent, 50 percent, or 60 percent) in a listed company, such acquisition shall be undertaken through a public offer of acquisition.

Stock Exchange

Stock exchanges are centralized mechanisms that simultaneously connect several buyers and sellers in order to negotiate securities transactions. Stock Exchange of Lima (Bolsa de Valores de Lima) is the only centralized mechanism in Peru at this time.

Stock Exchange Intermediaries

Stock exchange brokers are in charge of all transactions undertaken in the Lima Stock Exchange. Brokers are required to be authorized by CONASEV and are subject to its control and supervision.

CAVALI

CAVALI is the clearing entity for all transactions undertaken in the Lima Stock Exchange.

Tax Matters

Capital gains on listed securities are subject to a 5 percent preferential income tax rate when the seller is a nondomiciled entity provided that the securities are in fact traded in the Lima Stock Exchange (otherwise a 30 percent rate applies).

Secured Transactions

There are no restrictions on the holding of security interests in Peru by foreign individuals or entities. The most vastly used types of guarantees under Peruvian law are the mortgage and the pledge.

Mortgage

Real estate and any immovable assets can be mortgaged.

In order to create security under a mortgage the following essential requisites should be complied with:

1.   Expressed consent of the owner or its legal representative.
2.   Secured compliance of an already determined obligation or an obligation that can be determined.

3. Secured amount must be determined or able to be determined.
4. Registration of the public deed containing the mortgage agreement in the Registry of Real Estate Property.

Once the mortgage is registered in the above-mentioned registry, it is considered legally valid and effective.

Pledge (Garantía Mobiliaria)

The Garantía Mobiliaria creates a security interest on any personal goods or assets as long as there is written evidence thereof; however, registration of the security interest thus created will allow enforceability against third parties.

Enforcement of the Garantía Mobiliaria can be made directly by creditors without having to resort to courts if so agreed in the corresponding security agreement.

Litigation/Dispute Resolution Systems

Peruvian law allows for the resolution of disputes through either courts or arbitration. Foreigners are subject to the same rights and legal guaranties that apply to nationals. Due process and effective jurisdictional protection are recognized as constitutional rights.

Judicial System

The Judicial System is integrated by different types of courts that are specialized in different areas of law and have a determined jurisdiction on matters based on location and amounts involved in the dispute, among other factors. Civil courts are in charge of civil, commercial, and constitutional disputes, while criminal courts deal with any matter that is considered a crime under the Criminal Code or other applicable laws.

Procedural matters pertaining to civil and commercial matters are contained in the Code of Civil Procedure (Código Procesal Civil), while criminal procedures are dealt with by the Code of Criminal Procedure (Código de Procedimentos Penales). In turn, certain constitutional procedural matters are dealt with by the Code of Constitutional Procedure.

The judiciary is organized into 28 judicial districts around the country. First-instance courts include both civil and criminal judges. In each district, a Superior Court acts as a second-instance court of appeals (while in some criminal cases the court conducts oral trial). The Supreme Court is the highest court and acts as third-instance court.

In the case of protection of constitutional rights such as life, health, nondiscrimination, employment, due process, property, reunion, secrecy of communications and private documents, and bank secrecy, there is a higher court than the Supreme Court, in charge of reviewing last-instance and constitutional rights actions.

Enforcement of Foreign Judgments

Enforcement of foreign judgments in Peru is subject to compliance with the following requirements: (i) the judgment to be enforced does not resolve matters under the exclusive jurisdiction of Peruvian courts; (ii) the court rendering such judgment had jurisdiction under its own conflict of laws rules and under international rules on jurisdiction; (iii) the defendant was served with process in accordance with the law of the place where such court sits, was granted a reasonable opportunity to appear before such foreign courts, and was guaranteed due process rights; (iv) the judgment has the status of res judicata in the jurisdiction of the court rendering such judgment; (v) there is no pending litigation in the Republic of Peru between the same parties for the same dispute, which shall have been initiated before the commencement of the proceeding that concluded with the foreign judgment; (vi) such judgment is not incompatible with another enforceable judgment in the Republic of Peru unless such foreign judgment was rendered first; (vii) such judgment is not contrary to the public order or good morals of the Republic of Peru; and (viii) there is a treaty between the Republic of Peru and the country in which such judgment has been rendered, and the provisions of such treaty shall apply. In the absence of a treaty, the reciprocity rule is applicable (such reciprocity being presumed), under which a judgment given by a foreign competent court will be admissible in the Peruvian courts and will be enforceable thereby, except if according to such foreign law (a) judgments issued by Peruvian courts are not admissible in such foreign country, or (b) judgments issued by Peruvian courts are subject to re-examination by such competent court of the issues dealt with therein. As of this date, there is no treaty between the Republic of Peru and the United States of America on the enforcement of foreign judicial resolutions.

Arbitration

Any civil or commercial dispute can be submitted to arbitration if the parties thereto agree to do so. Any matters not expressly provided for by the parties shall be ruled by the Arbitration Law, which contains provisions regulating both domestic and international arbitration carried out in Peru.

Foreign arbitration awards will be recognized and enforced in Peru, according to the following instruments even if they are based on a foreign law:

1. Convention of Reconnaissance and Execution of Arbitral Decisions, approved in New York on June 10, 1958; or
2. Interamerican Convention of International Commercial Arbitration, approved in Panama on January 30, 1975.

CONTRACTS AND DOCUMENTS—FORMS AND ENFORCEABILITY

Contracts are regulated in the Civil Code, which sets forth the general rules applicable to a number of legal relationships with an economic content. Pursuant to these rules, parties to a contract can freely determine the contents of a contract as long as they do not contravene any mandatory provision, public order or good morals and provided that the relevant formalities (where applicable) are complied with.

The Civil Code establishes expressly that contract content set forth by the parties is considered as law and completely enforceable between the contracting parties, unless an imperative law says the contrary. The content must include all obligations that the parties must fulfill including obligations to give, do, or not do. Contracts are consider terminated by mutual consent from all parties or when all obligations are completely fulfilled.

The Civil Code also contains general provisions applicable to any breach of contract, liability arising therefrom, and termination, all of which apply as a supplement to the agreements of the parties contained in the contract.

ENDING/RESTRUCTURING A BUSINESS PRESENCE

Dissolution/Liquidation

The General Company Law establishes the causes and procedures for dissolution and liquidation of corporations and companies in general.

Dissolution

The dissolution of companies applies in any of the following scenarios:

1. Expiration of the term provided for in the bylaws of a company for its existence.
2. Conclusion of its corporate purpose or the manifested impossibility of fulfilling it.
3. Continued inactivity of the General Assembly of Shareholders.
4. Incurrence of losses that reduce the net assets value to less than one-third of the company's paid-in capital, unless such capital is duly increased or reduced.
5. Agreement approved by creditors in case of bankruptcy or insolvency, according to the procedure determined by law.
6. Lack of multiple shareholders.

7.   Judicial resolution adopted by the Supreme Court.
8.   Agreement approved by the shareholders.
9.   Any other cause established in the corporate bylaws or any other agreement between shareholders duly registered.

When a corporation falls into dissolution cause, the board of directors or any other shareholder must call within 30 days a general meeting for the corporation to decide whether to approve the dissolution agreement or to adopt all necessary measures that allow it to overcome the dissolution. Although corporations are run by the shareholders and its government bodies, the government can force the continuation of a company's activities due to domestic security or public necessity.

Once a decision is made to dissolve a company, all representation and responsibilities of directors, administrators, managers, and others representatives cease, and are transferred to the appointed liquidators. However, said former officers must provide information or assistance in order to facilitate the liquidation of the company.

Liquidation

The liquidation process is initiated with the adoption of the decision to dissolve the company, which maintains its corporate status until the liquidation process is duly finished and its extinction is recorded with the Companies Registry.

The liquidation process is conducted by one or more liquidators, whose main tasks include the elaboration of financial statements upon initiation of the liquidation, the keeping of proper accounting, paying all outstanding debts, enforcing and collecting all credits to shareholders and third parties, and preparing the final financial statements upon completion of the liquidation. Liquidators cannot distribute any remaining amounts to the shareholders until the corporate creditors are completely paid.

Liquidators must keep the shareholders informed about the financial statements and the good progress of the liquidation. Shareholders that represent at least 10 percent of the capital can require the liquidators to provide information regularly.

According to the General Company Law, once the remaining amounts have been distributed, the liquidators must request the extinction of the company before the Companies Registry. If there are pending debts to corporate creditors after the extinction, those creditors can enforce their payment to the shareholders but only up to the remaining amounts distributed thereto in the liquidation process. If unpaid obligations exist once the realization of all assets has been completed, the company falls into bankruptcy.

Insolvency/Bankruptcy/Restructuring

Peruvian law establishes that all insolvency, bankruptcy, and restructuring processes involving companies or individuals who are Peruvian residents shall be ruled by the Law of Insolvency System (Ley General del Sistema Concursal). INDECOPI is the government agency in charge of, and with exclusive and mandatory competence over, insolvency matters prior to bankruptcy.

Insolvency may be initiated at the request of a debtor or by its creditors when their credits are enforceable and mature in order to guarantee a methodic payment to all creditors from the debtor's insufficient patrimony.

A creditors committee is formed by all creditors who hold unpaid account receivables against the debtor; those creditors are entitled to decide on the outcome of the debtor, taking into account the following alternatives:

1. A debt restructuring plan that consists of continuing the debtor's activities with changes in its administration, establishing a payment schedule.
2. The dissolution and liquidation of the debtor.

Creditors committee agreements and decisions can be subject to questioning by the debtor or creditors that represent 10 percent of the total credits in the event of lack of compliance with legal formalities, legal mandates, or the abusive exercise of a right by creditors.

Payment of credits should be made according to the following preferences:

First: Salaries and labor benefits owed to workers, as well as contributions to pension funds.

Second: Credits secured by mortgage, mobiliary guaranties, pledges, warrants, or precautionary measures over the debtor patrimony as long as the guaranties were duly registered and the precautionary measures were attached before the beginning of the insolvency process.

Third: Tax debts including taxes, fees, rates, contributions, interests, and fines.

Fourth: All remaining credits that were not considered in the precedent orders.

If the dissolution and liquidation process ends with remaining credits to be paid, the debtor must be declared bankrupt.

CHAPTER 9

Uruguay

Sandra González Vila
Ferrere

COUNTRY OVERVIEW

Formerly a Spanish colony, Uruguay acquired an early independence in 1825 and quickly established a constitutional republic in 1830, being one of the first Latin American countries to adopt a democratic regime, which has remained one of the strongholds of the Uruguayan political system to this day.

With an area of approximately 68,000 square miles, Uruguay is a small coastal country located in South America, lying on the Atlantic coast between Brazil and Argentina, its only two neighboring countries.

The population of Uruguay is currently estimated at 3.4 million, of which some 1.3 million live in Montevideo, the capital and only large city, and neighboring areas, while the rest is distributed between the smaller cities and rural areas. Uruguay's population growth is 0.6 percent per year, one of the lowest in Latin America, similar to that of the majority of developed countries. The economically active population totals 1.5 million people. The average life expectancy is 76 years.

Being a former Spanish colony, and having received a strong influx of European immigrants, Uruguay's population is largely of European descent (93 percent), with other ethnic groups of African descent (5.9 percent) and indigenous descent. Uruguay

259

received a strong influx of European immigration between 1860 and 1920, mostly from Spain and Italy, and again after World War II from Central and Eastern Europe, which accounts for the country's current population composition.

Uruguay's official language is Spanish; however, English is widely spoken when conducting business, and other languages such as French, Portuguese, German, and Italian are also taught at primary, secondary, and university levels.

Traditionally, Uruguay has sustained a strong economy based mainly on agriculture and the primary sector exports, but with a rapidly growing predominance of the services sector, as shown by a thriving tourism industry and development of offshore banking and other services. Leading economic sectors include meat processing, agribusiness, wood, wool, leather production and apparel, textiles, and chemicals, together with a swiftly developing software industry.

Strategically located between the major consumer centers in Latin America, Uruguay is a member of MERCOSUR, an international trade zone. In 2009 the country's gross domestic product (GDP) was USD 31.5 billion with a per capita GDP of over USD 9.457 billion. The GDP annual growth rate was 2.9 percent in 2009. The annual inflation rate is currently 7.2 percent and the unemployment level is currently 7 percent. Exports for the year 2009 totaled USD 8.5 billion ($6.5 billion in goods and $2 billion in services), mainly directed to the major markets of Brazil, Argentina, China, Russia, Venezuela, the European Union, and the United States.

The country is also well known for its advanced education standards. The literacy rate is 98 percent and the secondary school attendance rate is 85 percent, the highest in Latin America.

Uruguay has a long-standing reputation for political stability, low corruption, and reliable institutions that create an environment of stability and overall confidence for investors. According to the World Bank, Uruguay leads in safety, transparency, government effectiveness, and control of corruption in Latin America.

Country	Voice & Accountability	Political Stability, No Violence
New Zealand	97.1	94.2
Chile	76.9	65.9
Uruguay	76.0	55.8
Brazil	59.1	36.5
Mexico	48.6	25.5
Argentina	57.2	49.5
Belgium	96.2	71.2
Australia	92.8	78.8

Since its inception, the country has been politically organized as a democratic republic under a presidential system of government with three traditional branches of power: executive, legislative, and judiciary. The executive branch is exercised by a president and a cabinet of 13 ministers, while the legislative power is represented by a General Assembly composed of a Chamber of Senators and the Lower Chamber of Representatives. Both the president and Parliament are elected for a fixed term of five years during the national elections, which take place every five years in October. The judiciary power is vested in the Supreme Court of Justice, lower courts, and judges on a nationwide basis. The decisions rendered by such courts do not constitute judicial precedent although they may provide guidance for future cases, being the main source of law that courts will apply.

Uruguay's strategic location in Latin America as one of the main regional ports, its political stability and democratic tradition, its high educational and living standards, its rapidly growing economy, and a favorable, investor-friendly approach to business create an ideal climate for the channeling of foreign investments.

ESTABLISHING A BUSINESS PRESENCE IN URUGUAY

Permanent Structures

Suitable Corporate Forms

The majority of business entities operating in Uruguay are organized either as corporations or foreign company branches. Some companies choose to operate as limited liability companies or partnerships limited by shares. For tax and legal purposes, most farming enterprises are organized as sole proprietorships.

Corporations can be open or closed. Open corporations are listed on the stock exchange and are created either through public offerings of shares or negotiable

Government Effectiveness	Regulatory Quality	Rule of Law	Control of Corruption
95.7	96.6	98.1	98.1
85.8	91.3	88.1	90.3
71.6	57.3	63.3	81.2
52.6	53.4	43.3	52.2
60.2	63.6	34.3	48.8
51.7	21.8	39.0	43.5
90.5	91.7	91.0	91.8
97.2	96.1	94.8	94.7

Source: World Bank

obligations, or are part of a structure in which the controlling or controlled company is also open.

When the entity's main purpose is to own assets in other companies, the appropriate corporate vehicle is an investment company. These are local (not offshore) companies whose main, but not exclusive, purpose consists of investing in other entities' assets.

Corporations located in free trade zones enjoy tax benefits insofar as their activities are exclusively carried out in or from free trade zones.

Wholly Owned Entities

Applicable Uruguayan regulations allow corporations to be wholly owned by a single shareholder.

However, for the purposes of completing the process of their incorporation, corporations are required to act with at least two shareholders. Once that process has been completed and the entity is finally incorporated, it can be wholly owned by a single shareholder without any further restrictions.

Joint Ventures

In addition to business companies of any type (normally corporations), joint ventures in Uruguay can be organized as follows:

a. Simple collaboration agreements between companies that may be more or less complex depending on the business involved. Such agreements are not subject to any formalities and hence require only signature of the pertinent contract. Liability of each of the parties will depend on the contract provisions, notwithstanding that in principle each party is liable for the acts it performs directly, and is not liable vis-à-vis third parties for acts performed by the other party.

b. Consortiums, which ultimately are an associative agreement for collaboration but are expressly regulated by Uruguayan legislation. Consortiums are set up by means of a contract between two or more persons (individuals or legal entities) temporarily linked to carry out work, or to provide certain services or certain goods. According to legal regulations, consortiums are not aimed at obtaining and distributing profits among their participants but rather at regulating activities in each of them. They do not have legal capacity and do not constitute companies independently from their members.

    The associative contract has to be set out in writing and should contain the main elements of the consortium (name, purpose, duration and domicile, participation of each member and inherent responsibilities, representation before third parties, and so on). Said contract must be subsequently registered and published.

    c.   Economic interest groups (EIGs), which involve an additional step beyond the above, given that they constitute a legal entity that is independent from their members, but whose activities are limited. EIGs may be established without any capital. The contract should set out the main elements characterizing the EIG, that is, identification of its members, duration and objective of the group, its domicile, and its management, and it must be registered with the competent registry. The participation of the members of this group may not be represented by negotiable securities, nor can participation be transferred to third parties or to other members of the group.

EIG members' liability vis-à-vis third parties for obligations contracted by the EIG involving acts included within its purpose is subsidiary, joint, and several. As for liability among EIG members, there is no legal limitation and hence the parties may freely agree to the rights and obligations of each of them according to their participation in the EIG.

Investments in and Mergers with Existing Entities

Uruguay has a specific legal treatment of the different alternatives for total or partial acquisition of a company. Such alternatives include the acquisition of shares, assets purchase, acquisition of a commercial establishment, or merger of companies.

In principle, the law does not prohibit the sale of the shares of a corporation. The disposal of stock can be limited, however, in the case of registered and book entry shares, if so established in the bylaws or by a shareholders' agreement, in compliance with the formalities set out by law.

In general the transfer of shares does not require prior consent or subsequent reporting to any public or private agency, with the exception of certain regulated activities (for example, banks, insurance companies and other activities under the supervision of the Central Bank, broadcasting, and so on).

Sale of a business establishment and company mergers involve a relatively complex and lengthy process.

In the case of sale of a business establishment or sale of companies, the process seeks to protect tax, labor, and commercial creditors of the transferred company, by avoiding disappearance of credits upon transfer due to the emptying out of the company, or due to the impossibility of identifying the acquirer, or if the latter does not assume the liabilities of the purchased company. Additionally, the regulations seek to protect the purchaser of the company, by allowing for limitation of its liability to debts claimed by creditors insofar as they comply with legal formalities. This protects purchasers from hidden liabilities of which they may be unaware upon making the purchase.

In company mergers, the process takes longer because of tax authority review of companies dissolved by the merger, to verify that no tax obligations are pending payment.

Agency, Reseller, Franchising, and Distribution Networks

Commercial distribution agreements are not specifically regulated in Uruguay; they are governed by general commercial contract rules. Consequently, there are no protectionist statutes for local distributors—as is the case in other countries in the region. In light of the above, the manufacturer and the distributor are considered independent parties on an equal footing when it comes to negotiating, executing, performing, and terminating commercial distribution agreements.

As regards termination of commercial distribution agreements, adoption of certain rules of doctrine and jurisprudence (nonbinding) is highly advisable to avoid detriment to the parties (especially the manufacturer). The spirit regarding termination of commercial distribution agreements should be that termination does not give rise to unjustified and excessive damage to the distributor. Hence contracts should clearly stipulate: (i) breaches authorizing the manufacturer to terminate the agreement (distributor's performance, noncompliance with manufacturer's corporate and/or local rules, or bad publicity or image of distributor); (ii) other reasons authorizing the manufacturer or distributor to terminate the agreement; (iii) existence of an advance notice period for termination; (d) regimen for goods in stock; and (e) regimen for other goods and investments.

Representative Offices and Other Nonpermanent Establishments

Foreign entities may perform isolated acts in Uruguay. In such cases they do not have to fulfill any requirements for acting in Uruguay, beyond accrediting their existence—that is, that they were duly organized and have complied with substantive and formal requirements of the law at their place of organization.

When such acts cease to be isolated and are part of the acts included in their corporate purpose, foreign companies must set up their business through a branch, agency, or other type of permanent representation.

Uruguay has recently introduced the concept of permanent establishments (PE) of nonresident entities. In this connection local rules reflect international guidelines, and consider a permanent establishment to exist when a nonresident person performs all or part of its activity through a fixed place of business in the country.

A PE begins to exist when a company performs its activities through a fixed place of business, including management offices, branches, offices, factories, mines, oil wells or quarries, and construction or installation works or projects having a duration in excess of three months.

Approvals and Registrations

Corporations can be incorporated in a single act by a group of founders or through public offerings of shares.

The process of incorporating a standard corporation takes three to four months. However, corporations may legally operate in the country even when procedures for incorporation are not complete. While these corporations are allowed to operate and conduct any kind of business, the law prescribes that their founders are held personally liable for any obligations assumed during this formation period and until the company, once duly incorporated, ratifies their performance.

In order to avoid any delays in the commencement of operations, it is possible to acquire an off-the-shelf corporation that has not engaged in any prior activity. In general, off-the-shelf companies are structured with broad corporate purposes and their bylaws and capital structure can be amended subsequently.

As for limited liability companies, their formation process is relatively simple. These companies are set up pursuant to an operating agreement entered into between a minimum of two and a maximum of 50 members, which can be either individuals or legal entities, including corporations. The procedures for incorporation are completed in one month.

Finally, a foreign investor may wish to operate in Uruguay through a branch. In order to establish a branch in Uruguay, the parent must complete a series of steps that include: (i) allocating branch capital, on which there are no limits; (ii) appointing an Uruguayan legal representative with sufficient authority; (iii) establishing a legal domicile in Uruguay; (iv) filing the branch's bylaws and the parent's resolution to set it up with the competent authorities; and (v) publishing an extract of the bylaws in the Official Gazette and in another newspaper. Incorporation procedures take one month.

Sensitive Economic Sectors/Restrictions on Foreign Ownership

There are no restrictions with respect to citizenship or domicile of shareholders and directors of corporations, except for certain specific activities considered to be of national interest that must be exclusively owned by Uruguayans (radio broadcasting and long-distance bus lines, among others). Aviation companies must be comprised of a majority of Uruguayan capital.

INVESTMENT ISSUES AND TAX INCENTIVES

Legal Treatment of Foreign Investment

Incentives

The main tax incentives for investments in the country stem from two different instruments: the Investment Law and the Free Trade Zone law.

Investment Law

Uruguay has adopted a specific legal framework for the promotion of investments. Relevant regulations establish that industrial, commercial, and service companies may obtain a government declaration granting promotional status that opens access to significant tax benefits.

The rules classify projects depending on the projected investment amount, measured in indexed units (UI) as small, medium, large, and high economic impact projects.

Following are the tax benefits granted to foreign investors under this promotional regimen.

Income tax: Companies with qualified projects can access an income tax (IRAE) exemption of up to 100 percent of the eligible investment (regardless of the source of financing), depending on the investment amount, which determines project category and position within the category.

Net worth tax: Companies can access a net worth tax exemption for the full useful life of movable assets applied to the project. In the case of investments in construction works, the term of the exemption is eight years if located in Montevideo (Uruguay's capital) and 10 years if located elsewhere.

Import duties and taxes: Companies can also benefit from an exemption from import duties and taxes on fixed assets certified as not competitive with Uruguayan industry by the Ministry of Industry, Energy and Mining.

Reimbursement of value added tax (VAT) on construction work: Eligible projects can benefit from reimbursement of VAT on local purchases of materials for construction and services hired in connection with construction work.

Free Trade Zones

This system has become an important tool for attracting investments to Uruguay. It has been utilized for carrying out traditional activities in the free trade zones (warehousing, logistics, and distribution) for providing services related to software, finance, call centers, and manufacturing.

Free trade zone users are exempt from all current and future national taxes, in connection with the activities performed within the free trade zone territory, as described below.

Treaties on Foreign Investment Protection

The promotion and protection of investments have been a consistent state policy in Uruguay, a practice reinforced in the past 20 years through the conclusion of a considerable number of bilateral investment treaties.

In the past few decades, Uruguay has seen a proliferation of these treaties, thus creating a suitable framework for the channeling of foreign investments, which essentially grant foreign investors customary protection in line with international standards. Many of these treaties incorporate one or more alternative dispute resolution procedures and more specifically arbitration, whether ad hoc or institutional (ICSID) is the preferred vehicle for investor-state dispute resolution.

In Uruguay, foreign investors receive the same treatment as domestic investors and generally enjoy most-favorable-nation and fair and equitable treatment standards, as well as protection against unlawful expropriation of their investment, all of which are built into the generality of the investment treaties in force.

Most treaties also provide for a broad definition of the term "investment," comprising all kinds of assets, tangible and intangible property including stock and other forms of company participation, loans, intellectual property rights, and business concessions owned or controlled by investors of one party, among others. Hence, protection granted under such instruments is ample and generally aims to contemplate all of investors' interests existing in the territory of the contracting states.

Following are some of the countries with which Uruguay has signed these agreements: Angola, Argentina, Australia, Belgium, Bolivia, Brazil, Bulgaria, Canada, Chile, the Czech Republic, Egypt, El Salvador, Finland, France, Germany, India, Israel, Italy, Malaysia, Mexico, Nicaragua, Panama, Paraguay, Romania, Saudi Arabia, Spain, Sweden, Switzerland, the United Kingdom, the United States, and Venezuela.

Publicly Held Companies—Capital Market Regulations

The Financial Market Act regulates the Uruguayan securities market and governs public offerings of securities, the activity of all agents who operate in the financial market (securities brokers, investment advisors, and so on), the basic structure of stock exchange, and the role of the Central Bank as a regulatory entity.

Public Offerings

To undertake a public offering of any securities in Uruguay (including the stock of publicly held companies) both the issuer and the securities to be issued must be previously registered with the Uruguayan Central Bank and their issuance has to be authorized by said entity.

Additionally, when the securities are registered to be traded in a stock exchange, the same also have to be filed with that stock exchange. In Uruguay, there are currently two stock exchanges: the Bolsa de Valores de Montevideo and the Bolsa Electrónica de Valores.

To evaluate the listing of securities, the Central Bank reviews the prospectus that will govern the issuance once it is authorized, and this will be the only prospectus that can be used in this market. All documents filed with the Central Bank are available to the public.

It is possible to request filings of securities programs to be implemented over a maximum of five years. Upon registering the program, the issuer must indicate the maximum amount to be issued in the different series over the course of the program.

This type of filing facilitates issuance of each series, as only supplements to the initial filing prospectus must be registered.

Private Offerings

Private securities offerings must be placed directly with specific individuals or legal entities interested in acquiring the stock. Existing regulations impose a series of requisites for private offerings that issuers should observe: (i) such offerings must contain express evidence of their private nature, (ii) the sale or offering cannot be the subject of any kind of advertising or divulgation to the public, and (iii) the offering cannot be made in a stock exchange in Uruguay. Unlike public offerings, the private placement of securities does not require any previous authorization or approval by the Central Bank.

International Offerings

In carrying out these offerings, the issuer must explicitly indicate their international nature.

Issuers may choose the law and jurisdiction of their preference to govern the issuance of securities to be offered internationally, in the setting of both private and public offerings. This is a remarkable exception to the long-standing domestic principle prohibiting the choice of law different to that mandated by the application of Uruguayan conflict of laws provisions.

Regardless of choice of law, securities holders always have the right to bring action in the jurisdiction of the issuer's domicile. Once jurisdiction is established and the parties have appeared before the pertinent courts, jurisdiction cannot be changed.

Debt Instruments

All local or foreign business companies, cooperatives, and entities of the state's industrial and commercial domain, as well as other nonstate public entities engaged in industrial or commercial activities, may issue negotiable obligations. Each issuer may issue different classes of negotiable obligations, bearing different rights, and within each class one or more series may be created, provided that prior to the issuance of a new series the preceding series has been totally subscribed or the unplaced balance has been cancelled.

There are no limits as to the amount of the debt that can be issued by each individual issuer. Financial institutions are authorized to invest in publicly offered securities and hence in publicly traded negotiable debt instruments, notwithstanding the limits set by the Central Bank regarding such investments.

Secured Obligations (Bonds)

The law permits the issuance of negotiable obligations with a guarantee feature, which may take the form of any real or personal security. Guarantees must be provided prior to or simultaneously with the issuance. The constitution of real guarantees must be publicly registered and subsequently accredited before the Uruguayan Central Bank.

The rights deriving from real and personal guarantees are automatically transferred to the new holder upon each conveyance of the guaranteed obligations. No registration is required for such purposes.

Alternate Investment Structure—Investment Funds

Trusts

The trust as a mechanism of the securitization of assets (money, credits, or personal and real property) is admitted and regulated by Uruguayan law. In Uruguay, trusts have proven to be highly useful vehicles for administering assets, channeling public and private investments, participating in privatizations and public concessions, constituting guarantees, providing business crisis solutions, and more recently for portfolio securitization.

Trusts are established through the execution of an agreement between the transferor and the trust manager, which must be registered in order to be enforceable vis-à-vis third parties.

Investment Funds

Uruguayan law characterizes investment funds as independent entities composed of contributions made by individuals or legal entities for their investment in securities or other assets.

Investment funds are managed by a fund manager and may have a limited duration and a maximum amount, or be unlimited. Their assets may consist of securities registered with the Central Bank of Uruguay, foreign securities, and time or demand deposits, among other instruments, as the joint property of the contributors that remains undivided during the fund's existence. Though not a corporation, their shares may be represented by bearer, registered, or book-entry securities. Uruguayan law has a built-in protection for these equity holders, which can never be held liable for debts incurred by fund contributors or fund managers.

OPERATIONAL LEGAL ENVIRONMENT

Foreign Exchange

Since September 1974, foreign exchange market operations have been completely free in Uruguay on the basis of fluctuating rates determined by supply and demand. This long-standing policy has been consistently upheld over the years and to date no new exchange controls have been put into effect.

Similarly, there are no current restrictions on such operations as the purchase and sale of foreign currency or payments made abroad in foreign currency.

Payment for imports may be made in foreign currency held either abroad or in the country, or by purchasing such currency within the country. Exporters may freely keep the foreign currency proceeds from their export sales.

There are no legal obstacles to commercial or financial agreements being drawn up in foreign currency. Legal enforcement of contracts may be made either in local currency or in the foreign currency originally agreed upon by the parties.

Immigration and Visa Requirements

A foreign person entering Uruguay as a tourist may remain in the country for three months, which can be extended once for the same period, before being considered an illegal immigrant. If such person wishes to extend his or her stay or is planning to work during that three-month period, and depending on the duration and purpose of the stay, existing laws and regulations mandate application for one of the following procedures: (i) the provisional identity document, or (ii) Uruguayan residence, in any of its two forms, legal or temporary.

In order to work in the country, all foreigners must file for one of the abovementioned procedures. The choice of procedure will depend on the personal situation of the applicant, the proposed stay, and the documents the applicant can obtain before arriving in Uruguay.

Provisional Identity Document

In principle, this document must be obtained by foreigners planning to work in Uruguay for a period of up to six months.

The procedure for obtaining the provisional identity document is simple, and requires only the presentation of a letter issued by the applicant's company, a certificate of good standing, and a copy of the applicant's passport before immigration authorities, after which the applicant is required to obtain a temporary ID card at the Civil Identification Office.

The provisional identity document is valid for six months, during which the foreigner may legally work in the country. Once expired, the applicant must file for any of the following procedures to maintain his or her legal status.

Uruguayan Residence Procedures

There are two different residence application procedures: (i) legal residence and (ii) temporary residence. While the first must be sought by foreigners entering the country with a view to staying indefinitely, the second is required for those who merely enter the country for the realization of temporary activities for up to two years. As such, the temporary residence enables these persons to hold their status of legal immigrant for the duration of the activities that gave rise to their entry with the above-mentioned two-year limit.

Application is completed upon the presentation of certain documents, including police certificates (indicating that the applicant bears no criminal record), a certified document evidencing the applicant's means of support in Uruguay (derived from activities abroad or in the country), identification document, tourist card given by the Immigration Office upon entry into the country, and birth and marriage certificates, among others. Additionally, once in Uruguay, applicants must undergo a physical examination and a series of tests to obtain a health card issued by a national medical center authorized for such purposes.

Once the procedures are initiated, legal residence may be obtained in approximately six to eight months while temporary residence will usually be granted two months after filing the pertinent documentation.

Visa Requirements

In general, persons visiting the country without a view to developing any working activities therein merely require a valid passport. In very specific cases and depending on the country of origin, a visa may be additionally required. Citizens from MERCOSUR member states may freely enter and leave the country carrying just their national identity document.

Import and Export Issues

Imports

There are no restrictions on the importation of goods into Uruguay, other than those imposed for petroleum, pharmaceuticals, medical products, and certain sensitive products. The importation of used goods is likewise not limited, with the exception of cars, trucks, and motorcycles.

The processing of imports is simple and takes only a few days, and there are abbreviated procedures for the importation of certain goods that can be completed after said goods have already been brought into the country.

Imported goods, with the exception of capital goods, information and telecommunications technology, sugar products, automotive industry products, and those contained on a list of some 100 products subject to exceptional regimens, are subject to the MERCOSUR common external tariff. The maximum duty currently applied under the common external tariff is 20 percent, and duties generally range between 10 percent and 16 percent.

Imports are subject to VAT and an aggregate tariff rate, which consists of various duties and charges. The aggregate tariff is calculated on the basis of GATT valuation rules. Valuation of used goods is based on the price of similar new products, less a deduction for the time of usage, with the exception of capital goods and information and telecommunications technology, which are valued at transaction value.

Temporary Admission of Inputs

Temporary admission of inputs for the export industry (raw materials, spare parts, components, engines, packaging, dies, and so on) is subject to a very favorable regimen. Under this system, imported goods are exempt from all customs and other import taxes. The importation of these goods for up to 18 months is normally authorized in less than a week, and authorization to import under this regimen may not be denied by the authorities on grounds of existence of local production of the same goods.

At the end of the authorized temporary admission period, the inputs imported must have been re-exported, either in the form in which they were imported or as inputs for other export goods. In exceptional cases, the goods may be permanently imported into the country by paying the regular customs and import duties.

All export industries can use this system. Under MERCOSUR provisions, however, temporary admission rules do not apply to exports to MERCOSUR countries. Nevertheless, in June 2000 the MERCOSUR member states agreed to allow the use of these mechanisms until the year 2010, subsequently extended until 2016.

Temporary Admission of Capital Goods

Authorization for the temporary importation of industrial equipment and tools is subject to the discretion of the Ministry of Economy and Finance, and may be granted for periods not exceeding 24 months (although it is possible to obtain renewals).

These authorizations are granted on a case-by-case basis, and the procedure to obtain them may take from three to six months. As authorization is discretionary, the request should constitute part of an overall industrial project submitted to the government.

Customs and other import duties are suspended during the validity of the temporary importation, and are completely waived once the goods are re-exported to a third country or to one of the Uruguayan free trade zones.

There are no regulations limiting temporary importation of used capital goods or other types of used equipment. The goods may also be permanently imported into the country, by paying the applicable customs and other import duties. Machinery and equipment whose temporary importation has been authorized may be used to produce for the domestic market.

Free Trade Agreements and Customs Unions

Uruguay is a member of MERCOSUR, a customs union comprising Argentina, Brazil, Paraguay, and Uruguay. As a consequence of this agreement, third-country imports not included on the list of exceptions for Uruguay are imported subject to the MERCOSUR common external tariff described above.

Uruguayan exports to Argentina, Brazil, and Paraguay are completely free from tariffs and similar duties in the country of importation. The tariff exemption, however, is subject to a set of rules of origin that make the MERCOSUR regimen inapplicable to products with high non-MERCOSUR content. In general terms, the special MERCOSUR treatment applies only to goods produced or manufactured in the exporting country with local or MERCOSUR inputs representing no less than 60 percent of the final value of the exported product.

Free Trade Zones

Activities Included in the Free Trade Zone Regimen

Free trade zones are duly isolated public or private areas within national territory that enjoy certain tax exemptions and other benefits specified by law, for the purpose of engaging in all types of industrial, commercial, and service activities, including:

a. Commercialization of goods, warehousing, storage, preparation, conditioning, selection, classification, division, assembly, disassembly, handling, or mixing of merchandise or raw materials of national or foreign origin;

b. Installation and operation of manufacturing establishments;

c. Provision of all types of services not restricted by national rules, both within free trade zones and from them to third-party countries;

d. Provision of the following telephone and IT services both to nonfree national territory and to third-party countries, respecting government monopolies and exclusivities and/or public concessions: international call centers, excluding those whose sole or main destination is national territory; electronic mailboxes; distance education; and issuance of electronic signature certificates.

e. Other activities, including banking activities, approved by the executive branch.

Free Trade Zone Users

Free trade zone users are individuals or legal entities who acquire the right to engage in any of the activities included in the free trade zone regimen in such areas. Although the law provides for two categories of users (direct and indirect), it does not establish differences as to the benefits and tax exemptions, or as to the legal obligations corresponding to each of them. Direct users acquire the right to operate in a free trade zone by means of a contract signed with the free trade zone operator. Indirect users acquire the right to operate in a free trade zone by means of a contract signed with a direct user.

User contracts must be filed with the free trade zone office and are enforceable against third parties as of their filing. Approval must be obtained from the free trade zone office for contracts between free trade zone users and operators, and between direct and indirect users.

Tax Exemptions and Other Benefits

Merchandise entering or leaving free trade zones from or to any third-party country are not subject to customs duties or taxes. Free trade zones are not subject to current or future requirements regarding obligatory inclusion of local components in manufactured goods, or other limitations with respect to entry or exit of goods from free trade zones, with the exception of those relative to control. Moreover, the law allows for the freedom of entry and exit from free trade zones of securities, national and foreign currencies, and precious metals for any purpose, and the holding, sale, circulation, and conversion or transfer thereof.

Legal monopolies granted to industrial and commercial utilities (electricity, fuels, communications, and insurance) are not applicable in free trade zones. Additionally, government corporations providing inputs or services to free trade zone users may establish special promotional rates.

Free trade zone users also benefit from a generic exemption from all current or future taxes on companies or sole proprietorships, with respect to activities performed in free trade zones. The government guarantees by law, under liability for damages, the maintenance of all tax exemptions and other benefits during effectiveness of the user contract, with the remarkable exception of social security contributions for Uruguayan personnel.

However, foreign personnel working in Uruguayan free trade zones are not required to pay social security taxes if they opt out of the Uruguayan social security system in writing.

Restrictions

Companies established in Uruguayan free trade zones may export to any destination, including the MERCOSUR countries. Nevertheless, exports to MERCOSUR countries are treated as imports to third-party countries (that is, non-MERCOSUR countries), and consequently are subject to the common external tariff.

Additionally, companies set up in free trade zones cannot engage in industrial, commercial, or service activities in nonfree Uruguayan territory; and a minimum of 75 percent of the persons employed by a company in free trade zone activities must be native or naturalized Uruguayan citizens in order to maintain free trade zone user status and the exemptions, benefits, and rights granted by law. This percentage may be reduced upon executive branch authorization. Retail trade is not permitted in free trade zones. The preferential treatment granted to Uruguayan exports by other countries in relation to certain products or for limited volumes or quantities will be applied preferentially to industries exporting such products and already operating in nonfree trade zones.

Taxation of Business and Cross-Border Transactions

Corporate Income Tax (IRAE)

Uruguay is one of the few countries in the region that still collects taxes following the source principle: all investments located and activities performed within the country are taxed, while those located outside Uruguayan territory are not subject to taxation. The corporate income tax (IRAE) is levied at a 25 percent rate on Uruguayan-sourced income obtained by Uruguayan resident entities (that is, entities incorporated in Uruguay) and permanent establishments of nonresidents. The definition of permanent establishment follows that of the OECD.

Income obtained in the agricultural sector (including forestry) is also in the scope of this tax; but, depending on the nature and size, those engaged in this type of activity may elect to be subject to the IMEBA agricultural products sales tax.

There is also an option to be taxed under IRAE rules available for those who obtain income subject to the IRPF individual income tax. For those who obtain income from personal services, taxation under IRAE may be mandatory depending on the level of fees effectively obtained.

To determine net taxable income, duly documented accrued expenses required for the generation of Uruguayan-sourced income are allowed as deductions. Transfer pricing rules (in line with the OECD guidelines) apply to transactions with foreign related parties or companies located in low tax jurisdictions.

In application of the so-called "padlock rule," the only expenses that can be deducted are those that constitute for the other party (resident or nonresident) income subject to income tax, and in the proportion resulting from applying to the expense the ratio between the maximum rate applicable to income of the other party and 25 percent corresponding to the IRAE rate. This rule is subject to some exceptions.

Personal Income Tax (IRPF)

Resident individuals are subject to personal income tax (IRPF). Individuals are considered Uruguayan tax residents when (i) they spend more than 183 days in Uruguay during the calendar year, or (ii) the core of their activities or interests are located in Uruguay (for instance, when the family—spouse and children—is settled in Uruguay or when more than 50 percent of the person's income is obtained in the country).

The income subject to tax is divided into two categories that are taxed separately: capital and labor income.

Capital income includes earnings obtained from holding movable and immovable property and transfers and is levied at a flat rate of 12 percent, with certain exceptions (for example, 3 percent to 5 percent on certain interests and 7 percent on dividends or profits paid by IRAE taxpayers).

Labor income includes earnings obtained from rendering personal services as an employee or as an independent contractor and is levied at progressive rates that range from 0 to 25 percent. Available deductions are minimal. However, taxpayers are given the option to pay this tax as a family unit, varying from the aforementioned rates and depending on the income of each member of the family unit.

As of January 1, 2011, interest on deposits and placements in foreign banks and other nonresident entities and dividends from foreign companies are subject to IRPF at a rate of 12 percent when received by a Uruguayan tax resident.

Nonresident Income Tax (IRNR)

Uruguayan-sourced income obtained by nonresidents (other than that obtained through a permanent establishment) is taxed by the IRNR at a general flat rate of 12 percent on gross income (with some reduced rates and exempt items). IRNR is basically collected by way of withholding.

Net Worth Tax (IP)

Net worth tax (IP) is an annual tax levied on net worth located in Uruguay, including all assets located, placed, or economically used in Uruguayan territory minus a short list of liabilities stipulated by law.

Business companies, foreign company branches, and other closed credit investment funds, as well as individuals and other companies subject to corporate income tax (IRAE), pay IP at a rate of 1.5 percent. IRAE taxpayers can deduct the amount paid for this tax against payment of up to 50 percent of IP generated during the fiscal year.

For assets belonging to individuals who are not IRAE taxpayers, IP is applied annually at progressive rates ranging between 0.7 percent and 2 percent, according to a scale, over a net worth valued for tax purposes at over approximately USD 100,000.

VAT

Uruguayan VAT is a noncumulative tax levied at a general rate of 22 percent on the provision of services and on the circulation of goods within the limits of Uruguayan territory. Imports of goods and value added in the construction of immovable assets are also within the scope of this tax.

A reduced 10 percent rate applies to goods integrating the family standard basket and certain services such as health services.

Some goods and services are exempt from VAT, such as foreign currency, real estate (different from initial sale), agricultural machinery and accessories, milk, books and magazines, newspapers and educational materials, interest on public and private securities and deposits, real estate rentals, and certain banking operations.

Export of goods is subject to 0 percent VAT and in all cases VAT credit of exportation can be recovered. Exports of services also benefit from a 0 percent rate when such services are included in the executive branch's restrictive list that includes consultancy services provided in relation to activities undertaken abroad, services for design or development of software to be used abroad, assignment of software use and exploitation rights in favor of persons abroad, services provided abroad by international call centers, services that must be provided exclusively within free trade zones, and so on.

The VAT operates according to the scheme of tax against tax, so that the tax payable shall arise from the difference between the output VAT and the input VAT included in the purchase of goods and services.

If the goods that a taxpayer sells or the services that a taxpayer renders are VAT exempted, the taxpayer has nothing to deduct from and the VAT it paid on its purchases of goods or services will become part of the costs (in case of exports—VAT rate of 0 percent—the VAT credit is still available to pay other taxes).

Excise Tax (IMESI)

In general, the excise tax (IMESI) applies on the first transaction made in the domestic market by manufacturers or importers of certain fixed goods.

Rates vary for each item (from 10 to 80 percent) and are generally set by the government within maximum parameters established by law. Goods subject to the highest rates are alcoholic beverages, tobacco, gasoline, fuel, lubricants, and other petroleum products.

Double Taxation Treaties

In April 2009 the Uruguayan government formally endorsed the OECD standards on transparency and exchange of information, as set out in the 2005 version of article 26 of the OECD model tax convention, and it committed to incorporate this standard in the treaties it is negotiating and in future agreements. Uruguay has double taxation treaties in force with Germany, Hungary and Mexico, and a Tax Information Exchange Agreement with France.[1]

Additionally, Uruguay has signed or is in the process of signing double taxation or exchange of information agreements with Belgium, Chile, Finland, India, Liechtenstein, Malta, Portugal, South Korea and Switzerland. Also, a new version of the treaty with Germany has been signed.

Transfer Pricing Regulations

As of July 1, 2007, transfer pricing has been regulated under the corporate income tax rules for fiscal years. These rules generally reflect the OECD transfer pricing directives, which can be used as a reference and relevant precedent when interpreting the Uruguayan rules.

As a general principle, transfer pricing rules are applicable to international transactions between related parties. However, the law has expanded the scope of these rules to transactions carried out with parties in low or zero-tax jurisdictions or regimens (either international or domestic), regardless of the relationship between them. Domestic transactions with Uruguayan free trade zones fall under this category.

The definition adopted by the law for determining related party status is quite broad, and may be applicable either directly or indirectly, and in matters of form or substance.

In case the terms and conditions do not follow normal market practices among independent entities, a situation that has to be proven by the competent tax authorities, taxpayers will have to make adjustments. In order to determine the adjusted prices, the following methods shall be applied (the method to be chosen shall be the more suitable for the relevant transaction): (i) comparable prices between independent parties method; (ii) resale prices between independent parties method; (iii) cost plus benefits method; (iv) profit split method; and (v) transactional net margin method.

For some commodity import and export transactions, the transfer price must be adjusted to the quotation for the commodity on an internationally recognized transparent market at the date of execution of the contract, provided the adjustment generates a higher taxable amount for income tax purposes.

The law has placed the burden of proof of the nonadjustment to market prices and terms on the tax authorities. However, the tax authorities can require production and filing of special sworn statements and documentation containing data considered necessary to analyze and verify the agreed-upon prices. The tax authorities have also been given the authority to enter into advance pricing agreements with taxpayers for periods not exceeding three years and to establish safe harbor regimes for specific activities.

Labor and Employment

Minimum Salary Requirements

Salaries are negotiated by salary boards by branch of economic activity. This obligatory collective bargaining process involves participation of the Ministry of Labor, along with labor and management organizations. Salary board decisions are binding upon the entire branch of activity once they are filed and published by the government. The agreements set minimum wages by job category, percentages of increases, and leave. In the event of an agreement between the parties, other work conditions can be negotiated.

Working Hours

The normal working day is eight hours, with a maximum of 48 hours per week for industrial workers and a maximum of 44 hours per week for commerce and office workers. These limitations are not applicable to managers, administrators, and executive personnel. Overtime is paid with a 100 percent surcharge when performed during business days, and a 150 percent surcharge when performed during holidays.

Vacation

All workers have the right to 20 business days of vacation after each year of work. After the fifth year of service, they have the right to one additional business day of vacation for every four years of service. Vacation may not be accumulated and should be taken by the worker in the year following that in which it is generated. Workers have the right to be paid an additional "vacation salary" prior to taking their vacation, equivalent to 100 percent of their net vacation pay.

The law provides for special leaves for education, the death of a direct family member of the employee, marriage, and maternity and paternity.

Annual Bonus

All workers are entitled to payment of an annual bonus ("aguinaldo") before each December 20, equivalent to one-twelfth of the aggregate sum collected by the employee during the entire year. In practice this payment is made in two install-ments, with the first half being due in June and the second before December 20.

Termination of Employment

If the worker's employment is terminated by the company's decision without cause, the worker has the right to receive compensation equal to one month's salary for each year (or fraction thereof) of service, up to a maximum of six months' remu-neration. This amount increases significantly in the case of dismissal during preg-nancy or illness or occupational accident. The statute of limitations for labor claims is one year following termination of employment, with five years' retroactivity.

Union Activity

Unions are not subject to specific regulations, although they are given the right to establish and operate freely. Collective bargaining has recently been fully regu-lated. The law provides that the parties may agree to conflict prevention and peace clauses. It establishes that collective agreements continue in effect beyond the estab-lished term until they are replaced by another agreement, unless otherwise agreed to by the parties.

Workers' right to strike is protected by law, and workers are likewise protected against dismissal for union activities. In particular, the law establishes nullity of dismissal due to union reasons.

The limits of lawful labor union activities are unclear, but major conflicts are restricted to a fairly limited number of areas.

In Uruguay opposition to legal regulation of strikes is strong. In practice the only limitation has consisted of the government's right to impose the obligation to maintain minimum levels of essential services.

Antitrust and Competition Issues

The purpose of the existing Antitrust Act is to foster the well-being of current and future consumers and users, through promotion and protection of competition, encouragement of economic efficiency, and freedom and equality of market access by companies and products.

These rules apply to all national and foreign public and private legal entities and individuals engaged in for-profit or nonprofit economic activities in Uruguayan territory. However, said rules also have an extraterritorial application: they are binding upon those engaging in economic activities abroad insofar as such activi-ties have total or partial effects in Uruguayan territory.

The Antitrust Act prohibits abuse of a dominant market position as well as all individual or concerted practices, conducts, or recommendations whose effect or purpose is to restrict, limit, hinder, distort, or prevent current or future competi-tion in the relevant market.

Under the Antitrust Act no conduct is illicit per se, but instead the rule of reason applies. This means that companies accused of violating the law are given the opportunity to allege that their conduct generates gains in economic efficiency that cannot be otherwise obtained, and that such gains operate to the benefit of consumers.

With regard to merger control, Uruguay also has a prior oversight system for mergers and acquisitions by companies bearing certain market power. When the transaction results in the possession of 50 percent or more of the relevant market, or when the combined gross annual billings in Uruguay of the parties to the transaction exceed approximately USD 70 million in any of the past three fiscal years, notice to the enforcement agency is required.

The law provides for certain exceptions to this notification requirement. However, in extreme cases involving de facto monopolies, authorization must be requested in advance.

Environmental Issues

Certain types of business activities or projects that could potentially have an environmental impact require specific environmental permits for their development.

For such projects, applicable laws and regulations require filing for a prior environmental permit, issued by the Ministry of Housing, Land Planning and Environment.

Some of the projects that require a prior environmental permit—among others—are:

- New forest plantations exceeding a given number of hectares.
- Industrial or agro-industrial structures or facilities for which production development areas exceed one hectare.
- Production, fractioning, and storage of chemically hazardous products or substances.
- Toxic and hazardous waste treatment and final disposal plants.
- Construction, repairing, or widening of national or provincial roads and railroad tracks.
- Construction or remodeling of bridges, public airports, and commercial and recreational ports.
- Oil or chemical transfer terminals, or oil or gas pipelines exceeding a given number of kilometers.
- Electricity generation plants and electric power transmission lines, among others.

Additional permits may be required for specific undertakings at different project stages during the process of obtaining the prior environmental permit. Examples are site suitability permits to obtain clearance of the proposed sites, and operational permits that must be requested once the construction phase is completed and before commencement of operations. Industrial or agro-industrial facilities must also file for special environmental permits if they were built, approved, or operational without requiring a prior environmental permit.

With regard to treatment of water and water usage, all industries whose industrial processes produce wastewater of any kind must file an application for an industrial drainage authorization permit, and comply with applicable dumping standards and parameters set forth by law.

Consumer Protection

Uruguay had adopted specific consumer protection legislation that applies to and regulates company relations with end-users of products or services. In addition to defining the basic structure of consumer relations and the scope of its application, existing legislation sets out a catalogue of basic consumer rights, with special emphasis on the protection of the health and safety of consumers, and compliance with minimum standards of information that must be made available to consumers prior to or at the time of purchase of products or services.

In line with the above, advertising of products and services is also regulated. The supplier of products or services is bound vis-à-vis the consumer by all information disseminated in its advertising. Additionally, while misleading advertising is expressly prohibited, comparative advertising is allowed; but in such cases the law places the burden of proof of truthfulness on the advertiser.

As in most consumer protection legislation, Uruguayan law grants consumers a brief period (five business days) to leave without effect the purchase of products and services through Internet, telephone, mail, or door-to-door channels.

Further protection to consumers is granted through the prohibition of including abusive clauses in adhesion contracts, and in this respect, consumers may petition for annulment of such clauses before the competent courts. Some commercial practices considered abusive are the failure to supply products or services when available, delivering unsolicited products or services to the consumer, and making the consumer appear to be the contract initiator when that is not the case.

Unlike more modern legislation, Uruguayan law does not establish the joint liability of all suppliers for manufacturing defects, and holds the importer and the manufacturer liable in the first degree, followed by the distributor and retailer. Products may be sold with no guarantee if the consumer is sufficiently informed of this fact.

This protective legislation is complemented by the limitation of financing and delinquency interest rates that can be set in consumer relations to 60 percent and 80 percent, respectively, over the average interest rates published by the Central Bank of Uruguay for the moving quarter preceding the date on which the obligation is created. When the principal amount of the loan—not including interest or charges—is equal to or greater than approximately USD 200,000, the limits on financing and delinquency interest are 90 percent and 120 percent, respectively.

More recently, a very abbreviated judicial proceeding was created enabling consumers to bring claims against companies for amounts up to approximately USD 2,400.

Land Use and Real Estate

Uruguay's real estate legal system is characterized by a general absence of restrictions on the ownership of private property, no discriminatory treatment of foreigners, and a clear scenario on taxation, as well as readily available information from public registries.

Foreign investors or companies willing to acquire real estate can act either as individuals or using any of the corporate vehicles previously outlined.

However, certain restrictions are in force with regard to the ownership of agricultural land. Corporations can own agricultural land only provided that their capital is composed entirely of registered stock owned by individuals. Certain noteworthy exceptions are granted in favor of a number of corporate forms (branches, trust funds, investment funds, cooperatives, and some corporations) when by virtue of the number of shareholders or the nature of their activities their capital cannot be owned exclusively by individual persons. However, in such cases, to acquire agricultural land these entities must file for the prior authorization by the executive branch, which must be renewed for every new acquisition of adjacent lands or extension of property.

Intellectual Property

Copyrights

Copyright law protects the rights of authors, artists, performers, phonogram and software producers, and radio broadcasters. The law distinguishes between economic and moral copyrights. Economic copyrights can be freely assigned or transferred, provided this is done in writing. Moral rights, such as paternity, integrity, and disclosure, cannot be assigned or waived, except in cases especially provided for by law.

Copyright protection covers works produced both locally and abroad; and such protection is afforded even in the absence of any registration. Copyright regulations include rules permitting confiscation of illegally reproduced software, and fines and criminal penalties for illicit reproduction of protected works for profit. Judicial actions have been particularly effective in cases of software piracy.

Trademarks

Protection of trademarks and service marks is granted for a period of 10 years following their registration, renewable indefinitely. The law provides that trademark rights may be licensed to third parties through license agreements that must be filed with a special registry. It also provides that mark rights are acquired only upon registration pursuant to law, although users of nonregistered marks are allowed to assert their rights vis-à-vis those seeking to file their marks with the registry. The use of registered marks is optional and may be declared mandatory by the executive branch only when there are compelling reasons attaining to the public interest.

Annulment of an already registered mark, on the grounds indicated by law, may be requested at any time, with few exceptions. The law also contemplates the possibility of the true holder bringing action for recovery of a mark in the event that its agent, representative, importer, distributor, or licensee registers said mark in its own name rather than the holder's.

Patents and Industrial Designs

That Patent Act protects inventors' and owners' rights to inventions, utility models, and industrial designs. In the case of patents on inventions, protection is for a 20-year nonrenewable period from the date of application. Utility models (minor inventions) and industrial designs are protected for a 10-year period from the date of application, which can be extended once for an additional five years.

Patenting of medicinal products is permitted. Nevertheless, the law regulates compulsory licensing for use of patents not used by their owners, as well as in cases of refusals to deal, anticompetitive practices, and for reasons attaining to public interest.

The law expressly excludes patenting of discoveries, scientific theories, mathematical models, plants and animals found in nature, marketing, advertising and raffling methods, literary and artistic works, computer programs, and biological or genetic materials found in nature, among others. Plant varieties, however, are protected through other special legislation and by UPOV 1978. The law allows for the patenting of micro-organisms, food products, chemical products, and agricultural chemicals.

Financing Issues
Financial Activities

Uruguay has adopted specific legislation, embodied in the Financial Intermediation Law, regarding the incorporation and functioning of public and private entities that act as financial intermediaries. The concept of financial "intermediation" is legally characterized as the regular and professional mediation between supply and demand of credit instruments, currency, or precious metals. Hence, all entities engaging in or performing any such activities qualify as financial institutions, subject to the aforementioned legal rules and under the control of the Uruguayan Central Bank.

In Uruguay, financial institutions may choose to incorporate and operate under any of these forms: banks (public or private), financial entities, offshore financial entities, investment banks, financial cooperatives, purchase plan management companies, and securities brokers.

Of these organizational structures, the most used and relevant are banks, financial houses, offshore financial entities, and investment banks.

a. Banks are full-license financial entities, specifically authorized by the regulatory authorities to use the term "bank" or "banking" in their trade names. Local law prescribes that certain operations may be exclusively performed by banks among all financial intermediaries, such as the opening of bank checking accounts, the taking of demand deposits (except those in foreign currency made by nonresidents), and the taking of time deposits by residents.

b. Financial houses (casas financieras) are limited-license financial institutions that may perform all regular banking operations except those reserved to full-license banks.

c. Offshore financial entities are limited-license banks (or offshore banks), authorized exclusively to perform banking operations outside Uruguay with nonresidents. These entities may take demand deposits and open checking accounts. Offshore banks are generally exempt from Uruguayan taxes.

d. Investment banks are also limited-license banks, authorized to make investments in shares, debentures, or negotiable instruments issued by companies, to own stock or equity interests in nonbanking companies, to own real estate or other assets for lease to third parties, to take long-term deposits, and to make long-term loans. Their purpose is to engage in activities usually not permitted for ordinary banks. However, we note that there are no such entities currently operating in Uruguay.

e. There are also representative offices of foreign entities, which are authorized to provide "consultancy services and technical assistance, with a view to preparing, promoting or facilitating business for their principals." Hence, representative offices cannot perform financial intermediation themselves, or take sums of money or securities of any kind, but merely prepare and facilitate the business of the parent entity.

Establishment of Financial Entities

Organization of financial entities of any kind is subject to authorization by the executive branch, upon the advice of the Central Bank on the legality and feasibility of the application submitted for consideration.

In the case of banks, the executive branch cannot approve new licenses in excess of 10 percent of the number of banks in existence during the previous year. The establishment of branches of foreign financial entities is not subject to any restrictions beyond those mentioned before.

Liabilities of Company's Directors and Officers

Uruguayan law does not make any distinction between directors and officers of companies. Only board members can be appointed chairperson, vice chairperson, treasurer, or secretary of the company.

Directors are jointly and severally liable vis-à-vis the company, the shareholders, and the creditors of the company for all violations of laws and regulations or acts contrary to the company bylaws committed with their knowledge or without their objection. This liability arises out of a breach of duty, such as the duty of diligence, when directors incur willful misconduct or gross negligence whether by way of act or omission.

Likewise, pursuant to several provisions, directors are personally liable vis-à-vis tax authorities for unpaid taxes, under certain pre-determined circumstances.

Applicable tax laws generally establish directors' joint and several liability for the company's unpaid tax obligations, a liability that arises from their position as company representatives and with respect to those matters under their knowledge and control. Said liability varies according to the level of knowledge and intention posed by the representatives during the discharge of their duties: when directors merely act with negligence, their personal liability is limited to the value of the company assets administered in their capacity; however, if directors act willfully they cannot benefit from such a limitation of liability.

Notwithstanding the former, current laws and regulations determine that directors are always jointly and severally liable for payment of company income tax (IRAE) before the competent tax authorities, thus configuring a harsher regime of strict and unlimited liability derived merely from their position as company directors.

Additionally, and from a labor standpoint, company directors can be made to respond, together with the company itself, for the company's nonfulfillment of the labor obligations attaining to safety norms in the workplace and failure to take out mandatory insurance with the state.

Litigation/Dispute Resolution Systems

Overview of the Uruguayan Litigation System

The civil litigation system in Uruguay is governed by a General Code of Procedure, which establishes a formal and structured proceeding, primarily in written form, with strict rules regarding the filing of briefs, evidence, and appeals. Civil cases are heard by a single judge, chosen randomly in most instances. Though briefly in force during the 1930s, there are currently no jury trials in Uruguay.

The basic structure of proceedings involves mandatory mediation hearings, the filing of a written complaint and an answer, a preliminary hearing in which a single judge rules on admissibility and production of evidence, followed by motions to dismiss and several evidence hearings in which witnesses and experts may testify. Once evidence has been produced, written closing arguments follow, and a final decision is rendered.

All decisions issued by a judge can be appealed before a three-member Appeals Court, and this decision can (in some cases involving judicial error) be appealed before the Uruguayan Supreme Court. Cases involving less than approximately USD 15,000 cannot be brought before an Appeals Court or the Supreme Court. Depending on its complexity, a case may take from two to five years until a final ruling is rendered. Occasionally, the losing party may have to pay for costs of the proceedings and the other party's legal fees if the court considers that it litigated maliciously or with gross negligence.

Provisional remedies and injunctions can be requested before and during every judicial proceeding provided there is initial evidence justifying them. The requesting party must post a sufficient counter-guarantee to cover any damages to the defendant in the event the complaint is finally dismissed. Pretrial production of evidence can be requested but is limited to specific documents since no discovery or similar procedure for the production of evidence exists in Uruguay.

Records and hearings in civil proceedings are public. Third parties and the public in general can attend the hearings and request access to the file and all briefs and evidence attached.

In the past few years, new technologies have become available in civil litigation. A system of electronic service of notice of judicial decisions and the possibility of having online access to information on all ongoing cases before the courts of most cities has made litigation more efficient. However, at this point there is still no electronic filing system in place for court documents.

Judges are selected among those finishing a two-year judiciary training program. After being assigned to different nonspecialized courts outside the capital for several years they are finally appointed in a specialized court. Specialized areas are labor, family, bankruptcy, civil, customs, and administrative.

Challenge of Administrative Decisions

A special five-member Administrative Claims Court hears challenges of decisions by public authorities and entities (such as those rendered by the Internal Revenue agencies or rulings on awards in public tenders). These proceedings are more formal than those described for civil proceedings, and usually take longer. Decisions by the Administrative Claims Court are final and cannot be appealed before any other court.

Bankruptcy Proceedings

New regulations on bankruptcy proceedings have recently become effective. These new regulations considerably simplified and unified bankruptcy procedures that under the former regime were extremely slow and complex. The new legislation provides for a general procedure (applicable to all companies and individuals) with an initial stage in which the evidence of the debtor's insolvency is produced and the judge eventually declares the bankruptcy, followed either by an agreement entered into between debtor and creditors (to allow for repayment and the continuation of business) or a liquidation stage. In the liquidation phase, auction of the whole company as an active business is sought, and only if that is not possible will the different assets belonging to the debtor be sold separately to pay the creditors.

Additionally, under Uruguayan law private restructuring agreements establishing debt-swaps, debt reductions, or different repayment schedules (among other stipulations) can be reached. These agreements, once approved by a certain majority of creditors, are binding on virtually all of them.

Jurisdiction of Uruguayan Courts in International Matters

Uruguayan courts do not generally accept choice of law and jurisdiction clauses in international contracts. Uruguayan courts may accept or decline jurisdiction based on provisions of law from which the parties cannot depart in most cases. Usually these rules state that a complaint can be filed in Uruguay if the defendant is domiciled there, if the assets involved in the contract are located in Uruguay, or—in the case of services contracts—if the service is to be provided in Uruguay (or the person who should provide it is domiciled in Uruguay).

However, choice of forum clauses are binding: (i) under the MERCOSUR Protocol on Jurisdiction in Commercial Contracts (applicable mainly between parties residing within the MERCOSUR countries), which allows the parties to submit to a court of one of the four member states for certain contracts; or (ii) if an international arbitration clause is included in the contract.

Enforcement of Foreign Judicial Decisions and Awards

The enforcement of foreign judicial decisions or awards is governed by the Code of Civil Procedure and several bilateral and multilateral International Conventions ratified by Uruguay (such as the 1958 New York Convention on Recognition and Enforcement of Arbitral Awards, or the Inter-American Convention on the Recognition of Foreign Judicial Decisions and Awards, or the MERCOSUR Protocol on Judicial Assistance).

Reciprocal recognition of decisions is not requested, and foreign decisions are recognized and enforced provided that they meet the following requirements: (i) the award must have been issued by a competent court, (ii) the defendant must have been properly served notice of the complaint, (iii) the defendant's right to due process of law must have been fulfilled, (iv) the decision must be final and binding, and (v) the decision must not plainly contradict the principles of Uruguayan public policy.

If enforcement of the decision is sought, exequatur must be previously requested from the Supreme Court of Justice. The defendant must be served notice of the request and has a 20-day term to oppose recognition and enforcement. Finally, the chief government attorney is heard. Once the Supreme Court grants exequatur, the decision can be filed with the competent court to proceed in accordance with the appropriate procedures for enforcement in line with the nature of the judgment.

Alternative Dispute Resolution in Uruguay

In recent years, Uruguayan courts have been prolific in decisions fully receptive to the conventions on foreign arbitral awards, and therefore, in support of international commercial arbitration. Domestic commercial arbitration, in addition, is fully accepted under Uruguayan law.

Unreserved ratification of the New York Convention on the Recognition and Enforcement of Foreign Arbitral Awards (New York Convention) and the Inter-American Convention on International Commercial Arbitration (Panama Convention) makes Uruguay an attractive site for international arbitration. Additionally, Uruguay has also ratified the MERCOSUR Agreement on Commercial Arbitration whose regulations are substantially similar to the Panama and New York Conventions but that expressly incorporate current, more modern international arbitration principles (such as autonomy of the arbitration clause or the "principle of kompetenz-kompetenz").

Indeed Uruguay is increasingly seen as a reliable "neutral site" in Latin America, and courts have accepted the changes brought by the New York and Panama Conventions. Decisions have consistently reflected, and continue to reflect, support for international commercial arbitration as well as criteria in line with the most modern international standards. More recently, courts have gone even further and established principles in line with most developed systems and clearly in favor of international arbitration.

In terms of local law, although Uruguay has not enacted an arbitration law, the General Code on Procedure specifically provides that foreign arbitral awards can be enforced in Uruguay in accordance with international conventions and local law, as applicable. Uruguayan courts will normally decline jurisdiction provided that a written arbitration clause was executed by the parties regarding a specific dispute.

Parties to domestic and international contracts today generally turn to arbitration as the preferred dispute resolution mechanism, being a comparatively quicker proceeding that enables the selection of arbitrators specialized in commercial and financial matters (a feature particularly relevant in Uruguay, due to the absence of courts specializing in such matters).

Arbitration clauses are also generally inserted in government contracts in order to preserve the neutrality in resolving potential disputes, and in recent years most of the major public works and services contracts entered with the state provided for arbitration.

As for other ADR mechanisms available in Uruguay, judicial mediation exists only for family matters, while private mediation is not very frequent.

CONTRACTS AND DOCUMENTS—FORMS AND ENFORCEABILITY

Uruguayan contract law, as embodied in the Uruguayan Civil Code, traces its origins back to the 1804 French Napoleonic Code. As such, the Uruguayan system of law adheres entirely to the civil law tradition, largely founded upon the scholarly developments and teachings of the most prominent 19th-century scholars of Continental Europe.

The rules that regulate contracts are to be found in the Civil and Commercial Codes, this last one containing provisions applicable to commercial contracts.

Both of these bodies of law lay out the cardinal principal of freedom of contract, under which parties can freely enter into negotiations and contract with each other with the only limitations being imposed by law. This principle derives from the constitutional rule that people's private actions that neither affect public policy nor damage third parties are exempt from judicial authority, and that the state cannot "force individuals to carry out what the law does not mandate, or abstain from what the law does not prohibit."

Concept of Contract

Uruguayan law characterizes the contract as a convention in which a party (be it an individual or multiple individuals) assumes an obligation with respect to another party (also individual or plural), or where both parties assume reciprocal obligations to one another. Such obligations may consist of actions (giving or doing something) or omissions (abstaining from doing something).

Constitutive Elements of a Valid Contract

Generally, a contract may be made orally, in writing, or by a course of conduct.

Certain contracts are required to be in writing or in a public deed, such as those relating to real estate transactions. The concurrence of the following elements creates a valid contract: (i) an offer made with the intent to be bound; (ii) an unqualified acceptance of the offer; (iii) legal capacity of the parties; (iv) a legal and determined object that constitutes the center of the obligation; (v) a licit and possible cause; and (vi) the observance of solemnities (for example, written form) when expressly required by law.

Challenges to the Validity or Enforceability of Contracts

Incapacity

Contracts are void, and such nullity may be invoked judicially, if one of the parties is a person (i) under the age of 18; (ii) mentally disabled; or (iii) deaf and mute who cannot communicate his or her will in writing or through sign language. Ultra vires acts of a company made by persons lacking the authority to bind it are valid and enforceable against the company unless the other party had knowledge of said lack of authority, or if the contract or act was notoriously counter to the company's corporate purpose.

Exception Clauses

Exception clauses in contracts are generally valid and enforceable provided that (i) the limitation of liability is reasonable; (ii) the exception clause is not inserted in a consumer-provider contractual relationship; (iii) it does not limit damages caused by gross negligence or willful misconduct; and (iv) it does not limit a party's liability for death or personal injury.

Certainty of Terms

To be enforceable, the terms of a contract must be certain or capable of being rendered certain, and the contract's objective must be possible.

Misrepresentation

A contract may be set aside on the grounds of misrepresentation (fraud) when a party makes a false statement of fact to the other contracting party as to a material fact, which induces that other party to enter into the contract.

Violence

A party that has been induced by the other contracting party to enter into a contract by means of violence, force, or intimidation or other forms of illegitimate pressure may have the contract set aside.

Mistake

A contract may also be annulled if it was entered into by mistake, when such mistake affects the parties' understanding of the type of contract being celebrated (for example, one party understood that the contract was a loan and the other one understood it was a donation), or whether the error falls upon the object of said contract.

Illegality

A contract is void if its objective or cause is illicit. Typical examples include contracts to commit a crime, tort, or fraud, or those whose objective goes against public policy. However, where the illegal contract term is severable, the rest of contract will remain valid excluding the illegal contract term.

RESTRUCTURING OR ENDING A BUSINESS PRESENCE

Restructuring

Restructuring is the process in which the company's type is modified, adjusting its bylaws and social contract to the characteristics and rules of the new type. Only completely regular companies may modify their type into another social type.

Restructuring does not imply that a new company is created. It is the same legal entity that already existed, although after the restructuring it changes its social type. The procedure for restructuring a company is as follows:

a. Company's internal resolution. Such decision may be taken by the administration body, a partner, or a group of partners or shareholders. In this last case, the administration body has to call for a partners' meeting or a shareholders' extraordinary meeting in order to decide about the proposed restructuring.

b. A special balance has to be presented to the shareholders meeting.

c. The resolution to restructure requires special majorities because it implies a modification of the social contract or bylaws. Act No. 16.060 establishes different majorities for each type of company.

d. The resolution to restructure must be published for three days, notifying partners and shareholders of such resolution. The restructuring decision can be seen and analyzed for 30 days together with the special balance. This step of the process is not needed if the restructuring is decided by the unanimity of partners or shareholders (Section 112 of Act No. 16.060).

e. In case nobody wants to leave the company, once the 30-day period is over the restructuring is documented according to the new company type adopted. The restructuring is communicated to the Corporate Oversight Authority requiring its approval (depending on the company type adopted), documents are registered with the National Registry of Commerce if applicable (depending on the company type adopted), and such documents must be communicated to the tax authority, social security authority, and to the Ministry of Work and Social Security. This same process must be followed in case someone leaves the company, once the departure is complete.

The right to leave the company in the case of restructuring can be exercised by those partners or shareholders who voted against the restructure or those who were absent. This right has to be exercised within 30 days after the last publication of the restructuring decision. The partner or shareholder has to make a certified notification to the company within the above-mentioned period.

Ending

In Uruguay the process to end a legal entity is not complicated, but it does take a long time. The longest delay consists of the analysis made by the tax authority of the ending enterprise for the purpose of verifying that no tax obligations whatsoever are pending payment.

A legal entity can liquidate itself as long as it is in compliance of its registrar, legal, accounting, and fiscal obligations.

The process of liquidation includes the following steps:

- The board of directors and shareholders' meetings shall resolve the company's liquidation and the appointment of the liquidator.
- The liquidator must make an inventory and a balance of the social patrimony.
- The liquidator must adopt the necessary measures in order to initiate and complete the liquidation of the company (conclude the company's pending business, extinguish corporate liabilities, duly guarantee payment of obligations not yet due or those that for just cause cannot be cancelled, prepare the proposal for distribution of remaining corporate assets, and execute the documentation necessary for such purposes).
- In case the company's social assets are insufficient to satisfy the debts, the liquidator has to order the shareholders to pay the contributions that are still due according to the company's bylaws and the type of company.
- The liquidator's performance and proposal of passive cancellation and of distribution of remaining corporate assets shall be approved by the company's shareholders.
- The enterprise must be closed before the tax authorities, and closing certificates must be obtained from the General Revenue Service, Social Security Administration, and Ministry of Work and Social Security.
- Finally, the liquidation must be filed with the Corporate Oversight Authority for its approval.
- Once approved, the liquidation procedure must be filed with the National Registry of Commerce.

NOTE

1. A double taxation treaty with Spain will be in force as of April 26, 2011.

CHAPTER 10

Venezuela

Fernando Pélaez-Pier
Paula Serra Freire
Hoet Pelaez Castillo & Duque

COUNTRY OVERVIEW

Venezuela is located in the northern part of South America. The country borders the Caribbean Sea to the north; Brazil to the south; the Atlantic Ocean and Guyana to the east; and Colombia to the west. The total area of the country is 917,450 square kilometers (354,227 square miles) and the estimated population is 28 million. The capital city is Caracas, which is located in the central-north part of the country and has approximately six million inhabitants. Other major cities are Maracaibo, Valencia, Maracay, Barquisimeto, Puerto la Cruz, Maturin, and Puerto Ordaz. Venezuela's official language is Spanish, although English is widely spoken in the tourism industry and the business environment.

According to the current Constitution of 1999, the Bolivarian Republic of Venezuela is a nation governed by laws with a democratic and participative government. The power of the state is divided into five branches: (i) executive, represented by the president of the republic, the executive vice-president, the ministers of the cabinet, and other officers of the public administration; (ii) legislative, represented by the National Assembly; (iii) judicial, represented by the Supreme Court and other courts created by law; (iv) moral, represented by the Attorney General; and

(v) electoral, represented by the National Electoral Council. In addition, there are three levels of territorial administration: federal, state, and municipal. Venezuela is organized as a decentralized federal state politically divided into 24 states, one capital district, and 650 municipalities. The city of Caracas is the capital of the republic and home for all the branches of government.

The Constitution guarantees citizens the right to engage in any lucrative or commercial activity. This right, however, is subject to the limitations stipulated in the Constitution and to those established by law with respect to security, health, or other matters of national interest. In addition, the state may reserve for itself the right to exploit certain industries or public services, for example, the oil and gas industry.

Nevertheless, Venezuela has opened its markets to foreign investment in important fields such as banking, insurance, telecommunications, and the oil sector. Foreign investors participate in the oil sector through joint venture agreements with the state-owned oil company and through profit-sharing association agreements. Similar regulations apply to activities of exploration, exploitation, and basic industrialization of iron, aluminum, and other mineral resources.

The Venezuelan financial system is under the supervision and regulation of the Superintendence of Banks and Other Financial Institutions. The Capital Market is under the supervision of the National Commission of Securities.

ESTABLISHING A BUSINESS PRESENCE IN VENEZUELA

Permanent Structures

The Venezuelan Commercial Code is the most important piece of legislation applicable to companies incorporated in Venezuela. In general terms, companies or business associations have as their corporate purpose one or more commercial activities. Nevertheless, corporations and limited partnerships are always attributed a business nature by law, whatever their purpose may be, except when they are engaged exclusively in agricultural activities.

Corporations are governed by the articles of incorporation agreed upon by the partners, as well as by the provisions of the Commercial Code, the Civil Code, and the provisions of special laws, which may be applicable to a particular business area.

Suitable Corporate Forms

The Venezuelan Commercial Code[1] provides for four different types of corporations: the stock corporation, which is the most common form of corporation used to carry out business in Venezuela; the limited liability company; the partnership; and the limited partnership.

The stock corporation does not require a minimum share of capital and the transfer of shares is not subject to the formalities applied to the limited liability company. The company can be managed by one or more administrators or a board of directors whose members could be foreigners.

The shareholders must subscribe the total capital stock and pay at least 20 percent of the stock subscribed by the time of incorporation. Although no minimum amount of capital stock is required, particular requirements may be applicable in certain business areas. The Commercial Code requires at least two shareholders for the purpose of incorporation, although immediately thereafter all shares may be transferred to a single shareholder.

With regard to capital contributions, limited liability companies are required to have their capital within a range established by law. However, the law does not require a minimum or maximum capital contribution for stock corporations. In any case, investments may be made in cash or by capitalization of goods.

Foreign investors may subscribe capital increases in any Venezuelan corporation. The foreign participation after the capital increase may not exceed the maximum proportion allowed by law in the particular economic sector.

Wholly Owned Entities

Foreign investors are allowed by law to incorporate wholly owned subsidiaries, except in those reserved sectors. As mentioned earlier, the Commercial Code requires at least two shareholders for valid incorporation of business organizations, although immediately thereafter all shares may be transferred to a single shareholder.

Another alternative is to establish a branch. Venezuelan Commercial Law[2] treats branches as local corporations; therefore, branches are authorized to carry out business without limitations other than the legal provisions applicable to companies organized in Venezuela with foreign participation.

Nevertheless, branches are not regarded as different or autonomous entities, so parent companies retain full liability for the branch's operations. In terms of limits of liability, even though an amount of capital must be allocated to the branch by the parent company, a branch's liability is determined by the parent company's capital.

Joint Ventures

Foreign investors may also enter into joint ventures. It is advisable to provide in detail all the rights corresponding to minority shareholders as there are very few minority protection provisions in the Commercial Code.

Investments in and Mergers with Existing Entities

The purchase of a business in Venezuela by a foreign corporation is subject to the requirement to file notice of the transaction with the appropriate agency. A foreign investor may (i) purchase the shares of another foreign investor in any Venezuelan company; (ii) purchase the shares of the national investor in any Venezuelan company; or (iii) purchase the assets of any company in Venezuela, assuming that the acquisition by the foreign investor does not contravene specific laws.

Similarly, a foreign investor may purchase the shares of another foreign investor in any offshore company holding shares in any Venezuelan company. In this case, it is not necessary to file notice of the transaction with the appropriate agency.

Except for the sectors reserved for national companies, foreign investors may freely purchase stock of listed companies in the stock exchange. In this case, registration with the appropriate agency has to be done for the stock owned by the foreign investor at the end of the calendar year. As a result, foreign investors may participate in the stock exchange and buy and sell shares during the year. They are compelled to comply only with the general regulations of stock exchange applicable to both national and foreign investors.

With regard to the sale of shares, the Foreign Investment Regulations[3] establish that the acquisition by foreign investors of shares owned by national investors is subject to registration within 60 calendar days from the execution of the commercial transaction.

Agency, Reseller, Franchising, and Distribution Networks

Although the concept of agency is not specifically regulated by the law, it is used as a convenient way through which a foreign corporation can carry out a certain level of operations in Venezuela. Under this kind of agreement, an individual or legal entity undertakes activities to initiate negotiations and promote business on behalf of a principal.

The agent is not considered a duly authorized officer of the principal and, therefore, may not assume any obligations on its behalf, unless a power of attorney has been granted in his or her name. Usually, the agent limits his or her activities to act as an intermediary between the company and local purchasers or potential clients, and to carry out marketing activities.

A distribution agreement is an agreement pursuant to which a person or legal entity (distributor) purchases goods in its own name and for its account from a manufacturer or wholesaler in order to sell them to third parties for a profit. There are no statutory rules specifically governing distribution agreements, so general principles of commercial law are applied to this kind of relationship.

Neither agents nor distributors are considered employees under Venezuelan Labor Law, unless the relationship includes subordination and other labor principles established in the country's labor laws.

Representative Offices and Other Nonpermanent Establishments

Representative offices are treated and permitted only in the scope of the General Law of Banks and Other Financial Entities,[4] serving as intermediates between their constituents and natural or legal persons who received credits granted by them.

In order to function legally in Venezuela, representative offices need an authorization issued by the Superintendence of Banks and Other Financial Entities,[5] and must fulfill every requirement and formality established by such Superintendence through general rules. In this matter, the Superintendence must admit the application within a term of two months from the date of its reception; if not, the Superintendence must inform the applicant of the status of such application and the reasons for the situation. In any event, the Superintendence may revoke the authorization given to any representative office, without prejudice of the sanctions established in the law.

It is important to note that Venezuela's legislation[6] prohibits representative offices from receiving deposits, from being intermediaries in passive operations related to fundraising, and from providing information or managing or treating any operation related to this matter; otherwise, a sanction will be applicable according to the provisions in the law.

Finally, the representative offices shall constitute and maintain a pledge with a financial institute or insurance company domiciled in Venezuela, in order to guarantee the fulfillment of the obligations acquired during its activities. Also, representative offices shall provide any information to the Superintendence in the period established for their activities in the country or in any opportunity requested by the Superintendence.

Approvals and Registrations

To legally incorporate a corporation in Venezuela, the law[7] requires registration of the articles of incorporation and bylaws before the Mercantile Registry Office and its subsequent publication in a local newspaper. Additionally, shareholders must file evidence of payment of the capital contribution.

Failure to fulfill all legal requirements results in the company not being considered legally incorporated and therefore the shareholders, administrators, and any other person who has acted on behalf of the company will be deemed personally liable for all ventures the company enters into.

There is a registration fee for incorporation of the company and registration of the branch equivalent to 1 percent of the capital stock or the capital allocated to the branch, plus administrative fees payable to the Registry Office.

Regarding administrative regulations, it is important to note that after incorporation of a business organization several requirements must be fulfilled, such as registration with the Venezuelan Internal Revenue Service in order to obtain a tax ID number (RIF); classification of the company by the appropriate agency; and registration of the foreign investment with the appropriate agency.

Sensitive Economic Sectors/Restrictions on Foreign Ownership

Some reserved sectors of the economy require local participation. These sectors fall into two main categories. The first category is sectors reserved for national enterprises by Foreign Investment Regulations. This includes television and radio broadcasting and Spanish-language newspapers, as well as services in areas requiring the participation of professionals whose practice is governed by national laws. The second category is areas reserved for national companies by special laws, including the oil and gas industry. Companies operating in all sectors other than the ones mentioned above may be formed with up to 100 percent of foreign ownership and may remain as foreign-owned companies indefinitely.

Political Risk and Related Issues

Current local conditions in Venezuela are challenging for private business. There is a clear Venezuelan governmental policy toward fostering a greater role of the state in all sectors of the economy, not just as a regulator, but also as an active participant in each area, by expropriating and taking over the activities of significant private players in different sectors of the economy such as banking, insurance, agro-industry, manufacturing, and retail.

In addition to the expropriations, the Venezuelan state has great participation in business; in fact it is the first and most important contracting party in the country. Actually, direct or indirectly, the government has an influence in every business in Venezuela. If it is not by its participation in the company, it is by controlling all permits, licenses, and authorization needed for the conducting of business activities in general and in particular imports and exports, exchange control, participation in public procurement procedures, and so on.

In addition, current politics indicate a trend of transition of the economic system from capitalism to socialism, which might have profound consequences in the way business will be conducted in the future. In this context, it is extremely important for foreign investors to seek out proper legal advice before entering the Venezuelan market and during their activities in the country.

INVESTMENT ISSUES AND TAX INCENTIVES

Legal Treatment of Foreign Investment

According to the regulations applied to foreign investment,[8] all foreign investments are deemed approved and are subject to registration with the appropriate agency provided only that they do not contravene any provision of general applicability under Venezuelan legislation.

A foreign investment may be made to create a new company or other business organization; however, it is also possible for foreign investors to acquire equity participation in local companies with no limitations other than those established for the particular economic activity in the applicable legislation.

The Superintendence of Foreign Investments (SIEX)[9] is the administrative office in charge of regulating foreign investments and technology transfer agreements; however, some exceptions may apply for particular sectors of the economy.

All foreign investments shall be registered before the SIEX within the first 60 days[10] following the registration of the company before the Commercial Registry Office or other act by which the investment is concluded. The company is allowed to start operations during the registration procedure before SIEX.

There are three possible classifications of investments: (i) foreign (more than 49 percent foreign equity); (ii) mixed (49 percent or less but more than 19.9 percent foreign equity); and (iii) national (less than 20 percent foreign equity). In order to classify the company as foreign, mixed, or national, the appropriate agency considers the percentage of equity held by the foreign investor. In addition, shares owned by foreign investors with no decision-making power in the technical, commercial, administrative, and financial management of the company are not computed for the purpose of classifying the company as foreign, mixed, or national.

The degree of control a foreign investor may exercise over a Venezuelan company depends on the sector of the economy in which the local company operates and the foreign investment classification assigned to the company by the appropriate agency.

According to applicable law, national, mixed, and foreign companies are authorized to repatriate 100 percent of their foreign investments, after payment of taxes due over the dividends at the closing of every fiscal year. The dividends declaration does not require a previous authorization, but the SIEX shall be notified of every payment of dividends.

On the other hand, the reinvestment of 100 percent of the dividends is legally possible in foreign and mixed companies. Once the reinvestment is completed, the SIEX shall be notified and the new investment shall be registered.

Treaties on Foreign Investment Protection

Venezuela has signed several treaties to protect foreign investment, such as multilateral treaties and bilateral treaties. The main multilateral agreements that can be used to protect foreign investments are the Multilateral Investment Guarantee Agency (MIGA),[11] the Convention on the Settlement of Investment Disputes between States and Nationals of Other States (ICSID);[12] and the Convention on the Recognition and Execution of Foreign Arbitral Awards (New York Convention, United Nations).[13]

Venezuela has also signed several bilateral agreements for the promotion and protection of investments with several countries.[14] It is important to take these agreements into consideration when investing in the country, as they bring a certain level of security to investors.

Publicly Held Companies—Capital Market Regulations

Publicly held companies are treated under the provisions of the Capital Market Law.[15] Under these rules, the National Executive regulates every operator of the capital market through the creation of general norms and provisions, in order to safeguard the transparency and the rights of the investors in every operation carried out in the capital market.

This law also regulates the public offering of securities, aiming for the control of the reception of public savings. This control guarantees an efficient capital market through the enforcement of laws aimed to protect the general interest.

Transparency is one of the main pillars in capital market regulations, since it is established to ensure clear and sufficient information for the investors, in which every investor is aware of the current information on the prices and economic conditions of the companies engaged in the capital market.

On the other hand, the rights of the investors constitute the other main pillar in the capital market regulations. The state, through the enforcement of laws, breaks the inequality between the major shareholders in control of the company and the minor shareholders, who are unable to manage the company and could be affected by the decisions of the major shareholders.

The capital market provisions also establish the participation of a National Securities Commission[16] vested with enough powers to regulate, guard, and supervise the capital market. This commission has to act according to the law, and its purpose is the public protection of investors' interests. In the case of an individual breach of the provisions of the law or the guidelines issued by the National Value Commission, a sanction will be applicable to this individual, since the provisions and guidelines are established in order to create a trustful and safe environment in which to invest.

Alternate Investment Structures—Investment Funds

Investment funds are understood by the legislation as entities of collective securities investment. An authorization is required in order to make a public offering of such securities, which cannot be the major equity participation of the company, in order to prevent a takeover in the financial or operative management of the company by the investor.

There are two distinct types of investment funds. The first is the entities of open equity, where equity may increase in consequence of new contributions by investors and partial or total withdrawal of contributions may be made without the need for a prior investor assembly. Its investment units are not negotiated in the stock market. The second type is entities of close equity, where an increase or decrease of equity must be approved by the investor assembly. Its investments units are negotiated in the stock market.

In order to buy investment units from investment funds the following steps and requirements must be fulfilled:

    a.   The investor must go to the Mutual Fund Management Society[17] registered in the National Securities Commission in order to make an investment and shall request the form authorized by the commission to make its decision on the investment.

b. With the approval of the commission, the investor shall fulfill the purchase form of the investment units with its personal information and the amount of investment units that he or she is buying.

c. The commission calculates the amount and after the payment, the commission will deliver a proof of the transaction.

It is important to note that the investor in an investment fund can withdraw his investment at any time, but the value of such will depend on the day value of the units; this operation is known as rescue. Some investment funds have special periods to withdraw or rescue the investment, and the person must respect the period established.

OPERATIONAL LEGAL ENVIRONMENT

Tips on Negotiations in Venezuela

Foreign investors should always be careful while negotiating or contracting in Venezuela or with Venezuelan parties. The following tips should always be followed:

- Make sure the companies involved are properly represented (by powers of attorney, proxies, or shareholders' resolutions);
- Make sure all important communications and decisions, as well as all agreements and contracts, are in writing;
- Make sure to get the best local legal advice every time you negotiate, contract, or make decisions, as it can save you time and money.
- Be patient—negotiations, execution of agreements, and even payments can take time.

Foreign Exchange

Since 2003, currency exchange has been controlled by the government. According to the limitations set forth in this matter, the Venezuelan Central Bank[18] has the exclusive right to perform currency exchange activities through its authorized dealers (banks and other financial institutions). The government fixes the exchange rate and the Currency Administration Commission (CADIVI)[19] is the government office in charge of the administration of the exchange control regime.

As of the publication of the Law against Illegal Exchange on October 15, 2005, currency exchange activities performed outside the authorized financial institutions are strictly forbidden and penalized. This law establishes several requirements for business transactions in foreign currency.

Nevertheless, there are a few operations that are not considered currency exchange and, for that reason, are outside the exchange control regime. These operations can be used to obtain foreign exchange using bolivars available in Venezuela. These operations imply the acquisition of Venezuelan bonds (titles of government debt) or gold, for instance.

Until May 2010, a swap system of securities titles was used. This system worked through local brokerages and implied the acquisition of Venezuelan titles denominated in bolivars and a subsequent exchange (swap) of such Venezuelan securities for foreign securities denominated in U.S. dollars. Nowadays, this option is not possible, since on May 17, 2010, a reform of the Law against Illegal Exchange[20] was published, having as a consequence the prohibition of the swap market.

Currently the exchange control is one of the main barriers to business. Without the swap system, and disregarding the other options that are either too complex or possible only sporadically, businesses have only one possible way to convert bolivars to foreign currency, which is via CADIVI.

The system implemented by CADIVI is meant to provide a controlled exchange instrument for companies and individuals. The exchange rate today is of 4.30 bolivars for one U.S. dollar or 2.60 bolivars for one U.S. dollar, depending on the case. For imports, for example, there are two lists of products. The Bs. 4.30/1 USD rate applies for one of the lists, and for the other, the list of essential products, the Bs. 2.60/1 USD rate applies.

However, in the case of companies, the system has so many limitations that sometimes it is impossible for some businesses to have access to foreign currency, either to import products or to repatriate dividends, for example.

On the other hand, foreign capital entering Venezuela must pass through the Central Bank, which will apply the official exchange rate of 4.30 bolivars for every U.S. dollar.

Immigration and Visa Requirements

Immigration and visa requirements in Venezuela are subject to Migration and Immigration Law[21] and to regulations from the Administrative Service for Identification, Migration and Immigration (SAIME).[22] Venezuelan authorities are allowed to issue several kinds of visa, but only two are relevant to business: the labor visa (visa de transeunte laboral) and the business visa (visa de transeunte de negocios).

The business visa is granted to merchants, executive employees, industry or corporate representatives, and micro-entrepreneurs, as well as nonmigrants who wish to enter the country in order to carry out activities and/or commercial transactions and mercantile, financial, or other lucrative activity related to their businesses. It is obtained directly by the person before the Venezuelan consulate in his or her country of origin or residence. It is granted for one year for multiple entries. The holder of this visa is not entitled to work for any local company.

The labor visa is the visa with which anyone can work in Venezuela and be hired by a company registered in Venezuela. It is recommended that the employee obtain the visa before entering Venezuela. In case there is the need to come to Venezuela before the visa is authorized, the employee shall enter Venezuela with the business visa (visa de transeunte de negocios). Once the labor visa is authorized, the employee shall withdraw it at the Venezuelan consulate in his country of origin or residence. The procedure to obtain the authorization to enter the country and the labor permission of the employee may take three to four months. It is granted for one year, and the holder is entitled to bring his or her family to Venezuela with a family visa (visa de transeunte familiar).

The procedures and the granting of a labor visa may be troublesome due to the number of documents to be filed and the need to obtain the work permit, which is a prerequisite for filing the application to obtain the labor visa.

Import and Export Issues

Venezuelan export tariffs are usually set on an ad-valorem basis. However, sometimes import duties are calculated on a specific or mixed basis. According to Regulation No. 989, which contains Venezuela's custom tariffs, there are four levels of tariffs applicable for imported goods. The highest range is up to 20 percent, the middle is 10 percent to 15 percent, and the lowest is 5 percent. Vehicles are an exceptional case, with tariffs up to 35 percent.

In 1990, Venezuela adopted the Harmonized Code on Nomenclature of Merchandise, which was incorporated into the customs tariff list. The Venezuelan tariff contains all specific legal data applied to every item imported into the country, including nontariff barriers.

The custom tariff's rule also expressly indicates that the agreements set forth in the integration treaties signed by Venezuela will prevail over the custom tariff. Therefore, a preferential treatment will take place in the event that the products are imported from any member country to these treaties to which Venezuela is a member. The applicable tariff would depend on the specific agreement.

There are also some special duties that might apply according to the case; for example, the customs services tax is 1 percent of the value of the merchandise imported into the country.

A company wishing to import must be duly incorporated in Venezuela and have as well a valid fiscal identification number (RIF) and fulfill all the requirements and procedures to obtain an importation license.

Regarding exporting policies, Venezuela has developed a policy of expansion and incentive for the exportation of nontraditional products (that is, products other than oil and gas, iron, and aluminum). In this sense, a special fund to finance nontraditional exports was created to grant loans with preferential conditions to Venezuelan exporters—the Bank of Foreign Trade (BANCOEX).[23]

Depending either on the destination or the nature of the product, an exporter may be requested to fulfill specific prerequisites such as export licenses, sanitary certificates, or certificates of origin.

Finally, the International Trade Unfair Practices Law enacted in 1992[24] prevents dumping and subsidiary practices by establishing policies to prevent harmful effects in the national production.

Taxation of Business and Cross-Border Transactions

The Venezuelan taxation system is based on the Constitution, which contains the fundamental principles on this matter, including the Equality Principle, the Legality Principle, the Generality Principle, and the Worldwide Income.[25]

Venezuela has entered into agreements with several countries to prevent double taxation.[26] When there are no treaties subscribed to by Venezuela with a given country, the income tax law[27] provides all the mechanisms to be applied.

The income tax law defines taxpayers as individuals, legal entities, and permanent establishments located in Venezuela. The law considers that a company carries out operations in Venezuela through a permanent establishment when either directly or indirectly (through a legal representative or an employee) such company owns any sort of office or established place of business in Venezuela, in which its activities are developed either in whole or in part. A foreign company will also be regarded as having a permanent establishment in Venezuela when there is evidence of the existence of a head office or branch in the country.

The legal form to determine the income tax is based on the taxpayer's gross income less the costs and deductions allowed by the law, that is, those normal and necessary expenses incurred in the country by taxpayers in order to obtain their income. The income tax law establishes that the annual income obtained by business entities is subject to a progressive tax rate from a minimum of 15 percent to a maximum of 34 percent.

Residents[28] are also subject to a progressive tax rate that ranges from a minimum of 6 percent for an annual taxable income of up to 1,000 fiscal units to a maximum of 34 percent for an annual taxable income of over 6,000 fiscal units.

Dividends are subject to a proportional tax applied only if they correspond to profits that have not been taxed at the level of the dividend distributing company. The net income is declared by the taxpayer through financial statements made in accordance with generally accepted accounting principles. The net income is the basis for the calculation of taxes. The proportional tax rate on dividends, when applicable, is 34 percent and it is subject to an anticipated withholding of 1 percent of the value of the dividend distributed in shares.

Exporting goods to Venezuela is not an activity subject to income tax as it is considered extraterritorial income for the foreign supplier since the source of income was not in the national territory. The importation of goods is subject to customs tax paid by the local importer.

The value added tax (VAT) is applied on the selling of goods, the rendering of services, and importation of goods and services. The VAT rate is established annually by law, and ranges from 8 percent to 16.5 percent. Currently, the VAT rate is set at 14 percent.

Other taxes are applicable to business organizations, such as social security contributions, registration taxes, the stamp tax, and, in particular, municipal taxes such as the Commercial Patent Tax, which is a tax applied by local governments to commercial or industrial activities carried out within their jurisdiction.

Labor and Employment

The Venezuelan Organic Labor Law (LOT) is the most important legal body that regulates labor and employment in Venezuela.

The general principles of the LOT are the following:

a. *Territoriality and Public Policy.* The provisions of the LOT are of territorial application and represent public policy, which means that the benefits provided by the law cannot be contractually modified. The law applies to employees of foreign enterprises for the services provided in Venezuela, even on a temporary basis.

b. *No Waivers.* The rights and obligations established in the labor legislation cannot be waived during the employment relationship. This means that any agreement between employer and employee that reduces or discards a right or obligation is null and void.

c. *Equality.* Any discrimination based on affiliation, age, sex, race, marital status, religious beliefs, or political or social condition is expressly forbidden. Nobody may be subject to discrimination in his or her right to work due to criminal records. It is also forbidden to include such conditions in job offers; however, labor contracts may include the normal references to nationality, sex, age, and marital status, which are customary, without breaking the law.

d. *Nationality Requirements.* Foreign employees shall not exceed 10 percent of the total workforce or 20 percent of the total payroll in any business. The Ministry of Labor may approve exceptions in particular cases. Additionally, certain positions are required to be filled by Venezuelans, such as human resources managers or ship and airplane captains.

e. *Prescription.* Rights arising from a labor relationship prescribe one year after the termination of the relationship and those arising from labor accidents or occupation disease prescribe five years after the accident. These statutes of limitations may be "interrupted" by various means such as claims filed before the courts or the Ministry of Labor.

According to the LOT, the parties of the labor relationship are the following:

a. *Employee and Worker.* An employee is an individual who mainly performs intellectual work. A worker is a person who performs manual work. A management employee is a person who intervenes in the company's decision-making or represents the employer before other employees or third parties and may substitute for the employer, partially or totally, in the exercise of his or her functions. A trustworthy employee is an employee who has supervision tasks, and has access to critical information vital for the business.

b. *Employer.* The employer is an individual or legal entity who in his or her own name is in charge of an establishment, exploitation, or task of any nature with the aid of employees. The employer's representative is a person who exercises functions of direction and administration such as director, manager, administrator, or head of industrial relations, and is considered by law the employer's agent in labor relationships.

c. *Intermediary.* An intermediary is a person who in his own name and normally for the benefit of another person uses the services of one or more employees. The intermediary is jointly liable with the beneficiary for the work regarding the rights of employees. The employees employed by intermediaries shall enjoy the same benefits as those of the employees employed directly by the beneficiary of the work.

d. *Contractor.* The contractor is an individual or legal entity who agrees in contract to perform works or services by his or her own means on behalf of somebody else. If the work carried out by the contractor is of the same or related nature as that of the beneficiary of the work or service, both the contractor and the beneficiary of the work are jointly liable for the obligations that arise in favor of employees.

The LOT establishes a few rules regarding labor contracts. The norm in Venezuela is for employers and employees to enter into indefinite term employment contracts. The work agreement is deemed for an undetermined period of time unless the parties clearly express their will to contract solely for the performance of a specific job or for a specific period of time. Labor contracts have no formalities and can be presumed for most kinds of work. It is advisable to draft labor contracts in writing, since they serve as evidence for critical issues such as obligations, conditions, salary, and date of incorporation.

Some employees enjoy absolute job stability, which means they cannot be dismissed unless previous authorization from the labor administration is obtained based on justified cause according to the law.

Relative job stability is granted by law to permanent employees with more than three months of service as long as they are not employed in the management of the company. Employees who do not enjoy job stability may be dismissed without justified cause, but then their severance payments are increased by law. Labor courts are authorized by law to determine whether an employee has absolute, relative, or no job stability and whether the cause of termination of contract is justified or not.

Agreements for fixed periods of time are also allowed. These kinds of agreements have a specific date of initiation and termination, and are limited by law only (i) when the nature of the service requires so; (ii) when its purpose is the provisional, legal substitution of an employee; and (iii) when Venezuelans are contracted in foreign countries. Contracts of this nature should be in writing as they evidence an exception to what the law generally presumes.

Fixed-term employment contracts are required to be in writing. In the case of qualified employees, a contract may not be subscribed for more than three years; in the case of normal employees it may not be subscribed for more than one year.

When the contract is extended more than once, or successive contracts of this nature are entered into by the same parties within 30 days of the expiration of the previous contract, the labor relationship must be considered to be for an undetermined period of time.

These contracts expire after their termination date. Should any party decide to terminate the contract prior to the termination date, this party must indemnify the damages caused to the other by the termination. The indemnity is set at the amount of salaries pending until the termination date.

The most important legal limitations according to Venezuelan labor law are the following:

a. *Working Hours.* The law establishes a maximum of 44 working hours a week for day work, 35 hours a week for night work, and 42 hours a week for mixed shifts. The daily shift may not exceed eight hours, and the night shift may not exceed seven hours. A maximum shift of 11 hours a day may be required for employees in management or "reliable employees" as well as those that perform surveillance or discontinuous or intermittent work.

b. *Overtime.* The law establishes a 50 percent surcharge on the basic hourly wage to be paid for overtime, and it may not legally exceed 10 weekly hours or a maximum of 100 hours a year.

c. *Holidays.* The law establishes a 50 percent surcharge on the basic daily wage in payment for work performed on holidays and days off.

d. *Participation in the Company's Benefits.* The employer should distribute among its employees 15 percent of the company's profits at the end of every fiscal year; however, this percentage may vary due to the employer's economic performance.

e. *Vacations and Vacation Bonus.* Every employee is entitled by law to 15 days of paid vacation after completion of his or her first year of employment. An employee is also entitled to an additional day of vacation for each subsequent year up to a maximum of 30 days of total vacation time. Employees are also entitled to a vacation bonus by law. This bonus is equivalent to seven days of salary for the first complete year of employment and then one additional day of salary for each year up to a maximum of 21 days.

f. *Seniority.* After three months of continued service, the employee is entitled to a seniority payment equal to five daily wages for each month worked. After the first anniversary the benefit increases to two additional daily wages per year, up to a maximum of 30. This bonus is deposited into a trust fund or may be kept by the company in its accounting and is paid only after termination of the employment or when requested after the rules of the LOT are complied with.

g. *Severance Indemnities.* Employees will be entitled to a severance indemnity in the event of dismissal without cause in the following terms:

- Ten days of salary if the employee has worked for more than 90 days but less than six months.
- Thirty days of salary for each year or fraction over six months worked by the employee up to a maximum of 150 days of salary.

Employees dismissed without cause are also entitled to indemnities in lieu of notice, calculated as follows:
- Fifteen days of salary if the employee was employed for more than one month but less than six months.
- Thirty days of salary if the employee was employed for more than six months but less than one year.
- Forty-five days of salary if the employee was employed for more than one year.
- Sixty days of salary if the employee was employed for more than two years but less than 10 years.
- Ninety days of salary if the employee was employed for more than 10 years.

There are also other labor obligations for companies, which must be registered before the regional office of the Ministry of Labor in the jurisdiction where they are located, before the National Institute of Technical Education to which applicable taxes must be paid, and before the Social Security Institute where applicable taxes must be paid for social security (unemployment taxes, housing policy taxes, and social security taxes).

Antitrust and Competition Issues

Competition issues are treated in the Venezuelan Constitution of 1999, and antitrust is regulated under the provisions of the Promotion and Protection of Free Competition Act of 1992,[29] known as the Procompetencia Act. Both establish the general framework for each matter and both are the current applicable law.

The purpose of the Procompetencia Act is to promote and protect free competition and efficiency in favor of manufacturers, merchants, and consumers. Procompetencia aims to protect the markets and not companies. However, this law is not applicable only to natural persons, since Procompetencia Act is also applicable to public or private corporations engaged in economic activities. It is important to note that certain public services-related sectors are excluded from the provisions established in the Procompetencia Act.

The authority in charge is the Superintendence for the Promotion and Protection of Free Competition.[30] This entity is an independent government agency attached to the Ministry of Light Industries and Commerce, vested with powers to conduct investigations.

The sanctions applicable to anyone who breaches the provisions established in the law are fines from 10 percent to 20 percent of the net sales of the offender and could reach 40 percent in the cases of reoffenders.

Finally, a new competition law has been under discussion by the Venezuelan National Assembly since 2006. The current draft includes several material changes in the current framework governing competition, such as the general prohibitions of anticompetitive behavior along with a wide range of particular prohibitions, the creation of the National Antimonopoly and Anti-oligopoly Institute, the creation of a distinction between cartels, and horizontal agreements. According to this bill, if the economic concentration is completed without notification or authorization of the competition authority, the transaction will be considered null and void, and an administrative sanction will be imposed. Finally, the percentages of the sanctions in the case of breaching the law would be increased and new criminal sanctions established.

Environmental Issues

The environment in Venezuela is regulated under the Organic Law of Environment.[31] According to this law, the environment is a grouping or a system of natural physical elements; chemical, biological, or cultural partners; in constant movement by human influence; ruling and conditioning the existence of humans and other living organisms.

The Environmental Issue is the administrative functionality of every activity engaged in the determination and development of policies, objectives, environmental duties, and their implementation through planning, control, conservation, and environmental development. Moreover, it comprehends:

a. *Responsibility.* It is the duty of the state, society, and the people to protect safety, health, and the ecological environment.
b. *Prevention.* Every measure applicable to the conservation of the environment prevails over any other criteria in environmental issues.
c. *Precaution.* The absence of scientific certainty cannot be claimed as a sufficient reason to evade the responsibility to apply protective and

efficient measures in activities that may cause a negative impact on the environment.

d. *Limitation of Individual Rights.* Environmental rights prevail over economic and social rights.

e. *Responsibility for Environmental Damages.* The responsibility is objective, and its reparation shall be carried out by the party responsible for the activity that caused the damage.

f. *Environmental Impact Evaluation.* All the activities capable of degrading the environment must be previously evaluated through a study of environmental and social impact.

g. *Environmental Damages.* Damages caused to the environment are considered damages to the public heritage.

Citizens and companies, private or public, shall execute their activities according to the plans established and the provisions of the law and any other legal instrument applicable to this matter. In addition, they are responsible for the formulation and execution of the projects engaged in the use of natural resources and biological diversity. Also, they shall create a permanent process of environmental education in order to allow the conservation of the ecosystem and a sustainable development.

Finally, environmental law establishes that every activity carried out by companies or individuals must be accomplished according to the provisions of the law, in order to safeguard the environmental stability and a peaceful place of living. Any citizen who breaches the provisions of the law and causes damage to the environment will be punished with the payment of up to 10,000 tax units and up to 10 years of prison.

Consumer Protection and Products Liability

In Venezuela consumer protection is regulated by the Constitution of the Bolivarian Republic of Venezuela and the Law for the People's Right to Access Goods and Services (LEDEPABIS).[32] In the Venezuelan Constitution, consumer protection is contemplated as a constitutional right to freedom of commerce and as the right of every man to access quality goods and services.

This protection contemplates basic consumer items, which are those that satisfy the basic necessities of the consumer, defining consumer as every natural or legal entity that acquires, uses, or enjoys goods and services of any nature. Consumer protection is thus defined as all those actions aimed at defending the economic and social interests of consumers in their relations with suppliers of goods or services.

The main purpose of LEDEPABIS is to protect the rights and interests, whether individual or collective, in the access to goods and services, and to satisfy the needs of consumers, establishing administrative procedures and sanctions. This law regulates all legal acts executed between suppliers and consumers. Under the LEDEPA-BIS, consumers have the right to the protection of their health, better quality and prices, judicial protection of their rights and economic interests, and the right to information and truthful advertising, among others.

The law also prohibits and sanctions every act of suppliers of goods or services that imposes abusive conditions or false advertising on consumers and sells goods at higher prices than those established by the corresponding authority.

The LEDEPABIS also provides the constitution of consumers' associations for the protection of their rights in accessing goods and services, and establishes the Institute for the Defense of People in the Access to Goods and Services (INDEPA-BIS),[33] whose main purpose is the protection and defense of the rights and interests of consumers in the access to goods and services and the execution of verification, inspection, and determination procedures to ensure compliance with the law.

It is important to mention that the LEDEPABIS provides administrative procedures, carried out before the INDEPABIS, to request preventive measures, which are ruled by the principles of direction and ex-officio acting, truth prevalence (the activities of the government official must be directed toward the truth), probation freedom (any kind of evidence can be used, as long as it is not prohibited), and publicity (the interested parties have the right to access any documents in the file), among others.

Land Use and Real Estate

Land use is treated in the Law of Land and Agricultural Development,[34] which establishes a different treatment for every type of land listed in the law. Also, the law ensures private property and ownership of land, but some restrictions are applicable, such as the obligation to maintain the harvesting of the land in order to safeguard the progress and productivity of the economic area; otherwise, the land can be expropriated by the National Executive in order to ensure the rightful use and disposal of the land.

Moreover, other regulations are applicable, such as the general rules issued by the National Institute of Lands; this Institute was created in order to regulate the land for agricultural purposes and to carry out every process needed to issue the declaration of vacant land and the certificate of an improved or productive farm. Also, it is the specialized organization to deal with the agrarian expropriation process and land recovery, and finally to intervene preventively in every unproductive land that might constitute a danger to the economic progress of the country.

The National Assembly recently approved a bill that establishes a partial reform of the Law of Land and Agricultural Development. This bill establishes that the public and private agrarian lands are under the full control of the state, differently from the current law, since today the control of private land belongs to the owner with certain limitations. It also establishes that the land can be used and enjoyed for its production but cannot be disposed, since the land disposal would belong to the state as the rightful owner.

Intellectual Property

The legislation regarding copyright[35] is enforced by the Ministry of the Popular Power for Trade[36] and the Autonomous Service for Intellectual Property (SAPI),[37] which is part of that ministry. There is also a centralized agency called the National Directorate on Copyright,[38] which is part of SAPI.

The provisions of the Copyright Law[39] shall protect all creative intellectual works, whether literary, scientific, or artistic in character and whatever their nature, form of expression, merit, or purpose, as well as neighboring rights.[40]

Regarding formalities, no requirement of copyright notice or deposit exists. There is a system for copyright registration. The works may be registered with the Registry of the Intellectual Property of the National Directorate of Copyright. The directorate evaluates the application during a period of approximately six months, and decides whether to grant the registration.

Regarding ownership, primarily, the author is the owner of the copyrighted work, but any person other than the author, whether a natural person or legal entity, may own the economic rights in the work in accordance with the provisions of the legislation. Rights can be transferred and the assignment of exploitation rights and licenses may be granted for legal use, but with the provision that they must be in writing.

In general, a copyright's duration is equal to the author's life, plus 60 years after his or her death; however, audio-visual and radio works, as well as software, expire 60 years after their first publication.

Any use of a work without the specific permission of the copyright owner can result in copyright infringement. The general measures intended to defend copyright are judicial inspections, expert studies, seizure, and sequestration. A term of imprisonment may also apply in some cases.

After Venezuela's withdrawal from the Andean Community on April 22, 2006, legislative matters related to intellectual property have changed in the country although no major changes have taken place regarding copyrights since the Copyright Law was implemented in 1993. Discussions have taken place regarding whether decisions issued by the Andean Community while Venezuela was a member country became part of its legislation or not. A petition for interpretation was filed at the Constitutional Chamber of the Supreme Court of Justice; however, the Supreme Court has still not rendered a decision.

In regard to trademark legislation, the withdrawal from the Andean Community must be taken in consideration, as well as that the Intellectual Property Law of 1955 is therefore back in force. According to this law, distinctive words and signs and combinations thereof that are capable of being graphically reproduced can be registered as trademarks, including numerals.

The time taken to obtain a trademark registration will depend on what occurs during the application process. If no official actions are issued by the Trademark Office, no oppositions are filed by third parties, and no ex-officio refusals are made by the Trademark Office, registration may be granted from 12 to 24 months after filing. The normal cost of obtaining a trademark can range from USD 1,400 to USD 2,000. The registration has a validity of 15 years from its granting date and can be renewed for successive 15-year terms, provided that the renewal is filed within six months prior to the expiration date of the registration.

Enforcements of trademark rights can be sought via both the criminal and civil jurisdictions. There are also border enforcement mechanisms. The most common way to proceed is the civil jurisdiction, as it entails less liability to the plaintiff. In order to do so, on a trademark basis, we would recommend that a valid trademark registration exist.

There is a project of reform in that the current industrial property law is being drafted. According to information received, this new legislation should be compliant with the World Trade Organization's agreement on Trade Related Aspects of Intellectual Property Rights (TRIPS) and other international agreements.

Regarding patents, to be patentable, the subject matter must be novel; however, there are some exceptions to this requirement such as an invention, improvement, or industrial model or design that, being patented abroad, has not been divulged, patented, or put into execution in Venezuela, which means it is not in the public domain.

Regarding Patent Office proceedings, generally a patent may take from four to five years to be granted. The filing, prosecution, and granting of a patent will generally cost around USD 2,000 in fees and USD 1,500 in expenses. Once granted, a yearly fee of USD 135 must be paid in order to maintain the validity of the patent.

In Venezuela, the enforcement of a patent right will generally be sought before a trial court (tribunal de primera instancia), which may issue, within the procedure, a wide range of injunctions to safeguard a legal right, provided that irreparable harm can be shown.

Following Venezuela's withdrawal from the Andean Community, the current situation in Venezuela relating to legislative issues has changed. The country is still awaiting a decision from the Supreme Court of Justice on the interpretation recourse filed before the Constitutional Chamber about the legislation in force regarding this matter.

Customs

The Organic Law of Customs[41] is the most important piece of legislation applicable to customs. In general terms, customs is a public entity with a national service supplier character, whose control activities intend to enforce the current law in matters related to foreign merchandise, national or nationalized.

In Venezuela customs are classified as follows:

a.   Hierarchy

- *Principal customs*, which have the jurisdiction in a specific judicial district and centralize the tax and administrative functions of the subordinates customs attached to them.
- *Subordinate customs*, which are attached to principal customs and are able to make specific customs operations for a selected judicial district.
- *Enabled customs*, which are authorized by the Financial Ministry in order to make certain operations, totally or partially, and customs services.

b.   Traffic

- *Entrance customs*, the customs office where the merchandise in traffic enters in customs territory and where the merchandise is declared for its nationalization.
- *Destination customs*, the office that ends the customs traffic operation.
- *Transit customs*, the office in which the merchandise transits all the way in the customs traffic operation.
- *Border-crossing customs*, the border customs office that intervenes in the control of the international traffic customs operation.

The administration related to this matter in Venezuela is distributed in two levels, a normative level and operative level, in order to guarantee an efficient customs organization and functionality. The operative level is constituted with 16 principal customs with their respectively subordinate offices, in charge of controlling the merchandise subject to declaration, as well as the physical verification of the merchandise, and related to liquidation and tax payments with its subsequent removal.

Finally, the normative level is constituted with the National Intendance of Customs,[42] which, as the executing unit of the national customs policies, is in charge of customs law enforcement and development of the customs procedures, in order to solve the claims established before the tax collection by this entity.

Internet Regulations/E-Commerce

The Internet and electronic commerce, known also as e-commerce, are treated in numerous laws of Venezuelan legislation, although there is not a specific law that regulates both matters, since the Internet is a relatively new communication service and e-commerce is a new business tool in society. E-commerce is considered any form of commercial transaction in which the parties exchange commercial views related to any economic activity, prepare purchase orders, negotiate prices for a certain services or objects, and more, all via the Internet.

E-commerce provides different types of commerce, such as the following:

a. *Business to Business.* In this case the companies are engaged in different electronic transactions, as service suppliers (Internet, security, etc.), financial institutions, or any other electronic transaction that can possibly be carried out through the Internet between companies.

b. *Business to Consumers.* The companies create websites, in which they publicly offer a number of products and services that people might need; therefore, people pay for them in order to satisfy their need.

c. *Consumers to Consumers.* In this case consumers use the Internet to buy or sell their own objects. In some cases it is possible that consumers become electronic merchants by auctioning objects online.

d. *Consumers to Executive Entities.* Entities from the administration interact with consumers through the establishment of tax payments; therefore, consumers use the Internet in order to acquire the correct information about tax payment rates or any other type of information that they need.

e. *Executive Entities to Business.* The administration establishes norms to regulate, support, and develop e-commerce, and it is a user of e-commerce.

The Venezuelan Chamber of e-commerce is a civil association in charge of grouping natural or legal persons, in order to support and develop their economic activities through the use of electronic media. This chamber was created to make electronic business more efficient and rentable, as well as promote innovation and necessary changes to develop every business engaged in e-commerce. It is important to note that this nongovernmental entity is a specialized association that represents and defends the interests of corporations engaged in e-commerce before national and international entities.

Financing Issues/Payments

The presence of a strict exchange control regime in Venezuela has a direct impact on financing and payments in Venezuela.

Pursuant to the exchange control regulations, government approvals are required to make payments in foreign currency to companies abroad or to companies of the same group. Sometimes, companies have no access to foreign currency through the official system because the products they need to import are not in the CADIVI lists. Other times, they go through the whole process but never receive the final approval to proceed with the exchange.

This has created difficult situations for companies that are unable to honor their international agreements or to do so on time. Some have their orders rejected from several international providers or have to pay a higher price in view of these problems.

Financing has also been affected as the payment of loans to foreign institutions is also limited by exchange control. This situation highly compromises the possibility of obtaining foreign financing in Venezuela.

Secured Transactions

The main law about guarantee rights is the Movable Mortgage and Pledge without Displacement of Possession Law (Movable Mortgage Law) enacted in 1973.[43] The other special law in this matter is the Sales with Title Reservation Law, enacted in 1959.

The Venezuelan legislation also establishes the possibility of granting guarantees over personal property through the commercial pledge or civil pledge, naval mortgage, financial lease transactions, and other transactions that can be considered forms of commercial guarantees.

Securities Laws Issues

The most important issue regarding securities laws in Venezuela is the announcement made by the president at the beginning of August 2010 that Venezuela was in transition toward a new securities system. He declared that the Law on the Stock Market was already approved by the National Assembly, and that this new law would create a new Public Securities System.

The new law will create a National Superintendence of Securities, as well as the Public Stock Exchange. The first will have its operation related with the National Public Debt bonds and the second with other securities operations. State and private companies will be able to place for sale their bonds, shares, and other securities.

This law will bring profound changes in the securities systems in the country, the consequences of which are still difficult to predict. It is certain though that this new law goes along with the current policy of socialization of the Venezuelan economy and its institutions.

Government Procurement

The main piece of legislation applicable to public procurement is the Public Procurement Act of 2009 (PPA)[44] and its Administrative Regulation established in Decree No. 6708.[45] There is no sector-specific procurement legislation supplementing the general regime, with the exception of concessions contracts, which are regulated by the Decree-Law for the Promotion of Private Investment Under Concessions Regime of 1999 (PPCR).

The PPA applies to the following subjects, which are the only contracting authorities:

a. All public bodies and government agencies of the national, state, and municipal levels of government, either centralized or decentralized;
b. Public universities;
c. The Venezuelan Central Bank;
d. Civil partnerships and mercantile companies in which the republic has an interest, which is equal to or above 50 percent of the patrimony or shareholding (state-owned companies in the first degree);
e. Civil partnerships and mercantile companies where state-owned companies in the first degree have an interest equal to or above 50 percent (state-owned companies in the second degree);
f. The foundations incorporated by any public entity;
g. Community councils or any other community organization handling public funds.

According to the PPA, the provisions of the procurement procedure must be construed according to the principles of economy, planning, transparency, honesty, efficiency, nondiscrimination, competition, and publicity. The same provisions also establish that the participation of the persons through any kind of partnership or association shall be motivated.

Finally, in matters related to conflicts of interest, there are several laws dealing with conflict of interest of public officials. In Venezuela, conflicts of interest of public officials give rise to disciplinary and administrative sanctions. The disciplinary sanctions are established in the Statute of Public Function Act, which provides for the removal of the public official. The administrative sanctions are provided in the General Controller's Office and National System of Accountability Act, which establishes sanctions that may vary from a fine, the suspension of the official up to 24 months, or his removal, and a prohibition for the performance of public functions for up to 15 years. The Administrative Proceedings Organic Act also provides for remedies in cases of conflicts of interest of public officials, who may be challenged by the participants in public procurement procedures.

Regarding Venezuela's anticorruption laws, it is important to note the approval and implementation of the Law against Corruption on April 7, 2003, substituting the Organic Law of Safeguard of public assets and funds. The law preserves the right of all citizens to access information and establishes the obligatory nature of providing information in relation to the use and expenditure of public funds and resources, through the quarterly publication of reports. It also prohibits public officials from opening secret accounts in foreign countries.

Liabilities of Company's Directors and Officers

According to the Venezuelan Commercial Code, the administrators are responsible only for the mandate execution and the obligations imposed by the law. Also, they are free of any personal obligation that may derive from the company's business. However, the administrators can act only according to the company bylaws; in case of breach, they are personally responsible before third parties.

A number of shareholders representing at least 20 percent of the capital stock may bring a claim before the Tribunal of Commerce based on the grounds of reasonable suspicion of serious irregularities in the fulfillment of duties by the administrators.

The administrators will also be responsible before the company and before third parties for infringement of the provision established in the law and bylaws, as well as of any other breach committed by management. However, the responsibility of the administrators for acts or omissions is not extended to those being free of guilt, if they stated in the minutes of the meeting their unconformity and notified the examiners, if any, immediately.

In the case of bankruptcy of a stock company or a limited liability company, the administrators can be punished if they did not pay attention to the provisions established in the law, or if they are in any way responsible for the bankruptcy of the company.

Litigation/Dispute Resolution Systems

Venezuela has developed its legal system in accordance with civil law, also known as continental law. This system contrasts with the common law system, or Anglo-American system prevailing in countries like the United States of America, Canada, and the United Kingdom, among others.

The head of the Venezuelan Judicial Power is the Supreme Court of Justice, the body in charge of controlling the legality of the actions of the public power, based on their constitutionality. As stipulated in Article 254 of the Constitution, this court has financial, functional, and administrative autonomy. It comprises seven chambers: plenary chamber, constitutional chamber, political-administrative chamber, electoral chamber, social chamber, criminal appellate chamber, and the civil appellate chamber. There are five magistrate judges in each of these chambers, with the exception of the constitutional chamber, where there are seven magistrate judges, and the plenary chamber, which is made up of 32 magistrate judges of the highest court, all of whom will serve for a period of 12 years.

Among its many powers, the Supreme Court of Justice is empowered to repeal laws if they are deemed unconstitutional, and it is also empowered to decide unfair competition disputes in courts of lower hierarchy, and it acts as a final appellate court. Decisions issued by the Supreme Court of Justice cannot be appealed.

The judicial power also comprises courts with ordinary jurisdiction: superior courts, first instance courts, and municipal courts for civil, mercantile, and transit matters. Processes involving amounts that do not exceed approximately USD 45,350 will be handled by municipal courts; and processes involving amounts higher than USD 45,350 will be handled by first instance courts for civil, mercantile, and transit matters. The decisions issued by municipal courts could be appealed before first instance courts; and the decisions issued by first instance courts could be appealed before superior courts.

The Special Jurisdiction works in parallel with the Ordinary Jurisdiction. The Special Jurisdiction is made up of courts that, according to the subject, will hear about certain matters, such as courts for the protection of children and teens, labor courts, contentious-administrative courts, courts for contentious and tax matters, measure enforcement courts, and maritime courts, among others.

The above describes how the Venezuelan justice system is distributed, starting from laws created under constitutional principles that must later be guaranteed under an effective judicial system, thus allowing access to justice.

Regarding alternative dispute resolution, Venezuela has one of the most modern commercial arbitration laws in Latin America. The Law on Commercial Arbitration (LCA) was enacted in 1998, and it substitutes the old rules contained in the Civil Procedure Code and represents an important improvement in Venezuelan arbitration.

One of the most important contributions of this law is that, in Article 11, it allows for the creation and development of private arbitration centers, and it also ensures that all centers created before its enactment will continue to work, provided that they follow the guidelines established in said law. The law also stipulates that arbitration centers, chambers of commerce, or any other organizations devoted to alternative dispute resolution shall be governed by their own rules; they can decide over their own authority, and they can also decide over the validity or existence of the arbitration agreement.

Today, in Venezuela, there are two main centers that offer their mediation and dispute resolution services at a commercial and institutional level: (i) the Arbitration Center of the Chamber of Caracas (CACC), and (ii) the Business Center of Conciliation and Arbitration (CEDCA), sponsored by the Venezuelan-American Chamber of Commerce. Both private institutions offer their services to important national and international companies involved in commercial disputes. Their purpose is to ensure, within arbitration processes, compliance with regulations provided in the Law on Commercial Arbitration, always guaranteeing the principle of due process.

In regard to the Arbitration Center of the Chamber of Caracas, it is the national version of the International Chamber of Commerce (ICC), it represents the International Arbitration Court in Venezuela, and it composes the national section of the Inter-American Commercial Arbitration Commission (IACAC).

It is important to highlight that, even if Venezuela has a Law on Commercial Arbitration, the country has executed treaties on this matter, which are binding and considered laws in Venezuela's legal system. One of them is the United Nations Convention on the Recognition and Enforcement of Foreign Arbitral Awards, also known as the New York Convention, which signals, in Article III, that each contracting state shall recognize arbitral awards and enforce them in accordance with the rules of procedure where the award is relied upon; the LCA has extended this precept.

Another important arbitration treaty is the Inter-American Convention on International Commercial Arbitration, also called the Panama Convention, published in 1985 in the National Official Gazette, which, just like the New York Convention, ensures the enforcement of arbitral awards, whether foreign or national.

CONTRACTS AND DOCUMENTS—FORMS AND ENFORCEABILITY

Contracts and obligations in Venezuela are ruled by the Venezuelan Civil Code.[46] The main rule in Venezuela regarding contracts is the freedom of the parties.

However, regarding forms and formalities, there are exceptions to this rule as some contracts must be concluded following certain form requirements (for example, in writing, requiring registration, or by public instrument). That is the case, for example, with real estate transactions and mortgages, which must be in writing and registered before the corresponding Real Estate Registry. Donations must also follow certain formalities; these contracts must be certified before a notary's office and registered before a Real Estate Registry when real estate is involved.

Any contract that fulfills the requirement for its existence and validity set forth in the Venezuelan Civil Code is enforceable according to its rules. There are no major difficulties regarding the enforceability of business contracts in Venezuela. These contracts can be enforced either by local courts or through arbitration proceedings (an arbitration clause or agreement is needed). As trials before Venezuelan courts can take several years, it is advisable to sign contracts with arbitration clauses, as arbitration proceedings tend to be much faster than court proceedings.[47]

However, it is important to note that enforceability can be highly difficult in what stands for contracts signed with public entities. Since a few years ago, there are hardly any judgments against the government, public entities, or state companies as the courts tend to be partial in this kind of trial. Therefore, investors willing to contract with the state or public entities must take this under consideration when evaluating risk.

ENDING/RESTRUCTURING A BUSINESS PRESENCE

Dissolution/Liquidation

According to the law, when a company has lost more than one-third of its capital stock value, the administrators must call a shareholders meeting to decide whether they will reimburse the capital, reduce it to the amount existing, or liquidate the company. The shareholders may decide to continue operations and not make any decision at that time.

However, when the loss has reached more than two-thirds of the capital stock, the company will necessarily enter into liquidation, if the shareholders do not reimburse the capital or limit it to the existing equity. Also, if the shareholders do not make any decision, the company has to be liquidated. In such a case, the administrators may not engage in new business operations to avoid personal liability. Administrators may be liable for criminal sanctions if they fail to call for a shareholders meeting when a company has incurred losses exceeding two-thirds of the capital stock.

Also, when a company has stopped making payments to its creditors and the liabilities do not exceed the assets, it can apply before the commercial court for an authorization to proceed with the liquidation of the company through a process called "benefit of moratorium relief."

During this amicable liquidation process, any pending legal proceedings and any enforcement of claims against the debtor will be suspended. Nonetheless, this suspension will not affect tax creditors, secured creditors, or privileged creditors with respect to their rights and credits.

The debtor will be given various opportunities by the court to liquidate assets and pay creditors, in a period that will not exceed 12 months. This can be extended once for another 12 months. The court can grant a freezing order or an embargo, or both, over any of the debtor's assets and can also order that the debtor not leave the country while the proceedings are pending.

Involuntary liquidations are also possible. The petitioning creditors must file their complaint with the relevant court. The debtor must have stopped making payments, and liabilities should exceed assets. The creditors' complaint should detail all the facts and circumstances relating to the suspension of payments.

Once the petition has been presented, the judge can grant, as a preventive measure, a freezing order or an embargo, or both, over any of the debtor's assets. The judge can also order that the debtor's business books, correspondence, and any documentation be safely placed with a third party. The making of payments and the delivery of assets to the debtor can also be forbidden.

Insolvency, Bankruptcy, and Restructuring

In Venezuela there are two insolvency proceedings: bankruptcy and benefit of moratorium relief. Generally speaking, bankruptcies are regulated by the Commercial Code of 1955, the Civil Code of 1982, and the Civil Procedure Code of 1987.

The Commercial Code distinguishes three kinds of bankruptcy: fortuitous, guilty, and fraudulent bankruptcy. Fortuitous bankruptcy occurs due to fortuitous events or force majeure that leads to a cessation of payments and the impossibility of continuing in business; a guilty bankruptcy occurs when there is negligent conduct by administrators; and fraudulent bankruptcy occurs when there are acts that may be considered willful misconduct.

Reorganization, as understood in common law jurisdictions, is not available in Venezuela. A similar proceeding for insolvency cases is available, known as the benefit of moratorium relief. This benefit allows any businessperson whose assets surpass liabilities, who cannot discharge obligations on time, and therefore is in default regarding payment of debts, to apply before a commercial court for an authorization to proceed to an amicable liquidation of the business within 12 months. This benefit is also governed by the Commercial Code, the Civil Code, and the Civil Procedure Code.

Bankruptcy and benefit of moratorium relief proceedings apply to those who qualify as "traders" under the Commercial Code. Traders are defined by the Commercial Code as individuals with the legal capacity to enter into legally binding agreements for which trading is the main business, and companies.

As a consequence, according to the Commercial Code, bankruptcy proceedings apply only to businesspeople or business companies (as defined above). If any of these have been the subject of a benefit of moratorium relief and have consequently stopped making payments, then bankruptcy proceedings cannot be commenced.

Individuals are excluded from bankruptcy and benefit of moratorium relief proceedings. This is because the Civil Code and the Civil Procedure Code establish two special proceedings designed for individuals, namely the "assignment for the benefit of creditors," and the "meeting of the general board of creditors to approve an insolvent's reorganization plan."

Bankruptcy may be declared only by a commercial court when a cessation or suspension of payments is present. This decision is important as the effects of the bankruptcy will be considered as of the date the cessation of payments occurred. The date of cessation of payments may not be more than two years before the court's decision. Gratuitous acts during the term of two years and 10 days prior to the declaration of bankruptcy are considered null and void. Onerous acts may also be considered null and void if the people who contracted with the bankrupt entity had knowledge of the insolvency when entering into the agreements.

Once bankruptcy proceedings have been initiated and prior to the issuing of a final decision, the court can, as a precautionary measure, grant a freezing order or an embargo, or both, over any of the debtor's assets. Any such measure given by the court will benefit all creditors equally.

None of the measures described above affects tax creditors, secured creditors, or privileged creditors with respect to the assets securing their respective credits or loans.

The above measures are available to all creditors and would normally be granted where the legal requirements are met. In such cases, the process for the granting of a preventive measure should not be difficult or time-consuming.

Once the commencement of bankruptcy proceedings has been accepted by the relevant court, all creditors will be required by the court to appear before the judge, even if the creditors are not located in Venezuela. This allows the creditors to prove their claims in the first creditors' meeting.

The notification issued by the court requiring all creditors to appear before the judge has to be published, in a particular format, in a recognized newspaper circulated throughout the country. Subsequent to the first creditors' meeting being held, the judge will call for a second creditors' meeting where the judge will qualify the claims presented by creditors before the court. Finally, a third creditors' meeting is called. This last meeting is commonly termed the "agreement meeting," as this is the meeting where creditors and debtors try to reach an agreement.

In a benefit of moratorium relief process a surveillance committee is appointed, integrated by bankers and businesspeople, among others. They will advise the court regarding liquidation of the company and payment of creditors.

Normally moratorium is granted for one year to allow a friendly liquidation, but nevertheless it is also possible to allow a merchant to recover, and the court may grant an extension for another year. All proceedings are conducted under the court's supervision.

In the case of corporate groups, as each subsidiary has its own corporate body under Venezuelan law, the parent company is not included in the insolvency proceedings. Each entity will be subject to an individualized insolvency proceeding, and creditors can pursue their claims only against the assets of the subsidiary, not the assets of the parent.

CONCLUSION

In summary, there is no doubt that current legal conditions in Venezuela are challenging for private business. There is a clear governmental policy leading to the transition of the economic system from capitalism to socialism, imposing a greater role of the state in all sectors of the economy as an active participant in each area.

Following this policy, businesses that are not yet controlled by the government are subject to more strict regulations that affect their activities. Besides, the risk of expropriation or having the activities taken over by the government is significant in different sectors of the economy such as chemicals, oil, banking, insurance, agro-industry, manufacturing, and retail.

In addition, the presence of a strict exchange control regime in Venezuela has a direct impact on business as government approvals are required to make payments to foreign suppliers of products or services, and to repatriate dividends and other proceeds of investments. This control creates investment and devaluation risks for businesses as approvals are delayed or denied. This situation also compromises the possibility of obtaining foreign financing, for example.

Nevertheless, despite all these barriers to business, Venezuela is still receiving foreign investments from countries like China, Brazil, Iran, and Russia. For some companies, several business activities like construction, mining, oil, and specialized services are still rentable regardless of the country risk.

All things considered, investors interested in the Venezuelan market must carefully study the current business conditions and be sure to have experienced local legal assistance, as being properly informed could be the key for better risk management.

NOTES

1. Venezuelan Commercial Code, Articles 200 to 375.
2. Venezuelan Commercial Code, Articles 354 to 358.
3. Reglamento del Régimen Común de Tratamiento a los Capitales Extranjeros y sobre Marcas, Patentes, Licencias y Regalías. Decree No. 2095, February 13, 1992, Article 13.
4. Decreto con Fuerza de Ley de Reforma de la Ley General de Bancos y Otras Instituciones Financieras, Decree No. 1.526, November 3, 2001, Articles 177 to 183.
5. www.sudeban.gob.ve.
6. Decreto con Fuerza de Ley de Reforma de la Ley General de Bancos y Otras Instituciones Financieras, Decree No. 1.526, November 3, 2001, Article 179.
7. Venezuelan Commercial Code, Article 212.
8. Foreign Investment is regulated by the Reglamento del Régimen Común de Tratamiento a los Capitales Extranjeros y sobre Marcas, Patentes, Licencias y Regalías. Decree No. 2095, February 13, 1992.
9. www.siex.gob.ve.
10. Reglamento del Régimen Común de Tratamiento a los Capitales Extranjeros y sobre Marcas, Patentes, Licencias y Regalías. Decree No. 2095, February 13, 1992, Article 13.
11. For MIGA projects in Venezuela see: www.miga.org/regions/index_sv.cfm?stid=1531&country_id=231&hcountrycode=VE.
12. For information regarding Venezuela membership and current cases see: www.icsid.worldbank.org.
13. For information regarding this convention see the website of the United Nations Commission on International Trade: www.uncitral.org/uncitral/en/uncitral_texts/arbitration/NYConvention.html.
14. Bilateral agreements have been signed with Argentina, Barbados, Belgium, Brazil, Canada, Chile, Costa Rica, Cuba, the Czech Republic, Denmark, Ecuador, France, Germany, Great Britain, Lithuania, Luxembourg, Iran, the Netherlands, Paraguay, Peru, Portugal, Russia, Spain, Switzerland, Sweden, Uruguay, and Vietnam.
15. Ley del Mercado de Capitales. Published in the Official Gazette No. 36.565 on October 22, 1998.
16. www.cnv.gob.ve.
17. www.avaf.org.
18. www.bcv.org.ve.
19. www.cadivi.gov.ve.
20. Ley contra los Ilícitos Cambiarios. Published in the Official Gazette No. 39.425, on May 17, 2010.
21. Ley de Extranjería y Migración. Published in the Official Gazette No. 37.944 on May 24, 2004.
22. For more information see the SAIME webpage: www.saime.gob.ve.
23. http://www.bancoex.gob.ve/.
24. Ley Sobre Practicas Desleales del Comercio Internacional. Published in the Oficial Gazette No. 4.441 Extraordinary on June 18, 1992.

25. The income obtained in the country is taxed, as well as the income obtained abroad for those considered residents or other parties domiciled in Venezuela. Nondomiciled entities with a permanent establishment in Venezuela must pay taxes based on the profits from territorial or extraterritorial sources from such permanent establishments.

26. Countries engaged in double taxation agreements with Venezuela are the United States, Italy, France, Germany, Portugal, the Czech Republic, Trinidad and Tobago, the Netherlands, Switzerland, the United Kingdom of Great Britain and North Ireland, Belgium, Denmark, and Barbados, among others.

27. Ley de Impuesto Sobre la Renta. Published in the Official Gazette No. 38.628 on February 16, 2007.

28. The income tax law defines nonresidents as those individuals who have not stayed in the country for more than 183 days during the calendar year or in the previous year. Nonresidents are taxed with a proportional rate of 34 percent of their gross income.

29. Ley para Promoteger y Promover el Ejercicio de la Libre Competencia. Published in the Official Gazette No. 34.880 on January 13, 1992.

30. www.procompetencia.gob.ve.

31. Ley Organica del Ambiente. Published in Official Gazette No. 5.833 Extraordinary on December 22, 2006.

32. Ley para el Derecho de las Personas en el Acceso de Bienes y Servicios. Published in Official Gazette No. 39.358 on February 1, 2010.

33. www.indepabis.gob.ve.

34. Ley de Tierras y Desarrollo Agrario. Published in Official Gazette No. 5.991 Extraordinary on July 29, 2010.

35. The relevant legislation affecting copyright includes the Copyright Law, October 1993; as well as Decision No. 351 of the Cartagena Agreement (October 1993) and Regulations of the Copyright Law and Decision No. 351 (March 1995), both of which establish a common regime on copyright and related rights for the member countries of the Andean Community.

36. www.mincomercio.gob.ve.

37. www.sapi.gob.ve.

38. www.sacven.org.

39. Ley sobre Derecho de Autor. Published in Official Gazette No. 4.638 on October 1, 1993.

40. The protection granted shall apply to (i) works expressed in writing; (ii) lectures, addresses, and sermons; (iii) musical compositions; (iv) dramatic and dramatic musical works; (v) choreographic and mimed works; (vi) cinematographic works and other audio-visual works; (vii) works of fine art; (viii) works of architecture; (ix) photographic works; (x) works of applied art; (xi) illustrations, maps, sketches, plans, diagrams, and three-dimensional works relating to geography, topography, architecture, or science; (xii) computer programs; and (xiii) anthologies or compilations of assorted works, and also databases, which, by the selection and arrangement of their contents, constitute personal creations.

41. Ley Organica de Aduanas. Published in Official Gazette No. 38.875 on February 21, 2008.

42. www.seniat.gov.ve.

43. Ley de Hipoteca Mobiliaria y Prenda sin Desplazamiento de Posesión. Published in Official Gazette No. 1.575 on April 4, 1973.

44. Official Gazette No. 39165 dated April 24, 2009.

45. Official Gazette No. 39189 dated May 19, 2009.

46. See articles 1133 to 1430 for general rules regarding contracts and the subsequent articles for special rules regarding certain kinds of contracts including donations and sales agreements.

47. See the section on Litigation/Dispute Resolution Systems.

Index